D0560343

Complex Organizations

A SOCIOLOGICAL READER

Amitai Etzioni
COLUMBIA UNIVERSITY

Complex Organizations

A SOCIOLOGICAL READER

HOLT, RINEHART AND WINSTON
NEW YORK · CHICAGO · SAN FRANCISCO
TORONTO · LONDON

September, 1964

Library of Congress Catalog Card Number: 61-7443

22550-0111

Printed in the United States of America

In memory of my father,

WILLI FALK

Preface

COMPLEX ORGANIZATIONS constitute one of the most important elements which make up the social web of modern societies. Most citizens of modern societies are born in a hospital, educated in a school, work in one organization or another; and to the degree that they participate in religious and political activities, these too, frequently, take place in complex organizations. In short, members of modern societies obtain a large part of their material, social, and cultural satisfactions from large-scale organizations. The way to the understanding of modern man and the society in which he lives leads, therefore, to the study of complex organizations. This volume is devoted to a review of some of the ideas, theories, and research findings concerning organizations, and concludes with a brief examination of some of the methods used in studying these social units.

By "organizations" we mean, following Parsons, social units which are predominantly oriented to the attainment of specific goals. The major types of organizations to be discussed are those which have bureaucratic characteristics, as specified by Weber. Thus, although our journey will lead us to the study of both formal and informal aspects of organizations, we shall not embark on the much longer voyage of presenting studies of "social organizations" in which all forms of patterned, regulated, or "organized" social behavior are explored.*

Some of our contributors, especially Howard S. Becker and Erving Goffman, refer to "institutions" when discussing the same category of social units designated here as organizations. Morris Janowitz sees the military as an "establishment." Whatever the term, the denota-

* For a recent discussion of this concept, see Scott A. Greer, *Social Organization* (Garden City, N.Y.: Doubleday, 1955), especially pp. 5–10.

tion seems to be similar. All the contributors discuss organizations—factories, prisons, offices, hospitals, churches, schools, military organizations, newspapers, voluntary associations, ships, trade-unions, governmental agencies, and universities—each of which is examined in detail by at least one contributor.

These readings were taken, as is customary, from a considerably large body of literature. One obvious criterion of selection was that of finding writings of high quality which were brief enough to be included or could be excerpted without becoming incomprehensible or distorting the author's thesis.* More specifically, an attempt was made to select material which could serve as a substitute for, or supplement to, a textbook for courses in organizational analysis. At the same time, efforts were made to refrain as much as possible from reprinting once more articles or parts of books which could be found on nearly everyone's desk. It is for this reason that some of the "classics" were not included. Omitting some of the standard selections left more room for newer contributions. Of thirty-nine selections collected here, seven have not been published before or have been revised for this volume. Many of the other excerpts are not easily available. A number of works have been reprinted from journals and publications which have only a limited circulation or do not regularly come to the attention of students of organizations.

These readings draw considerably on recent material because in the last decade organizational analysis has rapidly developed and expanded. For the same reason, young and somewhat less well-known authors are highly represented.

This collection, like others before it, does not lay claim to completeness. Quite a few aspects of organizational study are not represented, and many approaches could not be illuminated. An effort has been made to bring into the limelight new tendencies and recent developments. Considerable space has been devoted to the study of organizational *goals* and to the application of *research techniques* to organization research. Care has been taken to call attention to three dimensions of organizational analysis which still seem to be relatively neglected. These are the study of interaction between *organization and society;* intracultural *comparative* study of organizations; and analysis of *organizational change.*

The editor benefited from extensive comments offered by his colleagues at Columbia University and at the University of California

* The more important omissions are marked in the text by ellipsis dots (. . .).

at Berkeley. Their knowledge, generous advice, and encouragement—which are herewith gratefully acknowledged—made these readings possible. I am especially indebted to Robert K. Merton, Philip Selznick, and Erving Goffman for their valuable comments on earlier outlines of this volume The advice of John W. Riley, Jr., was most helpful, as well as the suggestions made by Renate Mayntz. Eva Etzioni served concomitantly as consultant, assistant, and companion.

A.E.
December, 1960
New York City

Contents

1. Toward a Theory of Organization

»»

Finding a balance between rational and nonrational elements of human behavior is a cardinal issue of modern life, society, and thought. It is also the central problem of organizational theory. All the scholars represented here make it their starting point or touch upon it in one way or another. The basic question is how best to coordinate human activities in order to make a highly rational unit, and at the same time maintain social integration, the normative commitments of participants, and their motivation to participate.

Weber sees three modes that authority, and in this sense, organizational structure, may take: two—traditional and charismatic authority—represent the nonrational elements; one, the legal-rational or bureaucratic type, represents of course the rational element. Each one of these modes of authority "is connected with a fundamentally different sociological structure of executive staff and means of administration."

Whereas Weber emphasizes the rational aspects of legal-rational or bureaucratic organizations, Barnard, examining a similar set of complex organizations, puts more stress on the psychological and social aspects. He sees organizations, first of all, as *cooperative* systems. Barnard's interest in conscious coordination of activities parallels Weber's interest in the systematic division of tasks and authority, and in the rational control of performance (see Hopkins, below). But at the same time, Barnard focuses on the motivational and nonrational aspects of behavior. How can actors be motivated to participate, to comply, and to perform?

Weber focuses on the sources and forms of rational structures; Barnard is more concerned with their nonrational aspects; Selznick's theory rests on both foundations. He studies organizations as economies and adaptive structures but also as cooperative systems. This compound approach leads Selznick to examine the formal roles of participants, as well as their personalities as a whole. It enables him to cast new light on phenomena such as leadership, informal relations, and the dynamics of interchange between personality and organization. The second part of Selznick's contribution is devoted to an examination of the structural-functional approach and its application to organizational analysis.

Parsons presents a general but elaborated model for the structural-functional analysis of organizations. He points out that organizations differ from other social units by being predominantly oriented to the attainment of specific goals. Two main reference points are adopted as central for examination of these units: first, the cultural and institutional patterns and, second, various role clusters which make up the organization structure. The key processes of organizations are defined as recruitment, allocation, and the coordination of activities. The selection included here (which constitutes the first part of Parsons' article on organizations), ends with a discussion of the ways in which the integration of the organization is established and maintained.

Parsons brings his general theory to bear on the study of organizations. A comparison of this article with Parsons' other work shows that the basic question illuminated here is the special form or structure which organizations employ in "solving" the generic functional problems of social units. The question of balance recurs: the instrumental processes of adaption to the environment and of goal implementation have to be balanced by the expressive processes of social and normative integration.

All the selections presented up to this point are concerned predominantly with organization as such and deal with individuals from the viewpoint of their effect on the organization. Merton, like March and Simon, focuses on the articulation between the personality as a system and the organization as a social unit. An examination of the *bureaucrat* leads Merton to modify the rationalistic model of bureaucracies by pointing out their inherent dysfunctions. The expert knowledge of the bureaucrat spells "trained incapacity" when the situation changes; discipline leads to devotion to means rather than devotion to ends; impersonal treatment of clients and cases is carried out by interacting persons who develop primary relations. These relations in turn may have dysfunctional effects. The study of organizations, it follows, is badly lacking without a study of the participants as persons, not just as incumbents of organizational roles.

March and Simon assert that "the Barnard-Simon theory of organization equilibrium is essentially a theory of motivation." It is concerned with the conditions under which participation is assured, including willingness to be recruited and trained, willingness to perform adequately in terms of quality and quantity, and willingness to obey. The organization is seen as an exchange system in which *inducements* are handed out in exchange for *contributions* supplied. The present selection examines mainly the participation criterion of employees. The extension of this analysis to other groups of participants is suggested by the authors. These groups include buyers, suppliers, agents, and investors. Thus the problem of organizational boundaries is brought into relief.

Gouldner and Hopkins make the *study* of bureaucracies, rather than bureaucracies themselves, the subject of their essays. Gouldner, examining the ideological perspectives of bureaucratic theories, finds them basically pessimistic and fatalistic. One approach finds the source of evil in the unavoidable complexity and large size of bureaucracies. Functionalists see it in the "technological" requirements of a highly rational organization.

Hopkins shows that Weber's and Barnard's theories of bureaucracy, usually considered quite different from each other, actually constitute complementary and convergent approaches. An examination of the concepts of authority, legitimation, organizational status, structure, and others—in both theories—shows the closeness of what were considered two distinct forms of analysis. Combining the insights of both scholars supplies a base for a general theory of bureaucratic authority, its basic concepts, and some of its major propositions.

Max Weber

The Three Types of Legitimate Rule

Translated by Hans Gerth

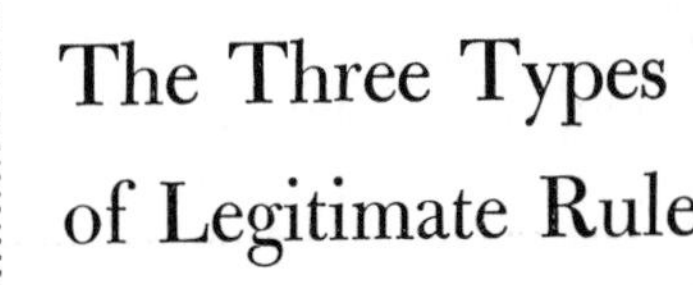

Authority means the probability that a specific command will be obeyed. Such obedience may feed on diverse motives. It may be determined by sheer interest situation, hence by the compliant actor's calculation of expediency; by mere custom, that is, the actor's inarticulate habituation to routine behavior; or by mere affect, that is, purely personal devotion of the governed. A structure of power, however, if it were to rest on such foundations alone, would be relatively unstable. As a rule both rulers and rules uphold the internalized power structure as "legitimate" by right, and usually the shattering of this belief in legitimacy has far-reaching ramifications.

There are but three clear-cut grounds on which to base the belief in legitimate authority. Given pure types each is connected with a fundamentally different sociological structure of executive staff and means of administration.

I

Legal authority rests on enactment; its pure type is best represented by bureaucracy. The basic idea is that laws can be enacted and changed at pleasure by formally correct procedure. The governing

 Weber's "Three Types of Legitimate Rule" appeared posthumously in the *Preussische Jahrbuecher* in 1922 (187: 1–12). This exposition was not included in the first editions of *Wirtschaft und Gesellschaft* (*The Theory of Social and Economic Organization*). In the 1956 edition of *Wirtschaft und Gesellschaft* (Tuebingen: J. C. B. Mohr, 1956), which was substantially revised by J. Winckelmann, "The Three Types of Legitimate Rule" appears as Section 2 of the "Sociology of Authority" (2: 551–558).

body is either elected or appointed and constitutes as a whole and in all its sections rational organizations. A heteronomous and heterocephalous sub-unit we shall call "public authorities" (Behörde). The administrative staff consists of officials appointed by the ruler; the law-abiding people are members of the body politic ("fellow citizens").

Obedience is not owed to anybody personally but to enacted rules and regulations which specify to whom and to what rule people owe obedience. The person in authority, too, obeys a rule when giving an order, namely, "the law," or "rules and regulations" which represent abstract norms. The person in command typically is the "superior" within a functionally defined "competency" or "jurisdiction," and his right to govern is legitimized by enactment. Specialization sets limits with regard to functional purpose and required skill of the office incumbent.

The typical official is a trained specialist whose terms of employment are contractual and provide a fixed salary scaled by rank of office, not by amount of work, and the right to a pension according to fixed rules of advancement. His administration represents vocational work by virtue of impersonal duties of office; ideally the administrator proceeds *sine ira et studio,* not allowing personal motive or temper to influence conduct, free of arbitrariness and unpredictability; especially he proceeds "without regard to person," following rational rules with strict formality. And where rules fail he adheres to "functional" considerations of expediency. Dutiful obedience is channeled through a hierarchy of offices which subordinates lower to higher offices and provides a regular procedure for lodging complaints. Technically, operation rests on organizational discipline.

1. Naturally this type of "legal" rule comprises not only the modern structure of state and city government but likewise the power relations in private capitalist enterprise, in public corporations and voluntary associations of all sorts, provided that an extensive and hierarchically organized staff of functionaries exists. Modern political bodies merely represent the type pre-eminently. Authority of private capitalist organization is partially heteronomous, its order is partly prescribed by the state, and it is completely heterocephalous as regards the machinery of coercion. Normally the courts and police take care of these functions. Private enterprise, however, is autonomous in its increasingly bureaucratic organization of management. The fact that, formally speaking, people enter into the power relationship (*Herrschaftsverband*) voluntarily and are likewise "free" to give

notice does not affect the nature of private enterprise as a power structure since conditions of the labor market normally subject the employees to the code of the organization. Its sociological affinity to modern state authority will be clarified further in the discussion of the economic bases of power and authority. The "contract" as constitutive for the relations of authority in capitalist enterprise makes this a pre-eminent type of "legal authority."

2. Technically, bureaucracy represents the purest type of legal authority. No structure of authority, however, is exclusively bureaucratic, to wit, is managed by contractually hired and appointed officials alone. That is quite impossible. The top positions of the body politic may be held by "monarchs" (hereditary charismatic rulers), or by popularly elected "presidents" (hence plebiscitarian charismatic rulers), or by parliamentary elected presidents. In the latter case the actual rulers are members of parliament or rather the leaders of the prevailing parliamentary parties. These leaders in turn may stand close to the type of charismatic leadership or to that of notabilities. More of this below.

Likewise the administrative staff is almost never exclusively bureaucratic but usually notables and agents of interest groups participate in administration in manifold ways. This holds most of all for the so-called self-government. It is decisive that regular administrative work is predominantly and increasingly performed by bureaucratic forces. The historical development of the modern state is identical indeed with that of modern officialdom and bureaucratic organization (cf. below), just as the development of modern capitalism is identical with the increasing bureaucratization of economic enterprise. The part played by bureaucracy becomes bigger in all structures of power.

3. Bureaucracy does not represent the only type of legal authority. Other types comprise rotating office holders or office holders chosen by lot or popularly elected officers. Parliamentary and committee administration and all sorts of collegiate and administrative bodies are included under the type if and when their competency rests on enacted rules and if the use they make of their prerogative follows the type of legal administration. During the rise of the modern state collegiate bodies have made essential contributions to the development of legal authority, especially the concept of "public authorities" (Behörde) originated with them. On the other hand, elected official-

dom has played an important role in the pre-history of the modern civil service and still does so today in the democracies.

II

Traditional authority rests on the belief in the sacredness of the social order and its prerogatives as existing of yore. Patriarchal authority represents its pure type. The body politic is based on communal relationships, the man in command is the "lord" ruling over obedient "subjects." People obey the lord personally since his dignity is hallowed by tradition; obedience rests on piety. Commands are substantively bound by tradition, and the lord's inconsiderate violation of tradition would endanger the legitimacy of his personal rule, which rests merely upon the sacredness of tradition. The creation of new law opposite traditional norms is deemed impossible in principle. Actually this is done by way of "recognizing" a sentence as "valid of yore." (the *Weistum* of ancient Germanic law). Outside the norms of tradition, however, the lord's sway in a given case is restricted only by sentiments of equity, hence by quite elastic bonds. Consequently the rule of the lord divides into a strictly tradition-bound sphere and one of free favor and arbitrariness where he rules at pleasure as sympathy or antipathy move him, following purely personal considerations subject especially to the influence of "good turns."

So far as principles are followed in administration and settlement of disputes, they rest on substantive considerations of ethical equity, justice, or utilitarian expediency, not on formal considerations characteristic of the rule of law. The lord's administrative staff proceeds in the same way. It consists of personally dependent men (members of the household or domestic officials), of relatives, of personal friends (favorites), or associates bound by personal allegiance (vassals, tributory princes). The bureaucratic concept of "competency" as a functionally delimited jurisdictional sphere is absent. The scope of the "legitimate" prerogatives of the individual servant is defined from case to case at the pleasure of the lord on whom the individual servant is completely dependent as regards his employment in more important or high ranking roles. Actually this depends largely on what the servant may dare do opposite the more or less docile subjects. Personal loyalty of the faithful servant, not functional duty of office and office discipline, control the interrelationship of the administrative staff.

One may, however, observe two characteristically different forms of positional relationships, the patriarchal structure and that of estates.

1. In the purely patriarchal structure of administration the servants are completely and personally dependent on the lord; they are either purely patrimonially recruited as slaves, bondsmen-serfs, eunuchs, or extra patrimonially as favorites and plebeians from among strata lacking all rights. Their administration is entirely heteronomous and heterocephalous, the administrators have no personal right to their office, there is neither merit selection nor status honor; the material means of administration are managed under, and on account of, the lord. Given the complete dependency of the administrative staff on the lord, there is no guarantee against the lord's arbitrariness, which in this set-up can therefore have its greatest possible sway. Sultanistic rule represents the pure type. All genuine "despotism" was of this nature. Prerogatives are considered . . . ordinary property rights of the lord.

2. In the estate system the servants are not personal servants of the lord but independent men whose social position makes them presumably socially prominent. The lord, actually or according to the legitimacy fiction, bestows office on them by privilege or concession; or they have contractually, by purchase, tenancy or lease, acquired a title to their office which cannot be arbitrarily taken away from them; hence within limits, their administration is autocephalous and autonomous. Not the lord but they dispose over the material means of administration. This represents estate rule.

The competition of the officeholders for larger bailiwicks (and income) then determines the mutual delimitation of their actual bailiwicks and takes the place of "competency." Privilege often breaks through the hierarchic structure (*de non evocando, non apellando*). The category of "discipline" is absent. Tradition, privilege, feudal or patrimonial bonds of allegiance, status honor and "good will" regulate the web of inter-relations. The power prerogatives of the lord hence are divided between the lord and the privileged administrative staff, and this division of powers among the estates brings about a high degree of stereotypy in the nature of administration.

Patriarchal rule (of the family father, sib chief, father of his people [*Landesvater*]) represents but the purest type of traditionalist rule. Any "authorities" who claim legitimacy successfully by virtue of mere habituation represent the most typical contrast, on the one hand, to the position of a contractually employed worker in business enterprise; on the other, to the way a faithful member of a religious community emotionally relates to a prophet. Actually the domestic group [*Hausverband*] is the nucleus of traditionalist power structures. The typical "officials" of the patrimonial and feudal state are domestic officers with originally purely domestic tasks (dapifer, chamberlain, marshall, cupbearer, seneschal, major domo).

The co-existence of the strictly tradition-bound and the free sphere of conduct is a common feature of all traditionalistic forms of authority. Within the free sphere, action of the lord or of his administrative staff must be bought or earned by personal relations. (This is one of the origins of the institution of fees.) It is decisive that formal law is absent and that substantive principles of administration and arbitration take its place. This likewise is a common feature of all traditionalist power structures and has far-reaching ramifications, especially for economic life.

The patriarch, like the patrimonial ruler, governs and decides according to the principles of "cadi justice": on the one hand, decisions are strictly bound by tradition; however, where these fetters give leeway, decisions follow juristically informal and irrational considerations of equity and justice from case to case, also taking individual differences into account. All codifications and laws of patrimonial rulers embody the spirit of the so-called "welfare state." A combination of social ethical with social utilitarian principles prevails, breaking through all rigor of formal law.

The sociological distinction between the patriarchal power structure and that of the estates in traditionalist rule is fundamental for all states of the pre-bureaucratic epoch. (The contrast will become fully clear only in connection with its economic aspect, that is, with the separation of the administrative staff from the material means of administration or with their appropriation by the staff.) This has been historically decisive for the question whether and what status groups existed as champions of ideas and culture values.

Patrimonial dependents (slaves, bondsmen) as administrators are to be found throughout the Mideastern orient and in Egypt down to the time of the Mamelukes; they represent the most extreme and what would seem to be the most consistent type of the purely patriarchal rule devoid of estates. Plebeian freemen as administrators stand relatively close to rational officialdom. The administration by literati can vary greatly in accordance with their nature: typical is the contrast between Brahmins and Mandarins, and both in turn stand opposite Buddhist and Christian clerics—yet their administration always approximates the estate type of power structure.

The rule of estates is most clearly represented by aristocracy, in purest form by feudalism, which puts in the place of the functional and rational duty of office the personal allegiance and the appeal to status honor of the enfeoffed.

In comparison to patriarchalism, all estate rule, based upon more or less stable appropriation of administrative power, stands closer to legal authority as the guarantees surrounding the prerogatives of the privileged assume the form of special "rights" (a result of the "division of power" among the estates). This rationale is absent in patriarchal structures, with their administration completely dependent on the lord's arbitrary sway. On the other hand, the strict discipline and the lack of rights of the administrative staff within patriarchalism is more closely related to the discipline of legal authority than is the administration of estates, which is fragmented and stereotyped through the oppropriation of the means of administration by the staff. Plebeians (used as jurists) in Europe's princely service have been pacemarkers of the modern state.

III

Charismatic authority rests on the affectual and personal devotion of the follower to the lord and his gifts of grace (charisma). They comprise especially magical abilities, revelations of heroism, power of the mind and of speech. The eternally new, the non-routine, the unheard of and the emotional rapture from it are sources of personal devotion. The purest types are the rule of the prophet, the warrior hero, the great demagogue. The body politic consists in the communal relationship of a religious group or following. The person in command is typically the "leader"; he is obeyed by the "disciple." Obedience is given exclusively to the leader as a person, for the sake of his non-routine qualities, not because of enacted position or traditional dignity. Therefore obedience is forthcoming only so long as people ascribe these qualities to him, that is, so long as his charisma is proven by evidence. His rule falls if he is "forsaken" by his god [1] or deprived of

[1] Translator's note: This allusion to Jesus' death and its interpretation as a downfall of his charismatic authority comes out more strongly in Weber's "Sociology of Charismatic Authority" ("Charismatismus," *Wirtschaft und Gesellschaft,* in *From*

his heroic strength, or if the masses lose faith in his leadership capacity. The administrative staff is selected according to charisma and personal devotion, hence selection does not consider special qualification (as in the case of the civil servant) nor rank and station (as in the case of administration by estates) nor domestic or other forms of personal dependency (as, in contrast to the above, holds for the patriarchal administrative staff). The rational concept of "competency" is lacking as is the status idea of "privilege." Decisive for the legitimation of the commissioned follower or disciple is alone the mission of the lord and his followers' personal charismatic qualification. The administration—so far as this word is adequate—lacks all orientation to rules and regulations whether enacted or traditional. Spontaneous revelation or creation, deed and example, decision from case to case, that is—at least measured against enacted orders—irrational decisions are characteristic of charismatic authority. It is not bound to tradition: "It is written but I say unto you" holds for the prophet. For the warrior hero the legitimate orders vanish opposite new creations by power of the sword, for the demagogue by virtue of his annunciation or suggestion of revolutionary "natural law." In the genuine form of charismatic justice and arbitration the lord or "sage" speaks the law and the (military or religious) following gives it recognition, which is obligatory, unless somebody raises a counter claim to charismatic validity. This case presents a struggle of leaders which in the last analysis can solely be decided by the confidence of the community; only one side can be right; the other side must be wrong and be obliged to make amends.

A. The type of charismatic authority has first been developed brilliantly by R. Sohm in his *Kirchenrecht* for the early Christian community without his recognizing that it represents a type of authority. The term has since been used repeatedly without recognition of its bearing.

Early history shows alongside a few beginnings of "enacted" authority, which are by no means entirely absent, the division of all power relationships under tradition and charisma. Besides the "economic chief" (sachem) of the Indians, an essentially traditional figure,

---

Max Weber: Essays in Sociology, H. H. Gerth and C. Wright Mills, trans. (New York: Oxford, 1946), p. 248. In his later work, *Ancient Judaism*, Hans H. Gerth and Don Martindale, trans. (Glencoe, Ill.: Free Press, 1952), p. 376, Weber reversed his position.

stands the charismatic warrior prince (corresponding to the Germanic "duke") with his following. Hunting and war campaigns, both demanding a leader of extraordinary personal endowments, are the secular; magic is the "sacred" place of charismatic leadership. Throughout the ages charismatic authority exercised by prophets and warrior princes has held sway over men. The charismatic politician—the "demagogue"—is the product of the occidental city state. In the city state of Jerusalem he emerged only in religious costume as a prophet. The constitution of Athens, however, was completely cut out for his existence after the innovations of Pericles and Ephialtes, since without the demagogue the state machine would not function at all.

B. Charismatic authority rests on the "faith" in the prophet, on the "recognition" which the charismatic warrior hero, the hero of the street or the demagogue, finds personally, and this authority falls with him. Yet, charismatic authority does not derive from this recognition by the subjects. Rather the reverse obtains: the charismatically legitimized leader considers faith in the acknowledgement of his charisma obligatory and punishes their violation. Charismatic authority is even one of the great revolutionary forces in history, but in pure form it is thoroughly authoritarian and lordly in nature.

C. It should be understood that the term "charisma" is used here in a completely value-neutral sense. For the sociologist the manic seizure and rage of the Nordic berserk, the miracles and revelations of any pettifogging prophecy, the demagogic talents of Cleon are just as much "charisma" as the qualities of a Napoleon, Jesus, Pericles. Decisive for us is only whether they were considered charismatics and whether they were effective, that is, gained recognition. Here, "proof" is the basic prerequisite. The charismatic lord has to prove his being sent "by the grace of god" by performing miracles and being successful in securing the good life for his following or subjects. Only as long as he can do so will he be recognized. If success fails him, his authority falters. Wherever this charismatic concept of rule by the grace of god has existed, it has had decisive ramifications. The Chinese monarch's position was threatened as soon as drought, floods, military failure or other misfortune made it appear questionable whether he stood in the grace of Heaven. Public self-impeachment and penance, in cases of stubborn misfortune, removal and possible sacrifice threatened him. Certification by miracles was demanded of every prophet (the Zwickau people demanded it still from Luther).

So far as the belief in legitimacy matters for the stability of basically legal structures of authority, this stability rests mostly on mixed foundations. Traditional habituation of "prestige" (charisma) fuse with the belief in formal legality which in the last analysis is also a matter of habit. The belief in the legitimacy of authority is shattered alike through extraordinary misfortunes whether this exacts unusual demands from the subjects in the light of tradition, or destroys the prestige or violates the usual formal legal correctness. But with all structures of authority the obedience of the governed as a stable condition depends above all on the availability of an administrative staff and especially its continuous operation to maintain order and (directly or indirectly) enforce submission to the rule. The term "organization" means to guarantee the pattern of conduct which realizes the structure of authority. The solidarity of its (ideal and material) interests with those of the lord is decisive for the all important loyalty of the staff to the lord. For the relation of the lord to the executive staff it generally holds that the lord is the stronger opposite the resisting individual because of the isolation of the individual staff member and his solidarity with the lord. The lord is weak opposite the staff members as a whole then they band themselves together, as has happened occasionally in the past and present. Deliberate agreement of the staff is requisite in order to frustrate the lord's action and rule through obstruction or deliberate counter action. Likewise the opposition requires an administrative staff of its own.

D. Charismatic rule represents a specifically extraordinary and purely personal relationship. In the case of continued existence, however, at least when the personal representative of charisma is eliminated, the authority structure has the tendency to routinize. This is the case when the charisma is not extinguished at once but continues to exist in some form and the authority of the lord, hence, is transferred to successors. This routinization of charisma proceeds through

1. Traditionalization of the orders. The authority of precedents takes the place of the charismatic leader's or his staff's charismatic creativity in law and administration. These precedents either protect the successors or are attributed to them.

2. The charismatic staff of disciples or followers changes into a legal or estate-like staff by taking over internal prerogatives or those appropriated by privilege (fiefs, prebends).

3. The meaning of charisma itself many undergo a change. Decisive in this is the way in which the problem of successorship is solved,

which is a burning question for ideological and indeed often material reasons. This question can be solved in various ways: the merely passive tarrying for a new charismatically certified or qualified master usually gives way to an active search for a successor, especially if none readily appears and if any strong interests are vested in the continuity of the authority structure.

Chester I. Barnard

Organizations as Systems of Cooperation

A cooperative system is a complex of physical, biological, personal, and social components which are in a specific systematic relationship by reason of the cooperation of two or more persons for at least one definite end. Such a system is evidently a subordinate unit of larger systems from one point of view; and itself embraces subsidiary systems—physical, biological, etc.—from another point of view. One of the systems comprised within a cooperative system, the one which is implicit in the phrase "cooperation of two or more persons," is called an "organization."

The number of cooperative systems having more or less definite purposes, and of sufficient duration to enlist attention and description or identification, is very large. They may be broadly classified by character of purpose or objective into a few groups which are widely different, such as churches, political parties, fraternal associations, governments, armies, industrial enterprises, schools, families. Between organizations classified in any one of these groups there are also wide differences.

The variations in concrete cooperative situations may be assigned to four preliminary classes: (a) those that relate to aspects of

Reprinted in part from Chester I. Barnard, *The Functions of the Executive* (Cambridge, Mass.: Harvard, 1938), pp. 65–74, by permission of the author and publisher.

the physical environment; (b) those that relate to aspects of the social environment; (c) those that relate to individuals; (d) other variables.

a. An inspection of the concrete operations of any cooperative system shows at once that the physical environment is an inseparable part of it. To the extent that there are variations in the physical aspects of cooperative systems an adjustment or adaptation of other aspects of cooperation is required. Whether such variations are significant for the general study of cooperation, or whether for most purposes the physical environment may be treated as a constant, is the first question at issue. By physical environment so far as we mean geographical aspects—that is, mere location, topography, climate, etc.,—it will readily be accepted that it may well be excluded from consideration for nearly all general purposes.[1] That part of the environment, however, which is regarded as the property of an organization is of different status; and that part which consists of structures, improvements, tools, machines, etc., pertains still more specifically to the organization which owns or works with them. All aspects of the physical environment are then regarded or most conveniently treated as the elements of other, physical and technical, systems between which and organizations the significant relationships may be investigated as may be required for the purpose in hand.

b. It is in most cases evident that the social elements are an important aspect likewise of a concrete cooperative situation. The social factors may be regarded as entering into the situation by several routes: (1) through being components of the individual whose activities are included in the system; (2) through their effect upon individuals, whose activities are not included, but who are hostile to the system of cooperation or whose activities potentially are factors in any way; (3) through contact of the system (either cooperative or otherwise) with other collateral cooperative systems and especially with (4) superior systems; and (5) as inherent in cooperation itself. Indirectly, social factors, of course, are also involved in the changes of the physical environment, particularly as effected by prior or other existing cooperative systems. . . .

We shall exclude all of the social environment as such from the definition of organization.

c. The exclusion of the physical and social environments from

[1] In special cases, however, this is not true; for example, where two manufacturing operations otherwise alike are conducted in two different climates. Climate may then be the most significant variable.

the definition of organization for general purposes will on the whole conform to ordinary usage and common sense, and will be accepted without great difficulty as a method of approach to a scientifically useful concept of organization. The question of persons, however, offers greater difficulty and doubt. Though with much vagueness and many exceptions, some of which have been already indicated, the most usual conception of an organization is that of a *group* of persons, some or all of whose activities are coordinated. The concept of the group as the dominant characteristic of cooperative systems is certainly also frequent in the literature of sociology, anthropology, and social psychology, although, as shown by Parsons,[2] systems in which at least the emphasis is upon *action* have been fundamental in the conceptual schemes of Durkheim, Pareto, and Weber.

As a working concept it may be made clear that "group" contains so many variables as to restrict the number and the firmness of any generalizations. It is unmanageable without the use of some more restricted concept. Hence, to the present writer, discussions of group cooperation often give the impression of vagueness, confusion, and implicit contradiction. The reason for this is apparent from the fact that both group and person require explicit definition. A group is evidently a number of persons plus some interrelationships or interactions to be determined. When the nature of these interrelations or interactions is described or defined, it at once appears that "person" is a highly variable thing, not merely in the sense that persons differ in many respects, but more especially because the extent and character of their participation in groups also widely varies. . . .

Now if, with reference to a particular system of cooperative action to which a person contributes, one examines all the acts of any person for even one day it will be at once evident in nearly all cases that many of these acts are outside *any* system of cooperation; and that many of the remainder are distributable among at least several such cooperative systems. The connection of any "member" with an organization is necessarily intermittent, and there is frequent substitution of persons. Again it is almost impossible to discover a person who does not "belong"—taking into account the intermittent character of his participation—at the same time to many organizations. . . .

It is evident from the foregoing that if persons are to be included within the concept "organization," its general significance will be

[2] Talcott Parsons, *The Structure of Social Action* (New York: McGraw-Hill, 1937).

quite limited. The bases or terms upon which persons are included will be highly variable—so much so that even within very restricted fields, such as a particular industry, "organizations" will mean a wide variety of entities. Hence, here again as when we included a part of the physical environment within the definition, the inclusion of persons may be most useful in particular instances, but of limited value for general purposes.

It nevertheless remains to consider whether it would actually be useful to adopt a definition from which persons as well as physical and social environments are excluded as components. If this is done, an organization is defined as *a system of consciously coordinated personal activities or forces.* It is apparent that all the variations found in concrete cooperative systems that are due to physical and social environments, and those that are due to persons or to the bases upon which persons contribute to such systems, are by this definition relegated to the position of external facts and factors,[3] and that the organization as then isolated is an aspect of cooperative systems which is common to all of them.

Organization will then mean a similar thing, whether applied to a military, a religious, an academic, a manufacturing, or a fraternal cooperation, though the physical environment, the social environment, the number and kinds of persons, and the bases of their relation to the organization will be widely different. These aspects of cooperation then become external to organization as defined, though components of the cooperative system as a whole. Moreover, the definition is similarly applicable to settings radically different from those now obtaining, for example, to cooperation under feudal conditions. Such a definition will be of restricted usefulness with reference to any particular cooperative situation, being only one element of such a situation, except as by its adoption we are enabled to arrive at general principles which may be usefully applied in the understanding of specific situations.

It is the central hypothesis of this book that the most useful concept for the analysis of experience of cooperative systems is embodied in the definition of a formal organization as a *system of consciously coordinated activities or forces of two or more persons.*

[3] That is, external to the organization but not external to the related cooperative system. It is to be borne in mind that we are dealing with *two* systems: (1) an inclusive cooperative system, the components of which are persons, physical systems, social systems, and organizations; and (2) organizations, which are parts of cooperative systems and consist entirely of coordinated human activities.

In any concrete situation in which there is cooperation, several different systems will be components. Some of these will be physical, some biological, some psychological, etc., but the element common to all which binds all these other systems into the total concrete cooperative situation is that of organization as defined. If this hypothesis proves satisfactory it will be because (1) an organization, as defined, is a concept valid through a wide range of concrete situations with relatively few variables, which can be effectively investigated; and (2) the relations between this conceptual scheme and other systems can be effectively and usefully formulated. The final test of this conceptual scheme is whether its use will make possible a more effective conscious promotion and manipulation of cooperation among men; that is, whether in practice it can increase the predictive capacity of competent men in this field. It is the assumption upon which this essay is developed that such a concept is implicit in the behavior of leaders and administrators, explaining uniformities observed in their conduct in widely different cooperative enterprises, and that its explicit formulation and development will permit a useful translation of experience in different fields into common terms.

Philip Selznick

Foundations of the Theory of Organization

Trades unions, governments, business corporations, political parties, and the like are formal structures in the sense that they represent rationally ordered instruments for the achievement of stated goals. "Organization," we are told, "is the arrangement of personnel for facilitating the accomplishment of some agreed purpose through the allocation of functions and responsibili-

Reprinted in part from Philip Selznick, *American Sociological Review*, 13 (1948), 25–35, by permission of the author and the publisher, The American Sociological Association.

ties."[1] Or, defined more generally, formal organization is "a system of consciously coordinated activities or forces of two or more persons."[2] Viewed in this light, formal organization is the structural expression of rational action. The mobilization of technical and managerial skills requires a pattern of coordination, a systematic ordering of positions and duties which defines a chain of command and makes possible the administrative integration of specialized functions. In this context *delegation* is the primordial organizational act, a precarious venture which requires the continuous elaboration of formal mechanisms of coordination and control. The security of all participants, and of the system as a whole, generates a persistent pressure for the institutionalization of relationships, which are thus removed from the uncertainties of individual fealty or sentiment. Moreover, it is necessary for the relations within the structure to be determined in such a way that individuals will be interchangeable and the organization will thus be free of dependence upon personal qualities.[3] In this way, the formal structure becomes subject to calculable manipulation, an instrument of rational action.

But as we inspect these formal structures we begin to see that they never succeed in conquering the non-rational dimensions of organizational behavior. The latter remain at once indispensable to the continued existence of the system of coordination and at the same time the source of friction, dilemma, doubt, and ruin. This fundamental paradox arises from the fact that rational action systems are inescapably imbedded in an institutional matrix, in two significant senses: (1) the action system—or the formal structure of delegation and control which is its organizational expression—is itself only an aspect of a concrete social structure made up of individuals who may interact as *wholes*, not simply in terms of their formal roles within the system; (2) the formal system, and the social structure within which it finds concrete existence, are alike subject to the pressure of an institutional environment to which some over-all adjustment must be made. The formal administrative design can never adequately or fully

[1] John M. Gaus, "A Theory of Organization in Public Administration," in *The Frontiers of Public Administration* (Chicago: University of Chicago Press, 1936), p. 66.

[2] Chester I. Barnard, *The Functions of the Executive* (Cambridge: Harvard University Press, 1938), p. 73.

[3] Cf. Talcott Parsons' generalization (after Max Weber) of the "law of the increasing rationality of action systems," in *The Structure of Social Action* (New York: McGraw-Hill, 1937), p. 752.

reflect the concrete organization to which it refers, for the obvious reason that no abstract plan or pattern can—or may, if it is to be useful—exhaustively describe an empirical totality. At the same time, that which is not included in the abstract design (as reflected, for example, in a staff-and-line organization chart) is vitally relevant to the maintenance and development of the formal system itself.

Organization may be viewed from two standpoints which are analytically distinct but which are empirically united in a context of reciprocal consequences. On the one hand, any concrete organizational system is an *economy;* at the same time, it is an *adaptive social structure.* Considered as an economy, organization is a system of relationships which define the availability of scarce resources and which may be manipulated in terms of efficiency and effectiveness. It is the economic aspect of organization which commands the attention of management technicians and, for the most part, students of public as well as private administration.[4] Such problems as the span of executive control, the role of staff or auxiliary agencies, the relation of headquarters to field offices, and the relative merits of single or multiple executive boards are typical concerns of the science of administration. The coordinative scalar, and functional principles, as elements of the theory of organization, are products of the attempt to explicate the most general features of organization as a "technical problem" or, in our terms, as an economy.

Organization as an economy is, however, necessarily conditioned by the organic states of the concrete structure, outside of the systematics of delegation and control. This becomes especially evident as the attention of leadership is directed toward such problems as the legitimacy of authority and the dynamics of persuasion. It is recognized implicitly in action and explicitly in the work of a number of students that the possibility of manipulating the system of coordination depends on the extent to which that system is operating within an environment of effective inducement to individual partipants and of conditions in which the stability of authority is assured. This is in a sense the fundamental thesis of Barnard's remarkable study, *The Functions of the Executive.* It is also the underlying hypothesis which

[4] See Luther Gulick and Lydall Urwick (editors), *Papers on the Science of Administration* (New York: Institute of Public Administration, Columbia University, 1937); Lydall Urwick, *The Elements of Administration* (New York, Harper, 1943); James D. Mooney and Alan C. Reiley, *The Principles of Organization* (New York: Harper, 1939); H. S. Dennison, *Organization Engineering* (New York: McGraw-Hill, 1931).

makes it possible for Urwick to suggest that "proper" or formal channels in fact function to "confirm and record" decisions arrived at by more personal means.[5] We meet it again in the concept of administration as a process of education, in which the winning of consent and support is conceived to be a basic function of leadership.[6] In short, it is recognized that control and consent cannot be divorced even within formally authoritarian structures.

The indivisibility of control and consent makes it necessary to view formal organizations as *cooperative* systems, widening the frame of reference of those concerned with the manipulation of organizational resources. At the point of action, of executive decision, the economic aspect of organization provides inadequate tools for control over the concrete structure. This idea may be readily grasped if attention is directed to the role of the individual within the organizational economy. From the standpoint of organization as a formal system, persons are viewed functionally, in respect to their *roles,* as participants in assigned segments of the cooperative system. But in fact individuals have a propensity to resist depersonalization, to spill over the boundaries of their segmentary roles, to participate as *wholes.* The formal systems (at an extreme, the disposition of "rifles" at a military perimeter) cannot take account of the deviations thus introduced, and consequently break down as instruments of control when relied upon alone. The whole individual raises new problems for the organization, partly because of the needs of his own personality, partly because he brings with him a set of established habits as well, perhaps, as commitments to special groups outside of the organization.

Unfortunately for the adequacy of formal systems of coordination, the needs of individuals do not permit a single-minded attention to the stated goals of the system within which they have been assigned. The hazard inherent in the act of delegation derives essentially from this fact. Delegation is an organizational act, having to do with formal assignments of functions and powers. Theoretically, these assignments are made to roles or official positions, not to individuals as such. In fact, however, delegation necessarily involves concrete individuals who have interests and goals which do not always coincide with the goals of the formal system. As a consequence, individual personalities may

[5] Urwick, *The Elements of Administration, op. cit.,* p. 47.

[6] See Gaus, *op. cit.* Studies of the problem of morale are instances of the same orientation, having received considerable impetus in recent years from the work of the Harvard Business School group.

offer resistance to the demands made upon them by the official conditions of delegation. These resistances are not accounted for within the categories of coordination and delegation, so that when they occur they must be considered as unpredictable and accidental. Observations of this type of situation within formal structures are sufficiently commonplace. A familiar example is that of delegation to a subordinate who is also required to train his own replacement. The subordinate may resist this demand in order to maintain unique access to the "mysteries" of the job, and thus insure his indispensability to the organization.

In large organizations, deviations from the formal system tend to become institutionalized, so that "unwritten laws" and informal associations are established. Institutionalization removes such deviations from the realm of personality differences, transforming them into a persistent structural aspect of formal organizations.[7] These institutionalized rules and modes of informal cooperation are normally attempts by participants in the formal organization to control the group relations which form the environment of organizational decisions. The informal patterns (such as cliques) arise spontaneously, are based on personal relationships, and are usually directed to the control of some specific situation. They may be generated anywhere within a hierarchy, often with deleterious consequences for the formal goals of the organization, but they may also function to widen the available resources of executive control and thus contribute to rather than hinder the achievement of the stated objectives of the organization. The deviations tend to force a shift away from the purely formal system as the effective determinant of behavior to (1) a condition in which informal patterns buttress the formal, as through the manipulation of sentiment within the organization in favor of established authority; or (2) a condition wherein the informal controls effect a consistent modification of formal goals, as in the case of some bureaucratic patterns.[8] This trend will eventually result in the formalization of erst-

[7] The creation of informal structures within various types of organizations has received explicit recognition in recent years. See F. J. Roethlisberger and W. J. Dickson, *Management and the Worker* (Cambridge: Harvard University Press, 1941), p. 524; also Barnard, *op. cit.*, c. ix; and Wilbert E. Moore, *Industrial Relations and the Social Order* (New York: Macmillan, 1946), chap. xv.

[8] For an analysis of the latter in these terms, see Philip Selznick, "An Approach to a Theory of Bureaucracy," *American Sociological Review*, Vol. VIII, No. 1 (February, 1943).

while informal activities, with the cycle of deviation and transformation beginning again on a new level.

The relevance of informal structures to organizational analysis underlines the significance of conceiving of formal organizations as cooperative systems. When the totality of interacting groups and individuals becomes the object of inquiry, the latter is not restricted by formal, legal, or procedural dimensions. The *state of the system* emerges as a significant point of analysis, as when an internal situation charged with conflict qualifies and informs actions ostensibly determined by formal relations and objectives. A proper understanding of the organizational process must make it possible to interpret changes in the formal system—new appointments or rules or reorganizations—in their relation to the informal and unavowed ties of friendship, class loyalty, power cliques, or external commitment. This is what it means "to know the score."

The fact that the involvement of individuals as whole personalities tends to limit the adequacy of formal systems of coordination does not mean that organizational characteristics are those of individuals. The organic, emergent character of the formal organization considered as a cooperative system must be recognized. This means that the *organization* reaches decisions, takes action, and makes adjustments. Such a view raises the question of the relation between organizations and persons. The significance of theoretical emphasis upon the cooperative *system* as such is derived from the insight that certain actions and consequences are enjoined independently of the personality of the individuals involved. Thus, if reference is made to the "organization-paradox"—the tension created by the inhibitory consequences of certain types of informal structures within organizations—this does not mean that individuals themselves are in quandaries. It is the nature of the interacting consequences of divergent interests within the organization which creates the condition, a result which may obtain independently of the consciousness or the qualities of the individual participants. Similarly, it seems useful to insist that there are qualities and needs of leader*ship*, having to do with position and role, which are persistent despite variations in the character or personality of individual leaders themselves.

Rational action systems are characteristic of both individuals and organizations. The conscious attempt to mobilize available internal resources (e.g., self-discipline) for the achievement of a stated goal—

referred to here as an economy or a formal system—is one aspect of individual psychology. But the personality considered as a dynamic system of interacting wishes, compulsions, and restraints defines a system which is at once essential and yet potentially deleterious to what may be thought of as the "economy of learning" or to individual rational action. At the same time, the individual personality is an adaptive structure, and this, too, requires a broader frame of reference for analysis than the categories of rationality. On a different level, although analogously, we have pointed to the need to consider organizations as cooperative systems and adaptive structures in order to explain the context of and deviations from the formal systems of delegation and coordination.

To recognize the sociological relevance of formal structures is not, however, to have constructed a theory of organization. It is important to set the framework of analysis, and much is accomplished along this line when, for example, the nature of authority in formal organizations is reinterpreted to emphasize the factors of cohesion and persuasion as against legal or coercive sources.[9] This redefinition is logically the same as that which introduced the conception of the self as social. The latter helps make possible, but does not of itself fulfill, the requirements for a dynamic theory of personality. In the same way, the definition of authority as conditioned by sociological factors of sentiment and cohesion—or more generally the definition of formal organizations as cooperative systems—only sets the stage, as an initial requirement, for the formulation of a theory of organization.

STRUCTURAL-FUNCTIONAL ANALYSIS

Cooperative systems are constituted of individuals interacting as wholes in relation to a formal system of coordination. The concrete structure is therefore a resultant of the reciprocal influences of the formal and informal aspects of organization. Furthermore, this structure is itself a totality, an adaptive "organism" reacting to influences upon it from an external environment. These considerations help to define the objects of inquiry; but to progress to a system of predicates *about* these objects it is necessary to set forth an analytical method which seems to be fruitful and significant. The method must have a relevance to empirical materials, which is to say, it must be more

[9] Robert Michels, "Authority," *Encyclopedia of the Social Sciences* (New York: Macmillan, 1931), pp. 319 ff.; also Barnard, *op. cit.*, c. xii.

specific in its reference than discussions of the logic or methodology of social science.

The organon which may be suggested as peculiarly helpful in the analysis of adaptive structures has been referred to as "structural-functional analysis."[10] This method may be characterized in a sentence: *Structural-functional analysis relates contemporary and variable behavior to a presumptively stable system of needs and mechanisms.* This means that a given empirical system is deemed to have basic needs, essentially related to self-maintenance; the system develops repetitive means of self-defense; and day-to-day activity is interpreted in terms of the function served by that activity for the maintenance and defense of the system. Put thus generally, the approach is applicable on any level in which the determinate "states" of empirically isolable systems undergo self-impelled and repetitive transformations when impinged upon by external conditions. This self-impulsion suggests the relevance of the term "dynamic," which is often used in referring to physiological, psychological, or social systems to which this type of analysis has been applied.[11]

It is a postulate of the structural-functional approach that the basic need of all empirical systems is the maintenance of the integrity and continuity of the system itself. Of course, such a postulate is primarily useful in directing attention to a set of "derived imperatives" or needs which are sufficiently concrete to characterize the system at hand.[12] It is perhaps rash to attempt a catalogue of these imperatives for formal organizations, but some suggestive formulation is needed in the interests of setting forth the type of analysis under discussion.

[10] For a presentation of this approach having a more general reference than the study of formal organizations, see Talcott Parsons, "The Present Position and Prospects of Systematic Theory in Sociology," in Georges Gurvitch and Wilbert E. Moore (ed.), *Twentieth Century Sociology* (New York: The Philosophical Library, 1945).

[11] "Structure" refers to both the relationships within the system (formal plus informal patterns in organization) and the set of needs and modes of satisfaction which characterize the given type of empirical system. As the utilization of this type of analysis proceeds, the concept of "need" will require further clarification. In particular, the imputation of a "stable set of needs" to organizational systems must not function as a new instinct theory. At the same time, we cannot avoid using these inductions as to generic needs, for they help us to stake out our area of inquiry. The author is indebted to Robert K. Merton who has, in correspondence, raised some important objections to the use of the term "need" in this context.

[12] For "derived imperative" see Bronislaw Malinowski, *The Dynamics of Culture Change* (New Haven: Yale University Press, 1945), pp. 44 ff. For the use of "need" in place of "motive" see the same author's *A Scientific Theory of Culture* (Chapel Hill: University of North Carolina Press, 1944), pp. 89–90.

In formal organizations, the "maintenance of the system" as a generic need may be specified in terms of the following imperatives:

1. The Security of the Organization as a Whole in Relation to Social Forces in Its Environment

This imperative requires continuous attention to the possibilities of encroachment and to the forestalling of threatened aggressions or deleterious (though perhaps unintended) consequences from the actions of others.

2. The Stability of the Lines of Authority and Communication

One of the persistent reference-points of administrative decision is the weighing of consequences for the continued capacity of leadership to control and to have access to the personnel or ranks.

3. The Stability of Informal Relations within the Organization

Ties of sentiment and self-interest are evolved as unacknowledged but effective mechanisms of adjustment of individuals and sub-groups to the conditions of life within the organization. These ties represent a cementing of relationships which sustains the formal authority in day-to-day operations and widens opportunities for effective communication.[13] Consequently, attempts to "upset" the informal structure, either frontally or as an indirect consequence of formal reorganization, will normally be met with considerable resistance.

4. The Continuity of Policy and of the Sources of Its Determination

For each level within the organization, and for the organization as a whole, it is necessary that there be a sense that action taken in the light of a given policy will not be placed in continuous jeopardy. Arbitrary or unpredictable changes in policy undermine the significance of (and therefore the attention to) day-to-day action by

[13] They may also *destroy* those relationships, as noted above, but the need remains, generating one of the persistent dilemmas of leadership.

injecting a note of capriciousness. At the same time, the organization will seek stable roots (or firm statutory authority or popular mandate) so that a sense of the permanency and legitimacy of its acts will be achieved.

5. A Homogeneity of Outlook with Respect to the Meaning and Role of the Organization

The minimization of disaffection requires a unity derived from a common understanding of what the character of the organization is meant to be. When this homogeneity breaks down, as in situations of internal conflict over basic issues, the continued existence of the organization is endangered. On the other hand, one of the signs of "healthy" organization is the ability to effectively orient new members and readily slough off those who cannot be adapted to the established outlook.

This catalogue of needs cannot be thought of as final, but it approximates the stable system generally characteristic of formal organizations. These imperatives are derived, in the sense that they represent the conditions for survival or self-maintenance of cooperative systems of organized action. An inspection of these needs suggests that organizational survival is intimately connected with the struggle for relative prestige, both for the organization and for elements and individuals within it. It may therefore be useful to refer to a *prestige-survival* motif in organizational behavior as a short-hand way of relating behavior to needs, especially when the exact nature of the needs remains in doubt. However, it must be emphasized that prestige-survival in organizations does not derive simply from like motives in individuals. Loyalty and self-sacrifice may be individual expressions of organizational or group egotism and self-consciousness.

The concept of organizational need directs analysis to the *internal relevance* of organizational behavior. This is especially pertinent with respect to discretionary action undertaken by agents manifestly in pursuit of formal goals. The question then becomes one of relating the specific act of discretion to some presumptively stable organizational need. In other words, it is not simply action plainly oriented internally (such as in-service training) but also action presumably oriented externally which must be inspected for its relevance to internal conditions. This is of prime importance for the understanding of bureaucratic behavior, for it is of the essence of the latter that action formally undertaken for substantive goals be weighed and transformed in terms of its consequences for the position of the officialdom.

Formal organizations as cooperative systems on the one hand, and individual personalities on the other, involve structural-functional homologies, a point which may help to clarify the nature of this type of analysis. If we say that the individual has a stable set of needs, most generally the need for maintaining and defending the integrity of his personality or ego; that here are recognizable certain repetitive mechanisms which are utilized by the ego in its defense (rationalization, projection, regression, etc.); and that overt and variable behavior may be interpreted in terms of its relation to these needs and mechanisms—on the basis of this logic we may discern the typical pattern of structural-functional analysis as set forth above. In this sense, it is possible to speak of a "Freudian model" for organizational analysis. This does not mean that the substantive insights of individual psychology may be applied to organizations, as in vulgar extrapolations from the individual ego to whole nations or (by a no less vulgar inversion) from strikes to frustrated workers. It is the *logic*, the *type* of analysis which is pertinent.

This homology is also instructive in relation to the applicability of generalizations to concrete cases. The dynamic theory of personality states a set of possible predicates about the ego and its mechanisms of defense, which inform us concerning the propensities of individual personalities under certain general circumstances. But these predicates provide only tools for the analysis of particular individuals, and each concrete case must be examined to tell which operate and in what degree. They are not primarily organs of prediction. In the same way, the predicates within the theory of organization will provide tools for the analysis of particular cases. Each organization, like each personality, represents a resultant of complex forces, an empirical entity which no single relation or no simple formula can explain. The problem of analysis becomes that of selecting among the possible predicates set forth in the theory of organization those which illuminate our understanding of the materials at hand.

The setting of structural-functional analysis as applied to organizations requires some qualification, however. Let us entertain the suggestion that the interesting problem in social science is not so much why men act the way they do as why men in certain circumstances *must* act the way they do. This emphasis upon constraint, if accepted, releases us from an ubiquitous attention to behavior in general, and especially from any undue fixation upon statistics. On the other hand, it has what would seem to be the salutary consequence of focusing inquiry upon certain necessary relationships of the type "if . . . then," for example: If the cultural level of the rank and file members of a formally democratic organization is below that necessary for participation in the formulation of policy, then there will be pressure upon the leaders to use the tools of demagogy.

Is such a statement universal in its applicability? Surely not in the sense that one can predict without remainder the nature of all or even most political groups in a democracy. Concrete behavior is a resultant, a complex vector, shaped by the operation of a number of such general constraints. But there is a test of general applicability: it is that of noting whether the relation made explicit must be *taken into account* in action. This criterion represents an empirical test of the significance of social science generalizations. If a theory is significant it will state a relation which will either (1) be taken into account as an element of achieving control; or (2) be ignored only at the risk of losing control and will evidence itself in a ramification of objective or unintended consequences.[14] It is a corollary of this principle of significance that investigation must search out the underlying factors in organizational action, which requires a kind of intensive analysis of the same order as psychoanalytic probing.

A frame of reference which invites attention to the constraints upon behavior will tend to highlight tensions and dilemmas, the characteristic paradoxes generated in the course of action. The dilemma may be said to be the handmaiden of structural-functional analysis, for it introduces the concept of *commitment* or *involvement* as fundamental to organizational analysis. A dilemma in human behavior is represented by an inescapable commitment which cannot be reconciled with the needs of the organism or the social system. There are many spurious dilemmas which have to do with verbal contradictions, but inherent dilemmas to which we refer are of a more profound sort, for they reflect the basic nature of the empirical system in question. An economic order committed to profit as its sustaining

[14] See R. M. MacIver's discussion of the "dynamic assessment" which "brings the external world selectively into the subjective realm, conferring on it subjective significance for the ends of action." *Social Causation* (Boston: Ginn, 1942), chaps. 11, 12. The analysis of this assessment within the context of organized action yields the implicit knowledge which guides the choice among alternatives. See also Robert K. Merton, "The Unanticipated Consequences of Purposive Social Action," *American Sociological Review,* I, 6 (December, 1936).

incentive may, in Marxist terms, sow the seed of its own destruction. Again, the anguish of man, torn between finitude and pride, is not a matter of arbitrary and replaceable assumptions but is a reflection of the psychological needs of the human organism, and is concretized in his commitment to the institutions which command his life; he is in the world and of it, inescapably involved in its goals and demands; at the same time, the needs of the spirit are compelling, proposing modes of salvation which have continuously disquieting consequences for worldly involvements. In still another context, the need of the human organism for affection and response necessitates a commitment to elements of the culture which can provide them; but the rule of the super-ego is uncertain since it cannot be completely reconciled with the need for libidinal satisfactions.

Applying this principle to organizations, we may note that there is a general source of tension observable in the split between "the motion and the act." Plans and programs reflect the freedom of technical or ideal choice, but organized action cannot escape involvement, a commitment to personnel or institutions or procedures which effectively qualifies the initial plan. *Der Mensch denkt, Gott lenkt.* In organized action, this ultimate wisdom finds a temporal meaning in the recalcitrance of the tools of action. We are inescapably committed to the mediation of human structures which are at once indispensable to our goals and at the same time stand between them and ourselves. The selection of agents generates immediately a bifurcation of interest, expressed in new centers of need and power, placing effective constraints upon the arena of action, and resulting in tensions which are never completely resolved. This is part of what it means to say that there is a "logic" of action which impels us forward from one undesired position to another. Commitment to dynamic, self-activating tools is of the nature of organized action; at the same time, the need for continuity of authority, policy, and character is pressing, and requires an unceasing effort to master the instruments generated in the course of action. This generic tension is specified within the terms of each cooperative system. But for all we find a persistent relationship between *need* and *commitment* in which the latter not only qualifies the former but unites with it to produce a continuous state of tension. In this way, the notion of constraint (as reflected in tension or paradox) at once widens and more closely specifies the frame of reference for organizational analysis.

For Malinowski, the core of functionalism was contained in the view that a cultural fact must be analyzed in its setting. Moreover, he apparently conceived of his method as pertinent to the analysis of all aspects of cultural systems. But there is a more specific problem, one involving a principle of selection which serves to guide inquiry along significant lines. Freud conceived of the human organism as an adaptive structure, but he was not concerned with all human needs, nor with all phases of adaptation. For his system, he selected those needs whose expression is blocked in some way, so that such terms as repression, inhibition, and frustration became crucial. All conduct may be thought of as derived from need, and all adjustment represents the reduction of need. But not all needs are relevant to the systematics of dynamic psychology; and it is not adjustment as such but reaction to frustration which generates the characteristic modes of defensive behavior.

Organizational analysis, too, must find its selective principle; otherwise the indiscriminate attempts to relate activity functionally to needs will produce little in the way of significant theory. Such a principle might read as follows: *Our frame of reference is to select out those needs which cannot be fulfilled within approved avenues of expression and thus must have recourse to such adaptive mechanisms as ideology and to the manipulation of formal processes and structures in terms of informal goals.* This formulation has many difficulties, and is not presented as conclusive, but it suggests the kind of principle which is likely to separate the quick and the dead, the meaningful and the trite, in the study of cooperative systems in organized action.[15]

The frame of reference outlined here for the theory of organization may now be identified as involving the following major ideas: (1) the concept of organizations as cooperative systems, adaptive social structures, made up of interacting individuals, sub-groups, and informal plus formal relationships; (2) structural-functional analysis, which relates variable aspects of organization (such as goals) to stable needs and self-defensive mechanisms; (3) the concept of recalcitrance as a quality of the tools of social action, involving a break in the continuum of adjustment and defining an environment of constraint, commitment, and tension. This frame of reference is suggested as providing a specifiable *area of relations* within which predicates in the

[15] This is not meant to deprecate the study of organizations as *economies* or formal systems. The latter represent an independent level, abstracted from organizational structures as cooperative or adaptive systems ("organisms").

theory of organization will be sought, and at the same time setting forth principles of selection and relevance in our approach to the data of organization.

It will be noted that we have set forth this frame of reference within the over-all context of social action. The significance of events may be defined by their place and operational role in a means-end scheme. If functional analysis searches out the elements important for the maintenance of a given structure, and that structure is one of the materials to be manipulated in action, then that which is functional in respect to the structure is also functional in respect to the action system. This provides a ground for the significance of functionally derived theories. At the same time, relevance to control in action is the empirical test of their applicability or truth.

Talcott Parsons

Suggestions for a Sociological Approach to the Theory of Organizations

For the purposes of this article the term "organization" will be used to refer to a broad type of collectivity which has assumed a particularly important place in modern industrial societies—the type to which the term "bureaucracy" is most often applied. Familiar examples are the governmental bureau or department, the business firm (especially above a certain size), the university, and the hospital. It is by now almost a commonplace that there are features common to all these types of organization which cut across the ordinary distinctions between the social science disciplines. Something is lost if study of the firm is left only to economists, of

This is the first article of a two-part series, reprinted in part from Talcott Parsons, *Administrative Science Quarterly*, 1 (1956), 63–85, by permission of the author and the publisher, Cornell University.

governmental organizations to political scientists, and of schools and universities to "educationists."[1]

The study of organization in the present sense is thus only part of the study of social structure as that term is generally used by sociologists (or of "social organization" as ordinarily used by social anthropologists). A family is only partly an organization; most other kinship groups are even less so. The same is certainly true of local communities, regional subsocieties, and of a society as a whole conceived, for example, as a nation. On other levels, informal work groups, cliques of friends, and so on, are not in this technical sense organizations.

THE CONCEPT OF ORGANIZATION

As a formal analytical point of reference, *primacy of orientation to the attainment of a specific goal* is used as the defining characteristic of an organization which distinguishes it from other types of social systems. This criterion has implications for both the external relations and the internal structure of the system referred to here as an organization.

The attainment of a goal is defined as a *relation* between a system (in this case a social system) and the relevant parts of the external situation in which it acts or operates. This relation can be conceived as the maximization, relative to the relevant conditions such as costs and obstacles, of some category of *output* of the system to objects or systems in the external situation. These considerations yield a further important criterion of an organization. An organization is a system which, as the attainment of its goal, "produces" an identifiable something which can be utilized in some way by another system; that is, the output of the organization is, for some other system, an input. In the case of an organization with economic primacy, this output may be a class of goods or services which are either consumable or serve as instruments for a further phase of the production process by

[1] There is already a considerable literature on organization which cuts across disciplinary lines. It is not the intention of this paper to attempt to review it. Three writers have been particularly important in stimulating the author's thinking in the field: Max Weber, Chester I. Barnard, and Herbert Simon. See particularly, Weber, *Theory of Social and Economic Organization* (New York, 1947), ch. iii; Barnard, *The Functions of the Executive* (Cambridge, Mass., 1938); Simon, *Administrative Behavior: A Study of Decision Making Processes in Administrative Organization* (New York, 1951).

other organizations. In the case of a government agency the output may be a class of regulatory decisions; in that of an educational organization it may be a certain type of "trained capacity" on the part of the students who have been subjected to its influence. In any of these cases there must be a set of consequences of the processes which go on within the organization, which make a difference to the functioning of some other subsystem of the society; that is, without the production of certain goods the consuming unit must behave differently, i.e., suffer a "deprivation."

The availability, to the unit succeeding the organization in the series, of the organization's output must be subject to some sort of terms, the settlement of which is analyzable in the general framework of the ideas of contract or exchange. Thus in the familiar case the economic producer "sells" his product for a money price which in turn serves as a medium for procuring the factors of production, most directly labor services, necessary for further stages of the productive process. It is thus assumed that in the case of all organizations there is something analogous to a "market" for the output which constitutes the attainment of its goal (what Chester I. Barnard calls "organization purpose"); and that directly, and perhaps also indirectly, there is some kind of exchange of this for entities which (as inputs into it) are important means for the organization to carry out its function in the larger system. The exchange of output for input at the boundary defined by the attainment of the goal of an organization need not be the only important boundary-exchange of the organization as a system. It is, however, the one most directly involved in defining the primary characteristics of the organization. Others will be discussed later.

The existence of organizations as the concept is here set forth is a consequence of the division of labor in society. Where both the "production" of specialized outputs and their consumption or ultimate utilization occur within the same structural unit, there is no need for the differentiation of specialized organizations. Primitive societies in so far as their units are "self-sufficient" in both economic and other senses generally do not have clear-cut differentiated organizations in the present sense.

In its internal reference, the primacy of goal-attainment among the functions of a social system gives priority to those processes most directly involved with the success or failure of goal-oriented endeavors. This means essentially the decision-making process, which controls the utilization of the resources of the system as a whole in the interest of the goal, and the processes by which those responsible for such decisions can count on the mobilization of these resources in the interest of a goal. These mechanisms of mobilization constitute what we ordinarily think of as the development of power in a political sense.

What from the point of view of the organization in question is its specified goal is, from the point of view of the larger system of which it is a differentiated part or subsystem, a specialized or differentiated function. This relationship is the primary link between an organization and the larger system of which it is a part, and provides a basis for the classification of types of organization. However, it cannot be the only important link.

This article will attempt to analyze both this link and the other principal ones, using as a point of departure the treatment of the organization as a social system. First, it will be treated as a system which is characterized by all the properties which are essential to any social system. Secondly, it will be treated as a functionally differentiated subsystem of a larger social system. Hence it will be the other subsystems of the larger one which constitute the situation or environment in which the organization operates. An organization, then, will have to be analyzed as the special type of social system organized about the primacy of interest in the attainment of a particular type of system goal. Certain of its special features will derive from goal-primacy in general and others from the primacy of the particular type of goal. Finally, the characteristics of the organization will be defined by the kind of situation in which it has to operate, which will consist of the relations obtaining between it and the other specialized subsystems of the larger system of which it is a part. The latter can for most purposes be assumed to be a society.

THE STRUCTURE OF ORGANIZATIONS

Like any social system, an organization is conceived as having a describable structure. This can be described and analyzed from two points of view, both of which are essential to completeness. The first is the "cultural-institutional" point of view which uses the values of the system and their institutionalization in different functional contexts as its point of departure; the second is the "group" or "role" point of view which takes suborganizations and the roles of individuals participating in the functioning of the organization as its point of departure. Both of these will be discussed, as will their broad relations to each other, but primary attention will be given to the former.

On what has just been called the cultural-institutional level, a minimal description of an organization will have to include an outline of the system of values which defines its functions and of the main institutional patterns which spell out these values in the more concrete functional contexts of goal-attainment itself, adaptation to the situation, and integration of the system. There are other aspects, such as technical lore, ideology, and ritual symbolization, which cannot, for reasons of space, be taken up here.

The main point of reference for analyzing the structure of any social system is its value pattern. This defines the basic orientation of the system (in the present case, the organization) to the situation in which it operates; hence it guides the activities of participant individuals.

In the case of an organization as defined above, this value system must by definition be a subvalue system of a higher-order one, since the organization is always defined as a subsystem of a more comprehensive social system. Two conclusions follow: First, the value system of the organization must imply basic acceptance of the more generalized values of the superordinate system—unless it is a deviant organization not integrated into the superordinate system. Secondly, on the requisite level of generality, the most essential feature of the value system of an organization is the evaluative *legitimation* of its place or "role" in the superordinate system.

Since it has been assumed that an organization is defined by the primacy of a type of goal, the focus of its value system must be the legitimation of this goal in terms of the functional significance of its attainment for the superordinate system, and secondly the legitimation of the primacy of this goal over other possible interests and values of the organization and its members. Thus the value system of a business firm in our society is a version of "economic rationality" which legitimizes the goal of economic production (specified to the requisite level of concreteness in terms of particular goods and services). Devotion of the organization (and hence the resources it controls) to production is legitimized as is the maintenance of the primacy of this goal over other functional interests which may arise within the organization. This is Barnard's "organization purpose."[2] For the business firm, money return is a primary measure and symbol of

[2] Barnard, *op. cit.*, pt. II, ch. vii.

success and is thus *part* of the goal-structure of the organization. But it cannot be the primary organization goal because profit-making is not by itself a function on behalf of the society as a system.

In the most general sense the values of the organization legitimize its existence as a system. But more specifically they legitimize the main functional patterns of operation which are necessary to implement the values, in this case the system goal, under typical conditions of the concrete situation. Hence, besides legitimation of the goal-type and its primacy over other interests, there will be legitimation of various categories of relatively specific subgoals and the operative procedures necessary for their attainment. There will further be normative rules governing the adaptive processes of the organization, the general principles on which facilities can be procured and handled, and there will be rules or principles governing the integration of the organization, particularly in defining the obligations of loyalty of participants to the organization as compared with the loyalties they bear in other roles.

A more familiar approach to the structure of an organization is through its constituent personnel and the roles they play in its functioning. Thus we ordinarily think of an organization as having some kind of "management" or "administration"—a group of people carrying some kind of special responsibility for the organization's affairs, usually formulated as "policy formation" or "decision-making." Then under the control of this top group we would conceive of various operative groups arranged in "line" formation down to the lowest in the line of authority. In a somewhat different relation we would also think of various groups performing "staff" functions, usually some kinds of experts who stand in an advisory capacity to the decision-makers at the various levels, but who do not themselves exercise "line" authority.

It seems advantageous for present purposes to carry through mainly with the analysis of the institutional structure of the organization. Using the value system as the main point of reference, the discussion of this structure can be divided into three main headings. The primary adaptive exigencies of an organization concern the procurement of the resources necessary for it to attain its goal or carry out its function; hence one major field of institutionalization concerns the modes of procurement of these resources. Secondly, the organization will itself have to have institutionalized procedures by which these resources are brought to bear in the concrete processes of goal-attainment; and, finally, there will have to be institutional patterns defining and regulating the limits of commitments to this organization as compared with others in which the same persons and other resource-controllers are involved, patterns which can be generalized on a basis tolerable to the society as a whole.

THE MOBILIZATION OF FLUID RESOURCES

The resources which an organization must utilize are, given the social structure of the situation in which it functions, the factors of production as these concepts are used in economic theory. They are land, labor, capital, and "organization" in a somewhat different sense from that used mainly in this paper.[3]

The factor of land stands on a somewhat different level from the other three. If we treat an organization, for purposes of analysis, as an already established and going concern, then, like any other social system, we can think of it as being in control of certain facilities for access to which it is not dependent on the maintenance of short-run economic sanctions. It has full ownership of certain physical facilities such as physical land and relatively nondepreciating or non-obsolescing buildings. It may have certain traditions, particularly involving technical know-how factors which are not directly involved in the market nexus. The more fully the market nexus is developed, however, the less can it be said that an organization has very important assets which are withdrawn from the market. Even sites of long operation can be sold and new locations found and even the most deeply committed personnel may resign to take other positions or retire, and in either case have to be replaced through the labor market. The core of this aspect of the "land" complex is thus a set of commitments of resources on value grounds.

The two most fluid factors, however, are labor and capital in the economic sense. The overwhelming bulk of personal service takes place in occupational roles. This means that it is *contracted for* on some sector of the labor market. It is not based on ascription of status, through kinship or otherwise, but depends on the specific terms settled between the management of the organization and the incumbent. There are, of course, many types of contract of employment. Some variations concern the agents involved in the settlement of terms; for example, collective bargaining is very different from individual bar-

[3] This possibly confusing terminological duplication is retained here because organization as a factor is commonly referred to in economic theory.

gaining. Others concern the duration of commitments, varying all the way from a casual relation terminable at will, to a tenure appointment.

But most important, only in a limiting case are the specific *ad hoc* terms—balancing specifically defined services against specific monetary remuneration—anything like exhaustive of the empirically important factors involved in the contract of employment. The labor market cannot, in the economic sense, closely approach being a "perfect market." It has different degrees and types of imperfection according to whether the employer is one or another type of organization and according to what type of human service is involved. A few of these differences will be noted in later illustrations. Here the essential point is that, with the differentiation of functionally specified organizations from the matrix of diffuse social groupings, such organizations become increasingly dependent on explicit contracts of employment for their human services.

Attention may be called to one particularly important differentiation among types of relation existing between the performer of services and the recipients of the ultimate "product." In the typical case of manufacturing industry the typical worker works within the organization. The end result is a physical commodity which is then sold to consumers. The worker has no personal contact with the customer of the firm; indeed, no representative of the firm need have such contact except to arrange the settlement of the terms of sale. Where, however, the "product" is a personal service, the situation is quite different; the worker must have personal contact with the consumer during the actual performance of the service.

One way in which service can be organized is the case where neither performer nor "customer" belongs to an organization. Private professional practice is a type case, and doctor and patient, for example, come to constitute a small-scale solidary collectivity of their own. This is the main basis of the sliding scale as a pattern of remuneration. A second mode of organization is the one which assimilates the provision of service to the normal pattern involved in the production of physical commodities; the recipient is a "customer" who pays on a value-of-service basis, with prices determined by commercial competition. This pattern is approached in the case of such services as barbering.

But particularly in the case of professional services there is another very important pattern, where the recipient of the service becomes an operative member of the service-providing organization. The school, university, and hospital are type cases illustrating this pattern. The phrase "member of the university" definitely includes students. The faculty are in a sense dually employed, on the one hand by their students, on the other by the university administration. The transition is particularly clear in the case of the hospital. In private practice the patient is unequivocally the "employer." But in hospital practice the hospital organization employs a professional staff on behalf of the patients, as it were. This taking of the customer *into* the organization has important implications for the nature of the organization.

In a society like ours the requirements of an organization for fluid resources are in one sense and on one level overwhelmingly met through financing, i.e., through the provision of money funds at the disposal of the organization.[4] This applies both to physical facilities, equipment, materials, buildings, and to the employment of human services —indeed, also to cultural resources in that the rights to use patented processes may be bought. Hence the availability of adequate financing is always a vital problem for every organization operating in a monetary economy no matter what its goal-type may be; it is as vital for churches, symphony orchestras, and universities as it is for business firms.

The mechanisms through which financial resources are made available differ enormously, however, with different types of organization. All except the "purest" charitable organizations depend to some extent on the returns they receive for purveying some kind of a product, be it a commodity, or a service like education or music. But even within this range there is an enormous variation in the adequacy of this return for fully meeting financial needs. The business firm is at one pole in this respect. Its normal expectation is that in the long run it will be able to finance itself adequately from the proceeds of sales. But even here this is true only in the long run; investment of capital in anticipation of future proceeds is of course one of the most important mechanisms in our society.

Two other important mechanisms are taxation and voluntary contributions. In a "free enterprise" economy the general principle governing financing by taxation is that organizations will be supported out of taxation (1) if the goal is regarded as important enough but organizations devoted to it cannot be made to "pay" as private enterprises by providing the service on a commercial basis, e.g., the care of large numbers of persons from the lower income groups who (by current standards) need to be hospitalized for mental illnesses, or (2)

[4] Weber, *op. cit.*, ch. iii.

if the *ways* in which the services would be provided by private enterprise might jeopardize the public interest, e.g., the provision of military force for the national defense might conceivably be contracted out, but placing control of force to this degree in private hands would constitute too serious a threat to the political stability of the society. Others in these categories are left to the "voluntary" principle, if they are publicly sanctioned, generally in the form of "nonprofit" organizations.

It is important to note that financing of organizations is in general "affected with a public interest" and is in some degree to be regarded as an exercise of political power. This consideration derives from the character of an organization as a goal-directed social system. Every subgoal within the society must to some degree be integrated with the goal-structure of the society as a whole, and it is with this societal goal-structure that political institutions are above all concerned.[5]

The last of the four factors of production is what certain economists, notably Alfred Marshall, have called "organization" in the technical sense referred to above. This refers to the function of *combining* the factors of production in such ways as to facilitate the effective attainment of the organization's goal (in our general sense, in its "economic" or factor-consuming aspects). Its input into the organization stands on a level different from that of labor services and financing, since it does not concern the direct facilities for carrying out defined functions in a relatively routine manner, but instead concerns readjustment in the patterns of organization itself. It is, therefore, primarily significant in the longer-run perspective, and it is involved in processes of structural change in the organization. In its business reference it is what J. A. Schumpeter referred to as "entrepreneurship."[6] Organization in this economic sense is, however, an essential factor in *all* organizational functioning. It necessarily plays a central part in the "founding" stages of any organization. From time to time it is important in later stages, since the kinds of adjustments to changing situations which are possible through the routine mechanisms of recruitment of labor services, and through the various devices for securing adequate financial resources, prove to be

[5] This general thesis of the relation between financing and political power and the public interest has been developed by Parsons and Smelser, *Economy and Society* (London, 1956), especially in chapters ii and iii.

[6] J. A. Schumpeter, *The Theory of Economic Development* (Cambridge, Mass.), 1934.

inadequate; hence a more fundamental structural change in the organization becomes necessary or desirable. This change would, in the present frame of reference, require a special input of the factor of organization in this technical sense.

The more generalized equivalent of the land factor is treated, except for the longest-run and most profound social changes, as the most constant reference point of all; its essential reference base is the stability of the value system in terms of which the goal of the organization is defined and the commitments involved in it are legitimized. It is from this reference base that the norms defining the broadly expected types of mechanism in the other respects will be derived, particularly those most actively involved in short-run operations, namely, the recruitment of human services through the labor market and the financing of the organization.

THE MECHANISMS OF IMPLEMENTATION

The problem of mobilizing fluid resources concerns one major aspect of the external relations of the organization to the situation in which it operates. Once possessing control of the necessary resources, then, it must have a set of mechanisms by which these resources can be brought to bear on the actual process of goal-implementation in a changing situation. From one point of view, there are two aspects of this process. First is the set of relations to the external situation centering around the problem of "disposal" of the "product" of the organization's activities. This involves the basis on which the scale of operations is estimated and on which the settlement of terms with the recipients of this product is arrived at. In the economic context it is the problem of "marketing," but for present purposes it is necessary to generalize this concept to include all products of organization functioning whether they are "sold" or not; for example, the products of a military organization may be said to be disposed of immediately to the executive and legislative branches of the government and through them to the public, but of course in no direct sense are they sold. The second aspect of the process is concerned with the internal mechanisms of the mobilization of resources for the implementation of the goal. For purposes of the present analysis, however, it will not be necessary to treat these internal and external references separately. Both, as distinguished from the mobilization of resources, can be treated together as governed by the "operative code" of the organization.

This code will have to have an essential basis in the value system which governs the organization. In the case of mobilization of resources, this basis concerns the problem of the "claims" of the organization to the resources it needs and hence the settlement of the terms on which they would be available to it. In the operative case it concerns the manner of their utilization within the organization and the relation to its beneficiaries. We may speak of the relevant value-implementation as centering about the question of "authorization" of the measures involved in carrying through the processes of utilization of resources.

There is an important sense in which the focus of all these functions is the process ordinarily called "decision-making." We have assumed that goal-attainment has clear primacy in the functioning of the organization. The paramount set of decisions then will be, within the framework of legitimation previously referred to, the set of decisions as to how, on the more generalized level, to take steps to attain the goal. This is what is generally thought of as the area of *policy* decisions. A second set of decisions concerns implementation in the sense of decisions about the utilization of resources available to the organization. These are the *allocative* decisions and concern two main subject matters: the allocation of responsibilities among personnel, i.e., suborganizations and individuals, and the allocation of fluid resources, i.e., manpower and monetary and physical facilities in accord with these responsibilities. Finally, a third set of decisions concerns maintaining the *integration* of the organization, through facilitating cooperation and dealing with the motivational problems which arise within the organization in relation to the maintenance of cooperation. The first two sets of decisions fall within the area which Barnard calls the problem of "effectiveness"; the third is the locus of the problem of "efficiency" in his sense.[7] Let us consider each of these decision areas in more detail.

Policy Decisions

By policy decisions are meant decisions which relatively directly commit the organization as a whole and which stand in relatively direct connection to its primary functions. They are decisions touching

[7] Barnard, *op. cit.*, pt. I, ch. V.

such matters as determination of the nature and quality standards of "product," changes in the scale of operations, problems of the approach to the recipients of the product or service, and organization-wide problems of modes of internal operation.

Policy decisions as thus conceived may be taken at different levels of generality with respect to the functions of the organization. The very highest level concerns decisions to set up a given organization or, conversely, to liquidate it. Near that level is a decision to merge with one or more other organizations. Then the scale descends through such levels as major changes in type of product or in scale of operations, to the day-to-day decisions about current operation. Broadly, this level of generality scale coincides with a scale of time-span of the relevance of decisions; the ones touching the longer-run problems of the organization tend to be the ones on a higher level of generality, involving a wider range of considerations and leading to more serious commitments. An important task for the theory of organization is a systematic classification of these levels of generality of decisions.

As has been noted, the critical feature of policy decisions is the fact that they commit the organization as a whole to carrying out their implications. This area of decisions is the focus of the problem of responsibility. One but only one major aspect of responsibility in turn lies in the fact that all operations of organization to some extent involve risks, and the decision-maker on the one hand is to some extent given "credit" for success, and on the other hand is legitimately held responsible for unfavorable consequences. One of the major features of roles of responsibility is the handling of these consequences; this becomes particularly complicated psychologically because it is often impossible to assess accurately the extent to which success or failure in fact stem from particular decisions or result from factors outside the control or predictive powers of the decision-maker. On high levels of responsibility conflicts of moral value may also operate.[8]

Because of the commitment of the organization as a whole, and through this of the interests of everyone participating in the organization to a greater or lesser degree, authorization becomes particularly important at the policy-decision level. This clearly connects with the value system and hence with the problem of legitimacy. It concerns not simply the content of particular decisions, but the right to make them.

[8] *Ibid.*, ch. xvii.

Different organizations, according to scale and qualitative type, of course, have different concrete ways of organizing the policy-making process. Often the highest level of policy is placed mainly in the hands of some kind of a board; whereas "management" has responsibility for the next highest levels, with the still lower levels delegated to operative echelons.

Allocative Decisions

Higher policy decisions will concern the general type and quantity of resources brought into the organization and the more general policies toward personnel recruitment and financing. But the operative utilization of these facilities cannot be completely controlled from the center. There must be some allocative organization by which resources are distributed within the organization, and responsibility for their utilization in the various necessary operative tasks is assigned. This means that specialization in the functions of administration or management precludes the incumbents of these functions from also carrying out the main technical procedures involved in the organization-goal, and hence making the main operating decisions at the "work" level. Thus, a commanding general cannot actually man a particular aircraft or command a particular battery of artillery; a university president cannot actively teach all the subjects of instruction for which the university is responsible.

From one point of view, these mechanisms of internal allocation may be treated as "delegations of authority," though this formula will have to be qualified in connection with various cross-cutting considerations of types of competence and so forth. Thus a general, who by training and experience has been an artilleryman, when he is in command does not simply "delegate" authority to the air element under his command; he must in some way recognize the special technical competence of the air people in a field where he cannot have such competence. Similarly a university president who by academic training has been a professor of English does not merely delegate authority to the physicists on his faculty. Both must recognize an independent technical basis for "lower" echelons performing their functions in the ways in which their own technical judgment makes advisable. The technical man can reasonably be held responsible for the *results* of his operations; he cannot, however, be "dictated to" with respect to the technical procedures by which he achieves these results.

Seen in this light, there are two main aspects of the allocative decision process. One concerns mainly personnel (organized in suborganizations, for example, "departments"), the other financial and, at the requisite level, physical facilities. In the case of personnel the fundamental consideration is the allocation of responsibility. Using decisions as the reference point, the primary focus of the responsibility problem is allocation of the responsibility to decide, i.e., the "decision who should decide," as Barnard puts it. Technical operations as such may then be treated as controlled by the allocation of responsibility for decisions.

The second main aspect of the allocation process is the budget. Though generally formalized only in rather large and highly differentiated organizations, analytically the budget is a central conception. It means the allocation of fluid financial resources which in turn can be committed to particular "uses," namely, acquisition of physical facilities and employment of personnel. Allocation of responsibility is definition of the *functions* of humanly organized subsystems of personnel. Budget allocation is giving these suborganizations access to the necessary means of carrying out their assignment. There is a certain important crisscrossing to the two lines in that at the higher level the decision tends to be one of budget, leaving the employment of the relevant personnel to the subsystem to which funds are allocated. The people responsible at the level in question in turn divide the resource stream, devoting part of it to personnel the employment of whom is, subject to general policies, under their control, another part to subbudget allocation of funds to the uses of personnel they employ. This step-down series continues until the personnel in question are given only various types and levels of control or use of physical facilities, and not control of funds.

Coordination Decisions

Two types of operative decisions have so far been discussed, namely, policy decisions and allocative decisions. There is a third category which may be called "decisions of coordination," involving what Barnard has called the problems of "efficiency." These decisions are the operative decisions concerned with the integration of the organization as a system. Our two types of fundamental resources have a sharply asymmetrical relation to these decisions as they do to the allocative decisions. Funds (considered apart from their lenders or other suppliers) and physical resources do not have to be motivated to cooperate in organizational tasks, but human agents do. Decisions of policy and decisions of the allocation of responsibility still leave open the question of motivation to adequate performance.

This becomes an integrative problem because the special types of performance required to achieve the many complex contributions to an organization goal cannot be presumed to be motivated by the mere "nature" of the participants independently of the sanctions operating in the organizational situation. What is coordination from the point of view of the operation of the organization is "cooperation" from the point of view of the personnel. The limiting case of noncooperation is declining to continue employment in the organization, a case of by no means negligible importance where a free labor market exists. But short of this, relative to the goals of the organization, it is reasonable to postulate an inherent centrifugal tendency of subunits of the organization, a tendency reflecting pulls deriving from the personalities of the participants, from the special adaptive exigencies of their particular job situations, and possibly from other sources.

In this situation the management of the organization must, to some degree, take or be ready to take measures to counteract the centrifugal pull, to keep employment turnover at least down to tolerable levels, and internally to bring the performances of subunits and individuals more closely into line with the requirements of the organization than would otherwise be the case. These measures can take any one or a combination of three fundamental forms: (1) coercion—in that penalties for noncooperation are set, (2) inducement—in that rewards for valued performance are instituted, and (3) "therapy"—in that by a complex and judicious combination of measures the motivational obstacles to satisfactory cooperation are dealt with on a level which "goes behind" the overt ostensible reasons given for the difficulty by the persons involved.[9]

[9] The famous phenomenon of restriction of production in the informal group as reported by F. J. Roethlisberger and W. J. Dickson (*Management and the Worker* [Cambridge, Mass., 1939], pt. IV) is a case of relative failure of integration and hence, from one point of view, of failure of management in the function of coordination. It could be handled, from the present point of view, neither by policy decisions (e.g., not to hire "uncooperative workers") nor by allocative decisions (e.g., to hold the shop boss strictly responsible for meeting high production quotas), but only by decisions of coordination, presumably including "therapeutic" measures.

Robert K. Merton

Bureaucratic Structure and Personality

A formal, rationally organized social structure involves clearly defined patterns of activity in which, ideally, every series of actions is functionally related to the purposes of the organization.[1] In such an organization there is integrated a series of offices, of hierarchized statuses, in which inhere a number of obligations and privileges closely defined by limited and specific rules. Each of these offices contains an area of imputed competence and responsibility. Authority, the power of control which derives from an acknowledged status, inheres in the office and not in the particular person who performs the official role. Official action ordinarily occurs within the framework of pre-existing rules of the organization. The system of prescribed relations between the various offices involves a considerable degree of formality and clearly defined social distance between the occupants of these positions. Formality is manifested by means of a more or less complicated social ritual which symbolizes and supports the pecking order of the various offices. Such formality, which is integrated with the distribution of authority within the system, serves to minimize friction by largely restricting (official) contact to modes which are previously defined by the rules of the organization. Ready calculability of others' behavior and a stable set of mutual expectations is thus built up. Moreover, formality facilitates the interaction of the occupants of offices despite their (possibly hostile) private attitudes toward one another. In this way, the sub-

Reprinted from *Social Theory and Social Structure*, rev. ed., pp. 195–206, by permission of the author and the publisher, The Free Press. Copyright 1957.

[1] For a development of the concept of "rational organization," see Karl Mannheim, *Mensch und Gesellschaft im Zeitalter des Umbaus* (Leiden: A. W. Sijthoff, 1935), esp. 28 ff.

ordinate is protected from the arbitrary action of his superior, since the actions of both are constrained by a mutually recognized set of rules. Specific procedural devices foster objectivity and restrain the "quick passage of impulse into action."[2]

THE STRUCTURE OF BUREAUCRACY

The ideal type of such formal organization is bureaucracy and, in many respects, the classical analysis of bureaucracy is that by Max Weber.[3] As Weber indicates, bureaucracy involves a clear-cut division of integrated activities which are regarded as duties inherent in the office. A system of differentiated controls and sanctions is stated in the regulations. The assignment of roles occurs on the basis of technical qualifications which are ascertained through formalized, impersonal procedures (*e.g.*, examinations). Within the structure of hierarchically arranged authority, the activities of "trained and salaried experts" are governed by general, abstract, and clearly defined rules which preclude the necessity for the issuance of specific instructions for each specific case. The generality of the rules requires the constant use of *categorization*, whereby individual problems and cases are classified on the basis of designated criteria and are treated accordingly. The pure type of bureaucratic official is appointed, either by a superior or through the exercise of impersonal competition; he is not elected. A measure of flexibility in the bureaucracy is attained by electing higher functionaries who presumably express the will of the electorate (*e.g.*, a body of citizens or a board of directors). The election of higher officials is designed to affect the purposes of the organization, but the technical procedures for attaining these ends are carried out by continuing bureaucratic personnel.[4]

Most bureaucratic offices involve the expectation of life-long tenure, in the absence of disturbing factors which may decrease the size of the organization. Bureaucracy maximizes vocational security.[5]

[2] H. D. Lasswell, *Politics* (New York: McGraw-Hill, 1936), 120–121.

[3] Max Weber, *Wirtschaft und Gesellschaft* (Tübingen: J. C. B. Mohr, 1922), Pt. III, chap. 6; 650–678. For a brief summary of Weber's discussion, see Talcott Parsons, *The Structure of Social Action*, esp. 506 ff. For a description, which is not a caricature, of the bureaucrat as a personality type, see C. Rabany, "Les types sociaux: le fonctionnaire," *Revue générale d'administration*, 1907, 88, 5–28.

[4] Karl Mannheim, *Ideology and Utopia* (New York: Harcourt, Brace, 1936), 18n., 105 ff. See also Ramsay Muir, *Peers and Bureaucrats* (London: Constable, 1910), 12–13.

[5] E. G. Cahen-Salvador suggests that the personnel of bureaucracies is largely

The function of security of tenure, pensions, incremental salaries and regularized procedures for promotion is to ensure the devoted performance of official duties, without regard for extraneous pressures.[6] The chief merit of bureacracy is its technical efficiency, with a premium placed on precision, speed, expert control, continuity, discretion, and optimal returns on input. The structure is one which approaches the complete elimination of personalized relationships and nonrational considerations (hostility, anxiety, affectual involvements, etc.).

With increasing bureaucratization, it becomes plain to all who would see that man is to a very important degree controlled by his social relations to the instruments of production. This can no longer seem only a tenet of Marxism, but a stubborn fact to be acknowledged by all, quite apart from their ideological persuasion. Bureaucratization makes readily visible what was previously dim and obscure. More and more people discover that to work, they must be employed. For to work, one must have tools and equipment. And the tools and equipment are increasingly available only in bureaucracies, private or public. Consequently, one must be employed by the bureaucracies in order to have access to tools in order to work in order to live. It is in this sense that bureaucratization entails separation of individuals from the instruments of production, as in modern capitalistic enterprise or in state communistic enterprise (of the midcentury variety), just as in the post-feudal army, bureaucratization entailed complete separation from the instruments of destruction. Typically, the worker no longer owns his tools nor the soldier, his weapons. And in this special sense, more and more people become workers, either blue collar or white collar or stiff shirt. So develops, for example, the new type of scientific worker, as the scientist is "separated" from his technical equipment—after all, the physicist does not ordinarily own his cyclotron. To work at his research, he must be employed by a bureaucracy with laboratory resources.

Bureaucracy is administration which almost completely avoids public discussion of its techniques, although there may occur public discussion of its policies.[7] This secrecy is confined neither to public

constituted by those who value security above all else. See his "La situation matérielle et morale des fonctionnaires," *Revue politique et parlementaire* (1926), 319.

[6] H. J. Laski, "Bureaucracy," *Encyclopedia of the Social Sciences.* This article is written primarily from the standpoint of the political scientist rather than that of the sociologist.

[7] Weber, *op. cit.*, 671.

nor to private bureaucracies. It is held to be necessary to keep valuable information from private economic competitors or from foreign and potentially hostile political groups. And though it is not often so called, espionage among competitors is perhaps as common, if not as intricately organized, in systems of private economic enterprise as in systems of national states. Cost figures, lists of clients, new technical processes, plans for production—all these are typically regarded as essential secrets of private economic bureaucracies which might be revealed if the bases of all decisions and policies had to be publicly defended.

THE DYSFUNCTIONS OF BUREAUCRACY

In these bold outlines, the positive attainments and functions of bureaucratic organization are emphasized and the internal stresses and strains of such structures are almost wholly neglected. The community at large, however, evidently emphasizes the imperfections of bureaucracy, as is suggested by the fact that the "horrid hybrid," bureaucrat, has become an epithet, a *Schimpfwort.*

The transition to a study of the negative aspects of bureaucracy is afforded by the application of Veblen's concept of "trained incapacity," Dewey's notion of "occupational psychosis" or Warnotte's view of "professional deformation." Trained incapacity refers to that state of affairs in which one's abilities function as inadequacies or blind spots. Actions based upon training and skills which have been successfully applied in the past may result in inappropriate responses *under changed conditions.* An inadequate flexibility in the application of skills, will, in a changing milieu, result in more or less serious maladjustments.[8] Thus, to adopt a barnyard illustration used in this connection by Burke, chickens may be readily conditioned to interpret the sound of a bell as a signal for food. The same bell may now be used to summon the trained chickens to their doom as they are assembled to suffer decapitation. In general, one adopts measures in keeping with one's past training and, under new conditions which are not recognized as *significantly* different, the very soundness of this training may lead to the adoption of the wrong procedures. Again, in

[8] For a stimulating discussion and application of these concepts, see Kenneth Burke, *Permanence and Change* (New York: New Republic, 1935), pp. 50 ff.; Daniel Warnotte, "Bureaucratie et Fonctionnarisme," *Revue de l'Institut de Sociologie,* 1937, 17, 245.

Burke's almost echolalic phrase, "people may be unfitted by being fit in an unfit fitness"; their training may become an incapacity.

Dewey's concept of occupational psychosis rests upon much the same observations. As a result of their day to day routines, people develop special preferences, antipathies, discriminations and emphases.[9] (The term psychosis is used by Dewey to denote a "pronounced character of the mind.") These psychoses develop through demands put upon the individual by the particular organization of his occupational role.

The concepts of both Veblen and Dewey refer to a fundamental ambivalence. Any action can be considered in terms of what it attains or what it fails to attain. "A way of seeing is also a way of not seeing —a focus upon object *A* involves a neglect of object *B*." [10] In his discussion, Weber is almost exclusively concerned with what the bureaucratic structure attains: precision, reliability, efficiency. This same structure may be examined from another perspective provided by the ambivalence. What are the limitations of the organizations designed to attain these goals?

For reasons which we have already noted, the bureaucratic structure exerts a constant pressure upon the official to be "methodical, prudent, disciplined." If the bureaucracy is to operate successfully, it must attain a high degree of reliability of behavior, an unusual degree of conformity with prescribed patterns of action. Hence, the fundamental importance of discipline which may be as highly developed in a religious or economic bureaucracy as in the army. Discipline can be effective only if the ideal patterns are buttressed by strong sentiments which entail devotion to one's duties, a keen sense of the limitation of one's authority and competence, and methodical performance of routine activities. The efficacy of social structure depends ultimately upon infusing group participants with appropriate attitudes and sentiments. As we shall see, there are definite arrangements in the bureaucracy for inculcating and reinforcing these sentiments.

At the moment, it suffices to observe that in order to ensure discipline (the necessary reliability of response), these sentiments are often more intense than is technically necessary. There is a margin of safety, so to speak, in the pressure exerted by these sentiments upon the bureaucrat to conform to his patterned obligations, in much the same sense that added allowances (precautionary overestimations)

[9] *Ibid.*, 58–59.
[10] *Ibid.*, 70.

are made by the engineer in designing the supports for a bridge. But this very emphasis leads to a transference of the sentiments from the *aims* of the organization onto the particular details of behavior required by the rules. Adherence to the rules, originally conceived as a means, becomes transformed into an end-in-itself; there occurs the familiar process of *displacement of goals* whereby "an instrumental value becomes a terminal value." [11] Discipline, readily interpreted as conformance with regulations, whatever the situation, is seen not as a measure designed for specific purposes but becomes an immediate value in the life-organization of the bureaucrat. This emphasis, resulting from the displacement of the original goals, develops into rigidities and an inability to adjust readily. Formalism, even ritualism, ensues with an unchallenged insistence upon punctilious adherence to formalized procedures.[12] This may be exaggerated to the point where primary concern with conformity to the rules interferes with the achievement of the purposes of the organization, in which case we have the familiar phenomenon of the technicism or red tape of the official. An extreme product of this process of displacement of goals is the bureaucratic virtuoso, who never forgets a single rule binding his action and hence is unable to assist many of his clients.[13] A case in point, where strict recognition of the limits of authority and literal adherence to rules produced this result, is the pathetic plight of Bernt Balchen, Admiral Byrd's pilot in the flight over the South Pole.

[11] This process has often been observed in various connections. Wundt's *heterogony of ends* is a case in point; Max Weber's *Paradoxie der Folgen* is another. See also MacIver's observations on the transformation of civilization into culture and Lasswell's remark that "the human animal distinguishes himself by his infinite capacity for making ends of his means." See Merton, "The unanticipated consequences of purposive social action," *American Sociological Review*, 1936, 1, 894–904. In terms of the psychological mechanisms involved, this process has been analyzed most fully by Gordon W. Allport, in his discussion of what he calls "the functional autonomy of motives." Allport emends the earlier formulations of Woodworth, Tolman, and William Stern, and arrives at a statement of the process from the standpoint of individual motivation. He does not consider those phases of the social structure which conduce toward the "transformation of motives." The formulation adopted in this paper is thus complementary to Allport's analysis; the one stressing the psychological mechanisms involved, the other considering the constraints of the social structure. The convergence of psychology and sociology toward this central concept suggests that it may well constitute one of the conceptual bridges between the two disciplines. See Gordon W. Allport, *Personality* (New York: Henry Holt & Co., 1937), chap. 7.

[12] See E. C. Hughes, "Institutional office and the person," *American Journal of Sociology*, 1937, 43, 404–413; E. T. Hiller, "Social structure in relation to the person," *Social Forces*, 1937, 16, 34–43.

[13] Mannheim, *Ideology and Utopia*, 106.

> According to a ruling of the department of labor Bernt Balchen . . . cannot receive his citizenship papers. Balchen, a native of Norway, declared his intention in 1927. It is held that he has failed to meet the condition of five years' continuous residence in the United States. The Byrd antarctic voyage took him out of the country, although he was on a ship carrying the American flag, was an invaluable member of the American expedition, and in a region to which there is an American claim because of the exploration and occupation of it by Americans, this region being Little America.
>
> The bureau of naturalization explains that it cannot proceed on the assumption that Little America is American soil. That would be *trespass on international questions* where it has no sanction. So far as the bureau is concerned, Balchen was out of the country and *technically* has not complied with the law of naturalization.[14]

STRUCTURAL SOURCES OF OVERCONFORMITY

Such inadequacies in orientation which involve trained incapacity clearly derive from structural sources. The process may be briefly recapitulated. (1) An effective bureaucracy demands reliability of response and strict devotion to regulations. (2) Such devotion to the rules leads to their transformation into absolutes; they are no longer conceived as relative to a set of purposes. (3) This interferes with ready adaptation under special conditions not clearly envisaged by those who drew up the general rules. (4) Thus, the very elements which conduce toward efficiency in general produce inefficiency in specific instances. Full realization of the inadequacy is seldom attained by members of the group who have not divorced themselves from the meanings which the rules have for them. These rules in time become symbolic in cast, rather than strictly utilitarian.

Thus far, we have treated the ingrained sentiments making for rigorous discipline simply as data, as given. However, definite features of the bureaucratic structure may be seen to conduce to these sentiments. The bureaucrat's official life is planned for him in terms of a graded career, through the organizational devices of promotion by seniority, pensions, incremental salaries, *etc.*, all of which are designed to provide incentives for disciplined action and conformity to the

[14] Quoted from the *Chicago Tribune* (June 24, 1931, p. 10) by Thurman Arnold, *The Symbols of Government* (New Haven: Yale University Press, 1935), 201–202. (My italics.)

official regulations.[15] The official is tacitly expected to and largely does adapt his thoughts, feelings and actions to the prospect of this career. But *these very devices* which increase the probability of conformance also lead to an over-concern with strict adherence to regulations which induces timidity, conservatism, and technicism. Displacement of sentiments from goals onto means is fostered by the tremendous symbolic significance of the means (rules).

Another feature of the bureaucratic structure tends to produce much the same result. Functionaries have the sense of a common destiny for all those who work together. They share the same interests, especially since there is relatively little competition in so far as promotion is in terms of seniority. In-group aggression is thus minimized and this arrangement is therefore conceived to be positively functional for the bureaucracy. However, the *esprit de corps* and informal social organization which typically develops in such situations often leads the personnel to defend their entrenched interests rather than to assist their clientele and elected higher officials. As President Lowell reports, if the bureaucrats believe that their status is not adequately recognized by an incoming elected official, detailed information will be withheld from him, leading him to errors for which he is held responsible. Or, if he seeks to dominate fully, and thus violates the sentiment of self-integrity of the bureaucrats, he may have documents brought to him in such numbers that he cannot manage to sign them all, let alone read them.[16] This illustrates the defensive informal organization which tends to arise whenever there is an apparent threat to the integrity of the group.[17]

It would be much too facile and partly erroneous to attribute such resistance by bureaucrats simply to vested interests. Vested interests oppose any new order which either eliminates or at least makes uncertain their differential advantage deriving from the current arrangements. This is undoubtedly involved in part in bureaucratic resistance to change, but another process is perhaps more significant. As we have seen, bureaucratic officials affectively identify themselves with their

[15] Mannheim, *Mensch und Gesellschaft,* 32–33. Mannheim stresses the importance of the "Lebensplan" and the "Amtskarriere." See the comments by Hughes, *op. cit.,* 413.

[16] A. L. Lowell, *The Government of England* (New York, 1908), I, 189 ff.

[17] For an instructive description of the development of such a defensive organization in a group of workers, see F. J. Roethlisberger and W. J. Dickson, *Management and the Worker* (Boston: Harvard School of Business Administration, 1934).

way of life. They have a pride of craft which leads them to resist change in established routines; at least, those changes which are felt to be imposed by others. This nonlogical pride of craft is a familiar pattern found even, to judge from Sutherland's *Professional Thief,* among pickpockets who, despite the risk, delight in mastering the prestige-bearing feat of "beating a left breech" (picking the left front trousers pocket).

In a stimulating paper, Hughes has applied the concepts of "secular" and "sacred" to various types of division of labor; "the sacredness" of caste and *Stände* prerogatives contrasts sharply with the increasing secularism of occupational differentiation in our society.[18] However, as our discussion suggests, there may ensue, in particular vocations and in particular types of organization, the *process of sanctification* (viewed as the counterpart of the process of secularization). This is to say that through sentiment-formation, emotional dependence upon bureaucratic symbols and status, and affective involvement in spheres of competence and authority, there develop prerogatives involving attitudes of moral legitimacy which are established as values in their own right, and are no longer viewed as merely technical means for expediting administration. One may note a tendency for certain bureaucratic norms, originally introduced for technical reasons, to become rigidified and sacred, although, as Durkheim would say, they are *laïque en apparence.*[19] Durkheim has touched on this general process in his description of the attitudes and values which persist in the organic solidarity of a highly differentiated society.

PRIMARY VS. SECONDARY RELATIONS

Another feature of the bureaucratic structure, the stress on depersonalization of relationships, also plays its part in the bureaucrat's

[18] E. C. Hughes, "Personality types and the division of labor," *American Journal of Sociology,* 1928, 33, 754–768. Much the same distinction is drawn by Leopold von Wiese and Howard Becker, *Systematic Sociology* (New York: John Wiley & Sons, 1932), 222–225 *et passim.*

[19] Hughes recognizes one phase of this process of sanctification when he writes that professional training "carries with it as a by-product assimilation of the candidate to a set of professional attitudes and controls, *a professional conscience and solidarity. The profession claims and aims to become a moral unit.*" Hughes, *op. cit.,* 762 (italics inserted). In this same connection, Sumner's concept of

trained incapacity. The personality pattern of the bureaucrat is nucleated about this norm of impersonality. Both this and the categorizing tendency, which develops from the dominant role of general, abstract rules, tend to produce conflict in the bureaucrat's contacts with the public or clientele. Since functionaries minimize personal relations and resort to categorization, the peculiarities of individual cases are often ignored. But the client who, quite understandably, is convinced of the special features of *his* own problem often objects to such categorical treatment. Stereotyped behavior is not adapted to the exigencies of individual problems. The impersonal treatment of affairs which are at times of great personal significance to the client gives rise to the charge of "arrogance" and "haughtiness" of the bureaucrat. Thus, at the Greenwich Employment Exchange, the unemployed worker who is securing his insurance payment resents what he deems to be "the impersonality and, at times, the apparent abruptness and even harshness of his treatment by the clerks. . . . Some men complain of the superior attitude which the clerks have."[20]

Still another source of conflict with the public derives from the bureaucratic structure. The bureaucrat, in part irrespective of his position with*in* the hierarchy, acts as a representative of the power and prestige of the entire structure. In his official role he is vested with definite authority. This often leads to an actually or apparently domineering attitude, which may only be exaggerated by a dis-

---

pathos, as the halo of sentiment which protects a social value from criticism, is particularly relevant, inasmuch as it affords a clue to the mechanism involved in the process of sanctification. See his *Folkways,* 180–181.

[20] " 'They treat you like a lump of dirt they do. I see a navvy reach across the counter and shake one of them by the collar the other day. The rest of us felt like cheering. Of course he lost his benefit over it. . . . But the clerk deserved it for his sassy way.' " (E. W. Bakke, *The Unemployed Man,* 79–80). Note that the domineering attitude was *imputed* by the unemployed client who is in a state of tension due to his loss of status and self-esteem in a society where the ideology is still current that an "able man" can always find a job. That the imputation of arrogance stems largely from the client's state of mind is seen from Bakke's own observation that "the clerks were rushed, and had no time for pleasantries, but there was little sign of harshness or a superiority feeling in their treatment of the men." In so far as there is an objective basis for the imputation of arrogant behavior to bureaucrats, it may possibly be explained by the following juxtaposed statements. "Auch der moderne, sei es öffentliche, sei es private, Beamte erstrebt immer und geniesst meist den Beherrschten gegenüber eine spezifisch gehobene, 'ständische' soziale Schätzung." (Weber, *op. cit.*, 652.) "In persons in whom the craving for prestige is uppermost, hostility usually takes the form of a desire to humiliate others." K. Horney, *The Neurotic Personality of Our Time,* 178–179.

crepancy between his position within the hierarchy and his position with reference to the public.[21] Protest and recourse to other officials on the part of the client are often ineffective or largely precluded by the previously mentioned *esprit de corps* which joins the officials into a more or less solidary in-group. This source of conflict *may* be minimized in private enterprise since the client can register an effective protest by transferring his trade to another organization within the competitive system. But with the monopolistic nature of the public organization, no such alternative is possible. Moreover, in this case, tension is increased because of a discrepancy between ideology and fact: the governmental personnel are held to be "servants of the people," but in fact they are often superordinate, and release of tension can seldom be afforded by turning to other agencies for the necessary service.[22] This tension is in part attributable to the confusion of the status of bureaucrat and client; the client may consider himself socially superior to the official who is at the moment dominant.[23]

Thus, with respect to the relations between officials and clientele, one structural source of conflict is the pressure for formal and impersonal treatment when individual, personalized consideration is desired by the client. The conflict may be viewed, then, as deriving from the introduction of inappropriate attitudes and relationships. Conflict with*in* the bureaucratic structure arises from the converse situation, namely, when personalized relationships are substituted

[21] In this connection, note the relevance of Koffka's comments on certain features of the pecking-order of birds. "If one compares the behavior of the bird at the top of the pecking list, the despot, with that of one very far down, the second or third from the last, then one finds the latter much more cruel to the few others over whom he lords it than the former in his treatment of all members. As soon as one removes from the group all members above the penultimate, his behavior becomes milder and may even become very friendly. . . . It is not difficult to find analogies to this in human societies, and therefore one side of such behavior must be primarily the effects of the social groupings, and not of individual characteristics." K. Koffka, *Principles of Gestalt Psychology* (New York: Harcourt, Brace, 1935), 668–669.

[22] At this point the political machine often becomes functionally significant. As Steffens and others have shown, highly personalized relations and the abrogation of formal rules (red tape) by the machine often satisfy the needs of individual "clients" more fully than the formalized mechanism of governmental bureaucracy.

[23] As one of the unemployed men remarked about the clerks at the Greenwich Employment Exchange: " 'And the bloody blokes wouldn't have their jobs if it wasn't for us men out of a job either. That's what gets me about their holding their noses up.' " Bakke, *op. cit.*, 80. See also H. D. Lasswell and G. Almond, "Aggressive behavior by clients towards public relief administrators," *American Political Science Review*, 1934, 28, 643–655.

for the structurally required impersonal relationships. This type of conflict may be characterized as follows.

The bureaucracy, as we have seen, is organized as a secondary, formal group. The normal responses involved in this organized network of social expectations are supported by affective attitudes of members of the group. Since the group is oriented toward secondary norms of impersonality, any failure to conform to these norms will arouse antagonism from those who have identified themselves with the legitimacy of these rules. Hence, the substitution of personal for impersonal treatment within the structure is met with widespread disapproval and is characterized by such epithets as graft, favoritism, nepotism, apple-polishing, etc. These epithets are clearly manifestations of injured sentiments.[24] The function of such virtually automatic resentment can be clearly seen in terms of the requirements of bureaucratic structure.

Bureaucracy is a secondary group structure designed to carry on certain activities which cannot be satisfactorily performed on the basis of primary group criteria.[25] Hence behavior which runs counter to these formalized norms becomes the object of emotionalized disapproval. This constitutes a functionally significant defence set up against tendencies which jeopardize the performance of socially necessary activities. To be sure, these reactions are not rationally determined practices explicitly designed for the fulfillment of this function. Rather, viewed in terms of the individual's interpretation of the situation, such resentment is simply an immediate response opposing the "dishonesty" of those who violate the rules of the game. However, this subjective frame of reference notwithstanding, these reactions serve the latent function of maintaining the essential structural elements of bureaucracy by reaffirming the necessity for formalized, secondary relations and by helping to prevent the disintegration of the bureaucratic structure which would occur should these be supplanted by

[24] The diagnostic significance of such linguistic indices as epithets has scarcely been explored by the sociologist. Sumner properly observes that epithets produce "summary criticisms" and definitions of social situations. Dollard also notes that "epithets frequently define the central issues in a society," and Sapir has rightly emphasized the importance of context of situations in appraising the significance of epithets. Of equal relevance is Linton's observation that "in case histories the way in which the community felt about a particular episode is, if anything, more important to our study than the actual behavior. . . ." A sociological study of "vocabularies of encomium and opprobrium" should lead to valuable findings.

[25] *Cf.* Ellsworth Faris, *The Nature of Human Nature* (New York: McGraw-Hill, 1937), 41 ff.

personalized relations. This type of conflict may be generically described as the intrusion of primary group attitudes when secondary group attitudes are institutionally demanded, just as the bureaucrat-client conflict often derives from interaction on impersonal terms when personal treatment is individually demanded.[26]

PROBLEMS FOR RESEARCH

The trend towards increasing bureaucratization in Western Society, which Weber had long since foreseen, is not the sole reason for sociologists to turn their attention to this field. Empirical studies of the interaction of bureaucracy and personality should especially increase our understanding of social structure. A large number of specific questions invite our attention. To what extent are particular personality types selected and modified by the various bureaucracies (private enterprise, public service, the quasi-legal political machine, religious orders)? Inasmuch as ascendancy and submission are held to be traits of personality, despite their variability in different stimulus-situations, do bureaucracies select personalities of particularly submissive or ascendant tendencies? And since various studies have shown that these traits can be modified, does participation in bureaucratic office tend to increase ascendant tendencies? Do various systems of recruitment (*e.g.*, patronage, open competition involving specialized knowledge or general mental capacity, practical experience) select different personality types?[27] Does promotion through seniority lessen competitive anxieties and enhance administrative efficiency? A detailed examination of mechanisms for imbuing the bureaucratic codes with affect would be instructive both sociologically and psychologically. Does the general anonymity of civil service decisions tend

[26] Community disapproval of many forms of behavior may be analyzed in terms of one or the other of these patterns of substitution of culturally inappropriate types of relationship. Thus, prostitution constitutes a type-case where coitus, a form of intimacy which is institutionally defined as symbolic of the most "sacred" primary group relationship, is placed within a contractual context, symbolized by the exchange of that most impersonal of all symbols, money. See Kingsley Davis, "The sociology of prostitution," *American Sociological Review*, 1937, 2, 744–755.

[27] Among recent studies of recruitment to bureaucracy are: Reinhard Bendix, *Higher Civil Servants in American Society* (Boulder: University of Colorado Press, 1949); Dwaine Marvick, *Career Perspectives in a Bureaucratic Setting* (Ann Arbor: University of Michigan Press, 1954); R. K. Kelsall, *Higher Civil Servants in Britain* (London: Routledge and Kegan Paul, 1955); W. L. Warner and J. C. Abegglen, *Occupational Mobility in American Business and Industry* (Minneapolis: University of Minnesota Press, 1955).

to restrict the area of prestige-symbols to a narrowly defined inner circle? Is there a tendency for differential association to be especially marked among bureaucrats?

The range of theoretically significant and practically important questions would seem to be limited only by the accessibility of the concrete data. Studies of religious, educational, military, economic, and political bureaucracies dealing with the interdependence of social organization and personality formation should constitute an avenue for fruitful research. On that avenue, the functional analysis of concrete structures may yet build a Solomon's House for sociologists.

James G. March
and
Herbert A. Simon

The Theory of Organizational Equilibrium

The Barnard-Simon theory of organizational equilibrium is essentially a theory of motivation—a statement of the conditions under which an organization can induce its members to continue their participation, and hence assure organizational survival. The central postulates of the theory are stated by Simon, Smithburg, and Thompson as follows:

1. An organization is a system of interrelated social behaviors of a number of persons whom we shall call the *participants* in the organization.

2. Each participant and each group of participants receives *from* the organization *inducements* in return for which he makes *to* the organization *contributions*.

3. Each participant will continue his participation in an organization only so long as the inducements offered him are as great or

Reprinted in part from James G. March and Herbert A. Simon, *Organizations* (New York: Wiley, 1958), pp. 84–93, 106, 107–108, by permission of the authors and the publisher.

greater (measured in terms of *his* values and in terms of the alternatives open to him) than the contributions he is asked to make.

4. The contributions provided by the various groups of participants are the source from which the organization manufactures the inducements offered to participants.

5. Hence, an organization is "solvent"—and will continue in existence—only so long as the contributions are sufficient to provide inducements in large enough measure to draw forth these contributions.[1]

The theory, like many theoretical generalizations, verges on the tautological. Specifically, to test the theory, and especially the crucial postulate 3, we need independent empirical estimates of (a) the behavior of participants in joining, remaining in, or withdrawing from organizations; and (b) the balance of inducements and contributions for each participant, measured in terms of his "utilities."

The observation of participants joining and leaving organizations is comparatively easy. It is more difficult to find evidence of the value of variable (b) that does not depend on the observation of (a). Before we can deal with the observational problem, however, we must say a bit more about the concepts of inducements and contributions.

Inducements

Inducements are "payments" made by (or through) the organization to its participants (e.g., wages to a worker, service to a client, income to an investor). These payments can be measured in units that are independent of their utility to the participants (e.g., wages and income can be measured in terms of dollars, service to clients in terms of hours devoted to him). Consequently, for an individual participant we can specify a set of inducements, each component of the set representing a different dimension of the inducements offered by the organization. Thus, each component of the inducement can be measured uniquely and independently of the utilities assigned to it by the participants.

Inducement Utilities

For each component in the set of inducements there is a corresponding utility value. For the moment we will not be concerned with the shape of the utility function; but we do not exclude from consideration a step function. The utility function for a given individ-

[1] H. A. Simon, D. W. Smithburg, and V. A. Thompson, *Public Administration* (New York: Knopf, 1950), pp. 381–382.

ual reduces the several components of the inducements to a common dimension.

Contributions

We assume that a participant in an organization makes certain "payments" to the organization (e.g., work from the worker, fee from the client, capital from the investor). These payments, which we shall call contributions, can be measured in units that are independent of their utility to the participants. Consequently, for any individual participant we can specify a set of contributions.

Contribution Utilities

A utility function transforming contributions into utilities of the individual contributor can be defined in more than one way. A reasonable definition of the utility of a contribution is the value of the alternatives that an individual foregoes in order to make the contribution. As we shall see below, this definition of contribution utilities allows us to introduce into the analysis the range of behavior alternatives open to the participant.

These definitions of inducements and contributions permit two general approaches to the observational problem. On the one hand, we can try to estimate the utility balance directly by observing the behavior (including responses to pertinent questions) of participants. On the other hand, if we are prepared to make some simple empirical assumptions about utility functions, we can make predictions from changes in the amounts of inducements and contributions, without reference to their utilities.

To estimate the inducement-contribution utility balance directly, the most logical type of measure is some variant of individual satisfaction (with the job, the service, the investment, etc.). It appears reasonable to assume that the greater the difference between inducements and contributions, the greater the individual satisfaction. However, the critical "zero points" of the satisfaction scale and the inducement-contribution utility balance are not necessarily identical. The zero point for the satisfaction scale is the point at which one begins to speak of degrees of "dissatisfaction" rather than degrees of "satisfaction." It is, therefore, closely related to the level of aspiration and is the point at which we would predict a substantial increase in search behavior on the part of the organism.

The zero point on the inducement-contribution utility scale, on the other hand, is the point at which the individual is indifferent to leaving an organization. We have ample evidence that these two zero points are not identical, but, in particular, that very few of the "satisfied" participants leave an organization, whereas some, but typically not all, of the "unsatisfied" participants leave.[2]

How do we explain these differences? The explanation lies primarily in the ways in which alternatives to current activity enter into the scheme (and this is one of the reasons for defining contribution utilities in terms of opportunities foregone). Dissatisfaction is a cue for search behavior. Being dissatisfied, the organism expands its program for exploring alternatives. If over the long run this search fails, the aspiration level is gradually revised downward. We assume, however, that the change in aspiration level occurs slowly, so that dissatisfaction in the short run is quite possible. On the other hand, the inducement-contribution utility balance adjusts quickly to changes in the perception of alternatives. When fewer and poorer alternatives are perceived to be available, the utility of activities foregone decreases; and this adjustment occurs rapidly.

Consequently, we can use satisfaction expressed by the individual as a measure of the inducement-contribution utility balance only if it is used in conjunction with an estimate of perceived alternatives available. Speaking roughly, only the desire to move enters into judgments of satisfaction; desire to move *plus* the perceived ease of movement enters into the inducement-contribution utility measure. Many students of mobility (particularly those concerned with the mobility of workers) have tended to ignore one or the other of these two facets of the decision to participate.[3]

Direct observation of the inducement-contribution utilities, however, is not the only possible way to estimate them. Provided we make certain assumptions about the utility functions, we can infer the utility balance directly from observations of changes in the inducements or contributions measured in nonutility terms. Three major assumptions are useful and perhaps warranted. First, we assume that the utility functions change only slowly. Second, we assume that each utility function is monotonic with respect to its corresponding inducement or contribution. Although we may not know what the utility of an increase in wages will be, we are prepared to assume

[2] L. G. Reynolds, *The Structure of Labor Markets* (New York: Harper, 1951).

[3] J. M. Rice, M. Hill, and E. L. Trist, "The Representation of Labour Turnover as a Social Process," *Human Relations,* 3 (1950), 349–372; J. Behrend, "Absence and Labour Turnover in a Changing Economic Climate," *Occupational Psychology,* 27 (1953), 69–79.

it will be positive. Third, we assume that the utility functions of fairly broad classes of people are very nearly the same; within a given subculture we do not expect radical differences in values. Also, we can expect that if an increase in a given inducement produces an increase in utility for one individual, it will produce an increase for other individuals.

There are other reasonable assumptions about individual utility functions; some will be indicated below when we relate individual participation to other factors. These three assumptions, however, in themselves lead to a variety of estimation procedures. Under the first assumption the short-run effect of a change in inducements or contributions will be uncontaminated by feedback effects. By the second assumption (particularly in conjunction with the third) a host of ordinal predictions can be made on the basis of knowledge of changes in the inducements and contributions. The third assumption permits us to estimate some of the cardinal properties of the inducements-contributions balance, avoiding the problem of interpersonal comparison of utilities.

Assumptions such as those listed have some a priori validity, but it is more important that much of the evidence currently available on the behavior of participants is consistent with them. Thus, predictions are frequently and often successfully made by businessmen as to the feasibility of proposed organizational plans.

Consider the analysis of a businessman exploring the feasibility of a business venture. His first step is to construct an operating plan showing what activities and facilities are required to carry on the proposed business, including estimates of the quantities of "inputs" and "outputs" of all categories. In the language of economics, he estimates the "production function." In the language of organization theory, the production function states the rates of possible conversion of contributions into inducements.[4]

His second step is to estimate the monetary inducements that will be needed to obtain the inputs in the amounts required, and the monetary contributions that can be exacted for the outputs—i.e., the prices of factors of production and of product. In estimating these monetary inducements, predictions are being made as to the inducements-contributions balances of various classes of participants. Let us give some hypothetical examples:

Salaries and wages. Information is obtained on "going rates of

[4] H. A. Simon, "A Comparison of Organizational Theories," *The Review of Economic Studies,* 20 (1952–53), 40–48.

wages" for similar classes of work in other companies in the same area. An implicit *ceteris paribus* assumption is made with respect to other inducements, or (if the work, say, is particularly unpleasant, if proposed working conditions are particularly good or bad, etc.) the monetary inducement is adjusted upward or downward to compensate for the other factors. If the problem is to attract workers from other organizations, it is assumed that a wage differential or other inducement will be required to persuade them to change.

Capital. Information is obtained on "the money market"—i.e., the kinds of alternative investment opportunities that are available, the weight attached to various elements of risk, and the levels of interest rates. It is then assumed that to induce investment, the terms (interest rates, security, etc.) must be at least equal to the inducements available in alternative investments.

The same procedure is followed for the inducements to other participants. In each case, information is required as to the alternative inducements offered by other organizations, and these establish the "zero level" of the net inducement-contribution balance. If nonmonetary factors are not comparable among alternatives, an estimated adjustment is made of the monetary inducements by way of compensation. Of course, the adjustment may just as well be made in the nonmonetary factors (e.g., in product quality).

If the planned inducements, including the monetary inducements, give a positive balance for all groups of participants, the plan is feasible. If the plan is subsequently carried out, a comparison of the actual operations with the estimates provides an empirical test of the assumptions and the estimates. If the outcomes fail to confirm the assumptions, the businessman may still choose which of the two sets of assumptions he will alter. He may interpret the result as evidence that the basic inducements-contributions hypothesis is incorrect, or he may conclude that he has estimated incorrectly the zero points of one or more of the inducements-contributions balances. The fact is, however, that such predictions are frequently made with substantial success.

The testing of the theory is not confined to predicting the survival of new enterprises. At any time in the life of an organization when a change is made—that (a) explicitly alters the inducements offered to any group of participants; (b) explicitly alters the contributions demanded from them; or (c) alters the organizational activity in any way that will affect inducements or contributions—on any of these occasions, a prediction can be made as to the effect of the change on participation. The effects may be measurable in terms of turnover rates of employees, sales, etc., as appropriate.

THE PARTICIPANTS

The theory of organizational equilibrium, as we have formulated it here, implies a structure—an organization—underlying the equilibrium. Specifically, there must exist a social system involving the participants that exhibits both a high degree of interrelationship and substantial differentiation from other systems within the total social milieu.

Up to this point, we have not tried to be precise in defining participation. In fact, we must necessarily be somewhat arbitrary in identifying some particular individuals as participants in a given organization. A number of individuals other than those we will identify as principal participants in a business organization receive inducements from the organization and provide contributions to its existence, and under special circumstances such "participants" may assume a dominant role in determining the equilibrium of the organization. But when we describe the chief participants of most business organizations, we generally limit our attention to the following five major classes: employees, investors, suppliers, distributors, and consumers.

Most obvious in any catalogue of organizational participants are the employees, including the management. Ordinarily, when we talk of organizational participants what we mean are workers, and membership in a business organization is ordinarily treated as equivalent to employment. Employees receive wages and other gratuities and donate work (production) and other contributions to the organization. As will become obvious below, employment is the area of participation in organizations in which the most extensive research has been executed.

The role of investors as participants in the organization is explicit in the economic theory of the firm but has rarely been included in other analyses of organizational behavior. A close analogue is found in some treatises on public administration where external power groups are dealt with specifically.[5] Although the participation of

[5] Simon, Smithburg, and Thompson, *op. cit.;* D. B. Truman, *The Government Process* (New York: Knopf, 1951); J. L. Freeman, *The Political Process, Executive Bureau–Legislative Committee Relations* (New York: Random, 1955).

investors in the activities of business firms is frequently less active than that of political power groups in the management of governmental units, the behavior of investing participants is not so insignificant in the general American business scene as to warrant excluding them from consideration.

The distinction between units in a production-distribution process that are "in" the organization and those that are "out" of the organization typically follows the legal definition of the boundaries of a particular firm. We find it fruitful to use a more functional criterion that includes both the suppliers and the distributors of the manufacturing core of the organization (or its analogue where the core of the organization is not manufacturing). Thus, in the automobile industry it is useful to consider the automobile dealers as component parts of an automobile manufacturing organization.

Finally, the role of consumers in an organization has, like the role of investors, been generally ignored except by economic theorists. Since consumers are clearly part of the equilibrating system, organization theory must include in its framework the major components of a theory of consumption.

Taken too literally, this conception of organizations incorporates almost any knowledge about human behavior as a part of organization theory. However, we will limit our primary attention here to the participation of employees. Labor mobility has been studied at some length by both economists and social psychologists. Consequently, we will be able to find at least some evidence for the propositions cited. In general, the areas of investment behavior, supplier behavior, and middleman behavior are less well developed; and their propositions less well documented. Consumer behavior presents a somewhat different case, being the subject of considerable research.[6] Nevertheless, we will limit ourselves in this area to the general observations made below.[7]

EMPLOYEE PARTICIPATION: THE PARTICIPATION CRITERION

In one respect an employee's relation to the organization is quite different from that of other participants. In joining the organization he accepts an authority relation; i.e., he agrees that within some limits

[6] L. H. Clark (ed.), *Consumer Behavior* (New York: New York Univ., 1958).
[7] See "Extension to Other Participants."

(defined both explicitly and implicitly by the terms of the employment contract) he will accept as the premises of his behavior orders and instructions supplied to him by the organization. Associated with this acceptance are commonly understood procedures for "legitimating" communications and clothing them with authority for employees. Acceptance of authority by the employee gives the organization a powerful means for influencing him—more powerful than persuasion, and comparable to the evoking processes that call forth a whole program of behavior in response to a stimulus.

On the assumption that employees act in a subjectively rational manner, we can make some predictions about the scope of the authority relation from our knowledge of the inducements and contributions of the employees and other organization members.[8] An employee will be willing to enter into an employment contract only if it does not matter to him "very much" what activities (within the area of acceptance agreed on in the contract) the organization will instruct him to perform, or if he is compensated in some way for the possibility that the organization will impose unpleasant activities on him. It will be advantageous for the organization to establish an authority relation when the employee activities that are optimal for the organization (i.e., maximize the inducement utility to other participants of the employee's activity) cannot be predicted accurately in advance.

These propositions can be restated in a form that permits them to be tested by looking at terms of the employment contract. A particular aspect of an employee's behavior can be (*a*) specified in the employment contract (e.g., as the wage rate usually is), (*b*) left to the employee's discretion (e.g., sometimes, but not always, whether he smokes on the job), or (*c*) brought within the authority of the employer (e.g., the specific tasks he performs within the range fixed by the job specification). The conditions that make it advantageous to stipulate an aspect of behavior in the contract are sharp conflict of interest (e.g., as to wage level) and some uncertainty as to what that interest is. It is advantageous to leave to the employee's discretion those aspects that are of little interest to the employer but great interest to the employee; and to subject the employee to the organization's authority in those aspects that are of relatively great interest to the employer, comparatively unimportant to the employee, and about which the employer cannot make accurate predictions much in advance of performance. . . .

[8] Simon, *loc. cit.*

To construct a series of hypotheses relating employee participation to external variables, we must first establish a criterion for "participation." Three methods of measuring participation yield substantially different results. First, we can measure the quantity of production by the individual worker. Second, we can use an absence criterion. Permanent physical absence associated with leaving the company payroll represents the extreme value on the low side. Differences in on-the-job productivity are not captured by the absence criterion, but employees are distinguished by their absence rates as well as their turnover rates. Third, we can use a turnover criterion: we can identify participation with the all-or-none phenomena of being on or off the organization payroll.

Although it may appear at first blush that these measures simply reflect different degrees of disassociation from the organization and, therefore, are simply different points on a common continuum, the available empirical evidence indicates no consistent relation among measures of production, absences, and voluntary turnover.[9] The correlations are sometimes high, sometimes low; and the antecedent conditions for each result are difficult to specify. Some reasons for these findings are suggested by the available research, although substantiation is difficult.

First, under what conditions should we expect to find low absence (and/or productivity) associated with high voluntary turnover? We might expect that if extreme penalties are imposed for absence (relative to those generally expected in the group employed), absence rates will tend to be low among those who choose to stay on the job. But we should also expect to find a high rate of exit from the job. Similarly, where the ability to leave the organization is restrained (e.g., by governmental fiat), we should expect to find low voluntary turnover rates but (particularly if labor is scarce) relatively high absence rates.[10]

Second, under what conditions should we expect to find a positive relation between absence and turnover? Assume (1) that motivation to avoid the demands (i.e., contributions) of the job situation stems primarily from dissatisfaction with the inducements-contributions bal-

[9] The Action Society Trust, *Size and Morale* (London: The Trust, 1953); N. C. Morse, *Satisfactions in the White-Collar Job* (Ann Arbor: Univ. of Michigan, Survey Research Center, 1953); A. H. Brayfield and W. H. Crockett, "Employee Attitudes and Employee Performance," *Psychological Bulletin*, 52 (1955), 396–424.

[10] E. Mayo and G. F. Lombard, *Teamwork and Labor Turnover in the Aircraft Industry of Southern California* (Boston: Harvard, Division of Research, 1944).

ance, (2) that for most people motivation to seek relief through temporary absence occurs at a point related consistently to the point at which motivation to quit occurs, and (3) that the factors contributing to individual dissatisfaction are general to the population of workers rather than specific to individual workers. Under these assumptions absence and voluntary turnover will be positively related when the penalties associated with absence and withdrawal are "normal."

Although we have scarcely touched the complexity of the relation among absenteeism, sickness, and turnover, we can see that the choice of a criterion of participation will significantly affect the propositions about participation. We propose here to use a turnover criterion, both because there is some intuitive sense in which such a criterion is most meaningful and because we have already dealt with the production criterion (which is closely related, at least conceptually, to the absence criterion) in the previous chapter. At the same time, however, we will attempt to point out how an absence criterion would support similar or different propositions.

Alvin W. Gouldner

Metaphysical Pathos and the Theory of Bureaucracy

The conduct of a polemic focusses attention on the differences between two points of view to the neglect of their continuity and convergences. No modern polemic better exemplifies this than the controversy between the proponents of capitalism and of socialism. Each tends to define itself as the antithesis of the other; even the uncommitted bystander, rare though he be, is likely to think of the two as if they were utterly alien systems.

Reprinted in part from Alvin W. Gouldner, *American Political Science Review*, 49 (1955), 496–507, by permission of the author and publisher, The American Political Science Association.

There have always been some, however, who have taken exception to this sharp contrast between socialism and capitalism and who have insisted that there are significant similarities between the two. . . .

Without doubt the most sophisticated formulation of this view was that conceived by the German sociologist, Max Weber. To Weber, the distinguishing characteristic of modern capitalism was the "rational organization of free labor." The pursuit of private gain, noted Weber, was well known in many earlier societies; what distinguishes present-day capitalism, he held, is the peculiar organization of the production unit, an organization that is essentially bureaucratic. This conception of capitalism, writes Parsons, "has one important concrete result; in contradistinction to Marx and most 'liberal' theories, it strongly minimizes the differences between capitalism and socialism, emphasizing rather their continuity. Not only would socialistic organization leave the central fact of bureaucracy untouched, it would greatly accentuate its importance." [1]

While Marx had dwelt largely on the interrelations *among* production units, that is, their market ties, Weber focussed on the social relations *within* the industrial unit. If social relations inside of socialist and capitalist factories are fundamentally alike, in that they are both bureaucratic, then, asked Weber, does a socialist revolution yield very much of an improvement for the capitalist proletarian? If Marx argued that the workers of the world had nothing to *lose* by revolting, Weber contended that they really had nothing to *gain.*

It is sometimes assumed today that the Weberian outlook is at bottom anti-socialist. In effect, the argument runs, Weber's viewpoint devitalizes the myth-like appeal of socialism, draining off its ability to muster immense enthusiasms. Weber's theses are therefore held to be an "ideology" serviceable for the survival of capitalism, while Weber himself is characterized as the "Marx of the bourgeoisie."

Now all this may be true, but it is only a partial truth; for, in actuality, Weber's theories cut two ways, not one. If it is correct that his theory of bureaucracy saps the fervor of the socialist offensive, it also undermines the stamina of the capitalist bastions. If socialism and capitalism are similar in being bureaucratic, then not only is there little *profit* in substituting one for the other, but there is also little *loss.*

[1] Parsons, Talcott, *The Structure of Social Action,* New York, 1937, Free Press. p. 509. See also the provocative fuller development of this argument as it applies to industrial organization: George C. Homans, "Industrial Harmony as a Goal," in *Industrial Conflict,* eds. Kornhauser, Dubin, and Ross (New York, 1954).

Considered only from the standpoint of its political consequences then, the Weberian outlook is not anti-socialist alone, nor anti-capitalist alone, it is both. In the final analysis its political slogan becomes "a plague on both your houses." If Weber is to be regarded as an "ideologist," he is an ideologist not of counter-revolution but of quiescence and neutralism. For many intellectuals who have erected a theory of group organization on Weberian foundations, the world has been emptied of choice, leaving them disoriented and despairing.

That gifted historian of ideas, Arthur O. Lovejoy, astutely observed that every theory is associated with, or generates, a set of sentiments which those subscribing to the theory could only dimly sense. Lovejoy called this the "metaphysical pathos" of ideas, a pathos which is "exemplified in any description of the nature of things, any characterization of the world to which one belongs, in terms which, like the words of a poem, evoke through their associations and through a sort of empathy which they engender, a congenial mood or tone of feelings." [2]

As a result, a commitment to a theory often occurs by a process other than the one which its proponents believe and it is usually more consequential than they realize. A commitment to a theory may be made because the theory is congruent with the mood or deep-lying sentiments of its adherents, rather than merely because it has been cerebrally inspected and found valid.

So too is it with the theory of organization. Paradoxically enough, some of the very theories which promise to make man's own work more intelligible to himself and more amenable to his intelligence are infused with an intangible metaphysical pathos which insinuates, in the very midst of new discoveries, that all is lost. For the metaphysical pathos of much of the modern theory of group organization is that of pessimism and fatalism.

I. EXPLANATIONS OF BUREAUCRACY

Among the serious goads to pessimism are theories explaining bureaucracy as the end-product of increased size and complexity in organizations. This is by far the most popular of the interpretations. Marshall Dimock and Howard Hyde, for example, in their report to the Temporary National Economic Committee (TNEC), state: "The

[2] Arthur O. Lovejoy, *The Great Chain of Being* (Cambridge, Mass., 1948), p. 11.

broadest structural cause of bureaucracy, whether in business or in government, is the tremendous size of the organization. Thus with capital or appropriations measured in hundreds of millions and in billions of dollars and personnel in tens and hundreds of thousands, it is difficult to avoid the obtrusion of the objectionable features of bureaucracy."[3]

While suggesting varied causes for the development of bureaucracy, Max Weber also interpreted it as a consequence of large size. For example, in discussing the ubiquity of bureaucratic forms, Weber adds: "The same [bureaucratic] phenomena are found in the large-scale capitalistic enterprise; and the larger it is, the greater their role."[4] He underscores the role of size by emphasizing that "only by reversion in every field—political, religious, economic, etc.—to small-scale organization would it be possible to escape its influence."[5] Despite his consideration of other possible sources of bureaucracy, these comments suggest that Weber regarded organizational size as the controlling factor in the development of bureaucracy.

Weber's emphasis on size as the crucial determinant of bureaucratic development is unsatisfactory for several reasons. First, there are historic examples of human efforts carried out on an enormous scale which were not bureaucratic in any serious sense of the term.[6] The building of the Egyptian pyramids is an obvious example. Second, Weber never considers the possibility that it is not "large size" as such that disposes to bureaucracy; large size may be important only because it generates other social forces which, in their turn, generate bureaucratic patterns.

Of course, in every analysis there are always intervening variables—the unknown "x"—which stand between any cause and effect. Scientific progress depends, in part, on moving away from the gross causes and coming closer to those which are more invariably connected with the object of interest. The point is that when a social

[3] Monograph #11, Temporary National Economic Committee, *Bureaucracy and Trusteeship in Large Corporations* (Washington, D. C., 1940), p. 36.

[4] *Max Weber: The Theory of Social and Economic Organization,* translated and edited by A. M. Henderson and Talcott Parsons (New York, 1947), p. 334.

[5] *Ibid.,* p. 338.

[6] See Reinhard Bendix, "Bureaucracy: The Problem and Its Setting," *American Sociological Review,* Vol. 12, pp. 502–7 (Oct., 1947). On the other hand, there are theoretically significant cases of small organizations which are highly bureaucratized, for example, the Boulton and Watt factory in 1775–1805. This "case illustrates the fact that the bureaucratization of industry is not synonymous with the recent growth in the size of business enterprises." Reinhard Bendix, "Bureaucratization in Industry," in *Industrial Conflict,* p. 166.

scientist accepts "size" as an explanatory factor, instead of going on to ask what there is *about size* that makes for bureaucracy, he is making an analytic *decision.* It is not a formulation unavoidably dictated by the nature of the data itself.

Significantly, though, it is a decision that conduces to bleak pessimism. For to inform members of our society that the only way out of the bureaucratic impasse is to return to the historical past and to trade in large- for small-scale organizations is, in effect, to announce the practical impossibility of coping with bureaucracy. Moreover, many people in our society believe that "bigness" symbolizes progress; to tell them that it also creates bureaucracy is to place them on the horns of a dilemma which gores no matter which way they turn. In such a position the most painless response is inaction.

II. THE STRUCTURAL-FUNCTIONALISTS

The fuller ramifications of this approach to bureaucracy can best be explained by turning to the analyses of industrial organization made by some of the "structural-functionalists," who are still the dominant, albeit now seriously challenged, school of American sociologists, which has grown directly out of the theories of Durkheim, Weber, and others, and whose most elaborate expression is to be found in the work of Talcott Parsons.

Parsons' recent analyses of industrial bureaucracy are of sufficient importance to be quoted in full. "Though with many individual exceptions [which he does not examine], *technological advance* almost always leads to increasingly *elaborate division of labor* and the concomitant requirement of increasingly elaborate organization." He continues:

> The fundamental reason for this is, of course, that with elaborate differentiation of functions the need for *minute coordination* of the different functions develops at the same time. . . . There must be a *complex organization of supervision* to make quite sure that exactly the right thing is done. . . . Feeding the various parts into the process, in such a way that a modern assembly line can operate smoothly, requires very *complex organization* to see that they are available in just the right quantities at the right times and places. . . . One of the most important phases of this process of change is concerned with the necessity for *formalization* when certain points of complexity are reached. . . .

> *Smaller* and simpler organizations are typically managed with a high degree of particularism (i.e., personal consideration) in the relations of persons in authority to their own subordinates. But when the "distance" between points of decision and of operation increases, and the number of operating units affected by decisions with it, uniformity and coordination can be attained *only* by a high degree of formalization. . . .[7]

Surprisingly enough, this is an atavistic recurrence of technological determinism in which characteristic bureaucratic traits—such as an elaborate division of labor, complex organization, and formalization—are held to stem directly from technological advance. This is a form of *technological* determinism because bureaucracy is seen as the result of technological change, without inquiring into the motives and meanings which these changes have for the people involved, and without wondering whether technological change would have a different impact on the formal organization of a group that had a high motivation to produce and therefore did not require close supervision. This is a form of technological *determinism,* because no alternative solutions are appraised or deemed possible and coordination is seen as attainable "*only* by a high degree of formalization. . . ."

Here once again we are invited to draw the conclusion that those who want modern technology must be prepared to pay for it with a minute and even stultifying division of labor.

All this, though, is a theoretical tapestry devoid of even the plainest empirical trimmings. Even on logical grounds, however, it is tenuous indeed. For it is evident that organizational patterns, such as a high division of labor, are found in spheres where modern technology has made comparatively little headway. This, in fact, is a point that Weber was at pains to insist upon. And if, as he maintained, bureaucratic forms are also found in charitable, political, or religious organizations—and not solely in industry—then they certainly cannot be explained as a consequence of modern machine technology.

Beyond these logical considerations, there are some *empircal* grounds for questioning the adequacy of Parsons' analysis. Peter Drucker, for example, became extremely doubtful about the necessity of a minute division of labor while observing large-scale American industry during World War II. (This is crucial for Parsons' argument, because he holds that it is through increased specialization that tech-

[7] Talcott Parsons, *The Social System* (Glencoe, Illinois, 1951), pp. 507–8. Italics added.

nology evokes the other elements of bureaucratic organization.) Drucker comments that

> we have learned that it is neither necessary nor always efficient to organize all mass production in such a manner as to have the majority of workers confine themselves to doing one and only one of the elementary manipulations. . . . It was impossible [because of wartime shortages of skilled labor] to "lay out" the job in the usual assembly-line fashion in which one unskilled operation done by one unskilled man is followed by the next unskilled man. The operation was broken down into its unskilled components like any assembly-line job. *But then the unskilled components were put together again with the result that an unskilled worker actually performed the job of a highly skilled mechanic*—and did it as reliably and efficiently as had been done by skilled men.[8]

In short, lower degrees of specialization than those normally found in large-scale industry are not necessarily forbidden by modern technology. Drucker's observations must, at the very least, raise the question as to how much of the minute division of labor is attributable to technological causes. Parsons, though, gives no consideration to other factors contributing to an extreme division of labor. However, Carl Dreyfuss, a German industrial sociologist, has advanced an array of keen observations and hypotheses which meet this question directly. He writes: "the artificial complication of the rank order . . . permits numerous employees to feel that they hold high positions and are to a certain extent independent." Moreover, he notes that a complicated division of labor is "with its unwarranted differentiations, telescoped positions, and ramifications, diametrically opposed to efforts of rationalization." [9] In other words, Dreyfuss suggests that much of the complex division of labor today is not to be explained by technological requirements, but rather in terms of the prestige satisfactions, the "psychic income," that it presumably provides workers.

In Dreyfuss' view, the "minute division of labor" also stems from management's needs to *control* workers and to make themselves independent of any specific individual or group of workers. A high division of labor, said Dreyfuss, means that "individual workers and employees can be exchanged and replaced at any time." [10] Through its use,

[8] Peter Drucker, *Concept of the Corporation* (New York, 1946), pp. 183–84.

[9] Carl Dreyfuss, *Occupation and Ideology of the Salaried Employee*, trans. Eva Abramovitch (New York, 1938), p. 17.

[10] *Ibid.*, p. 75.

"dependence of the employee upon the employer is greatly increased. It is much more difficult for today's employee, trained in only one particular function, to find re-employment than it was for his predecessor, a many-sided, well-instructed business man, able and fitted to fill a variety of positions." [11]

It is unnecessary for our purpose here to resolve this disparity between Dreyfuss, on the one hand, and Parsons, on the other. What may be suggested, however, is that there is considerable reason for holding Parsons' position to be both logically and empirically inadequate and to recognize that it has, without compelling scientific warrant, accommodated itself to the metaphysical pathos of organizational theory, which sees no escape from bureaucracy.

III. THE TRADITION OF MICHELS

There is another offshoot among the structural-functionalists which is distinguished by its concern for the problems bequeathed by Robert Michels, and, as such, it is even more morosely pessimistic than others in the school. Michels, it will be remembered, focussed his empirical studies on the Social Democratic parties of pre-World War I Europe. He chose these, quite deliberately, because he wanted to see whether groups which stood for greater freedom and democracy, and were hostile to authoritarianism, were not themselves afflicted by the very organizational deformity to which they were opposed.

Michel's conclusions were, of course, formulated in his "iron law of oligarchy," in which he maintained that always and everywhere a "system of leadership is incompatible with the most essential postulates of democracy." [12]

Focussing, as Michels did, on an apparently democratic group, Philip Selznick examined the TVA, which many Americans had long believed to be an advanced expression of democratic values. Like Michels, Selznick assumes that

> wherever there is organization, whether formally democratic or not, there is a split between the leader and the led, between the agent and the initiator. The phenomenon of abdication to bureaucratic directives in corporations, in trade unions, in parties, and in cooperatives is so widespread that it indicates a fundamental weakness of democracy.[13]

[11] *Ibid.*, p. 77.

[12] Robert Michels, *Political Parties* (Glencoe, Ill., 1949), p. 400. Michel's work was first published in 1915.

[13] Philip Selznick, *TVA and the Grass Roots* (Berkeley and Los Angeles, 1949), p. 9.

Selznick's study concludes that the TVA's emphasis on "decentralization" is to be best understood as a result of that agency's needs to adapt to suspicious local communities and to survive in competition with older governmental agencies based in Washington. "Decentralization" is viewed as a "halo that becomes especially useful in countries which prize the symbols of democracy." [14] In its turn, the TVA's emphasis on "participation" is explained as a catchword, satisfying the agency's needs to transform "an unorganized citizenry into a reliable instrument for the achievement of administrative goals. . . ." [15]

Selznick, like Michels, is impressed with the similarity in the organizational devices employed by different groups, whether they are democratic or authoritarian in ideology. He asserts

> . . . there seems to be a continuum between the voluntary associations set up by the democratic (mass) state—such as committees of farmers to boost or control agricultural production—and the citizens' associations of the totalitarian (mass) state. Indeed, the devices of corporatism emerge as relatively effective responses to the need to deal with the mass, and in time of war the administrative techniques of avowedly democratic countries and avowedly totalitarian countries tend to converge.[16]

In Selznick's analysis human action involves a commitment to two sets of interests: first to the *goals* intended, and second to the organizational *instruments* through which these goals are pursued. These tools are, however, recalcitrant; they generate "needs" which cannot be neglected. Hence if men persist in their ends, they are forced to satisfy the needs of their organizational instruments. They are, therefore, as much committed to their tools as to their ends, and "these commitments may lead to unanticipated consequences resulting in a deflection of original ends." [17]

For these reasons, organizational behavior must be interpreted not so much in terms of the *ends* that administrators deliberately seek, as in terms of the organizational "needs" which their pursuit engenders.

> The needs in question are organizational, not individual, and include: the security of the organization as a whole in relation to social forces in its environment; the stability of the lines of authority and communication; the stability of informal relations within the organization; the continu-

[14] *Ibid.*, p. 220.
[15] *Loc. cit.*
[16] *Loc. cit.*
[17] *Ibid.*, p. 259.

ity of policy and of the sources of its determination; a homogeneity of outlook with respect to the means and role of the organization.[18]

Selznick chose to focus on those social constraints that *thwart* democratic aspirations, but neglected to consider the constraints that enable them to be *realized,* and that foster and encourage "good will" and "intelligence." Are these, however, random occurrences, mere historic butterflies which flit through events with only ephemeral beauty? Or are they, as much as anything else, often the unanticipated products of our "commitments"? Why is it that "unanticipated consequences" are always tacitly assumed to be destructive of democratic values and "bad"; why can't they sometimes be "good"? Are there no constraints which *force* men to adhere valorously to their democratic beliefs, which *compel* them to be intelligent rather than blind, which leave them *no choice* but to be men of good will rather than predators? The neglect of these possibilities suggests the presence of a distorting pathos.

It is the pathos of pessimism, rather than the compulsions of rigorous analysis, that leads to the assumption that organizational constraints have stacked the deck against democracy. For on the face of it there is every reason to assume that "the underlying tendencies which are likely to inhibit the democratic process" are just as likely to impair authoritarian rule. It is only in the light of such a pessimistic pathos that the defeat of democratic values can be assumed to be probable, while their victory is seen as a slender thing, delicately constituted and precariously balanced.

When, for example, Michels spoke of the "iron law of oligarchy," he attended solely to the ways in which organizational needs inhibit democratic possibilities. But the very same evidence to which he called attention could enable us to formulate the very opposite theorem—the "iron law of democracy." Even as Michels himself saw, if oligarchical waves repeatedly wash away the bridges of democracy, this eternal recurrence can happen only because men doggedly rebuild them after each inundation. Michels chose to dwell on only one aspect of this process, neglecting to consider this other side. There cannot be an iron law of oligrachy, however, unless there is an iron law of democracy.

Much the same may be said for Selznick. He posits certains organizational needs: a need for the *security* of the organization, for *stable* lines of authority and communication, for *stable* informal relationships.

[18] *Ibid.*, p. 252.

But for each of the organizational needs which Selznick postulates, a set of contrary needs can also be posited, and the satisfaction of these would seem to be just as necessary for the survival of an organization. If, as Selznick says, an organization must have security in its environment, then certainly Toynbee's observations that too much security can be stultifying and corrosive is at least as well taken. To Selznick's security need, a Toynbee might counterpose a need for a moderate *challenge* or *threat.*

A similar analysis might also be made of Selznick's postulated need for homogeneity of outlook concerning the means and role of the organization. For unless there is some *heterogeneity* of outlook, then where is an organization to find the tools and flexibility to cope with changes in its environment? Underlying Selznick's need for homogeneity in outlook, is there not another "need," *a need that consent of the governed be given—at least in some measure—to their governors?* Indeed, this would seem to be at the very core of Selznick's empirical analysis, though it is obscured in his high-level theoretical statement of the needs of organizations. And if all organizations must adjust to such a need for consent, is there not built into the very marrow of organization a large element of what we mean by democracy? This would appear to be an organizational constraint that makes oligarchies, and all separation of leaders from those led, no less inherently unstable than democratic organization.[19]

These contrary needs are just as real and just as consequential for organizational behavior as those proposed by Selznick. But they point in a different direction. They are oriented to problems of change, of growth, of challenging contingencies, of provoking and unsettling encounters. Selznick's analysis seems almost to imply that survival is possible only in an icy stasis, in which "security," "continuity," and "stability" are the key terms. If anything, the opposite seems more likely to be true, and organizational survival is impossible in such a state.

Wrapping themselves in the shrouds of nineteenth-century political economy, some social scientists appear to be bent on resurrecting a

[19] See Arthur Schweitzer, "Ideological Groups," *American Sociological Review,* Vol. 9, pp. 415–27 (Aug., 1944), particularly his discussion of factors inhibiting oligarchy. For example, "A leadership concentrating all power in its hands creates indifference among the functionaries and sympathizers as well as decline in membership of the organization. This process of shrinkage, endangering the position of the leaders, is the best protection against the supposedly inevitable iron law of oligarchy" (p. 419). Much of the research deriving from the Lewinian tradition would seem to lend credence to this inference.

dismal science. Instead of telling men how bureaucracy might be mitigated, they insist that it is inevitable. Instead of explaining how democratic patterns may, to some extent, be fortified and extended, they warn us that democracy cannot be perfect. Instead of controlling the disease, they suggest that we are deluded, or more politely, incurably romantic, for hoping to control it. Instead of assuming responsibilities as realistic clinicians, striving to further democratic potentialities wherever they can, many social scientists have become morticians, all too eager to bury men's hopes.[20]

Terence K. Hopkins

Bureaucratic Authority: The Convergence of Weber and Barnard

Organizational theory today contains two different views of systems of bureaucratic authority. In one, which has its source in the writings of Max Weber, they are power structures operating in a quasi-judicial fashion: rational values legitimate them, trained experts run them, and the principle of hierarchy, prescribing a positive relation between the rank of a unit and its power, defines their shape. In the other, developed most fully by Chester I. Barnard, they are communications processes. Here they function to apprise decision makers of relevant matters of fact and to

I am grateful to Professors Daniel Bell, William J. Goode, Renate Mayntz, Morris Zelditch, Jr., and, especially, Amitai Etzioni and Robert K. Merton for their critical comments on earlier versions of this paper. The ideas presented here were initially developed in 1957–1958, when I held a Pre-Doctoral Research Training Fellowship from the Social Science Research Council, and its support during that period is gratefully acknowledged.

[20] We have sought to develop the positive implications of this approach to bureaucratic organization in *Patterns of Industrial Bureaucracy* (Glencoe, Ill., 1954).

inform those who execute the decisions of their responsibilities. In this conception neither legitimacy nor hierarchy plays a particularly central role. Both occur, but individual self-interests rather than shared moral commitments provide the main motivations, and the lateral extension of the system in physical space is more salient than its vertical extension in stratified social space. If the first view suggests the image of a pyramid, the second suggests a wheel, with the lines of communication as so many spokes radiating from the few persons at the organization's center who make the decisions to the many along the outer rim who finally carry the decisions out. In one, then, the outstanding elements are power, hierarchy, and legitimacy; in the other, decision making, communication, and rational self-interest. Taken together, they comprise the major concepts currently used in the study of bureaucratic authority.

In point of fact, however, they are seldom taken together. Either one view or the other is used but not usually the two in combination. In consequence, many studies of communication systems read as though the exercise of authority depended upon the good will and rationality of the participants, and many studies emphasizing power leave the impression that, so far as the effectiveness of the system is concerned, the processes through which authority is exercised are of little consequence. So much is more implicit than explicit, of course—few proponents of one point of view would actually deny the relevance of the other—but since the researcher usually takes a part for the whole to begin with, it is not surprising that he sometimes ends up with incomplete, and to that extent misleading, conclusions.

Moreover, the two types of findings, once in, remain unrelated—conclusions about power structures and communication systems are rarely seen to have implications for one another—with the result that theoretical developments have been relatively few and far between and, when they do occur, limited to commentaries on the views or additions to them.[1] In short, partly owing to their separation from one another, neither conception has developed very far in the direction of a coherent propositional theory of bureaucratic authority. Rather, each

[1] Perhaps the best of these are Robert K. Merton, "Bureaucratic Structure and Personality," in *Social Theory and Social Structure* (Glencoe, Ill.: Free Press, 1957), pp. 195–206; Talcott Parsons' discussion of authority in his "Introduction" to Max Weber, *The Theory of Social and Economic Organization,* trans. A. M. Henderson and Talcott Parsons (New York: Oxford, 1947), especially n. 4, pp. 58–60; and Talcott Parsons, "Authority, Legitimation, and Political Action," in Carl J. Friedrich (ed.), *Authority* (Cambridge, Mass.: Harvard, 1958), Chap. 12.

has remained in this respect largely as it was when originally formulated—a loosely related set of assumptions, concepts, and implicit propositions.

It therefore seems reasonable to attempt to integrate the two views of bureaucratic authority. One way of doing this is to turn back to Weber and Barnard, systematically compare their accounts, and then outline the resulting composite picture of bureaucratic authority structures. This paper attempts to carry out such a review. It first demonstrates that, so far as both the definition of authority and the explanation of the stability of bureaucratic authority structures are concerned, Weber and Barnard develop similar ideas. Their convergence on these two points gives the essay its title. Subsequently it suggests where and in what degree their explanations of the effectiveness of authority systems differ. The principal propositions of their theories, and thus the main sources for the two views of bureaucratic authority just described, occur in these explanations, and for this reason only a summary of them is given here. The essay concludes with an outline of their combined conceptions.

THE DEFINITION OF BUREAUCRATIC AUTHORITY

For Weber, authority of any kind is exercised when a given order is obeyed, when the recipient's action "follows in essentials such a course that the content of the command may be taken to have become the basis of action for its own sake." [2] For Barnard bureaucratic authority is exercised when a communication is accepted, which occurs when the communication governs "the action he (the recipient) contributes" or determines "what he does or does not do so

[2] Weber, *op. cit.,* p. 327. A certain difficulty attends the interpretation of Weber's theory. In its original version it applies to whole societies, and states that differences in the way control is exercised result from differences in beliefs about the nature of authority. Naturally only a part of this theory is employed in current organizational studies, the part that describes the rational-legal conception of authority and its organizational form, bureaucracy: focusing on particular, concrete organizations, located in societies where this conception is highly institutionalized, these studies use Weber's categories as approximate descriptions of the organizations being examined. But owing to these shifts—from societies to organizations as the units being analyzed, and from cross-cultural comparisons to detailed studies of a particular organizational form—Weber's theory has acquired a second set of meanings and so can now be read in two broadly different ways. For this reason it should be said explicitly that its interpretation here reflects its use in current organizational research, not its original use.

far as the organization is concerned."[3] Both men, then, see the problem of authority as primarily a problem of compliance, they define compliance in the same general way, and, in consequence, their theories are addressed to the same range of problems, the determinants of stable structures of compliant actions.

The setting within which this compliance takes place, and which gives it its specifically bureaucratic character, is, in Weber, the rationally organized "corporate group" and, in Barnard, the formally organized "cooperative system."[4] These are not equivalent concepts, since corporate groups by definition have both a restricted membership and rules enforced by specific persons, whereas neither is a necessary feature of cooperative systems. But if the corporate group and the cooperative system have rational, formalized, and complex organizations, they are sufficiently alike to permit the remaining differences to be ignored here because, first, both theories focus on the internal structure and operation of units—their organization—not on their particular goals or social contexts, and, second, both assume, so far as these rationally organized units are concerned, that the grounds for compliance and the qualities that make a system of authority effective are in principle everywhere the same. Owing to this focus and its parallel assumption, Weber and Barnard use the same criterion to judge the effectiveness of bureaucratic authority systems, namely, the extent to which those subject to the organization's formalized rules and orders actually obey them.[5]

[3] Chester I. Barnard, *The Functions of the Executive* (Cambridge, Mass.: Harvard, 1938), p. 163.

[4] On corporate group, see Weber, *op. cit.*, Chap. 1, Sections 12–17. On cooperative systems, see Barnard, *op. cit.*, pp. 65 ff. Barnard attempts to distinguish between the concept of "organization" and the concept of "group" (e.g., p. 112). A number of difficulties beset this distinction; but it does catch up one very important point, namely, that the edges ("boundaries") of the organization, as marked out by the line between participants and nonparticipants, does not necessarily coincide with the edges ("boundaries") of the group anchoring the organization, as marked out by the line between group member and nonmember. (On "group" and "member," see Merton, *loc. cit.*, pp. 285–286.) Generally, the organization is the more inclusive; there are participants who are not members, but not usually vice versa. This distinction, between the concepts of participant and member, has an important bearing on the "legitimation" of particular authority structures (see below, pp. 95–96).

[5] Some confusion may arise here because neither writer consistently distinguishes between the effectiveness of the authority system and the effectiveness of the total organization. In Weber, the criterion of the latter is the extent to which the substantive goals of the corporate group are achieved. In Barnard, it is this attainment of goals plus the extent to which personnel are motivated to continue participating in the cooperative system.

The concern with compliance further restricts the scope of the theories. Because of it one might think these authors slight the part of authority that pertains to its exercise. In their theories, however, the giving of orders or the sending of communications are themselves forms of compliance, because the orders a participant gives are assumed to derive directly from those he receives. True, in a rationally organized system this sort of chain of command ends eventually in a set of established general rules or policies and a policy-making body. But at this point both theories cease to have relevance. Neither includes as part of its subject matter the actions by which general rules are initially established or intentionally changed. Both pertain only to the command-obedience sequences by which already formulated policies are translated into routine operations and continually maintained in effect.

So much, then, for the subject matter and scope of the theories, the further development of which thus falls naturally into two parts, one dealing with the grounds for compliance in a general way and the second, with the properties of social structure which presumably affect the degrees of compliance and therefore serve to distinguish between authority systems that are more and less effective.

THE GROUNDS FOR COMPLIANCE: MOTIVES AND VALUES

The "motivation" to obey seemingly receives a good deal of attention, for Weber begins with a discussion of it and Barnard talks about it in various places. But in point of fact neither says anything important about the social psychology of compliance.[6] Instead, both introduce the element of shared values and conclude, each in his own way, that the participants in an organization must to some extent hold in common certain "legitimating" beliefs or "fictions" if obedience is to occur regularly and the chain of command to prove stable.

Legitimacy

As was said, Weber begins his discussion of authority by mentioning a number of motives that may come into play in particular circumstances. But almost immediately he turns from these to "the belief in legitimacy." This, he holds, provides the only "sufficiently reliable

[6] Compare either's writings with, say, the rigorous paper by Hans Zetterberg, "Compliant Actions," *Acta sociologica*, 2(1957), 179–201.

basis" for a stable and effective system of authority.[7] Different types of value system provide this belief and so enable different systems of authority to exist.

For bureaucratic authority, the value system providing the required legitimation is rational-legal and contains, *inter alia,* the following ideas: obedience is an obligation of statuses, not of persons as such; an issued command is an interpretation or application of a general rule; such rules (whether established unilaterally by the governing group or voted into being by a majority of the participants) apply in principle to all participants, no one being above the law; the rules may be changed.[8]

This concept of legitimacy designates an essentially moral element. By introducing it Weber is claiming that, in general, people obey when they do because they feel a moral obligation to do so, because, specifically, they and everyone else define the statuses they occupy as allowing or requiring them to do so. To put it in contemporary terms, a system of authority has the property of legitimacy to the extent that the statuses and roles are institutionalized: an act of commanding and its reciprocal act of obeying do not form a specific and stable pattern unless both are appropriate actions within a well-defined role relation.[9]

The Fiction of Superior Authority

When Barnard discusses "motives" he does not move directly to the sphere of values but first introduces the concept, "zone of indifference." Among all the orders a person in a particular position in an organization might conceivably receive, some he would consider unacceptable, some would be on the borderline of acceptability, and some would be "unquestionably acceptable." These last fall within that particular person's "zone of indifference," and these he will readily obey.[10]

[7] Weber, *op. cit.,* p. 325.

[8] *Ibid.,* pp. 329–330. Since the point has been misunderstood on at least one occasion, it bears emphasizing that these are *not* Weber's own ideas about legal authority but the ideas that, in the typical case, the people subject to a system of legal authority must hold if it is to prove stable and effective.—*Ibid.,* p. 329. For the misunderstanding, see Alvin W. Gouldner, *Patterns of Industrial Bureaucracy* (Glencoe, Ill.: Free Press, 1954), pp. 19–20.

[9] On the concept of institutionalization, see Talcott Parsons, *The Social System* (Glencoe, Ill.: Free Press, 1951), pp. 36–45. For a more exact rendering of "legitimacy," and a distinction between "legitimation" and "institutionalization," see Parsons, "Authority, Legitimation, and Political Action," *loc. cit.*

[10] Barnard, *op. cit.,* pp. 168–169.

The "zone," then, is a characteristic of the person. Its scope is determined, not by characteristics distinctive to him as an individual, however, but by characteristics common to all who occupy a similar position in the organization's structure. Turning first to the order itself, Barnard says an acceptable order is usually one which

> . . . lies within the range that in a general way was anticipated [by the person] at the time of undertaking the connection with the organization.[11]

These anticipations, he next suggests, are socially determined and form elements of a normative consensus:

> The common sense of the community informally arrived at affects the attitude of individuals, and makes them, as individuals, loath to question authority that is within or near the [community's] zone of indifference.[12]

What begins conceptually as a personal zone of indifference becomes in this way part of the definition of the person's status in the organization: he can usually be counted upon to accept any communications or to obey any orders which, because of this status, he both expects to accept and is expected by others to accept. Barnard then introduces the rank structure and the rational-legal ideology and thus arrives at the position taken by Weber:

> The formal statement of this common sense is the fiction that authority comes down from above, from the general to the particular. This fiction merely establishes a presumption among individuals in favor of the acceptability of orders from superiors. . . . [It] makes it possible normally to treat a personal question impersonally.[13]

Basic to both men's conceptions, then, are shared values. In effect, each applies to a particular class of actions, the giving and obeying of orders, the general theorem that motivational and cultural elements of action are integrated.[14] Their conceptions thus contain at this point, besides the earlier definitions, the proposition that in a rational and complex organization compliance with the rules varies with the institutionalization of the roles through which commands are issued

[11] *Ibid.*, p. 169.

[12] *Ibid.*

[13] *Ibid.*, pp. 169–170. "Fiction," it might be noted, means here a nonlogical construct in Pareto's sense, one which participants use to explain their behavior and which they believe in. Hence the ideas this "fiction" contains "have validity" for those in the system. Barnard himself notes in this regard, "Either as a superior officer or as a subordinate, . . . I know nothing I actually regard as more 'real' than 'authority.' "—*Ibid.*, p. 170, n. 5.

[14] Parsons, *The Social System,* pp. 36–45.

and obeyed. This statement should be regarded, not as an hypothesis within the theory, however, but as the basis for a further restriction of its subject matter: in order to apply the theory in particular cases, one must be able to assume that compliance is to some extent an institutionalized pattern; otherwise no authority system exists, and therefore no question of its effectiveness arises.

The two views of bureaucratic authority are alike, then, in the following ways. Both define the exercise of authority in terms of compliance; locate the compliant actions within social systems that exhibit a rationalized, formalized, and complex type of organization; define the effectiveness of authority systems as the extent to which those subject to the organization's rules in fact comply with them; assume that for all such systems the grounds for compliance and the qualities that make an authority system effective are in principle the same; and postulate that an authority system exists in so far as compliance is an aspect of the actions of institutionalized roles.

BUREAUCRATIC STRUCTURES OF AUTHORITY

By definition, all authority structures are institutionalized at least to some extent; presumably, therefore, a system with an authority structure exhibits a higher degree of compliance than a system without one, other things being equal. In addition, though, some authority structures secure higher degrees of compliance than others do, and it is differences of this latter kind, differences in the relative effectiveness of authority structures, that both theories attempt to explain.

The explanations are not so much alike as complementary, however, a fact which accounts for the two views of bureaucratic authority described briefly in the introduction to this paper. Weber and Barnard analyze social structures in somewhat different ways and predicate properties of somewhat different structural units, and in consequence their hypotheses also differ. Weber examines the status of administrator (the office), attributes authority to this unit, and explains the effective exercise of authority mainly in terms of other attributes of the office or in terms of attributes brought to it by officials. Barnard, in contrast, examines the role relation (channel of communication), attributes authority to communications (which thus become more or less authoritative), and explains effectiveness in terms of other attributes of communications or in terms of attributes of role relations that transmit communications. In principle, what is true of a role relation should be translatable into something that is true of a status, and vice versa. The necessary definitions have yet to be formulated, however, and the two conceptions thus appear to differ more than they actually do.

The Administrative Office

From the first Weber employs the principle of hierarchy to divide the participants in the corporate group into three ranked strata: there are the rulers who establish the rules, the administrators who interpret and apply them, and the "subjects" or subordinates (so far as the authority system is concerned) who only comply with them.[15] In the theory of legal authority he pays little attention to the first and third strata and concerns himself instead with the administrative staff. This he describes in two ways, first, in terms of the organizational features that are necessary if the staff as a unit is to perform effectively in its pivotal position between the rulers and the subjects and, second, in terms of the characteristics of officials that make it likely they will do what they are supposed to do as staff members and nothing else.

With respect to the first list, Weber claims in effect that subjects who hold to a rationalistic ideology obey more readily and frequently if the administrative staff's organization can be described by "the fundamental categories of rational-legal authority." [16] These include the following: an explicit and specific statement of the purposes of the corporate group; a set of well-defined statuses differentiated in the light of these purposes; and the arrangement of the statuses in a single hierarchy in which "each lower (ranking) office is under the control and supervision of a higher (ranking) one." [17] Despite the language in which these statements are couched, they constitute a complex proposition, not a definition, and so could conceivably be wrong in part.

In the second set of statements Weber deliberately confines analysis to the structure of authority *within* the administrative staff itself.[18] Officials who are personally free, subject to organizational authority

[15] Weber does not say so, but these should be conceived as roles or statuses, not concrete persons. Especially in analyzing political systems is this important, because in the democratic type there is in principle a reversibility of the ruler-subject roles, just as in the perfect market there is a reversibility of buyer-seller roles. See below, n. 39.

[16] Weber, *op. cit.*, pp. 330–331.

[17] *Ibid.*, p. 331. "Office" may mean "unit organization" in Barnard's sense, for Weber speaks in this context of "administrative organs," but he is usually interpreted as referring to a status. For example, see Merton, *loc. cit.*, pp. 195–196.

[18] Weber, *op. cit.*, p. 332.

only within specified spheres, appointed according to their technical qualifications, contractually related to the organization, free to resign, and paid by salary; who treat the office as their primary occupation, view it as integral to their careers, and work without owning or appropriating the means of administration—officials in such a system, Weber asserts, are more likely to comply with the organization's rules than officials in systems that lack one or more of these characteristics.[19] Again, this is a complex proposition, not a definition, and could be wrong in whole or in part.

Weber's detailed attention to the structure of the administrative staff seems justified, since the extent to which those lowest in the full hierarchy comply with the rules, and hence the effectiveness of the authority system, depends directly on the administrators' compliance with the rules. However, his neglect of the lowest stratum suggests what surely is not so, that the effectiveness of an authority system is unaffected by the type of social structure among those only subject to it. Substantial differences in organization distinguish the clients or publics of a government agency from the students of a college or the workers of factory, for example, and such differences, it would seem, can hardly help affecting the degree of compliance typically found in each case. Barnard's approach has in this respect a distinct advantage over Weber's, because it prevents the analyst from committing just this sort of error of omission.

The Channels of Communication

Basic to Barnard's idea of organizational structure is the concept, "unit of organization."[20] Composed of one superior and several subordinates, these units are in other respects much like Weber's offices. They have clearly defined and specific purposes within the total organization; are marked out as part of the rational division of labor; and, in particular, are arranged hierarchically. Moreover, in Barnard's view *all* activities of the organization take place within the context of one or another of its units, and so *all* participants, whatever their place in the authority system, occupy definite positions in relation to one another. The analyst is thus unlikely to overlook the type of social structure found among those lowest (or highest, for that matter) in the hierarchy he is examining.

These units form a coherent whole in Barnard's scheme because of

[19] *Ibid.*, pp. 333–334.
[20] Barnard, *op. cit.*, pp. 109 ff.

the double location of their higher-ranking positions. That is, ranked pairs of units have in common one status which in the subordinate unit has high rank and in the superior unit low rank.[21] The foreman, for instance, is simultaneously located in a lower managerial unit and a work unit. A status so located is Barnard's equivalent of Weber's office, and the aggregate of such statuses is the equivalent of the administrative staff. But at this point an important difference between the two modes of analysis shows up.

Because he pictures a structure divided into three distinct strata, Weber is able to isolate his administrative staff, to view it as if it were a detachable part of a total organization. Barnard cannot do this. Exactly this sort of abstraction is precluded by his view of organizational structure. For if one looks at the total organization as a set of interlocking units of organization, neither an administrative status nor an administrative staff so stands out that it can be easily separated from the structure as a whole. What Barnard does abstract, what for him is a relatively free element of structure, is the role relation between two positions within a unit, e.g., the foreman-supervisor relation of the lower managerial unit or the foreman-worker relation of the work unit. These relations taken collectively, however, constitute, not one particular stratum of participants, but the communications structure of the total organization. (In turn, therefore, the organization may be viewed as a network of such relations.) In effect, authority here "flows" to those subject to it through the communications system; it is not exercised "over them" by a well-defined administrative staff.[22]

As might be expected, Barnard describes first what he takes to be the characteristics of an acceptable communication (an order that will

[21] *Ibid.*, pp. 111–112.

[22] Neither Weber's nor Barnard's approach to structures is in general the better one. Weber provides a more useful scheme for depicting structure as such; Barnard, for depicting process. If one wants to characterize the relatively stable differences among the units of a social system on the (complex) dimension of authority, then Weber's is the more useful. If one wants to examine the process(es) through which these differences are continually re-created—through which "authority" is, so to speak, continually redistributed among the units—then Barnard's is the more useful. It is only a special case of the more general choice between viewing the units of a system as having constant (differential or equal) degrees of a property for the period of the analysis, or viewing them as having degrees of it that vary over this period. For many sociological problems this formal difference becomes the difference between using status as the unit of the system, or using role. See, for example, Talcott Parsons, "A Revised Analytical Approach to the Theory of Social Stratification," in Reinhard Bendix and Seymour Martin Lipset (eds.), *Class, Status, and Power* (Glencoe, Ill.: Free Press, 1953), esp. p. 97.

be obeyed). These, he says, are four: from the recipient's point of view the communication must be understandable, consistent with the purpose of the organization, compatible with his personal interests, and capable of being executed.[23] Later he adds that the communication must also be authenticated: the recipient must believe that it comes from a particular position and that this position has the right to send such a communication.[24] Since this whole topic receives no attention from Weber, it is worth pointing out that the characteristics listed by Barnard fit well with Weber's characterization of the office. For example, trained officials should be more capable of understanding and executing orders than untrained officials should; and officials who are dependent on the office for their income and style of life should find a wider range of orders compatible with their personal interests than less dependent officials should. Nevertheless, whether or not Barnard's characteristics are considered to derive from Weber's, they are, like his, parts of hypotheses about effective authority structures, not parts of a definition. That orders "consistent" with the purposes of the organization are more readily or more often obeyed than those which are not, for example, is a statement of fact in the present context, not a definition.

Barnard next concerns himself with the "channels of communication" or "lines of authority." [25] Here his analysis is less compact, but again there are several places where his assertions directly parallel statements by Weber, as, for example, in his claim that ". . . individuals are able to exercise authority only when they are acting officially." [26] At the same time, though, owing to his concern with the processes on which the exercise of authority depends, he is able to suggest an important property of office which Weber fails to mention: "Objective authority is only maintained if the positions or leaders continue to be adequately informed." [27] With respect to the lines of authority proper, Barnard lists six properties. Two of these are like two of Weber's: that the persons serving as "communications centers" must be "competent" [28] corresponds directly to Weber's similar statement;

[23] *Ibid.*, pp. 165–166.

[24] *Ibid.*, pp. 180–181. Before "authenticity" can become a property of communications, participants must view "authority" as a property of positions; the "fiction of superior authority" leads them to take such a view.

[25] *Ibid.*, p. 175.

[26] *Ibid.*, p. 172.

[27] *Ibid.*, p. 174.

[28] *Ibid.*, pp. 178–179. On the matter of "competence," Weber and Barnard emphasize somewhat different contents, but the gist of what each says is similar.

and that the "channels of communication should be definitely known" [29] is similar in content, though not in phrasing, to Weber's requirement that each office consist of a "specified sphere of competence." [30] In addition, Barnard asserts that effective channels formally connect every participant to the organization; that they are as short as possible between any two positions but once set up are never "jumped" by a "communication from the head of an organization to the bottom"; and that they are not broken by a temporary or permanent absence while the organization is in operation.[31]

In summary, then, although they focus on different units of social structure, Weber and Barnard list properties of effective authority systems that are either similar or complementary but never contradictory. Their versions of effective systems are, however, different, because Barnard describes primarily the process through which such a system operates, and Weber, primarily its structure.

A COMPOSITE VIEW

The following outline of a theory of bureaucratic authority systems is directly based on what has gone before, but it necessarily departs in several respects from the two views taken separately. There are three parts to it, the concept of an authority system, the concept of bureaucratic authority systems, and some propositions about the latter. The usual qualifications that precede an attempt such as this apply here: the approach taken is only one of several that could be followed; only a few of the more important parts of the theory are discussed and these only sketchily; a more satisfactory formulation would emphasize the matters of fact for which there is systematic evidence on hand.

The Concept of Authority Systems

This concept can be described in four steps.

The exercise of authority consists of one person issuing a command and a second complying with it, and thus it is a form of interaction. This statement holds whether the interaction is a specific command-and-obedience sequence, or the more enduring and inclusive kind of sequence where one party establishes general rules which the other con-

[29] *Ibid.*, pp. 175–176.
[30] Weber, *op. cit.*, p. 330.
[31] Barnard, *op. cit.*, pp. 176–180.

tinually conforms to. Proclaiming a general policy and issuing a single piece of advice are thus equally "commands," and the appropriate responses, equally "compliance."

Authoritative role relations. A role relation is authoritative to the degree that it exhibits a stable distribution of commanding actions to one role and the reciprocal complying actions to the other.[32] Relations so differentiated are of two primary types: simple, which do not directly implicate third parties (most professional-client authority relations), and complex, in which a command from A to B implies a subsequent command from B to C (most bureaucratized authority relations).

Complex structures of authority. Ordered sets of complex relations form complex structures of authority, and the interactions within them (or, more precisely, with respect to them) constitute the operation of authority systems. Such structures normally include three principal classes of participants, although in concrete circumstances it may not always be easy to distinguish them clearly: a ruling group from which general orders issue forth, an administrative staff which interprets and transmits the orders, and "subjects," that is, those who only comply. (This, of course, is an extremely simplified formulation, but there is not space to qualify or to expand these statements.)

Legitimation. A structure of authority of this complex sort is always embedded in some kind of group, at least in part.[33] Expressed otherwise, an authority system is only an abstracted aspect of some concrete social system.[34] The principal significance of this embedded-

[32] Predicated of a role, then, authority is always relational: a role "has" a certain degree of authority only in virtue of the relation which defines it. If one predicates authority of a position independently of its relational context, as for example Parsons seems sometimes to do, then what is here called "authority" is equal to the *difference* between the two positions' degrees of authority *in relation to* one another. I do not think it especially useful, however, to conceive of every position in a structure as "having" *some* authority.

[33] "Group" is used here as defined by Merton, *loc. cit.*, pp. 285–286. It refers "to a number of people who interact with one another in accord with established patterns" (p. 285), who define themselves as members, and who are defined as members by others.

[34] Actually, the authority system is at least at two removes from the concrete group. At the first level of abstraction is the type of social system which best "fits" the group. The authority system is, in turn, an abstract aspect of this social system. It enters as one of the important ways in which units of the system differ from one another, but it is only one; and as one of the important processes constituting the operation of the system, but again as only one. In short, no type of social system is composed of "pure" authority roles; rather, social systems are composed of roles of which authority is only one of the properties or basic di-

ness is the "legitimation" of the authority system: the members of the group share various values and norms, among which are the values that justify the existence of the authority system and the norms that define its roles and interactions. The same general condition that largely determines the stability of any type of social structure therefore determines also the stability of authority structures, namely, their degree of institutionalization.

Not all who occupy statuses in an authority system, however, need be members of the group whose values legitimate it.[35] Aliens are not "members" (citizens) of the country they are visiting, but they nevertheless occupy a definite status in relation to those who enforce its laws. Again, Weber comments in passing that those subject to an authority system may not even consider it legitimate; in this event the ruling group and the administrative staff alone comprise the membership of the group whose values legitimate it.[36] From the point of view of nonmembers, then, the structure may or may not be legitimate. If it is not, it is less highly institutionalized (and so will probably prove less stable and less effective) than if it were. But the concept requires only that some group's values legitimate the authority system, not that all who occupy positions in the hierarchy consider it legitimate, much less that they be members of that group.

Bureaucratic systems of authority. In principle any form of group may provide values legitimating an authority structure. Bureaucratic systems of authority occur in the context of groups having a certain type of value system and a certain type of organization and are themselves in turn characterized by certain distinctive structural features.

Rational-legal values. The values legitimating the bureaucratic system of authority conform to Weber's description of the rational-legal ideology and have the effect noted by Barnard, that they "make it possible normally to treat a personal question impersonally." [37]

---

mensions. Thus the roles of student and professor differ on the dimension of authority, but they contain much more; the "commanding" and "complying" aspects of the actions of each role hardly exhaust the significant content of the roles.

[35] For the basis for this distinction, see above, n. 4.

[36] Under certain conditions, says Weber, an authority structure ". . . can afford to drop even the pretence of a claim to legitimacy. But even then the mode of legitimation of the relation between the chief and his staff may vary widely according to the type of basis of the relation of authority between them . . ."—Weber, *op. cit.*, p. 327. See also the opening paragraph of David Hume's "Of the First Principles of Government."

[37] Barnard, *op. cit.*, p. 170.

Formal organization. Correspondingly, the group has a relatively specific and explicit set of aims; a body of explicit rules intentionally established in order to realize these aims (or rationalized as being in support of them); and several specialized units of organization, which together contain all the activities deemed necessary to achieve the aims. Universities, factories, hospitals, modern armies, these are all in this sense formally organized groups.

Bureaucratic structures of authority. The authority system itself is a product of this rational allocation of labor. The actions which compose it are among those formally assigned to the units and, within the units, to the roles. That is, the units of the rationally organized group are differentiated with respect to responsibility for coordinating the activities carried on within or by the group as a whole; and within each unit the roles are differentiated with respect to coordinating the activities carried on within or on behalf of the unit. Paralleling this is the differentiation of both units and roles with respect to rank: in general, the higher the rank, the greater the coordinating responsibility, and vice versa. (This is the principle of hierarchy.)

A higher-ranking unit is joined to each of the units immediately subordinate to it by a common status: the highest-ranking status within each subordinate unit is at the same time a low-ranking status within the superior unit.[38] The set of these linking statuses constitutes the group's administrative stratum, and it is the activities of these administrators which constitute the heart of the authority system. For, in bureaucratically organized systems, neither the making of policy decisions, which is the specific task of the ruling group, nor the patterns of compliance among those who are only subject to authority (and who may perform any of a very large number of activities), is as such central to the authority system.

Bureaucratic authority thus always operates relative to a given set of rules and produces compliance with them; its systematic exercise is specifically unidirectional; [39] and the measure of its effectiveness

[38] "This is clearly seen in practice, it being customary to recognize a foreman, or a superintendent of a shop section, or a captain, at one time or from one point of view as a 'member' of his gang, shop crew, or company, at another time or from another point of view as a member of a 'district management group,' or the 'shop executives' group,' or the 'regimental organization.' "—Barnard, *op. cit.*, p. 111.

[39] Unidirectionality marks "democratic" systems, it might be noted, as much as it does authoritarian systems, although it may not appear to at first. To make the point briefly, as an aside here, it is necessary to phrase it in an overly simple form. In democratic systems the ideology states that there exists a fourth and

is the degree of compliance with the group's formal rules or with the administrators' interpretations of them.

Two Types of Proposition

Not all actual formal organizations exhibit structures conforming to this model, of course. For concrete systems which do, Weber's and Barnard's conceptions contain a number of propositions which, because they assert matters of fact, can in principle be tested. One kind refers to the authoritative role relation and describes the characteristics of acceptable orders and of effective superior-subordinate lines of communication. A second kind describes the characteristics exhibited by the administrative position or its occupants in effective bureaucratic systems of authority.

CONCLUSION

Current studies of formal organizations tend to fall into two groups, those in which the authority system is viewed as a power structure and those in which it is viewed as a communications process, a division which this essay has tried to show is neither useful nor necessary. The principal theorists for each view, Weber on the one hand and Barnard on the other, converge in their ideas about the nature of bureaucratized systems of authority, and their explanations of effectiveness are mutually supporting, not mutually exclusive. Together they develop a conception of bureaucratic authority built around the important tautology that every imperative communication is both imperative and a communication.

---

highest stratum, the citizenry, from which ultimate authority flows. Of course, for the most part this authority is latent as a structural matter, but at certain times (elections, referenda, and the like), the system changes phases: the "subject" status becomes temporarily latent, and the citizenry collectively issues "commands" to the next echelon, the ruling group. Consequently, in this sense, democratic processes are not the opposite of authority processes, as they are sometimes made to seem, but a particular kind of authority process.

2. Organizational Theory Applied

»»»

Organizational theories, and research guided by these theories, offer a wide base for applied work in fields ranging from personnel administration to planning of mental hospitals. The approach most often and most widely applied seems to be that of the so-called Human Relations School. Drawing from works by Elton Mayo, Kurt Lewin, and many others, it has influenced the means and techniques of control in factories, offices, schools, prisons, armed forces, and many other organizations. But at the same time the Human Relations approach arouses considerable criticism on moral, theoretical, and empirical grounds. Three of the following selections discuss the pros and cons of this approach.

Whyte, himself an influential leader of the Human Relations tradition, presents a "progress report." He first examines the original contributions of the Human Relations approach; he then considers their advantages and disadvantages; finally, he draws the contours of a new pattern emerging in this field. In "the New Look of Human Relations" the significance of money as a motivational factor is reemphasized; the place and effect of labor unions are fully recognized; the fact that not all workers are members of cohesive groups is taken into account; the structure of communities in which workers participate enters the picture, and so do many other factors. Thus the Human Relations approach becomes considerably more encompassing and analytically sound. It also comes closer to other frames of reference applied by social scientists.

One of Bendix's major interests, well represented in his *Work and Authority in Industry,* concerns bureaucratization, industrialization, and their effects on managerial ideologies. Bendix and Fisher examine the

Human Relations approach from this viewpoint in their presentation. What functions does this school fulfill for management? Which aspects of social reality does the approach emphasize, and which does it neglect? Why is conflict seen as a social disease? Why is management assigned the role of "enlightened leadership" and savior of modern society? Why is the role of the trade-union not analyzed? These and other cogent questions concerning the Human Relations School are raised and answered.

Homans joins the debate with "some corrections" to the critique of Bendix and Fisher. He wonders whether Mayo himself had the intentions others found in his work; he suggests that it would be best to settle part of the argument by empirical research.

In the concluding selection, Etzioni applies a tentative outline of a general organizational model to one particular type: economic organizations, such as factories, banks, and offices. An effort is being made to demonstrate that one applied field, Industrial Sociology, can be fruitfully delineated and codified, with the use of this model. Etzioni hopes that when further developed, and when applied to other types of organizations as well, the suggested model will make possible the systematic transfer of concepts and theorems from the study of one organizational type to another.

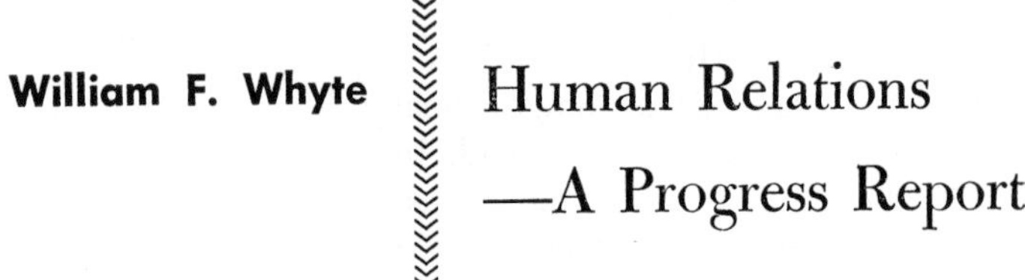

William F. Whyte

Human Relations —A Progress Report

OUTLINE OF PROGRESS

In oversimplified form, the progress in human relations theory can be outlined in three stages:

Reprinted in part from *Harvard Business Review*, 34 (1956), 125–132, by permission of the author and publisher, the Graduate School of Business Administration, Harvard University.

1. *Staking out the claims*—This new field of study was opened up by the research that Elton Mayo and his associates in the Department of Industrial Research at the Harvard Business School, F. J. Roethlisberger and W. J. Dickson, carried on at the Western Electric Company. Through experimentation, observation, and interviewing, they demonstrated the fallaciousness of the old established theories of human behavior in industry.

2. *Following the leads*—For some years, we all followed Mayo's leads; we accepted and elaborated on his assumptions as we worked along the lines of our particular interests. But what we had learned from Mayo was, to a large extent, clarification of what was *not* true about behavior in industry rather than information as to what *was* true. So, while sometimes we came to fruitful conclusions, more and more we found ourselves going up blind alleys.

3. *Developing a new pattern*—Realizing we did not have all the answers, we were forced to rethink the work we had been doing. This led us toward a new pattern of theory and research. The pattern is not yet clear enough to provide many practical conclusions. It is emerging, nevertheless, and that emergence promises a brighter future both for the development of research and for its application to human problems in industry.

As I see it, we have now advanced beyond Mayo in several important ways, each of which deserves independent evaluation.

We know how to use money more effectively as an incentive. We have gone beyond the simple "work group" concept to discover some of the different forms of group behavior actually to be found in industry. We are learning how the structure of the organization can affect morale and productivity. We have learned some of the limitations of human relations training—a necessary step in the development of more effective action.

OLD THEORIES DISCREDITED

Mayo attacked a theory of human behavior and a theory of organization. According to the established management theory, the working man was thought to be an individual who responded to management's actions upon a completely individualistic basis. Money was thought to be the main, if not the only, incentive to which he responded.

On the organization side, the theories that went under the name of "scientific management" dominated the scene. Two points stood out—"functionalization" and the "span of control":

> 1. *Functional specialization* was equated with efficiency. The more specialization on the part of the worker or supervisor, the more effective he was supposed to be.
>
> 2. The concept of *span of control* involved an essentially mechanical theory of organization. It placed emphasis upon the formal structure and upon building control into the organization from the top down. It assumed that one man could supervise adequately only a small number of people. . . .

It was Elton Mayo and his associates who made the first effective challenge to the prevailing theories of individual and organizational behavior. They did so by establishing the following propositions:

> 1. *The economic incentive is not the only motivating force to which the worker responds.* In fact, he often holds back his production to a point well below his physical capacity even when he is on piece rates and could make more money with more production. His production is importantly influenced by his relations with other workers and by his personal problems inside and outside the plant.
>
> 2. *The worker does not respond as an isolated individual.* He is a member of a work group, and the face-to-face relations he experiences have a great effect upon his behavior. Wherever men work together, they tend to build up an informal organization which may not follow the lines of the formal organization as established by management.
>
> 3. *Extreme functional specialization does not necessarily create the most efficient organization.* Mayo and his associates did not give great attention to this point, but, in their study of the bank wiring room, they noted that the wiremen and soldermen frequently exchanged jobs, contrary to management's policy. These job exchanges had no adverse effects upon production and seemed to raise the morale of the entire work group.

We can accept Mayo's assumption regarding functional specialization without modification. A good deal of research and experience since Mayo's day leads us to believe that extreme functional specialization results in lower productivity and lower morale. In a number of cases it has been found that both morale and productivity have been raised by job enlargement (giving the worker more tasks to perform) and by allowing the worker to change jobs from time to time. . . .

NEW APPROACH TO INCENTIVES

Mayo and his associates performed an important service in demonstrating that the economic incentive is not all-important. But where do we go from there?

Money Still Vital

Some researchers in the field have gone on to assume that money—far from being all-important—is really not very important at all. This viewpoint is based on various questionnaire surveys which indicate that workers rank "good wages" seventh or eighth among the desirable conditions of work. Since items having to do with "fair treatment" by supervisors are consistently ranked higher, some people have come to think that workers are primarily concerned with human relations and do not worry very much about their take-home pay.

However, it has not been possible for us in human relations research to remove money from factory life. We have been forced to recognize that although workers may be thinking of other things too whenever they complain about wages, they are still most certainly concerned about money. Also, we have learned that the pattern of human relations in an organization can be such as to promote—or block—an enthusiastic response to an economic incentive.

It is futile to argue about the relative importance of money and human relations. We might just as well argue whether the engine or the gasoline is more important in making an automobile run. Our problem in research is to determine how the economic incentive and human relations fit together. More work has been done on this in recent years than can be summarized here, but I can point up two important areas of current research interest: the effect of incentives on intergroup relations and experimentation with new types of incentives.

Disrupting Influences

Industry today is full of strife growing out of intergroup problems created by incentive systems. For instance, look at the now time-honored struggle between workers on incentive pay and those on hourly rates:

> Take the skilled people in the maintenance department, who usually are more skilled than any other workers in the plant. Normally,

they hold relatively high status or prestige in the plant community. But since their work is not directly measurable, they are not generally included in incentive plans. Yet a piece-rate system for production workers is likely to eliminate part or all of the differential in earnings between the two groups. In some cases, the production workers actually come out ahead in pay. This narrowing or reversal of the differential inevitably generates severe pressures within the union and from the union to management.

Even within production departments, incentives often give rise to intergroup problems. For example,

> Suppose the production department consists of "grinders" and "polishers." The hourly rate for grinders is $1.90, that for polishers, $2.00. The polishing job is thought to require somewhat more skill and enjoy a higher status, and the promotional ladder calls for workers to move up from grinder to polisher.
>
> Now suppose that incentives are introduced into the department. To make it easier for management, let us assume that the rates for grinders and polishers are set up at approximately the same time—a situation that is often *not* found in practice. Ideally, the incentive system will turn out so that the polishers maintain approximately the same earnings differential as they enjoyed on day rates. However, almost as often as not—and regardless of the rate-setting methods used—the incentive earnings will turn out something like this: polishers, $2.45; grinders, $2.65.
>
> In other words, the incentive system has turned upside down the relative positions of the two jobs. What happens now is easy to predict. The polishers put pressure on union and management in order to get a loosening of the rate and re-establish the pre-existing differential. And the grinders become very reluctant indeed to "promote" into the polisher position.

Management must anticipate the changes that incentives are likely to produce in the relative positions of work groups in the plant status system. It must be prepared to deal with the pressures that arise in response to such changes. On the basis of what we already know, there is no excuse for management to be taken by surprise by the intergroup problems that piece rates generate.

Plant-wide Incentive

One way to by-pass the intergroup problems produced by piece rates is to abandon piece rates altogether. This does not necessarily mean giving up financial incentives. In recent years a few companies, following the lead of the late Joseph Scanlon, have been experimenting with incentives based on the performance of an entire plant. If the plant-wide formula does not eliminate whatever "inequities" workers may think exist, it at least has the merit of not introducing *new* inequities.

It is important to note that the plant-wide plan does not, in and of itself, produce results. Since the individual worker has so little direct effect on the payoff he receives, the success of a plant-wide formula depends on a new approach to motivation. Where the plan has been successful, it has been used as a symbol around which to reorganize human relations throughout the plant. The individual must feel that he is an important part of the organization, and he does not get this feeling simply by having management tell him how important he is. He feels appreciated only when he has an opportunity to contribute his ideas as well as his manual skills to the organization.

The plant-wide incentive program requires, therefore, a continuing program of discussion and action, whereby the individual can bring up ideas within his own department and whereby these ideas are carried for action to as high an organizational level as is necessary for decision making. This means stimulating workers to offer production ideas through the union channels. However, management people cannot just sit back and wait for union suggestions; they must also present production and cost problems to workers and union officers for discussion.

Without going into the mechanics of the system, some general comments can be made about its effectiveness. Under a successful plant-wide incentive, men will work more steadily, although it is not this harder work which accounts for most of the payoff. The successes have been achieved largely through a more effective mobilization of the knowledge and ideas of all members of the organization.

Elton Mayo destroyed the orthodox economic theory of worker motivation. For a time we tried to develop a theory of motivation that would leave out money altogether. That too was found wanting, and we are now building a new theory that integrates economic incentives *and* human relations.[1]

[1] For more on this subject, see W. F. Whyte *et al., Money and Motivation* (New York: Harper & Brothers, 1955); also William Foote Whyte, "Economic Incentives and Human Relations," *Harvard Business Review,* March–April 1952, p. 73.

ACCENT ON FACE-TO-FACE RELATIONS

Mayo and his associates showed that we cannot afford to think of an isolated individual employee. We must consider him as part of a work group. But where do we go from there?

Misleading Conclusions

We have elaborated upon Mayo's assumption in ways that have led toward misleading conclusions. Let us examine the steps here.

At first, we took it for granted that in *every* factory department there was a work group, and furthermore that it had a well-organized structure that tended to have a good deal of stability. In this conclusion we were, of course, influenced by the classic Western Electric study of the bank wiring room, which did have a well-organized work group with a definite and stable structure. Neither Mayo nor any of his associates ever wrote that *all* factory departments must be organized in this pattern, but, when we had no comparable studies of other work groups, there was a natural tendency to assume that this was a universal pattern.

If there were such a work group structure, then it would follow that the foreman could supervise most effectively if he understood the structure of the group and dealt with it through the informal leadership that had arisen. We therefore focused our attention on the relations between the foreman and the *informal organization* of his workers. Without being fully aware of what we were doing, we sought to discover the factors that would make for good relations between foremen and workers—regardless of the technology involved, the distribution of job skills, the over-all structure of the organization, and so on.

The assumption underlying all this work was that the nature of human relations in the plant was primarily determined by the human relations skills of the people in leadership positions. It followed that training efforts to improve the skill and understanding of these people would result in more harmonious relations.

This line of thinking has been severely jolted by three sets of studies.

More Powerful Forces

Clark Kerr and Abraham Siegel put to us the following embarrassing question: If cooperation in industry depends primarily on the skill and understanding of the key people involved, how do you explain the fact that there has been consistent conflict in the longshore industry in this country, and even internationally, while relations in the clothing industry have been reasonably peaceful?[2] Can it be that the key people in Industry A just happen to be skilled in human relations whereas their opposite numbers in Industry B are a bunch of bunglers?

This would be hard to believe, and as a matter of fact we do not believe it. We have had to recognize that there are certain forces operating that are more powerful than the human relations techniques of individual executives or union leaders. Along this line, Kerr and Siegel emphasize the homogeneity or heterogeneity of worker groupings on the job or in the community:

> Strike-prone industries, they argue, are those in which most workers work in close proximity on the same or similar jobs, and in which they live in close association in communities where they are cut off from intimate contact with other types of workers or with management people.
>
> At the other extreme, heterogeneity leads to more peaceful union-management relations: workers who do a wide variety of jobs and are scattered through the community, among other types of people, are less likely to strike.

This is an oversimplification of the Kerr-Siegel argument, but, for our purposes, it need not be presented in detail. It is enough to note that they have drawn our attention to the powerful influence of job structure and community organization upon human relations on the job.

Multigroup Relations

The work of Leonard Sayles and George Strauss has served to broaden our understanding of work groups.[3] A great variety of possible organizational patterns may be found among such groups. There are groups with stable organizations such as in the bank wiring room. There are also groups which may at times be so disorganized that it is hard even to speak of them as groups. Furthermore, we cannot think

[2] "The Interindustry Propensity to Strike—An International Comparison," *Industrial Conflict,* edited by A. Kornhauser, R. Dubin, and A. M. Ross (New York, McGraw-Hill Book Company, Inc., 1954), p. 189.

[3] *The Local Union* (New York, Harper & Brothers, 1953). See also their article, "Conflicts within the Local Union," *Harvard Business Review,* November–December 1952, p. 84.

simply in terms of the supervisor in relation to *the* work group. In a department of any size, the supervisor must relate himself to *several* work groups. At any given time these groups may be in competition and conflict with each other, so the supervisor must deal in intergroup relations as well as in his own relations to each group.

Sayles is now pushing ahead in an effort to discover some of the laws of work group behavior. He has tentatively identified four types of work groups, in terms of their characteristic behavior patterns:

> The *apathetic* group, whose members may be dissatisfied but are so divided against themselves they are unable to take concerted action. The *erratic* group, which swings from passivity to outbursts of aggressive action—and often on issues that seem to management and union leaders too small to account for the emotional heat involved. The *strategic* group, which constantly seeks to improve its position through carefully calculated, united action. The *conservative* group, whose members are capable of concerted action but who are generally satisfied enough so that they do not take the trouble to make themselves heard.[4]

Affixing a label has no value in itself, but Sayles is finding that the groups whose behavior fits a given label are reacting to very similar conditions of technology, level of skill, and arrangement of jobs. In other words, if we find groups in two different factories that fit the "erratic" behavioral description, we can expect to find them facing similar conditions in the social and technological work environment.

Study along this line is still in an early stage; within a few years we can expect to know a good deal more about work groups than we do today. Such knowledge can be invaluable in improving supervisory leadership and in increasing the effectiveness of local union leaders in their dealings with work groups. It will take us far beyond the simple work group concept.

The Odds on Training

The third force in upsetting our old conceptions of human relations has been provided by research evaluations of the impact of supervisory training programs.

In recent years, two solid pieces of research have been done along this line. In each case, the workers under the supervisors who were to be trained were given a questionnaire dealing with their relationship with the supervisors before the program began. The same

[4] Leonard R. Sayles, *Behavior of Industrial Work Group* (New York: John Wiley & Sons, 1958).

questionnaire was administered some months after the conclusion of the program. The result? Disappointing, to say the least.

Edwin A. Fleishmann, Edwin F. Harris, and Harold E. Burtt at Ohio State found that the International Harvester Company program had effected no gain in these supervisor-worker relationships—and perhaps it had even resulted in a slight loss.[5] The University of Michigan Survey Research Center's study of a training program in two divisions of the Detroit Edison Company showed a small over-all gain.[6] However, it was found that there had been a loss of ground in one division which was more than compensated for by a gain in the other.

How can we account for these results? Were the programs in themselves no good? No doubt better training can be given, but probably these courses were a good deal better than the average in industry today.

We find the best explanation by looking at the two divisions in the Detroit Edison study. The researchers found that in the division where progress had been made, the foremen were led by a higher management which supervised them very much in line with the principles developed in the course. On the other hand, in the division which lost ground the foremen were under superiors who directed them in a manner which was entirely out of harmony with the program.

These findings suggest that the effectiveness of a training program for lower-level supervisors depends in very large measure on the way that program is supported at higher levels in the organization. Nor can that support be simply verbal. Real success depends on the actions of top management in its day-to-day behavior.

What about training in human relations for the higher-ups? Years ago management tended to make the foreman a sort of scapegoat for all human relations difficulties. It was assumed that if the foreman were only as good a leader of men as the president or vice president of the company, then there would be no problem. Today few management people are that naive. They are ready to recognize that a change in behavior at higher levels may be necessary too, if the foreman is to do the skillful job of supervision expected of him. So it makes sense to direct training at these higher levels.

[5] *Leadership and Supervision in Industry: An Evaluation of a Supervisory Training Program* (Columbus, Bureau of Educational Research, The Ohio State University, Monograph No. 33, 1955).

[6] See Norman A. Maier, *Principles of Human Relations* (New York, John Wiley & Sons, Inc., 1952), pp. 184–192.

Nevertheless, we are becoming increasingly doubtful whether training can do the job here. We often assume that people high up in management are free agents. If they put pressure on their subordinates in a way that hinders cooperation and lowers morale, we may assume that this is because they do not have the necessary human relations skills or because they have some personality difficulties. But the truth is that the big wheels are not free to do as they please. They too are under pressure.

The plant manager is in competition for advancement with other plant managers. He is struggling to meet a budget that is deliberately set tight so as to demand his best efforts. He works with accountants and cost control people who, as Chris Argyris has explained, gain their successes through discovering and reporting the failures of production people.[7] Faced with rising material costs and wages, the manager must spur his organization to greater efficiency, so that the plant produces in greater volume and still keeps prices down and profits up. He has design engineers, industrial engineers, personnel men, and other specialists to help him and his production men do this, and yet he finds much of his time and energy devoted to untangling the snarls that arise among the people who make up the complex and sensitive organism which he directs.

At still higher levels, the company executive may be under less direct pressure from above, but he generates his own pressure in response to his ideal of the successful American executive. That ideal demands that he not be content with today's achievement, that he be constantly pushing to improve or expand the organization. Progress may require him to gamble millions of dollars on projects whose payoff is years away. Responsibility is a heavy weight in itself.

Our problem involves certain things that are bigger than the individual and his social skills. What are these things? We are only beginning to understand them, but one of the important factors seems to be the formal structure of the organization.

RE-ENTER FORMAL ORGANIZATION

Stimulated by research that has come out of Sears, Roebuck and Co. under the leadership of James C. Worthy (later Assistant Secre-

[7] "Human Problems with Budgets," *Harvard Business Review,* January–February 1953, p. 97.

tary of Commerce and now back at Sears as Director of Public Relations), we are busy taking a new look at organization structure.

We find that the way you build your organization has a great influence on its pattern of human relations. If you follow the span of control theory, you will build a long, narrow hierarchy with many levels of authority from bottom to top. Since supervisors will have few people reporting to them, they will tend to supervise those people closely. Under such conditions, the subordinate will concentrate on pleasing the boss and will have little opportunity to display initiative and assume the responsibilities necessary to developing his capacities.

The span of control theory is irrefutable if you accept the assumption about behavior on which it is based: that men perform best when they are under close supervision. The fact is that research (especially at Rensis Likert's University of Michigan Institute for Social Research) has been demonstrating the falsity of such an assumption. A number of studies have shown that both morale and productivity are higher under light, general supervision.

This means that the boss should delegate responsibility and authority to the men under him, giving them the chance to exercise their own capabilities. But can you get the boss to do this? Experience has shown that this is exceedingly difficult when the organization is based on the span of control concept and the boss has only a few people reporting to him. Despite training and management policy, he tends to keep close track (and control) of the work of his subordinates. It is easy for him to do so, and what else should he do with his time?

Flat Structure

If we really want delegation of authority and the improved morale that seems to go with it, we might adopt the organization structure approach of giving the boss so many subordinates that he cannot possibly supervise them closely. Such a course means building a broad, flat structure with relatively few levels of authority from bottom to top. This management philosophy—the exact opposite of the span of control concept—is practiced by Sears and is becoming increasingly popular in American industry.

I am not suggesting that it is impossible to achieve a healthy degree of delegation of authority without changing the structure of the organization. And certainly not all companies would be able to model themselves after the Sears department store structure. The organizational pattern most appropriate for a particular business will depend on what it produces, its technology, the types of staff groups that must work with the line, and a number of other factors we are just beginning to investigate.

Nor am I trying to bury for all time the thinking that has gone into the span of control theory—which is still very much alive today, if we are to judge from the recent cogent statement of Lyndall Urwick.[8] My only claim is that we have come again to recognize the importance of formal structure—but now with a difference. Instead of theorizing in an *a priori* manner, we are beginning to carry on the empirical research that may some day enable us to plan the structure of the company so as to predetermine, in some degree, the nature of its human relations.

HUMAN RELATIONS IN PERSPECTIVE

In this article, I have pointed out the important influences upon human relations exercised by the pay system, the technology, the organization of work, and the formal structure. Does this mean that face-to-face relations are unimportant? Does this mean human skills and understandings do not really count for much?

The answer to both questions is *no*. However, research and experience have placed face-to-face relations in a new perspective. Both the morale and the productivity of an organization are tremendously influenced by the nature of face-to-face relations in that organization, but we have come to recognize that the relations we observe tend to be channeled within certain limits by the organization's structure, technology, and so on. . . . As research begins to trace out the human relations patterns that go with different structural and technological arrangements, we can look for greater achievements through applying a human relations knowledge to industrial problems.

[8] "The Manager's Span of Control," *Harvard Business Review*, May–June 1956, p. 39.

Reinhard Bendix
and
Lloyd H. Fisher

The Perspectives of Elton Mayo

The small number of Elton Mayo's writings [1] belies the extent of his influence since coming to Harvard in 1926. Many social scientists and businessmen in the United States are indebted to him. His ideas have stimulated both social science research and factory management.

The influence of Mr. Mayo has been notable in the work of those social scientists who apply to their study of modern society the techniques and concepts developed in the analyses of simpler cultures. He has imparted to this anthropology of the modern life his strong feeling for the necessity of the stable social relationships which characterize traditional societies [2] and are commonly so lacking in our own. However, the influence of Mayo's work has been greatest in the promotion of a sociological or anthropological approach to industrial management. Much of the content of those courses in the universities

Reprinted from *Review of Economics and Statistics,* 31 (1949), 312–319, by permission of Reinhard Bendix and the publisher, Cambridge, Mass., Harvard University Press.

---

[1] The late Elton Mayo was Professor of Industrial Research at the Harvard University School of Business Administration. His written work consists of six books: *Democracy and Freedom, An Essay in Social Logic* (1919); *The Human Problems of an Industrial Civilization* (1933, new ed. 1946); *The Social Problems of an Industrial Civilization* (1945); *The Political Problem of Industrial Civilization* (1947); *Some Notes on the Psychology of Pierre Janet* (1948); and, together with George Lombard, *Teamwork and Labor Turnover in the Aircraft Industry of Southern California* (1944). In addition, Mayo has written some 30 articles and numerous forewords to the books of his colleagues, collaborators, and disciples.

[2] See the numerous writings of W. L. Warner, B. Gardner, S. Kimball, C. Arensberg, G. Homans, A. Davis, W. F. Whyte, and others.

catalogued as "Human Relations in Industry" consists of the work of Mayo, his colleagues, and his students. It is not yet possible to assess the effect of this approach on the personnel practices of factory managers. It may be that a later age will compare Mayo's work with that of Frederick W. Taylor, and indeed the "human relations approach" and "scientific management" are not unrelated. At any rate, Mayo's emphasis on the human side of worker-management relations has had a considerable effect upon the literature and perhaps the practices of personnel relations. This influence has already been substantial enough to warrant an attempt to consider its major tendencies. It is to this end that the present article is addressed.

BASIC ORIENTATIONS

There is consistency in the writings of Mayo. From his earliest book in which he reviewed the social and political scene in Australia to the last of his trilogy on the problems of industrial society, a sense of imminent danger pervades his writing. It is not an unequivocal prophecy of doom, for escape from the cataclysm is open to those who are not too blind to see.

Spontaneous Cooperation

What one must see in order to be saved is that the essence of a healthy society is a sound social organization. And the requirement of a sound social organization is the *spontaneous* cooperation of its members within the various enterprises in which they are organized. Conflict in human society, and especially political conflict, is always a symptom of social disease.

An understanding of the term "spontaneous" reveals the main drift of Mayo's work. Spontaneous does not mean voluntary. If Mayo gave to the term "spontaneous" the meaning of voluntary he would belong in a different political current altogether. He would appear as one in a long line of liberal theorists who have attempted to find a reconciliation in industrial society between the function of authority and the liberal requirement of individual consent. But this would have raised problems which Mayo has shown no intention of dealing with—problems of agreement on the nature and the ends of industrial organization itself.

Man's conduct in society, according to Mayo, is primarily determined by tradition. It is this reliance upon tradition that distinguishes spontaneous behavior from voluntary behavior. For it is precisely traditional behavior which can be spontaneous without being voluntary.[3] Thus, individual happiness and the social "growth and health" of society are dependent not upon freedom from unreasonable restraint nor upon any rational calculus of pleasure and pain, nor upon the opportunity for self-development, but upon whether or not the individual has a sense of "social function."

In his earliest book, *Democracy and Freedom, An Essay in Social Logic,* published in Australia in 1919, Mayo laid down the thesis which remained the core of his subsequent work.

> Viewed from the standpoint of social science, society is composed of individuals organized in occupational groups, each group fulfilling some function of the society. Taking this fact into account, psychology . . . is able to make at least one general assertion as to the form a given society must take if it is to persist as a society. It must be possible for the individual to feel, as he works, that his work is socially necessary; he must be able to see beyond his group to the society. Failure in this respect will make disintegration inevitable. (p. 37.) [4]

As a diagnosis of the plight and problem of industrial man this is neither novel nor in itself politically revealing. This is indeed the sin of bourgeois society. Both socialists and fascists excoriate it. It is denounced by the agrarian and by the medievalist. It is the attack of Ruskin and Morris upon nineteenth century capitalism. It is the case for conservatism as Burke made it.

The Decline of Civilization

In the hands of Mayo the charge becomes really comprehensive. Australia as Mayo saw it in 1919 exhibited on all sides the growth of conflict and the decline of civilization. The belief that government could aid in the development of social cooperation he stigmatized as a dangerous illusion. Government can only "record and enforce existing moral relationships," it cannot initiate or change them. Those who think that social cooperation can be achieved by political means help to intensify class conflict and thus bring closer the disintegration of society. Hence party politics and democracy deserve to be condemned because they sanction the conception of a class society and thereby feed the forces of social disorder.

[3] Social behavior, to be sure, is not exclusively or even predominantly voluntary and rational. However, Mayo proposes the further cultivation and extension of traditional behavior as a positive social objective.

[4] For a similar comment see Mayo, *Human Problems,* p. 166.

> The recent growth of interest in political matters in Australia is by no means a sign of social health. (*Democracy and Freedom*, p. 43.)
>
> Revolution or civil war is the only outcome of the present irreconcilable attitude of Australian political parties. The methods of "democracy," far from providing a means of solving the industrial problem, have proved entirely inadequate to the task. Political organization has been mistaken for political education; the party system has accentuated and added to our industrial difficulties. Democracy has done nothing to help society to unanimity, nothing to aid the individual to a sense of social function. Under its tutelage, social development has achieved a condition of perilous instability, a condition which democracy as such can apparently do little or nothing to cure. (*Ibid.*, p. 44.)

Government and Industrial Relations

All of this is most clearly seen in the field of industrial relations. Mayo deplores industrial conflict, but any government intervention to relieve it is an empty if not a dangerous delusion. The state cannot "produce by regulation [the cooperation] which can only be the result of spontaneous growth." [5]

> The office of rules and regulations is to express a static relation; prohibition can do nothing to bring about a condition of wholehearted and spontaneous cooperation. Collaboration in the complex purposes of civilization is the mark of social health; any ideal which aims at less than this is dangerous. Civilization has passed beyond nineteenth century individualism to twentieth century class rivalry. Its capacity to survive depends upon its capacity to achieve a social condition that will subsume castes and classes under a community of interest and purpose. To achieve this, artificial restrictions must be eliminated and "common rules" revoked—except where common rules undoubtedly express the social mind. Human nature may be trusted to work out a gradual solution once the attempt to find political nostrums and ad hoc remedies is abandoned. (*Ibid.*, pp. 49–50.)

The political devices which have been developed under democratic institutions to regulate industrial relations are but an "artificial substitute for (the spontaneous growth of) human cooperation." (*Ibid.*, pp. 51–52.)

These opinions of three decades ago are essentially similar to the views which Mayo has expressed in recent years. In his *Human Problems* he concludes a chapter on "Government and Society" with the statement that

[5] *Democracy and Freedom*, p. 48.

> No form of political action can ever substitute for this loss (of social function). Political action in a given community presumes the desire and capacity of individuals to work together; the political function cannot operate in a community from which this capacity has disappeared. (p. 167.)

Again in his book of 1945 he quotes with approval the assertion of Figgis that the state has never created "in any real sense" the social institutions of modern society. And he denounces with Figgis any thought of the constructive role which politics and government may play in our society as that monstrous idea of "an omnipotent state facing an equally unreal aggregate of unrelated individuals." [6] It is difficult to understand Mayo's work unless one realizes how much he abhors conflict, competition, or disagreement. Conflict is a "social disease" and cooperation is "social health." But many forms of cooperation, especially those initiated or aided by political means (e.g., collective bargaining), are not cooperation after all, but artificial substitutes for it. In 1919 Mayo wrote that only "spontaneous cooperation" is socially healthy,[7] and more recently he has held that this ideal of social health can only be found in the Middle Ages, when society was characterized by a community of purpose among all its members.[8]

For Mayo the conditions necessary for a healthy social organism are present when each individual has a sense of social function and responsibility. Tradition assigns him his role in the group. Cooperation is assured because the purposes of each are the purposes of all. And this basic unanimity is the social foundation of all human collaboration. Unanimity and cooperation are traditional rather than deliberate, spontaneous rather than voluntary. Any effort to achieve cooperation deliberately in the absence of a basic identity of purpose (within the group) is the beginning of social disintegration. In his elaboration of this view, Mayo draws heavily on the work of the anthropologist.

On this basis, Mayo passes adverse judgment on many facets of contemporary life. He deplores competition as well as the class struggle, politicians as well as election campaigns, economic self-interest as well as interest in political affairs. He deplores them all because they do not contribute to "spontaneous cooperation." Cooperation is easy

[6] *Social Problems*, pp. 54–55.

[7] *Democracy and Freedom*, p. 49.

[8] *Political Problem*, p. 23. Whether the Middle Ages did in fact possess this community of purpose is open to serious doubt. The idealization and even falsification of the past appears to be a characteristic response to present discontents.

enough, he writes in a recent work, in the face of an emergency. However, "the real problem is that of the maintenance of *spontaneous cooperation* in times of peace." [9]

> The immense changes of the last two centuries have disturbed all the traditional social balances. Material and technical achievements have outpaced free communication between groups and the capacity for spontaneous cooperation. Study of the social facts is only now beginning—at a critical moment when the general ignorance of the facts of social organization has become alarming. Owing to this general ignorance, the political leaders in many countries have introduced another unfortunate complication by relapsing on the ancient idea of compulsion by central authority. This has affected even those countries that nominally retain the forms of democratic government. . . . Compulsion has never succeeded in rousing eager and spontaneous cooperation. [Under compulsion] the popular will to collaborate ultimately withers. . . . The will to survive and cooperate must come from within. (*Political Problem*, p. 24.)

Thus, government is nearly synonymous with "compulsion by central authority." In 1947, as in 1919, Mr. Mayo creates a dichotomy between the spontaneous cooperation which is inherent in society, and the dangerous and destructive effect which politics and governmental action have on the will of the people to cooperate. He acknowledges that in modern society cooperation must be deliberately organized, since the force of tradition has weakened in our day.[10] Yet that deliberate planning of cooperation, as Mayo sees it, is not to be achieved by governmental institutions, but rather through the development of administrative elites within the private, and more particularly the industrial, organizations of our society.

A great many scientists and citizens share Mr. Mayo's concern over the bitter and dangerous conflicts which beset modern society. But not only does Mayo misconceive the remedy, he misconceives the disease as well. Political conflicts do not necessarily cause a civilization to decline; they may as readily be the necessary condition of a free society, and except upon the radical hypothesis that freedom and civilization are mutual enemies, the charge cannot be supported. Government for natural man may indeed be an artifice, but so is the industrial society in which he will be either slave or master. Competition, with its conflict of interest, lacks the order and discipline of a tra-

[9] *Political Problem*, p. 12.
[10] Cf. *Social Problems*, p. 9.

ditional society; but the more conventional complaint is that we have too little competition rather than too much. We know very little about the requirements of the "social health" of an entire society to make pronouncements upon it—too little, in fact, to be sure that even the concept has meaning. To assert, as Mayo does, that competition, self-interest, and politics will destroy civilization, and that a society is doomed unless it can "restore" to the individual a sense of his "social function" is only to assert his preference for the social organization of the Middle Ages. Many will agree that important and difficult problems arise from the conflicts of modern society, but many will question that the solution lies with the re-establishment of the traditional society of the past. How, then, does Mayo propose to deal with the problem of cooperation in modern society?

SMALL WORK GROUP

Mayo repeatedly criticizes social scientists, businessmen, and politicians for their failure to solve the problem of human cooperation. Their various attempts have come to naught (if in fact they have not made matters worse) because they have been based either upon insufficient evidence or upon political nostrums which have served to arouse human passions and make constructive solutions impossible. These errors may be avoided only by an insistence upon the need for a detailed investigation of the social and psychological stucture of cooperation. Only empirical research into how men act in concert can lead to the basic "knowledge-of-acquaintance" without which cooperation cannot be organized effectively. Social scientists have been satisfied with "knowledge about" facts rather than knowledge of the facts at first hand. Impelled by these convictions, Mayo was occupied for many years with careful and painstaking research of the Hawthorne Plant of the Western Electric Company. This work led to the now famous conclusions that work output is a function of the degree of work-satisfaction, which in turn depends upon the informal social pattern of the work group.

It will be assumed that the Hawthorne studies are familiar to the reader in a general way. They have now become part of the established findings of industrial management. They concern us here only because of a certain looseness with which Mayo interprets his findings, and because of certain ambiguities and elisions which result.

The work groups which Mayo observed in the Hawthorne experiments were separated from the factory proper. To test the effect of separation itself, output records were taken for each member of the group before and after isolation. Since output did not change it was concluded that isolation in itself had no effect upon output.[11] It was not until the several workers under the sympathetic ministrations of skillful supervisors became a cohesive group that output rose. Thus the increased output was the fruit of spontaneous cooperation and the sense of social function its cause. In evaluating the experiment as a whole, Mayo concluded that a sense of personal futility pervaded the ordinary work situation and prevented the effective cooperation of workers with management.[12]

It is by no means clear that the conditions or supervision achieved for the isolated work group could ever be reproduced for the factory. Isolation, though perhaps in itself insufficient to produce increased output, may yet have been a necessary condition for successful supervision. It is conceivable that the "sense of social function" depended as much in the end upon separation from the common run of the factory as upon the non-invidious attachment of the group members to each other. In any event, there are opportunities for illusions on the part of a small work group that would not be possible for a factory as a whole. The isolation of the small work group, however essential for purposes of observation, disguises the interdependence of group with factory and the factory with the economy as a whole. To sever the ties which related the work group to the process of production may make observation of the group manageable. It will obscure the fact, however, that the worker is subject to the authority of the employer. If the factory were not in some measure an authoritarian institution, production would break down. The "sense of social function," however valuable in itself, will have a limited range of acceptable manifestations in the factory.

It would appear also that there is considerable ambiguity as to whether social cooperation and the sense of social function are always signs of "social health." Clearly Mayo regards cooperation for objectives defined by management, e.g., increased production, as a high order of self-fulfillment. But what may be an even more spontaneous form of cooperation, e.g., trade union activities, seems to stand on a different footing.[13]

[11] *Human Problems,* p. 59.

[12] *Ibid.,* p. 120.

[13] Trade unions are mentioned twice in Mayo's writings, once when he alludes to the resistance of trade unions to technological change (*Human Problems,* p.

Mayo's writings are open to the interpretation that the cooperation of workers with management is "socially healthy," while cooperation among workers for ends of their own is not. It is certainly true that the mechanization and routinizing of the working day is a basic source of discontent. A number of social scientists today are preoccupied with the manifold consequences of the problem. But in the entire literature of the nineteenth and twentieth centuries, only the proponents of the corporative state have suggested that work satisfaction can be regained only by integrating the worker into the plant-community under the leadership of management.

ELITE OF INDUSTRIAL MANAGERS

The implicit denial of the inevitably authoritarian aspects of a factory system plays a strategic role in Mr. Mayo's philosophy. He seeks to restore "spontaneous cooperation." The men he charges with this task of restoration are the industrial managers. According to Mayo, they have used their authority in the past in a manner which has created a widespread sense of futility. Can they now be expected to "create a sense of social function"? The answer to this question takes the form of exhortation.

> The world over we are greatly in need of an administrative elite, who can assess and handle the concrete difficulties of human collaboration. As we lose the non-logic of a social code, we must substitute a logic of understanding. If at all the critical posts in communal activity we had intelligent persons capable of analyzing an individual or group attitude in terms of, first, the degree of logical understanding, second, the non-logic of social codes in action, and, third, the irrational exasperation symptomatic of conflict and baffled effort; if we had an elite capable of such analysis, very many of our difficulties would dwindle to vanishing point. (*Human Problems*, p. 185.)

This is indeed an ancient quest. It started with Plato's unsuccessful attempt to persuade the tyrant Dionysius of the virtues of philosophy. It ends—for the time being—with the attempt to persuade businessmen that they are able and ought to be willing to rescue our civilization.

Mayo's confidence is this ability of our industrial managers derives from the evidence of the Hawthorne studies. He suggests to the

---

181) and a second time when he states that trade unions repeat the mistake of management in organizing for industrial warfare rather than cooperation (*Political Problem*, p. 22).

managers that they adopt the Human Relations Approach, because the "sense of social function," which was created in the experimental work group without much exercise of authority, is to him the model solution. Whether industrial managers can run a whole factory on the model of a work group of five girls is a question Mayo has not faced. He simply assumes that managers can organize production with a minimum exercise of authority and a maximum attention to the individual's work-satisfaction. And since the cooperation of the workers in the experimental group was convincing evidence of "spontaneous cooperation," he calls upon the managers to organize the factory accordingly. In this manner Mayo has come to advocate an approach to industrial relations which overlooks the role of authority in the organization of production. It is unfair to charge an author with the use which other people make of his ideas. But it is not entirely fortuitous that managers, having adopted the Mayo approach but who nonetheless must exercise authority to meet production quotas, are often found to engage in verbalisms which disguise the exercise of authority in the vocabulary of the Human Relations Approach.

A good deal of Mayo's writings has been devoted to persuading industrial managers that the future of our civilization depends upon them. They are told that in modern society cooperation cannot be left to chance. They must organize cooperation, since most forms of organized cooperation so far tried are artificial, political, and part of the unfortunate legacy of the nineteenth century. To do so successfully, the managers must become aware "that it is a human social and not economic problem which they face." [14] Furthermore, the barriers between administrators and social scientists should be broken down. Administrators should have a knowledge of the social sciences, while social scientists should have an acquaintance with the facts.

> We have failed to train students in the study of social situations; we have thought that first-class technical training was sufficient in a modern and mechanical age. As a consequence we are technically competent as no other age in history has been; and we combine this with utter social incompetence. This defect of education and administration has of recent years become a menace to the whole future of civilization. (*Social Problems*, p. 120.)

The intense hostilities which modern society engenders demand "intelligent attention."

[14] *Human Problems*, p. 188.

> The administrator of the future must be able to understand the human-social facts for what they actually are, unfettered by his own emotion or prejudice. He cannot achieve this ability except by careful training—a training that must include knowledge of the relevant technical skills, of the systematic ordering of operations and of the organization of cooperation. (*Ibid.*, p. 122.)

This knowledge of the "human-social facts" will enable the factory manager, according to Mayo, to organize the "spontaneous" cooperation of workers and in that way he may rescue our civilization.

We shall pass over the logical problem involved in organizing "spontaneous" cooperation. In calling upon the industrial manager to organize cooperation, Mayo has in mind the type of cooperation which existed among men during the Middle Ages and in primitive societies.[15] In these societies, custom and tradition prompted men to agree on the goals of their actions. Tradition also gave them a feeling of their social function, in that the rights and duties which were theirs by birth established a meaningful relationship between the individual and his society.

This theme is applied to the problems of modern industry. Men of a primitive tribe cooperate "spontaneously" because they do not question the authority of tradition. In an analogous way, Mr. Mayo appears to believe that workers cooperate only when they accept the objectives of management. How else can we account for his assertion that since the industrial revolution there has been no effective collaboration between managers and workers?[16] Once workers agree with the objectives of management, it becomes the task of the latter to organize the plant in a cooperative manner. But here Mr. Mayo assumes what he has yet to prove: that there is a natural community between worker and manager. Where that is true, managers may well mitigate industrial discipline by attending to the job satisfaction of their workers; but if "spontaneous cooperation" is *not* characteristic of industrial relations, as Mayo never tires of pointing out, then the human relations approach is only an embellishment of the antagonistic cooperation between workers and managers. As such it may serve its modest function, but as such it will not enable the elite of industrial managers to play the large role which Mayo assigns to them.

[15] This idea had had an important influence on modern social science research. Cf. Mr. Mayo's comments on the study of Newburyport, Mass., by W. L. Warner and his colleagues, *Human Problems,* pp. 138–43.

[16] *Human Problems,* p. 179.

ASSETS OF CONFLICT AND DANGERS OF UNANIMITY

In most fields of social science it is important that the writer's basic values be clearly stated. In the study of industrial relations it is essential. Mr. Mayo has not done that, although it is evident that he prefers cooperation to conflict. But one may share that preference without condemning all kinds of conflict. And the desire for cooperation should be limited by the recognition that a certain measure of conflict is the inescapable accompaniment of an individual's freedom of choice.

Mr. Mayo makes distinction between the established society of the Middle Ages and of primitive tribes, and the adaptive society of today. He speaks of the need to develop social skills to supplement our technical skills. He says that cooperation must be organized rather than be left to chance. These and similar statements are in themselves plausible; but they are made with a certain bent for overstatement. To demand spontaneous cooperation in a society in which cooperation must be organized is meaningless. To demand unanimity of purpose in a society in which voluntary associations abound is to ask too much. To say that the individual must have a sense of social function or our civilization will perish, is a play with dangerous symbols. We really do not know how happy mankind must be in order to preserve its civilization.[17] It is the fashion today, and Mayo has contributed his share to the vogue, to become transfixed by gazing at the pathologies of our age. But nothing is gained, it seems to us, by making the modern dilemma worse than it is. Much may be lost if alarmist views provoke alarming social and political "remedies."

Yet the modern dilemma *is* serious, cooperation *is* difficult to attain. Organized labor is pitted against organized capital, and their cooperation is interrupted from time to time by a peaceable or combative re-definition of organizational prerogatives. In this situation Mr. Mayo has offered us a political nostrum despite his own rather vehement denunciation of such remedies. His appeal is clearly directed to the elite of industrial managers, whom he charges with the task of organizing cooperation in their plants through the "human relations approach." From this Mayo apparently expects that workers would cooperate with management without organizing in trade unions and

[17] In fact, we have the testimony of Dr. Freud, whom Mayo quotes approvingly in other connections, that any civilization leads to discontent.

precipitating industrial conflicts. If the strongest need of industrial workers is to have a sense of their social function, and if the "human relations approach" can provide this sense while membership in a trade union (at the price of intermittent industrial conflict) cannot, then Mayo would be correct in his diagnosis. But what evidence is there to prove this contention? The difficulty is that Mr. Mayo seeks to prove too much; he seeks to rescue our civilization as a whole by advocating remedies which might alleviate but not cure some of its ailments. He has shown that a good bit can be said for mitigating the harshness of industrial discipline by a more understanding cultivation of human relations within the plant. And his appeal is directed to the correct address, since it is the elite of industrial managers which is peculiarly equipped to act upon Mayo's insight. But the Goliath of industrial warfare cannot be slain by the David of human relations.

If we want rather to preserve the freedom of association, we must run the risk of industrial warfare. Mr. Mayo has indicated that many of our social and industrial conflicts would be avoided if managers, workers, and the people generally had more of a sense of social responsibility. But most people in modern society express their sense of social responsibility by their participation in such associations as the National Association of Manufacturers, the Chamber of Commerce or the Congress of Industrial Organizations. These and other associations will conflict. The crucial issue is not to avoid all conflict, but to contain that conflict within the limits of a broad pattern of common purposes—and that occurs daily in every industrial community of the land. It is the peculiar blindness of Mayo and others who have seen the medieval vision, that they do not understand that it is precisely the *freedom* to conflict which establishes the boundaries within which the actual conflicts can be contained.

An appeal to the leaders in unions and management to do their share is entirely appropriate. But Mr. Mayo forgets—in his appeal to the elite—that these leaders are both the servants and the masters of their respective organizations. *Their* success in helping our society and economy retain the middle ground between the enforced cooperation of dictatorship and a destructive frequency of conflicts, is a small although essential element. It is intimately related to a variety of factors such as the total productivity of a country, its security from outside attack, the "temper" of a people in periods of acute crisis, the role of the military, and others. Such factors add up to a quality of flexibility in a society, which cannot easily be measured but which constitutes its capacity for enduring internal conflicts relatively unimpaired. The human relations approach, if it were purged of its false metaphysic and its tendency to become the empty slogan of the advertising man, might make a very modest contribution to that capacity. In his claims for this approach, Mr. Mayo suffers from a widespread delusion of modern intellectuals, who believe that knowledge is power in the direct sense that they can instruct a powerful elite and "rescue" society.

Mr. Mayo has left no doubt that he regards the failure to achieve complete cooperation and a meaningful life for the individual as the outstanding failure of democracy. In this he ranges himself alongside other critics of democracy. These others, conservatives like Burke and revolutionaries like Marx, were usually at some pains to make clear the different standards according to which they found democracy and industrial society wanting, and to make plain the ethical platforms from which their criticisms were launched. Theirs were moral and ethical visions. Mr. Mayo is apt to try to pass as a technical prophet and to justify the ethical assumptions implicit in his prescription on an "else we perish" basis. But if one should choose to regard the emergency as a trifle less critical than Mayo believes it to be, then the urgency of survival no longer is a justification in itself for the means adopted. The means of survival may be various, and there may be some grounds less imperative than survival which become relevant. If we can defer the cataclysm for a while, it will not be inappropriate to inquire rather deeply into the terms of this unanimity which Mayo believes to be the condition of survival itself, and into the objects of the cooperation which it is the function of industrial managers to organize. There is a question or two to be answered.

Mayo's failure as a social scientist arises in large measure from his failure to define sharply the ethical presuppositions of his scientific work. Without these presuppositions made clear, the knowledge and skill which Mayo finds so undervalued in democratic societies deserve no higher rating than they get. Knowledge and skill have no implicit direction, no necessary ethical content. With equal efficiency and dispatch they may take us where we do or where we do not want to go. Until the ethical credentials pass critical scrutiny, democratic societies do well to keep their powder dry.

George C. Homans

Some Corrections to "The Perspectives of Elton Mayo"

"The Perspectives of Elton Mayo" has left out the foreground: the concrete research in industry that Mayo did and that others did with him. This research brought to the light of explicit understanding some—not all—of the determinants of workers' behavior, the importance of which had been appreciated only intuitively before his time. Later research, even in fields somewhat different from the one in which he worked, has abundantly confirmed his findings.[1] If this is "failure as a social scientist," then most of us would be happy to fail.

No rounded appraisal of Mayo's work can neglect the concrete research findings. Bendix and Fisher are not talking about them but about their broader "interpretation." This brings up two kinds of questions: (1) Are the findings applicable for action in situations other than the ones in which they were reached? (2) How did Mayo himself interpret his findings? The first question can, I think, be answered only by further research. The second can easily be answered wrong. A man is always able, if he wishes, to find in another's statements a meaning that the other, himself, did not place in them.

On the first point, I shall take just one example. Bendix and Fisher rightly point out that most of the Western Electric researches concerned small, isolated groups, and they go on to say: "It is by no means clear that the conditions or supervision achieved for the isolated work group could ever be reproduced for the factory." Of course it is not clear, and the question can be answered, not by debate, but by trying the experiment. It literally never has been tried, at least in a big factory. Mayo only asserted that it ought to be tried. Whatever its result we could not fail to learn by it, but if we do not try we shall never learn.

There is, by the way, in Mayo's work no implication that he

Reprinted from *Review of Economics and Statistics,* 31 (1949), 319–321, by permission of the author and the publisher.

[1] See, for example, W. F. Whyte, *Human Relations in the Restaurant Industry.*

studied all the problems and has all the answers. He did not study the social relationships within labor unions or between unions and management. It is often forgotten that there was nothing more than a company union at Hawthorne in the years when the research was being carried on. Some of his students are now working on labor relations. We also need, for example, a study of top management as a small work group. "There is a question or two to be answered"; so let us get to work.

On the second point, anyone is at liberty to disagree with Mayo's own interpretation of his findings. As a former student of Mayo's, I am only concerned here with making clear what that interpretation was, as it came out in his conversation and his writings. Bendix and Fisher are mistaken about it at certain crucial points.

Mayo is interested in discovering how spontaneous cooperation can be achieved. But Bendix and Fisher say that for him "spontaneous does not mean voluntary." I wholly disagree. That is just exactly what it does mean, and a description, such as Malinowski's, of a primitive society shows that cooperation can be both traditional *and* voluntary in the highest degree.

But it is, again, a misreading of Mayo to attribute to him a "preference for the social order of the Middle Ages." In making his distinction between an "established" and an "adaptive" society, he was careful to point out that any society we can look forward to at present is one in rapid change. The problem, he argued, is that of achieving spontaneous cooperation in a society that cannot leave cooperation to tradition. Failure to solve the problem will in fact take us back to an "established" society like that of the Middle Ages. He was always interested in studies of traditional cooperation, but it was not his model for our society, which he hoped could become "adaptive." [2]

Nor can Mayo be exposed as an anarchist—someone who believes in "the dangerous and destructive effects which politics and governmental action have on the will of the people." Bendix and Fisher put him in the position of opposing government when faced with the simple question, "Are you for government or against it?" But this is not the question, and Mayo would say that such an "all or nothing" choice is characteristic of obsessive thinking. His real position is well stated in a remark that Bendix and Fisher quote without seeing its significance: "Political action in a given community presumes the desire and capacity of individuals to work together; the political function

[2] See especially *The Social Problems of an Industrial Civilization* (1945), p. 12.

cannot operate in a community from which this capacity has disappeared." This does not imply that political conflict is inevitably destructive; it does imply that politics cannot work for growth in a society unless certain conditions hold, among others, a range of consensus among the members of the society. If the consensus does not exist, Mayo certainly holds that enforced cooperation, ultimately by dictatorship, destroys the capacity for spontaneous cooperation on which, he feels, the maintenance of civilization rests. But this view is not the same thing as opposition to governmental action. Since his retirement from Harvard, Mayo has found nothing in his convictions to prevent his working, as a consultant on industrial problems, with the labor government of Great Britain.[3]

As for the elite of industrial managers, Mayo did his work in industry, and it was natural for him to address himself to its leaders, especially as industry is obviously a key sector of modern society. He does not, one way or the other, express "confidence in the ability of our industrial managers," except to underline their competence in the merely technological field. He does point out that they, among others, have a responsibility and an opportunity. He feels that legislation is not going to help us out of our difficulties if it is not accompanied by an increased capacity for and a new conception of administration. He wants "intelligent persons capable of analysing an individual or group attitude" at "all the critical posts of communal activity." The emphasis is on the *all*. Here again he is not in the position of opposing political action but of stating its necessary concomitants. And as for authority, Mayo would hold that authority, far from being necessarily in conflict with spontaneous cooperation, can exist at a high level only if spontaneous cooperation is achieved. And it is too often forgotten, among the existing conflicts of our industrial life, that, after all, workers and management do share one common activity: both together are producing goods and services for the use of the public.

Mayo never "condemns all kinds of conflict." He does not think in absolute but in relative values. He feels that there is, quantitatively, enough unresolved conflict in our civilization to put it in danger of a collapse backward to the Middle Ages he is supposed to admire so much. This belief is certainly not hard to hold nor original with Mayo. Indeed, concern about our social and international conflicts is so widely shared that, if Bendix and Fisher do not share it, perhaps it is they who ought to make their "ethical presuppositions" clear.

[3] Elton Mayo died while this article was in press.

Amitai Etzioni

Industrial Sociology: The Study of Economic Organizations

Industrial sociology is a field of applied sociology, and has grown mainly out of interests in such issues as productivity, motivation, and unionization. In many cases, however, the theoretical relevance of the studies is evident, and often it is explicitly discussed by those who conducted the research. "Overcoming Resistance to Change,"[1] a frequently quoted study, is a case in point: while the problem studied is how to introduce frequent changes into the system of production in a pajama factory without reducing productivity, it is discussed from the point of view of its contributions to Kurt Lewin's field theory.[2] The studies of Mayo, Roethlisberger, Whyte, Warner, and many others have a theoretical perspective, and are not predominantly focused on practical problems. The applied nature of industrial sociology is revealed not so much in a lack of theoretical implications of the various studies as in a lack of conceptual codification and of systematic delimitation of the field. The accumulation of studies in this area seems now to have reached the stage at which one may attempt to offer such a systematic delimitation and to spell out the main dimensions of the field.

An important justification for this effort is that a successful con-

Reprinted in part from *Social Research,* 25 (1958), 303–324, by permission of the publisher, The New School for Social Research.

[1] Lester Coch and John R. P. French, Jr., "Overcoming Resistance to Change," in *Human Relations,* vol. 1 (1948), pp. 512–23.

[2] Kurt Lewin, "Group Decision and Social Change," in Guy E. Swanson, Theodore M. Newcomb, and Eugene L. Hartley, eds., *Readings in Social Psychology,* rev. ed. (New York, 1952), pp. 459–73.

ceptual delimitation of industrial sociology will make research in the field more economical. When it can be shown that an applied field is congruent with a theoretical area, and to determine its systematic boundaries, it becomes possible to see its relations to other fields of study (such as political sociology) and to make use of their hypotheses and concepts. Thus industrial sociologists have had a better understanding of the process of supervision and the role of the foreman since the concept of leadership, taken from other areas, has been introduced. Military sociology, on the other hand, has benefited from the idea of informal organization, first used by industrial sociologists. Such "translations" of concepts are not possible unless it becomes clear that soldiers and officers on the one hand, and workers and foremen on the other, are phenomena that have some elements in common. This is where theory enters into applied fields. It will be attempted below to point out some general parallelisms between industrial sociology and other areas of study, in order that sets of concepts and hypotheses can be translated. And another reason for attempting to spell out the theoretical dimensions of a field is that this effort may fulfill the function that Mendeleev's table fulfilled in chemistry: it may help to point out the missing elements, the uncovered, neglected areas.

I

I would like to suggest that what is usually regarded as industrial sociology can be fruitfully conceived of as a branch of organizational sociology. Industrial sociology has an implicit delimitation which, when made explicit and somewhat rearranged, fits neatly into the model of organizational sociology.

The latter is concerned with roles, and with processes of interaction, communication, and authority, that are *specialized* in serving specific social goals. Thus it studies civil service as pursuing the goals set by the government; and industry as creating goods and services, or as making profit. It has a relatively well developed theoretical model based on Max Weber's theory of bureaucracy, which has been significantly remodeled and improved by supplementing the study of rational aspects with the study of non-rational and irrational aspects of organizations.[3]

[3] See, for example, T. Parsons, "Suggestions for a Sociological Approach to the Theory of Organizations," in *Administrative Science Quarterly,* vol 1, nos. 1–2 (June–September 1956).

Organizational sociology is potentially able to develop sound bases for a generic as well as a comparative study of organizations, and it has greatly benefited from the interchange of concepts and hypotheses among its various sub-fields. Thus, while there are many significant differences between a church, an army, a university, a factory, and a trade union, sociologists have found it helpful to treat all these organizations as having common problems that may serve as a basis for a generalized discussion of organizations and also for differentiating the various organizational structures. The various types of organizations seem to have common functional problems, but different structural solutions, though fortunately the number of alternative solutions seems to be limited, and this makes a fruitful study of the field possible. Considering the present state of knowledge in this area, the following discussion of some of the common problems and alternative solutions must be very tentative.

All organizational structures, for example, have to face the problem of recruiting, training or socializing, and motivating their personnel, that it may function in accordance with the organization's regulations and norms. All organizations have to create and maintain among their personnel a motivation adequate to the role expectations of the organizational structure. Many of the studies on leadership, informal organization, small groups in organizational structures, morale, and other phenomena deal with this set of problems. Another element common to all organizational structures is the dynamic relationship among the organization's goals, inner needs, and need to adapt to a changing environment.

These common problems, as well as many others, can serve also as a basis for differentiation, that is, for classification and comparison of the various organizations. Thus one of the common functional problems of all organizations is the need to obtain resources from the outside, through exchange, taxation, or private endowments. For the analysis of certain organizational processes (such as efficiency, social control, services to the clientele) it is of interest to compare organizations according to the ways they obtain their resources. Again, all organizations have some goals they serve or pretend to serve, and therefore are confronted with the problem of creating and maintaining some personal commitment to these goals in at least part of their personnel. These commitments may be established and reinforced by coercion, material sanction, or social and symbolic rewards or deprivations. Which type of sanction is mainly applied is an important characterizing factor in the comparative study of organizations.

Presumably the subject matter of industrial sociology is industry. But "industry" seems to be a concept with no direct sociological meaning, and it is difficult to specify a theoretical orientation along its lines. The term "industry" has been taken over from commonsense language, economics, and the census of occupations, without sociological scrutiny. It has been used mainly in two ways: as synonymous with factory; and as covering any large-scale employment of labor and capital.

In the first use industry is seen as the manufacturing unit. Sociologists who have used the term in this manner have called industrial sociology "plant sociology." [4] This seems to be a too exclusive delimitation. There are many studies that fruitfully apply the ideas and concepts of industrial sociology to the study of offices, transportation, restaurants, and grocery stores, and to exclude these organizations from industrial sociology seems a rather arbitrary decision.

The second use of the term is widespread. Industry, according to Webster, is "any department or branch of art, occupation, or business; especially, one which employs much labor and capital and is a distinct branch of trade," or, in economics, "systematic labor or habitual employment." The census follows the same lines and classifies every field of full-time work as industry, including public administration, professional services, education, and private household work. All these demarcations of the field are obviously much too inclusive.

Therefore I suggest a middle way, the delimitation of industrial sociology to an area of sociological study of economic organizations, as these will presently be defined. Thus industrial sociology will include the study of offices, restaurants, and other economic organizations that are not factories, but will exclude the study of universities, schools, hospitals, and other non-economic organizations. Many industrial sociologists seem to have implicitly drawn the lines of the field in this way.

The proposed delimitation has an additional advantage: it classifies organizations according to a systematic conceptual scheme. Were we to classify study areas according to their subject matter, we would

[4] See C. Kerr and L. H. Fisher, "Plant Sociology: The Elite and the Aborigines," in M. Komarovsky, ed., *Common Frontiers of the Social Sciences* (Glencoe, Ill., 1957), pp. 281–304.

end up with an endless and unsystematic list: a sociology of industry, of financial institutions, of offices, services, mining, agriculture, and what not. For the purpose of systematizing an applied field we have to find an analytical base for delimiting it, which means in the present case an analytical basis on which organizational sociology can be subdivided.

That basis is provided by the functions that an organization fulfills for society, or for the social unit in which it is embedded. . . . The typology can be further refined by classifying organizations according to their primary *and* secondary functions. This raises two questions: first, how to distinguish between economic and noneconomic organizations; second, how to determine what is an organization's primary or dominant orientation and what is its secondary one.

Economic organizations are those whose primary aim is to produce goods and services, to exchange them, or to organize and manipulate monetary processes. The profit motive as an institutionalized primary goal may often serve as a helpful empirical indicator, but it is not reliable because, on the one hand, some schools, hospitals, and social clubs are geared mainly to the maximizing of profit, while on the other hand, publicly owned or managed industries may not be profit oriented.

The dominant orientation can be determined in several ways. What is considered to be the legitimate primary orientation can be established by communicating with the appropriate group of people. What the dominant functions actually are may be determined by studying the goals that receive the preponderance of efforts, funds, and time. It would be even better to study critical decisions and the incidence of conflicts between two or more sets of considerations: if economic considerations are usually decisive, this may be considered an indicator of the dominant orientation. From this point of view the study of top management decisions is very significant, because secondary or even tertiary orientations may dominate on the lower levels.

Another clue may be gained from the structure of the hierarchy. In most economic organizations, technological considerations are usually subordinated to economic criteria and there is no room for the domination of expert perfectionism and pure technological achievement that cannot be geared to production under the existing economic conditions, or those predicted for the near future. This is reflected in the fact that those who make economic decisions are usually in higher positions of authority than the experts. In universities, on the other hand, where serving the goals of knowledge and following such "unproductive" interests as basic research are considered one of the main aims, and where economic considerations (such as decisions concerning the allocation of funds) are subordinated to these "expert" considerations, it is legitimate, and according to this analysis also functional, to subordinate the administration to the "experts," for instance, to the academic senate or other faculty bodies. Thus by studying the distribution of activities, critical decisions and incidences, conflict situations and organizational hierarchies, we can determine which orientation is primary, which secondary, and so on.

If it is agreed that industrial sociology be defined as a part of organizational sociology, dealing specifically with those organizations whose primary function is economic, it remains to consider how the generic concerns of organizational sociology apply to the study of economic organizations in particular. It will be seen that industrial sociologists have already studied some of the areas that legitimately belong to the field, but have neglected others.

II

Organizational sociology focuses on the study of organizations from four levels or points of view. On the first level, organizations are studied as social units, and interest here is divided between the study of the formal and the informal structure. The formal dimension, often studied by administrators, is in itself of little interest to the sociologist of organizations. The latter usually focuses on the informal relations and their connection to the formal system. He is interested in the formal only as it impinges on the social process and sets a stage for the more "real" processes of interaction.

On the second level the study of organizations deals with the relation of an organizational structure as a unit to other organizational structures and to non-organizational social units (collectivities), such as families, communities, ethnic groups, social classes, and the society.

On the third level organizations are studied from the point of view of their relations to what would be called, in Parsons' frame of reference, personality and culture. The organization-personality studies are concerned with the interrelationships between the needs of the organizational structure and the needs of the personalities of the actors; problems of motivation and involvement, mentioned above, are cases in point. The study of the relations of organizations to cultural systems focuses on two main concerns. Some scholars are interested in value orientations, and inquire into the sources of the legitimation of authority and into the dynamic relations between the ideals and goals of the organization and the needs of the organizational structure itself. Others are more interested in the ways in which knowledge (mainly scientific knowledge) is recruited and institutionalized within the organization. Other aspects of culture, such as myth, are also studied in relation to organizational behavior.[5]

The fourth level, the relations between organizations and their environment, has thus far received relatively little attention, but theoretically there is place for this focus of interest. It would include the study of relationships between organizational behavior and the biological and physiological capacities and needs of the actors, and the study of the respective adaptations between the organization and its geographical-physical environment.

Not all of these levels are of equal interest to sociologists, and not all of them have been equally explored. As regards the actual study of organizations, it can be said—and this is applicable also to the sociology of economic organizations—that most studies tend to focus on the organizational unit and the interrelations among its elements, and tend to neglect its relations to other social units, even such significant ones as other organizations and collectivities. The emphasis is often on the generic characteristics and processes of organizational units, rather than on the specific structures and processes of the various organizational subtypes. These points will be extensively illustrated in the following discussion of how the four levels of interest apply specifically to the study of economic organizations.

Economic Organizations as Social Units

Study of the formal structure of economic organizations—the division of labor and the lines of communication and authority—is conducted mainly as part of the study of administration. Although this type of investigation is relatively well developed in regard to some kinds of organizations, such as hospitals, its application to economic organizations leaves much to be done. Often it is assumed that because the latter are close to the generic model of organization, there is little need to study the specific nature of their administrative struc-

[5] See Richard C. Myers, "Myth and Status Systems in Industry," in *Social Forces,* vol. 26 (1948), pp. 331–37.

ture. Therefore the sociologist, though interested mainly in the relationship between the formal and the informal aspects, is quite often compelled to spell out the nature of the formal structure he is dealing with.[6]

Analysis of the informal structure of economic organizations is one of the most important contributions of industrial sociology to the study of organization in general. The findings of Mayo, Roethlisberger, Dickson, Whyte, Homans, K. Lewin, and many others are too well known to be repeated here. It seems more fruitful to point out the directions in which these findings have to be further elaborated, since there is a strong tendency to repeat the work already done and to ignore other areas.

One such area is very similar to that neglected by the administrative studies: the *specific* nature of the informal aspects of economic organizations. We know by now that informal organization exists and influences the functioning of industries as well as armies, schools, and churches. But we know little about the significant differences in the amount of informal organization, or about the different ways in which informal factors function in various organizational contexts. We can make guesses. We may presume, for instance, that informal organization in the army is much more developed than in a bridge club, because army life is more encompassing (includes more spheres of life) —that, other things being equal, the more encompassing an organization, the more involving and powerful its informal organization. It may well be that different economic organizations have different types of informal organizations; thus in a small industry the informal organization of the workers may be more strongly related to that of the foremen, and even to that of the management, than in a larger industry, and similar differences may exist between a unionized and a nonunionized plant. But all such possibilities are necessarily speculations, as so few comparative studies exist.

Even such a basic question as the conditions under which informal organization of workers supports, withholds support from, or is hostile to management, striving to undermine the formal structure, has not been satisfactorily answered. Whereas we know something about "human relations" factors, such as two-way communication, leadership by the supervisor, participation, it seems that the study

[6] See, for example, Rose Laub Coser, "Authority and Decision-Making in a Hospital: A Comparative Analysis," in *American Sociological Review*, vol. 23, no. 1 (February 1958), pp. 56–63.

of other factors, such as distribution of rewards, the cultural background of workers, the social structure of the community, and many further structural factors that affect workers' attitudes to work and management, is relatively neglected.

The same holds true for the study of informal relations and groups on various levels in the hierarchy of economic organizations. A great deal of repetitious research is conducted on groups of workers, but relatively little is known about informal relations in middle and top management. The difficulties of studying primary relations on these levels are obvious, but the extra effort may be rewarded by an extra premium in terms of significant findings, for these elites occupy crucial positions in the organizational structures and the decision-making processes.

Examination of the relations between the two aspects of organization, the formal and the informal, constitutes a source of many interesting insights into the functioning of organizations, and has become an integral part of the approach of industrial sociologists to economic organizations. Thus we need not discuss it here.

Most industrial sociologists regard the factory as a social system; some even go so far as to see it as a "small society." But it is not enough to state that an industry is a social system, because the same is true of a family, a community, and a nation. What has to be explored is the specific nature of those social systems that are economic organizations, the characteristics that distinguish them from other social systems. It may well be that the differentiating line is to be found in the nature of the integration of rational and non-rational (or instrumental and expressive) elements. Moreover, some industries seem to be not a "small society," but a part of other systems—for example, part of the social system of a community. In these cases some basic functions, which every social system or sub-system has to fulfill in order to exist, are carried on for the industry by the community.

Economic Organizations and Other Social Units

The significance of studying inter-organizational relationships, especially those between economic and non-economic organizations, has lately been emphasized by economists as well as by students of administration. But the examination of inter-organizational relationships from a sociological point of view leaves much to be desired. Even the relations between two organizations that are often studied—corporations and trade unions—are frequently seen from a legal or economic point of view, only rarely from a sociological perspective; also, many of the studies on this subject are merely descriptive and suffer from a lack of theoretical sophistication. Relations between corporations and other organizations are rarely studied.

Thus, as regards specifically economic organizations, we know very little about the sociological meaning of their relations with one another—for example, the relations between financing and manufacturing institutions; the role of inter-organizational mobility; the functions of social contacts among the economic elites in maintaining informal monopolistic price regulations and "price leadership." And we know even less about the relations between economic and non-economic organizations. After centuries of abstract arguments concerning the influence of governmental control on economic organizations, there are only a handful of sociological studies on the subject, many of which are predominantly concerned with the sociology of law and not with the study of inter-administrative relations. When one turns from the Western world and studies industries and other economic organizations in newly developed countries or in countries of the Soviet orbit, one can make little progress, however, without taking into account at the very least the relations among economic organizations, governmental agencies, and political parties.

In turning now to the relations between economic organizations and collectivities, it should be repeated that by the latter term is meant social groups that have strong elements of solidarity, such as families, communities, ethnic groups, social classes, and society as a whole. All economic organizations are *partial* systems, in the sense that they do not regulate all the basic needs of the actors. Therefore they are always embedded in collectivities, which serve certain social and symbolic requirements. Economic organizations differ according to the degree and ways in which they are related to these collectivities.

The collectivities provide at least elementary socialization and exercise a considerable degree of social control over the behavior of their members, also in their role as organizational personnel. Thus the meaning of the pay check depends on the attitude of the worker's family and neighbors, his status in the community, and so on. Some industrial sociologists, following certain of Durkheim's and Mayo's ideas on the disintegration of collectivities, have expected the industry to take over the social functions of the collectivities, by becoming a community and a family to the worker. In recent years, however, industrial sociologists seem to agree that workers' peer groups are supplementing rather than substituting for collectivities. There are not enough studies that focus on this subject, or on the relationship between work groups and other collectivities. We have a number of studies on the relationship between industrial organizations and families, ethnic groups, or communities, but while most of these contribute a great deal to our understanding of workers and of the functioning of economic organizations, they stimulate our interest in this field more than they satisfy it.

Organizations are not only related *to* collectivities; they are also *in* collectivities, in the sense that a factory is in a community and the NAM and AFL-CIO are in the American society. It is not easy to spell out exactly what this "being in" means. From the legal point of view it means that the laws and regulations of the political organs of the collectivity apply to the organization that is in it. But this is only a formal aspect of the more basic phenomenon: economic organizations are integrated with other organizations, and into the society, through collectivities.

Warner demonstrated this when he showed that the relations between the upper and lower classes in a community have an integrative effect on the work relations among managers and workers recruited from these classes.[7] The power structure and the net of instrumental relations in the industry are embedded in the net of solidaric relations of the community. The managers, who are also the leaders of the community, display more than mere economic "exploitative" interests in the workers, and the latter have ways and means, other than grievances and strikes, of conveying their feelings and needs to management and of exerting pressure on it. When this balance is disturbed by a transference of the center of power outside the community's solidaric framework, first a "pure" power relation emerges (the strike occurs), and then a new balance on the national level between a trade-union center and an employer is established, with the directing aid of a government agency (the State Board of Arbitration and Conciliation). Gouldner reports a similar case in which relations in the community impinge on the labor-foremen relations in the industry, and describes the disturbance caused by the interference of an external center of power.[8]

[7] W. L. Warner and J. O. Low, *The Social System of the Modern Factory* (New Haven, 1947).

[8] Alvin W. Gouldner, *Wildcat Strike* (Yellow Springs, Ohio, 1954).

A full multi-factor analysis, which would take into account all of the major organizational structures and all the significant collectivities to which organizations are related and in which they are embedded, may be far beyond the reach of industrial sociology at its present state. But a study of the interrelations of three or more organizations and collectivities, instead of the traditional examination of the relationship between corporations and trade unions, does not seem to be an exaggerated demand.

As for the relations between economic organizations and society as a whole, this is one of the most significant as well as best covered fields of sociology. It was one of the main interests of Marx and Weber, to name only two. Modern society is often said to be characterized by the supremacy of economic units, institutions, and values. Since the term industry is loosely applied, it is only one step further to speak of modern society as "industrial society" and to call its study "industrial sociology." The historical and psychological reasons for this use of the term are of no interest here, as they cannot justify this doubtful extension. It obscures the fact that its subject matter is a major type of society and hence involves a general theory of societies and not a theory of social units or organizations within society. It obscures also the fact that modern society is characterized by many traits, and the supremacy of economic institutions is only one of them; modern society would be better described as characterized by the supremacy of rational values and institutions. The term "modern," since it is associated with the supremacy of science, technology, and secular ideology, no less than with the supremacy of the market system and industry as a mode of production, is preferable to the term "industrial," which brings up mainly economic associations.

Similarly, in order to avoid identifying the study of society (sociology) with the study of economic organizations (industrial sociology), the study of "industrial societies" *as such* should be conceived of not as part of industrial sociology but as a study in itself, the study of modern societies. Industrial sociology has a direct interest in the study of society only in the following cases: first, when the problem is the relations of economic organizations to other organizations and to collectivities, and the extent to which society regulates or directs these relations; and second, when there is direct interaction between economic organizations and integrative structures of the society itself, as in the political organs of modern society.

3. Organizational Goals

»»

Organizations are social units oriented toward the pursuit of specific goals. In this sense they can be conceived as tools which gain their meaning and direction from their function. But one of the most important observations of students of organizations is that often the "tools" in part determine the goals to which they are applied. This process takes several forms: initial goals may prove to be "utopian," and organizational personnel may adjust these goals by making them more "realistic." The organization's original goals may be neglected without being changed officially; the organization may develop alternative or competing goals which are more in line with the interests of its staff. Or the organization may see its predominant task in maintaining and expanding itself.

A considerable number of studies have been conducted on this subject. They seek to determine the conditions under which goals are served, in contrast to the conditions under which they are neglected or adapted; to clarify the mechanisms through which goals are formulated and changed; and to establish the effect of goal changes on the organization's structure and its relation to the social environment.

Sills reports the conclusion of his study on the changing goals of an organization and surveys the findings of several other studies conducted in this area. He studied the National Foundation for Infantile Paralysis which, when it came close to realizing its major goal, had to decide whether it ought to disband or whether it should persist and work toward a new goal. Since it became evident through Sills' research that the members' commitment to the organization itself was high, and was not necessarily based on the goal of fighting polio, the organization was in a position to pursue a new, though similar, goal without risking the loss of its membership.

Sills reviews a number of other studies of voluntary associations in order to examine the conditions under which organizations abandon old goals and develop new. Whereas success was a major factor in goal succession in the case of the National Foundation for Infantile Paralysis, lack of success in recruiting membership, funds, prestige, and public support made for goal succession in the case of the Woman's Christian Temperance Union and the Townsend Organization. Other organizations, such as the Y.M.C.A., the Red Cross, and the Planned Parenthood Federation, increased or renewed their public appeal, not by dismissing their old goals, but by reinterpreting them and by adding new ones. This solution seems to allow for more organizational continuity than a complete substitution of goals would provide. Continuity seems to be valued because of its function in legitimating organizational activities; abrupt changes in goals seem to endanger such legitimation. Thus the analysis of goals has made a full cycle, from considering goals as guides and ends for organizational activities to viewing them as means employed by organizations to improve their position in their social environment.

In his study of the Adult Education system, Clark points out some of the factors which make for the "weakness" or "strength" of goals in terms of their ability to resist pressures to adapt to various organizational and environmental needs. Goals tend to be precarious when they are undefined, when the positions of those in charge of their implementation are not fully legitimized, and when the members of the organization are committed to other values. The vagueness of such goals as "cultural development" and "self-expression," the marginality of Adult Education in a child-oriented school system, and the part-time, relatively uncommitted students, made the initial goals of Adult Education precarious. These conditions also determined to a considerable degree the direction of the organizational adaptation, namely, toward a client-oriented, vocational training system.

Cressey brings up problems arising from the fact that organizations serve more than one goal at a a time, and serve unofficial as well as official goals. He found not only that the prisons he studied were custody- or treatment-oriented but that they also were oriented to the protection of inmates from society. Inmates needed protection from "the stares of organized groups of tourists," which undermined their therapy in the treatment-oriented prison, as well as from the ridicule of employees in the more segregated and impersonal custody-oriented prison. In assessing organizational effectiveness, therefore, official policy, interaction with staff and with outsiders, and variations in structure have to be examined from the viewpoint not only of the declared but also of unstated goals, such as protection of the inmates.

Thompson and McEwen examine the effect of interaction between organizations and their environment on organizational goals; they point out that the constantly changing environment requires organizations continuously to reappraise their goals. Reappraisal, in turn, is dependent upon the measurability of goal requirements and the organization's accomplishments. The more difficult an appraisal, the more likely it is that the organization will evade societal controls.

Thompson and McEwen identify four forms of organizational interaction within its environment: competition, and three forms of cooperation—bargaining, co-optation, and coalition. The authors specify the effect of each form of interaction on the way the environment influences the selection of organizational goals. Competition eliminates organizations which insist on catering to goals that society is not willing to accept. Bargaining means that representatives of the environment become actual partners in the decision-making process within the organization. Co-optation enables the organization to control those who are supposed to control it and therefore opens avenues for arbitrary or unilateral decisions. Coalition reduces the organization to the level of a committed partner in a larger unit and therefore curtails its freedom of decision.

Like the authors of the other three studies, Thompson and McEwen emphasize the fact that organizations, in order to assure the realization of their goals, attempt to control the environmental factors which supposedly control them. Thus this study also underlines the major issues in the analysis of organizational goals: who will guard the organizations to keep them from becoming ends in themselves, and who will guard the guards?

David L. Sills

The Succession of Goals

Any analysis of a goal-directed organization cannot be confined to things as they are, since the future state of affairs toward which the organization's activities are oriented is very much a component of the contemporary organization. It must, in the very nature of the case, inquire into the relationship of present activities to future developments.

The relevance of this statement to the present analysis is rooted in the fact that the Foundation's * major goal is by definition a finite one. A fundamental assumption underlying the original establishment of the Foundation was that infantile paralysis was a disease which medical science would eventually be able to bring under control, and a major reason for the capacity of the Foundation to maintain through the years its high ratio of goal-related activities has been the very real possibility that the organization's goal would be realized—perhaps within the lifetime of the participants. The recent development of the Salk vaccine, and its use on a nationwide scale, serve as dramatic evidence that the full achievement of the Foundation's major goal will be realized in the not too distant future. In fact, Dr. Jonas E. Salk, who developed the vaccine, and Dr. Leonard E. Scheele, former Surgeon General of the United States Public Health Service, recently reported to the American Medical Association that by the middle of 1959 paralytic polio should be completely eliminated as a threat to both children and adults.[1]

The imminence of this full achievement of its major goal naturally raises the question of what will happen to the Foundation at that time.

Reprinted in part from *The Volunteers,* pp. 253–268, 270, by permission of the author and the publisher, The Free Press. Copyright 1957.

* The National Foundation for Infantile Paralysis [Ed.].

[1] *New York Times,* June 12, 1956, p. 37.

Will it simply go out of existence, will it continue on a more limited scale, providing assistance to persons already afflicted by polio, or will it—taking advantage of experience gained in conquering polio—turn its attention to another health or welfare problem? The seriousness of these questions, as they apply to organizations generally, has been noted by a number of students of voluntary associations and social movements. Wendell King, for example, states that "an apparently unanticipated and rarely desired outcome of achieving goals can be the abrupt demolition of the whole organization. Unless additional objectives are devised, the movement lies robbed of its reason for existence."[2]

In order to achieve a perspective through which to approach the topic of the future of the Foundation it is helpful to recall the major conclusions reached by Philip Selznick in his analysis of the relationship between doctrine and action in the Tennessee Valley Authority. Organizations, Selznick notes, develop obligations over a period of time to act in a certain way, obligations which Selznick terms "commitments." He summarizes the importance of these commitments as follows:

> The systematized commitments of an organization define its character. Day-to-day decision, relevant to the actual problems met in the translation of policy into action, create precedents, alliances, effective symbols, and personal loyalties which transform the organization from a profane, manipulable instrument into something having a sacred status and thus resistant to treatment simply as a means to some external goal. That is why organizations are often cast aside when new goals are sought. . . .
>
> So long as goals are given, and the impulse to act persists, there will be a series of enforced lines of action demanded by the nature of the tools at hand. These commitments may lead to unanticipated consequences resulting in a deflection of original goals.[3]

Although Selznick's research was restricted to one organization, he clearly intended his conclusions to apply to other organizations as well. For this reason, it is appropriate to examine the extent to which this formulation of the consequences of organizational commitments may be said to characterize the situation which may soon confront the Foundation.

[2] C. Wendell King, *Social Movements in the United States* (New York: Random House, 1956), p. 114.

[3] Philip Selznick, *TVA and the Grass Roots* (Berkeley and Los Angeles: University of California Press, 1949), pp. 258–59.

The passage cited is composed of two parts. First, it states that "day-to-day decisions" (i.e., those made in order to solve immediate and pressing problems) lead to "commitments," which in turn define the "character" of an organization. Second, it states that this process may have two consequences: an organization may be "deflected from its original goals" and it may be "cast aside when new goals are sought."

Although the major focus of this study has been the current membership and activities of the Foundation, rather than the details of its history, sufficient attention has been given to the circumstances surrounding the original emergence of various features of the organization to document the first of these two statements—that decisions made for the purpose of solving immediate problems often determine the ultimate character of an organization. It has been noted, for example, that the Foundation's almost total dependence upon a fund-raising strategy based upon obtaining small gifts from large numbers of people emerged from two decisions made in the Depression year 1933: to solicit gifts from the people of Georgia in order to finance the construction of a new building at Georgia Warm Springs, and to raise funds nationally by sponsoring President's Birthday Balls; that the characteristically middle-class composition of the Foundation's Volunteer membership may be traced in large part to the decision to ask postmasters, Democrats, and persons of civic prominence generally to organize these Birthday Balls; and that the patient care program is a direct outgrowth of the decision to permit local Committees for the Celebration of the President's Birthday to retain for use in their own communities a portion of the funds raised in 1935. This brief listing of examples suggests the general applicability to the Foundation of this aspect of Selznick's thesis: the Foundation's "character" today is clearly in many respects the result of decisions made with other ends in view.

The second part of Selznick's statement concerns the consequences which may result from the emergence of organizational commitments —goal displacement and the destruction of the organization itself. Sufficient evidence from other studies has been cited throughout this volume to suggest the near-universality of the phenomenon of goal displacement within organizations, and a number of reasons underlying the Foundation's capacity to maintain itself as a goal-oriented organization have been cited. But what of the Foundation's capacity to maintain itself as an organization after its initial goals have been realized, and "new goals are sought"? Will its organizational structure be "cast aside"? It is to a consideration of these questions that the discussion now turns.

Evidence from Other Organizations

Two important voluntary associations in our early history, the Sons of Liberty and the Committees of Correspondence, were dissolved when the anti-British purposes for which they were established culminated in the American Revolution and the establishment of the Continental Congress. Sometimes organizations decline long before their goals are achieved, as, for example, the American Anti-Slavery Society, which split through internal dissension and controversy over policy matters some twenty years before the Emancipation Proclamation. And sometimes they are dissolved when their functions are taken over by governmental bodies, as happened to the Public School Society of New York City when the public school system was established.

The succession of goals. Dissolution, however, is not the only course of action open to an organization when its purposes are either achieved or become irrelevant because of changes in the social environment; in fact, it is equally easy to find examples of organizations which have remained intact for the purpose of working toward new or sharply modified objectives. Peter Blau has called this process the "succession of goals." [4]

The American Legion, to cite one example, was originally established in order to preserve the spirit which characterized the American Expeditionary Force in World War I, but it very soon included in its objectives the protection of the rights of veterans and, particularly among local Posts, the instigation of community service projects. Dartmouth College, to cite another example, was originally founded primarily in order to educate and Christianize the Indians of New England, but it experienced no great difficulty in transforming itself into a general liberal arts college.

Voluntary health and welfare agencies exhibit similar tendencies. The Birth Control Federation, for example, in 1942 adopted the more

[4] Peter M. Blau, *The Dynamics of Bureaucracy* (Chicago: University of Chicago Press, 1955), p. 195. See also Peter M. Blau, *Bureaucracy in Modern Society* (New York: Random House, 1956), pp. 95–96.

comprehensive name of the Planned Parenthood Federation of America, and has since that time expanded its objectives to include treatment for infertility, education for marriage, and marriage counseling.[5] The American Social Hygiene Association, which has traditionally concerned itself with combating both prostitution and venereal diseases, has in recent years adjusted to the decline in organized prostitution and the drastic lowering of the incidence of venereal diseases, and has established such new objectives as supporting family life education and preparing high school boys for the social and psychological strains which they will undergo during military service.[6] In fact, thousands of organizations of all kinds have adapted in one way or another to external conditions affecting the relevance of their objectives, but there have been very few systematic analyses of such organizations from this point of view. It is therefore instructive to examine briefly the process of organizational adaptation as it has taken place in organizations for which relatively complete information is available. Two of these organizations, the Woman's Christian Temperance Union and the Townsend Organization, have failed to adjust themselves to a changed environment, and exist today as fossil remains of their previous life. The other two, the Young Men's Christian Association and the American National Red Cross, have made highly successful adaptations.

The Young Men's Christian Association. Although there have been a number of organizational histories of the Y.M.C.A., Owen Pence's volume, *The Y.M.C.A. and Social Need,* is most useful for an examination of the Y.M.C.A. as an illustration of the process of organizational adaptation.[7] The book is sub-titled "A Study of Institutional Adaptation"; more specifically, it is an examination of how the goals of the Y.M.C.A. have changed in response to various changes in the social environment, particularly the secularization of American society which has taken place in the past century.

Today the Y.M.C.A. places a great deal of emphasis upon the opportunities for recreation and physical exercise which it offers, but the first Association in London stated that its objective was "to improve the spiritual condition of young men engaged in the drapery and other trades"; the first Association in America, in Boston, expanded its ob-

[5] Planned Parenthood Federation of America, *Birth Control U.S.A.: Highlights of the Program,* p. 8; *The Most Important Thing,* p. 3.

[6] American Social Hygiene Association, *Social Hygiene News,* April, 1955.

[7] Owen E. Pence, *The Y.M.C.A. and Social Need* (New York: Association Press, 1939).

jective to include "the improvement of the spiritual and mental condition of young men"; and the first New York Association included in its objectives the following:

> The object of this Association shall be the improvement of the spiritual, mental, and social condition of young men . . . to bring them under moral and religious influences, by aiding them in the selection of suitable boarding places and employment. . . .[8]

With the passing years, as Pence shows, the Y.M.C.A. has devoted increasing attention to its physical and social goals, and less attention to its original religious and spiritual aims. This transition is summarized in these terms:

> In contrast with the conception of earlier years, when the principal concern of the Association was with the securing of individual commitments to the Christian life, the realization has steadily grown in recent years that religious living and interest are so gravely conditioned by the total social experience that the two cannot be dealt with separately.[9]

And again, in more direct language:

> In time, the Associations began to take their objectives for granted. In their place activity (that is, whatever met and satisfied expressed interests of members) became the real objective.[10]

The Y.M.C.A., therefore, is an example of an organization whose goals have changed, not because they were achieved, but rather because of fundamental changes in the social environment in which its activities were carried out. . . .

The Woman's Christian Temperance Union. The central problem which led Joseph Gusfield to study the W.C.T.U. is the fact that changes in American drinking habits and the increased acceptance of drinking as a part of general social life "have presented the W.C.T.U. with an environment more hostile to the doctrine of total abstinence than was true in the years of the organization's formation and development."[11] In the face of this situation, Gusfield sought both to

[8] *Ibid.*, p. 12.
[9] *Ibid.*, p. 315.
[10] *Ibid.*, p. 236.
[11] Joseph R. Gusfield, "Social Structure and Moral Reform: A Study of the Woman's Christian Temperance Union," *American Journal of Sociology*, 61 (1955), pp. 221–32. The discussion in the text is based entirely upon this study.

determine "whether the change in environment has led to changes in the goals and doctrine of the movement" and to explain "changes, or lack of change, in the organization." [12]

In many respects, the Y.M.C.A. and the W.C.T.U. have had similar histories. Both organizations were established at a time when a powerful middle class believed that its mission was to improve the social conditions under which the lower class lived. The Y.M.C.A. sought to improve these conditions by Christianizing and educating young men; the W.C.T.U. believed that working class people could enjoy the benefits of middle class life if they stopped drinking—"drink is the curse of the working classes" was a popular slogan of the 19th Century temperance movement.[13] And both organizations have survived in spite of a sharp decline in the popularity of these theories of humanitarian reform. But they differ greatly in the manner in which they have survived.

As previously indicated, the Y.M.C.A.'s history has been characterized by successive adjustments to its social environment. The W.C.T.U., on the other hand, has not adjusted:

> Today the W.C.T.U. is an organization in retreat. Contrary to the expectations of theories of institutionalization, the movement has not acted to preserve organizational values at the expense of past doctrine.[14]

How has this been possible? As Gusfield shows, the W.C.T.U. has not abandoned its goal of establishing temperance norms, but has instead shifted its attention to a new audience. Originally the organization was composed largely of middle- and upper middle-class women who sought both to dissuade working class people from drinking and to improve their general welfare in other ways; today it is less upper middle-class and more lower middle- and working-class in composition, and its chief target is the drinking habits of middle-class groups. In short, the W.C.T.U. has elected *not* to change its goals to meet changed conditions. Instead, the organization has changed the composition of its membership, limited its goals to the discouragement of middle-class drinking, and shifted its strategy from active campaigning against intemperance to indulging in what Gusfield terms "moral indignation." [15]

[12] *Ibid.*, p. 222.
[13] *Ibid.*, p. 225.
[14] *Ibid.*, p. 232.
[15] *Ibid.*

The Townsend Organization. The Y.M.C.A. is an example of an organization which has succeeded through successive adaptations to its social environment; the W.C.T.U. is an organization which is in a state of decline because of its failure to adjust to changes in its environment; and the Townsend Organization, as Sheldon Messinger has demonstrated, is one which has nearly vanished because its major goal, alleviating or preventing economic dislocation, has at least temporarily been achieved—not, however, through the efforts of the organization.[16]

Dr. Francis E. Townsend first proposed his plan to end the Depression by retiring all United States citizens at the age of sixty on a monthly pension of $200 in September, 1933; by 1936 the Townsend Organization had 2,250,000 members. In 1935, however, the Social Security Act was passed, and by 1951 the organization had only 56,656 members, a loss of more than 97 per cent.[17] In the intervening years, the expansion of social security legislation, of pension plans by private employers, and of the national economy itself largely eliminated public interest in a program designed to end the Depression of the 1930's. In the face of these changes in the relevance of its original goals, how has the Townsend Organization survived at all?

Messinger outlines three organizational transformations which have taken place. First, there has been a tendency to support other measures affecting the aged, a tendency which the leaders themselves have checked since they realized it could lead only to a break-up of the organization. Second, there has been a tendency to obtain financial support by selling consumer goods of one kind or another, e.g., vitamin pills. Finally, there has been a tendency to convert membership meetings into social gatherings, and to hold other social events as well. On the basis of these tendencies, as well as of other aspects of the transformation of the Townsend Organization, Messinger draws this conclusion:

> The organized arms of declining social movements will tend to adapt to these changed conditions in characteristic ways. We can broadly describe this adaptation by asserting that the dominating orientation of leaders and members shifts *from the implementation of*

[16] Sheldon L. Messinger, "Organizational Transformation: A Case Study of a Declining Social Movement," *American Sociological Review*, 20 (1955), pp. 3–10. The discussion which follows is based largely upon this study. See Arnold W. Green, *Sociology* (New York: McGraw-Hill Book Co., 1956), pp. 547–55, for further details of the Townsend Movement.

[17] Messinger, *op. cit.*, p. 4.

the values the organization is taken to represent (by leaders, members, and public alike), *to maintaining the organizational structure as such,* even at the loss of the organization's central mission.[18]

The Townsend Organization, in short, has adjusted to changes in its environment in ways quite different from those followed by the W.C.T.U. Instead of modifying its membership and its goals, it has virtually abandoned its original goals and has concentrated its attention, not very successfully, upon maintaining its organizational structure.

The American National Red Cross.[19] Like the Y.M.C.A., the Red Cross is a highly successful organization, and for much the same reasons: it has made successive adjustments to changes in its social environment. Its initial objective, as set forth in its first constitution, was "to hold itself in readiness in the event of war or any calamity great enough to be considered national, to inaugurate such practical measures in mitigation of the suffering and for the protection and relief of sick and wounded as may be consistent with the objects of the Association. . . ."[20] The organization was small in its early years, and floods and other disasters, the Spanish-American War, and most importantly, World War I, provided sufficient challenges to its resources to make any expansion of its objectives unnecessary. The end of World War I, however, found a greatly expanded Red Cross without an objective of sufficient scope to maintain the organization. There was a decline in membership interest, and the leaders feared the organization would suffer. Foster Dulles has summarized this crisis in the Red Cross's history in these terms:

> The officers of the Red Cross, discouraged but not dismayed, were determined to find a way out in spite of chapter apathy. There was a natural desire on their part to see the American Red Cross maintain its position and still further broaden its field of usefulness, not only for the sake of whatever contributions could be made toward improving the conditions of American life, *but for the sake of the organization itself.*[21]

This crisis was surmounted by adopting a new program—"the preservation and improvement of the public health"[22]—and the Red

[18] *Ibid.*, p. 10.

[19] The discussion of the Red Cross in the text is based entirely upon Foster R. Dulles, *The American Red Cross: A History* (New York: Harper and Brothers, 1950).

[20] Cited in Dulles, *op. cit.*, p. 16.

[21] *Ibid.*, p. 218. Italics supplied.

[22] *Ibid.*, p. 219.

Cross had no need to question the adequacy of its objectives until the Depression of the 1930's, when there was disagreement among the leaders concerning the role the organization should play in dispensing unemployment relief.[23] But the most severe test to date of the adequacy of the Red Cross's objectives came at the end of World War II, when again a greatly expanded organization found that its capacity to act outpaced its goals. Furthermore, there now existed a new threat to the organization—the increased intervention of the Government in welfare and relief activities as a result of the responsibilities it had assumed during the Depression and War years.

. . . it was necessary to establish new objectives and new activities. These were found in "the adoption of a national blood donor program as the core of its peacetime activities apart from disaster relief." [24] In this way the most recent crisis has been met, and the Red Cross has both maintained an active program and obtained adequate volunteer and public support in the postwar years. . . .

This brief review of the history of four organizations has of necessity mentioned only a few of the major conclusions reached by the authors cited. Nevertheless, it has called attention to the fact that organizations are by no means necessarily "cast aside when new goals are sought" and indicated some of the ways in which organizations have adjusted to changes in their environment and the relevancy of their goals. Furthermore, the histories of these four organizations suggest that the fate of an organization after its goals have been either achieved or rendered irrelevant cannot be determined on *a priori* grounds, but is rather a resultant of a given set of forces. "What," Blau asks, "determines whether displacement of goals or succession of goals predominates in an organization?" [25] Although he admits that this crucial question can be answered only in part, Blau does suggest two determining factors: "structural constraints in the organization" and acceptance on the part of the community. "When the community permits an organization . . . to become established and attain at least some of its first objectives in a relatively short period, it will probably find new fields to conquer in the course of its development." [26] It goes without saying that American society has permitted the Foundation to be established and to attain its first objectives; in fact, it has given it more encouragement and support than it has given any comparable organization. Accordingly, in order to pursue the inquiry

[23] *Ibid.*, pp. 276–94.
[24] *Ibid.*
[25] Blau, *Bureaucracy in Modern Society*, p. 95.
[26] *Ibid.*, pp. 95–96.

implied in Blau's formulation of the problem of goal succession, it is necessary to examine what structural constraints might impede the Foundation from seeking new goals.

The Foundation's Structure and the Future

The relevance of the Foundation's corporate-type structure to its capacity to carry out its program has been stated in some detail throughout this volume, and need only be summarized here. Local Chapters, for example, being *ad hoc* instrumentalities of the Board of Trustees, are subject to all rules, regulations and policies of the National Headquarters—a situation which enables National Headquarters, if the need should ever arise, to exert considerable authority over the activities of a local Chapter. The March of Dimes is officially directed by National Headquarters, and local Campaign Directors are appointed by the State Chairman, who is in turn appointed by National Headquarters. Here again, the structural machinery exists through which National Headquarters can exercise control over the activities of local organizations. The patient care program, although financed largely by the 50 per cent of all campaign receipts which is retained in the local community, is dependent, for its effective operation, upon the redistribution of funds by National Headquarters. The research program is entirely under the direction of National Headquarters, and Chapters are specifically prohibited from making grants to support research projects. In short, if National Headquarters (i.e., the Board of Trustees) should decide to embark upon a new program, there is no organizational machinery to stand in the way. The new program would not need to be ratified by local Chapters, and there are no effective sub-groups within the organization which could offer effective resistance to it. The Foundation, in other words, has an organizational structure which would make "the succession of goals" quite feasible.

VOLUNTEERS AND THE FUTURE

The statement that the Foundation's structure would permit "the succession of goals," although true in a legal sense, does not of course acknowledge the fundamental fact that the Foundation is a voluntary association. Its members are free to leave at any time, and no one is obliged to join. For this reason, no program sponsored by National Headquarters could possibly be successful if it did not command the enthusiastic support of Volunteers throughout the county. Witness, for example, the ill-fated attempt of National Headquarters in the first year of the Foundation's existence to have full authority over the expenditure of all the funds raised during the March of Dimes. In order to examine the Foundation's future prospects it is therefore necessary to examine the potential support for a new program which exists among the Foundation's Volunteer membership. . . .

Objectively speaking, the Foundation has obviously served as an instigator of change. Not only has it pioneered in developing a coordinated mode of attack upon a specific disease, but it has also introduced new concepts of fund-raising, of patient care, and of community responsibility. The mass field trials of the Salk vaccine, which the Foundation sponsored, to cite another example of innovation, were a completely new development as far as the history of immunological verification is concerned—never before has the efficacy of a newly developed vaccine been tested on such a mass scale. It is of some interest, accordingly, to note that a considerable number of Volunteers are alert to the fact that the Foundation, in keeping with its character both as a social movement and a voluntary association, has served as a "pacesetter" in American society.

This broad theme has a number of variations. For some Volunteers, the most important precedent-setting aspect of the Foundation is the fact that it has mobilized laymen in a coordinated attack upon a disease. A March of Dimes Chairman in Defense Town, for example, adopted what he termed "the sociological viewpoint," saying "we can fight polio if we can organize people. If we can organize people like this, we can fight anything." This opinion was echoed by that of the Harbor City Campaign Director, who asked rhetorically, "Wouldn't it be a wonderful story to get polio licked, and then go on to something else and get that licked and then go on to something else?" Pausing a moment, he added the comment, "It would be a challenge, a career."

Other Volunteers focused their remarks more sharply upon specifically organizational accomplishments and potentialities. For example, after verbally exploring the possibilities of other diseases which might be conquered by techniques similar to those employed against polio, the Steamboat City Campaign Director concluded with this affirmation:

> I really believe in this type of organization when people get together and get things done. I would like to see other organizations set

> up or something done in other fields . . . like mental health. But no one has had the organization that the Foundation has had. . . . I don't think this unique organization should pass out of existence. It should be utilized.

. . . Finally, for some Volunteers the policy of the Foundation which permits funds to remain in the community for assisting polio victims is a precedent of such importance in terms of achieving public support that they believe it could and should be applied to the battle against other diseases. As a Wheat County March of Dimes Volunteer pointed out,

> They could take over heart and cancer and do the same thing. The money could stay in the community and that should be the basis of the talk that would be given on it. You can say, "it stays here for your protection."

Not all of the Volunteers interviewed, needless to say, were as articulate as these in expressing either their judgments of the Foundation's role as an innovating organization or their own hope that the organization would continue to exist after its objective of eliminating epidemic polio is achieved. Since Volunteers were not questioned concerning their views of the Foundation's future, only those who had given some thought to the matter prior to the interview took occasion to express their views. In fact, some Volunteers explicitly stated that in their opinion the Foundation should *not* undertake a new program. After polio has been conquered, according to the Chapter Vice-Chairman in Gas City, the Foundation "should get a big loving cup from the general population of the country and call it quits." Opinions of this kind were expressed only rarely, however, while thirty-five Volunteers—15 per cent of those interviewed—spontaneously recommended that the Foundation should continue to exist even after its major objective had been achieved. In the light of this evidence it seems reasonable to conclude that a considerable portion of the Volunteer membership of the Foundation has found its organizational characteristics sufficiently appealing, and its activities sufficiently rewarding, to be willing and anxious to take part in the organization should it seek to realize new goals.

. . . In the final analysis, however, the most compelling reason for predicting that the Foundation will in the future make a successful adjustment to the achievement of its major goal is that the organization has in fact *already* been transformed, in large part by its Volunteers, into something other than a special purpose association. For those

Volunteers who, in spite of the fact that they may initially have been recruited as Polio Veterans or Good Citizens or Joiners, have come to regard the organization as a "social movement" or a "pacesetter" have altered not only the character of their own participation but the character of the Foundation as well. Implicit in these perceptions is the notion that the Foundation has an institutionalized status which transcends its current goals. Since the Foundation includes among its Volunteers so many who are able to conceptualize their involvement in terms of its ultimate implications (for themselves, or for society as a whole), rather than only in terms of a limited, pragmatic goal, it has already become an organization as deeply committed to its mode of operation as to its current purposes. In a word, it is an organization which is as committed to a means as it is to an end.

Burton R. Clark

Organizational Adaptation and Precarious Values

With the proliferation of formal organizations in modern bureaucratic society it is apparent that the fate of various social values may be affected by the action of administrative agencies. Organizational analysis has shown that rationally contrived structures may transform their initial values in the process of adjusting to emergent problems. Where a number of organizations undergo a similar value transformation, the change may shape a value system of the larger society. The processes by which organizations shape values, however, are only dimly understood and difficult to discern. It is proposed that such effects can be seen most clearly by studying organizations that are tied to weakly established values. The purpose of this paper is, first, to identify some of the conditions of weakness in social values, and secondly, to present a case study of one

Reprinted in part from Burton R. Clark, *American Sociological Review,* 21 (1956), 327–336, by permission of the author and the publisher, The American Sociological Association.

type of value modification. The case materials have been taken from research on the adult education movement in California.

PRECARIOUS VALUES

Social values may be defined as conceptions of the desirable that that are distinctive of some human group.[1] These conceptions are usually voiced in goals and standards of action—in relatively specific notions of *what* should be obtained and *how*. The aspect of values that concerns us here is the degree to which they are secure. The degree of security will, of course, be determined by many conditions of the social and cultural context. The following are several general grounds for value insecurity that are identifiable in a wide range of situations.

1. *Social values tend to be precarious when they are undefined.* This concerns the link between general value conceptions and a proximate set of goals and norms. Values are *undefined* when they are not embodied in existing goals and standards of committed groups. They lack specific normative reference and no one knows what various symbols really mean. Values may be precarious, then, when there is a strong need for definition of behavioral cues, for identification of what is proper in the name of given symbols. This may be referred to as content weakness, or weakness in the normative system.

2. *Social values tend to be precarious when the position of functionaries*[2] *is not fully legitimized.* This concerns the grounding of a value in a firm social base. A surrounding population may be so hostile to the value conceptions of a smaller group that the group must struggle even to gain a position within relevant arenas from which to work. In such extreme cases, e.g., the Jehovah Witnesses, the right to act must be won. A search for legitimacy in this sense is a central tactical problem for highly deviant political groups, such as the Communist Party of the United States. The point is that in specific organizations or in the general society, values may be precarious because of the weak position of custodians in the social structure.

3. *Social values tend to be precarious when they are unacceptable*

[1] Clyde Kluckhohn, "Values and Value-Orientations in the Theory of Action," in Talcott Parsons and Edward A. Shils (editors), *Toward a General Theory of Action*, Cambridge: Harvard University Press, 1952, p. 395 and p. 417.

[2] A term used by Hertzler in describing those chiefly responsible for the "active implementation" of institutions. Used in this way, functionary refers to activists outside of organizations as well as organizational agents. Joyce O. Hertzler, *Society in Action*, New York: The Dryden Press, 1954, pp. 200–201.

to a "host" population. This condition, the most apparent source of weakness, is usually related to the second factor above. Groups supporting a new set of values, for instance, are likely to obtain a legitimate status only as their goals and practices became minimally accepted, i.e., seen as in general accordance with the value systems of the larger society. But to some degree these two conditions are separable. Pluralistic societies "tolerate" minority values. Thus functionaries may have a legitimate status even when their values are somewhat disliked by other groups. Then value weakness stems solely from lack of support by the general membership of the larger social system. Hence, the unacceptability of certain values to a host population can be taken as an analytically distinct factor in the precariousness of those values.

Secure values, then, are those that are clearly defined in behavior and strongly established in the minds of many. Such values literally take care of themselves. Precarious values, on the other hand, need deliberately intentioned agents, for they must be normatively defined, or socially established, or both.

This poses the general problem of how groups attempt to implement their values when they are precarious, and what changes in meaning and acceptance are incurred. The case in point concerns adult education administrators in a state school system. While adult education has had some acceptance in the American society as a general conception, functionaries have generally found themselves working with a weakly established set of values. As will be seen below, the goals and standards of this field have been somewhat undefined for several decades. In addition, adult education has had a marginal existence within the public schools, with its administrative agencies forced to search diligently for a secure operational base. An organizational adaptation has ensued that involves a transformation in values. This adaptation may be understood by recapitulating the core problems of adult education departments and the general response they have made.

THE CASE OF THE ADULT SCHOOL

Conditions of Administrative Action

Adult education emerged as a movement in the United States in the 1920's with newly acquired organizations and a corps of spokesmen.

Within the public schools the movement meant a changed conception of adult participation. Before 1925 "night school" was emphasized, with programs restricted mainly to elementary and high school work, vocational training, and Americanization-Citizenship classes. The schools were heavily "remedial" in orientation, based originally on an extended-day definition.

Since 1925 there has been a steady drift away from these characteristics, with a trend toward diversification of effort and broadening of clientele.

1. *The manifest ends of action.* The philosophy that became prevalent in the late 1920's with the emergence of an adult education movement had, in retrospect, two sharply divergent aspects: first, as an outgrowth of the Americanization effort, purpose was frequently voiced in the language of "enlightenment." This connoted a commitment to liberal education and a sense of educational mission. But the attempt to tie adult education to the ideals of liberal education did not prove viable. Grass-roots administrators were not in step with this doctrine but increasingly stressed a tenet related to the means of administration—that a proper conception of adult education could be implemented only by breaking away from formal patterns and clientele restrictions. For a quarter of a century this liberation theme has been growing within administrative circles, with the result that administrative units have increasingly worked with diffuse purpose. The program should be extremely diversified in order to meet a host of present individual, group, and societal problems. Such "purposes" hardly constitute directives, however, and officials are under pressure to establish more specific aims. The specific objectives of adult education in California are stated as follows:

> 1. To make adults aware of their civic responsibilities to one another and to the community
> 2. To make them economically more efficient
> 3. To develop an understanding of the attitudes and personal adjustments required for successful home life and family relationships
> 4. To promote health and physical fitness
> 5. To provide an opportunity for cultural development
> 6. To supplement and broaden educational backgrounds
> 7. To provide for the development of avocational interests through opportunities for self-expression.

Generality of purpose remains, however, with "cultural development," "self-expression," etc., covering a wide range of possibilities. Also, the different objectives do not receive priority or emphasis, since a selective approach would reflect the tendency toward restriction and formalization from which adult education officials have sought to escape. Selective aims have not been forthcoming, and statements about specific objectives merely reaffirm that purpose is to be as broad as possible. Openended purpose is a basic characteristic of California adult schools.

The more indefinite purpose becomes, however, the less can ends intervene in administrative choice. For goals to influence decision-making, they must provide cues for what should be done. When the administrator is confronted with the recurrent question of what courses to add to his program, his diffuse aims leave him without criteria. He works within a milieu where there is no *educational* reason for the administrator to favor one subject over another. Thus stated objectives are likely to become simply a rationale for a program broadly conceived and flexible in administration. The manifest ends of action function to widen administrative discretion.

2. *Organizational marginality.*[3] Since the basic purposes of the public schools center on the training of the young, various levels of education have become legitimized by relevance to this concern. Elementary schools, high schools, and junior colleges form an educational ladder in the public schools, and in California they all come under the doctrine of free public education. It is with these major units, comparatively well established within the school hierarchy and in the public image of education, that adult schools compete for position, budget, and support.

Within this organizational complex, adult education resides as an activity that is disconnected from the primary endeavor. It is not a part of the sequence of grades, its "students" exist completely outside of the range of compulsory attendance and have other occupations. These attributes leave adult education as a peripheral, non-mandatory effort of the schools, and its officials typically find themselves organizationally marginal. This marginality stems from the program's comparatively low degree of legitimacy as an important school activity and charge on public funds. A school program needs acceptance from various groups—its own personnel, other school units, the state legislature, politically potent interest groups, and the unorganized public.

[3] The "organizations" under analysis are adult schools, units of school systems that have adult education as their only program commitment. Multi-program organizations which may include adult education (e.g., junior colleges) are here excluded.

Only in the eyes of its own administrators and some of its teachers has the adult education activity had the level of acceptance that would guarantee its stability. The California Congress of Parents and Teachers, for example, is a strong supporter of adult education and is closely tied to adult schools through co-sponsorship arrangements, but when pressed PTA will maintain that the "compulsory education program" should not be jeopardized by "volunteer programs in which category we place adult education." [4]

The marginality of the program may thus be seen as the *basic source of insecurity for administrative units.* Without a firmly legitimized status, the adult schools have little control over the conditions of their existence. Their position as "low man on the totem pole" is dangerous not only in times of depression, but whenever school finances are under pressure, for they stand to be "cut the first and the most severely when financial support runs low." [5] To win a permanently secure niche, administrative strategy needs to be oriented toward ultimately achieving a "peer" status (the ideal), or a fixed partial parity of status that is clearly defined and respected by all. Short-run tactics, however, must be oriented to the problem of justifying a peripheral activity. The schools need "results." Thus marginality within the larger, host educational systems heightens the effect of the following conditions.

3. *Operating pressures.* The most important pressures bearing upon these schools in day-to-day administration arise from *the enrollment economy.* First, school income is largely set by student attendance. Financial support from the state is figured by the hours of attendance logged the previous year, producing a direct relation between student turnout and level of state aid.[6] Unless a school maintains and preferably increases attendance, future support is likely to stagnate, and a major slump in attendance constitutes a serious threat to organizational welfare. The closeness of this relationship depends upon the degree of *local* support, that is, whether local authorities will back the program out of their own tax levy if state aid decreases.[7]

[4] Testimony of PTA representative in *Partial Report of the Senate Interim Committee on Adult Education,* The Senate, State of California, March, 1953, p. 461.

[5] Bureau of Adult Education, *Report and Proceedings of the Montecito Workshop in Adult Education,* California State Department of Education, 1952, pp. 85–86.

[6] Five hundred and twenty-five hours of student time are equal to one unit of "average daily attendance," the basic unit in state apportionments.

[7] State apportionments and local tax levies are the two main sources of school revenue. Thus there is an inverse relationship between the proportion of costs

The less likely this guarantee, the more budget and support rests on a quantity-of-clientele basis.[8] Since marginality is the common condition, *the appropriations process sets incentives for action in the direction of building attendance.* There are no dependable sources of financial support independent of student turnout. Therefore everything is staked on the search for clientele.

A second important aspect of the enrollment economy is the tenuous tie of student participants. The student body is part-time, voluntary, and highly susceptible to casual attendance and easy termination. Participation is sharply affected by outside events beyond the control of the organization, e.g., warm weather, holiday seasons, and community events. Of all student groups, part-time adult students are surely the most difficult to maintain, and any adult education agency, public or private, has to solve the problem of sustaining a noncaptive student body. The point is that the enrollment economy becomes a double-barreled pressure for adaptation to outside interests. On the one hand administrators are faced with an uncommitted clientele, on the other, with the fact that students are the rationale for existence, and in California their attendance the basis for appropriations. These conditions converge to define the prime short-run problem to be that of creating and sustaining a clientele base. An adaptation is called for that will reasonably guarantee the attraction, retention, and replacement of students. The needs of the enrollment economy generate persistent pressures to which administrators and teachers must make a number of adaptive responses.

These pressures cannot be ignored, for they are reflected in policies set by school boards and top professional staffs. For example, minimum size requirements for both the introduction and the continuation of classes are widespread throughout the state. Their effect is to make enrollment *the* criterion by which courses are initiated and continued.

The organizational adaptation. These conditions of an organized system induce the following tendencies. Irrespective of intent, *the enrollment economy* renders the adult school highly sensitive to public likes and dislikes. Since "the public" is quite heterogeneous in both

---

covered by one source as compared to the other. Local boards of education and professional administrators tend to view "cost" as the share of total outlay that is shouldered by the local tax levy, for which they are directly responsible.

[8] Some adult education officials are allowed only as much money as their enrollment brings into the local school system from state aid, i.e., *no* support from local tax funds. . . .

educational background and part-time interest, ready adjustment to it entails a conglomerate, "cafeteria" program. At the same time, the *manifest ends of action* are permissive and allow the school to adapt freely. Stated ends interpose no objection to the tendency that follows from practical pressures; in fact, they favor an effort to do all things for all men. There is an absence of specific missions from which standards and professional authority might flow. In addition, *marginality* deepens the need for administrators to assume an "other-directed" orientation. Insecurity fastens attention on building support by means at hand.

With these conditions lying behind administration, the cumulative effect of decision-making is to adjust the program rapidly to expressed interests of the population. The adult education program that has developed in California may therefore be characterized as dominantly *a service enterprise,* for the key feature of this adaptation is the attempt of the schools to service consumers in an immediate way. Here several features of the schools may be adduced as evidence of a normatively unrestricted activity. (1) The main instruments of program building have become "the sign-up list" and "the group petition." These devices are simply objective ways of gauging demand. If demand is of the magnitude where the survival of a proposed class becomes probable, then its initiation is feasible. If the number of recruits increases, then more classes can be added and that part of the course assortment will grow. Thus the schools have an extreme version of what is known elsewhere in education as the elective system, and the relatively unlimited play of student choice determines the evolution of the collection of courses. (2) The structure of the teaching force is accommodated to the requirements of a service enterprise. Such a high degree of staff flexibility is needed that full-time work and guaranteed employment become administratively undesirable. Adaptation to a heterogeneous clientele involves considerable specialization in subject-matter and the hiring of the part-time specialist, e.g., a welder, a gardener, a dental technician, a housewife skilled in lamp-shade-making. In Los Angeles in 1952, for example, over 90 per cent of the adult teachers were part-time, with one-fourth working four hours a week or less.[9] Less than 20 per cent had tenure in adult education and less than 5 per cent possessed tenure at a fulltime level of employment.[10]

Building programs by consumer preference, however, produces

[9] Source: *Adult Education Branch Files, Los Angeles School System.*
[10] Source: *Personnel Division Files, Los Angeles School System.*

an administrative dilemma. Located within school systems, adult education officials find their practices scrutinized by others in the light of school norms that are professional or "inner-directed" in kind, i.e., that educators should plan, initiate, and control changes on the basis of research and the assessment of experts. When laymen challenge school practices, for instance, the administrator ordinarily rests his case on expert opinion. Moreover, the drive for higher professional status on the part of teachers and administrators reinforces these sentiments. Thus there are school values, central to the self-image of the educator, that are against ready adjustment to student demands.

When this professional orientation is brought to bear upon the adult activity, the administrators do not fare well. They are judged to be in a posture of expediency, with much of their work seen as having little relationship to "education." From outside the school system, state legislators and economy-minded interest groups repeatedly challenge the propriety of what is done. Cake-decorating, rug-making, and square dancing are some of the classes that bring the adult schools under fire. In one recent case of opposition, the entire state program underwent a hostile, sustained scrutiny by an investigating committee of the State Senate.[11] The current program was challenged as one saturated with frills, with 55 per cent of total enrollment placed in the frill category.[12] This investigation resulted in unfavorable publicity and restrictive legislation.

Thus in many ways a service enterprise, uncontrolled by school norms, sorely tries the educational respectability of the agencies involved. But the service tendency cannot be turned off easily since it is impelled by basic pressures of an organizational system. Classes of a questionable nature continually crop up when field administrators work with *ad hoc* demand, under pressure for an enrollment payoff. The crux of the matter is that the adult schools labor under incompatible needs. Their central dilemma is that the short-run need for clientele, set by the enrollment economy, strains against the long-run need for educational respectability as the basis for legitimacy. The adult schools are torn between being a service facility and a school enterprise. . . .

[11] See Partial Report of the Senate Interim Committee on Adult Education, *op. cit., passim.*

[12] *Ibid.,* pp. 171–174.

Donald R. Cressey

Achievement of an Unstated Organizational Goal

It is customary for both sociologists and correctional workers to adopt the viewpoint of society, rather than of the prisoner, when discussing the goals of prisons and other correctional institutions. In general, prisons, like mental hospitals, are seen as performing an integrative function for society.[1] Usually, they are said to do this by incapacitating criminals, thus directly protecting society from them; by punishing them, thus protecting society both by reinforcing the system's anti-criminal values and by deterring potential criminals; and by reforming them, thus protecting society by restoring social integration.[2] In short, a society assigns *incapacitation, retribution, deterrence* and *reformation* goals to prisons.

THE GOALS OF PRISON

Under the leadership of "professional" personnel such as social workers and psychiatrists, the conception of the criminal as a bad man or outlaw is giving way to a conception of him as a needy or sick person who deserves help. Both these changes are expressions of concern for the welfare of inmates and have led to the assignment of a new goal to prisons—protection of inmates from society. Although criminology textbooks and institutional policy-statements are silent

Reprinted in part from *Pacific Sociological Review,* 1 (1958), 43–49, by permission of the author and the publisher, The Pacific Sociological Society.

[1] See Talcott Parsons, "Suggestions for a Sociological Approach to the Theory of Organizations, II," *Administrative Science Quarterly,* 1 (September, 1956), pp. 225–239.

[2] For discussion of these institutional goals, which are sometimes called *functions,* see Edwin H. Sutherland and Donald R. Cressey, *Principles of Criminology,* Fifth Edition, New York: J. B. Lippincott, 1955, pp. 460–462.

regarding this relatively new goal, contemporary prisons are expected both to protect society from inmates and to protect inmates from society.

In the course of a year spent observing the structure and functioning of two prisons,[3] we are able to document such an extension of the protective goal, just as it has been documented in reference to mental hospitals and in the area of probation and parole.[4] This was done by extensive interviews with samples of all categories of employees and a sample of inmates and by firsthand observations of the institutions in action. Although neither institution had an explicit policy regarding protection of inmates, the staffs showed considerable concern for protecting them. This protection took two principal forms.

First, there was concern for protecting inmates from the ostracism, ridicule, exploitation and even physical attack which they might have experienced had they been left in the free community. Criminals whose cases were well publicized and whose crimes were horrendous were viewed as in most need of such protection but some interviewees in both prisons said that all prisoners should be protected (a) from exploitation by gangsters, high pressure salesmen, overzealous attorneys and other individuals; (b) from ministrations of amateur "reformers" or "researchers"; and (c) from observation and ridicule by the morbidly curious. One guard pointed out, for example, that in some states criminal statutes prohibit the "exhibition" of criminals.

Second, over half the interviews in each prison indicated, and personal observation verified, that in both institutions concerted effort was made to protect inmates from each other and from staff members. This included protection from dishonesty, ridicule and physical harm.

Generally speaking, both institutions efficiently provided the two kinds of protection. Such similarities between the two prisons indicate that both are organized, at least unofficially, for the protection of inmates. Even though unstated, this goal is achieved with considerable

[3] This paper is based on field research conducted between July, 1955, and September, 1956, when the author was attached to the Center of Education and Research in Corrections, University of Chicago. The results of this research project are now being prepared for early publication and are being integrated with the results of other research conducted at the Center during the years 1953–1956. The author is greatly indebted to Lloyd E. Ohlin, Director of the Center, to Donnell M. Pappenfort and Herman Piven, who were research assistants, and to the Russell Sage Foundation, which financed the Center.

[4] Alfred H. Stanton and Morris S. Schwartz, *The Mental Hospital,* New York: Basic Books, 1954, pp. 48–55, 233–234; Lloyd E. Ohlin, Herman Piven, and Donnell M. Pappenfort, "Major Dilemmas of the Social Worker in Probation and Parole," *National Probation and Parole Association Journal,* 2 (July, 1956), pp. 211–225.

efficiency. However, some differences were observed between the two institutions in the kind and amount of protection offered. As we shall show below, inmates in one prison were more effectively protected from observation by curious outside groups, while inmates in the other were more effectively protected from ridicule by staff members. These differences are of greater sociological significance than are the similarities, for their presence illustrates three things of concern to students of social organization: (1) the effect of official policies on accomplishment of unstated organizational goals, (2) the effect on organizational behavior of relationships which must be maintained with authority outside the system, and (3) the effects on both official and unstated goals of officially substituting informal control mechanisms for formal ones.

VARIATIONS IN OFFICIAL POLICY

The two prisons are located in the same state but their institutional "climates" were quite different. One was characterized by a "relaxed discipline" for inmates and staff alike. The administrators were "professional" persons and viewed inmates as men in need of "treatment" rather than, or in addition to, punishment and close supervision. Generally speaking, guards and other employees were expected to *understand* inmates, to help them with their problems, to avoid being "rigid" or "punitive" and to refer inmates with serious problems to professional personnel for therapy. Thus in this prison, which is for youthful offenders, official emphasis was on the fourth goal which society assigns to prisons: the reformation of criminals. Although the institution's walls, guntowers, bars, locks and lines of marching inmates revealed official concern for protecting society, the stated policy was to "coordinate all the institution's facilities in a program of individualized treatment."

The other prison housed older but not necessarily more dangerous offenders and its routine was not as "relaxed." Inmates were officially viewed as dangerous and conniving and, accordingly, were expected to obey explicit rules which were stated in advance. The principal duty of guards and other employees was to maintain "discipline" among inmates by enforcing rules. While administrators expressed and implemented concern for rehabilitation and treatment, the institutional routine attempted to insure that a maximum number of inmates were under close surveillance at all times. Official emphasis was on the first goal which society assigns to prisons: the *incapacitation* of criminals. The official policy of this prison was stated as follows: "First of all, our purpose is protection of society; that is first and foremost."

Although the policy-statement of the first prison specifies a single goal, treatment or rehabilitation, and that of the second prison indicates the possibility of multiple goals, it must be emphasized that both statements are expressions of the *priority* to be given to the rehabilitation goal and to the incapacitation goal. Both institutions had both a rehabilitation and a custodial goal. In the first there was greater official emphasis upon meeting inmates' needs by "individualized treatment" in an effort to reform them. In the second there was more emphasis upon protecting society from inmates. Because the difference is one of emphasis, we have called the first institution a "treatment-*oriented*" prison and the second a "custodially-*oriented*" prison.

However, the differences in official policy had important implications for achieving the unstated goal of protecting inmates. Despite the fact that the treatment-oriented institution had to protect society, the commitment to individualized treatment required that inmate deviations within the prison, like criminal acts themselves, be interpreted as a consequence of *inability* to conform rather than as *intentional* and *deliberate* violation. The trend toward the "professional" view that criminals are sick rather than bad has had as one of its consequences the kind of policy characterizing the treatment-oriented prison and the attendant concern for inmates rather than, or in addition to, concern for society.[5]

On the other hand, in our culture when deviation is perceived as *intentional* or *deliberate* the reaction is punishment and/or close surveillance. It is this principle which is emphasized in the custodially oriented prison. Although some inmates are to be "treated" and all are to be handled "humanely," the goal of protecting society from the majority of inmates is the one emphasized in the official policy-statement.

The observed difference in official policies was found to be reflected in the degree to which inmates in the two prisons were protected from ridicule and humiliation by outsiders. In the state in question, as in others, a large number of citizens want to tour penal institutions in order to "educate" themselves or, perhaps more realisti-

[5] See Donald R. Cressey, "Rehabilitation Theory and Reality, I, The Pain of Restriction," *California Youth Authority Quarterly*, 10 (Spring, 1957), pp. 6–9.

cally, to "amuse" themselves. During the year of observation, inmates at the treatment-oriented prison were more carefully protected from such curious tourists than were those at the custodially oriented prison.

Such tours are much more frequent at the custodially oriented prison than they are at the treatment-oriented prison. During one month in a recent year over one hundred man-hours were devoted to guiding about one thousand visitors through the custodially oriented institution. Inmates complained about being put on exhibition, guards complained about the threat to security and the administration found it necessary to maintain in the central lobby a large sign reading "Visitors must not speak to or point out prisoners." In the treatment-oriented prison, on the other hand, groups other than college classes or members of professional organizations somehow related to penology rarely were taken on tours. While nonacademic and nonprofessional groups were not prohibited from touring this prison, they were somehow discouraged from applying for tours.

The official policy-statements, thus, had important consequences for accomplishing the unstated goal. The official emphasis upon treatment and the concomitant view that deviation is unintentional meant that inmate welfare, including protection from curious tourists, had to be given high priority, while the official emphasis on protecting society from inmates made this unnecessary. . . .

VARIATIONS IN STRUCTURE

Because the custodially oriented prison's official policy and relationships with external authority stressed the importance of protecting society, a maximum number of treatment, educational and industrial activities were made subservient to custodial routines. Consistently, guards were expected to follow rules which had been designed to maximize safe custody of inmates. For example, they were not expected to use "discretion" in deciding whether or not behavior was an infraction of rules.

Thus, the system of control was formal. Employees were trained to view inmates as dangerous and conniving men from whom society must be protected even at risk of life. They were to maintain social distance between themselves and inmates at all times and, like inmates, were to follow rules which had been specified in advance. These rules were, generally speaking, instructions for "enforcing" rules for inmates. As indicated earlier, the general duty of guards was to "maintain discipline" among men who were, by definition, inferior to them and in need of control. "Enforcing rules" and "maintaining discipline" meant that guards were to report deviations to the central court in a routine way; captains and lieutenants gave demerits to guards who were caught deviating from this formal procedure. In a sense the prison was organized to emphasize inmate inferiority to guards and guard inferiority to officers and administrators. Although some guards occasionally withdrew from this formal system and entered into co-operative alliances with inmates, such behavior did not seem to be as extensive as it was in the institutions observed by McCorkle and Korn, and by Sykes.[6]

Stated in another way, emphasis upon protecting society from inmates led to implementation of a system for controlling men who were feared. Just as a community hires policemen because it fears unapprehended criminals, it maintains prisons in part because it continues to fear these men after they have been apprehended and convicted. Within a prison which emphasizes protecting this outside community, the organizational response is a formal system designed to minimize inmate autonomy and to minimize opportunities for inmate rebellion. To this end, guards and others were trained to be alert to conditions which might stimulate inmate retaliation of either an individual or collective nature. One such condition, administrators believed, was informal relations with inmates. Again, control systems were to be formal and emotionally neutral. For example, even if ridiculing inmates works as a short-term control measure, in the long run ridiculing men who are in a system which defines them as bad and dangerous can only be an irritant leading to individual or collective violence, both of which threaten institutional security. Further, if controls are formal any inmate hostility might be directed toward "the system," but informal control by ridicule might direct hostility toward the ridiculer and thus be personally dangerous.

At the treatment-oriented institution, on the other hand, employees were expected to view inmates as essentially maladjusted or "sick," as not entirely responsible for their actions and as in need of individualized "treatment" rather than, or in addition to, "discipline." This individualized treatment policy has definite organizational implications. Most significantly, it calls for a "relaxed discipline" in which

[6] Lloyd W. McCorkle and Richard Korn, "Resocialization within Walls," *The Annals of the American Academy of Political and Social Science*, 293 (May, 1954), pp. 88–98; Gresham M. Sykes, "The Corruption of Authority and Rehabilitation," *Social Forces*, 34 (March, 1956), pp. 257–262.

nonprofessional employees assist professional treatment personnel with the task of treatment.

Guards were expected to be receptive, passive and relaxed. They were to think for themselves, use discretion in deciding whether an action is a rule violation and be "professional." Relationships with inmates were to be personal and friendly rather than formal. In their roles as treatment agents, guards were expected informally to give rewards to inmates showing signs of improvement.

At the same time, however, guards had to function as guards. While they were relaxing in their relationships with inmates so as to contribute to rehabilitation, they were to maintain order and insure that inmates performed the work tasks which had to be performed if the institution were to continue operating. Although institutional policy and reference groups stressed inmate welfare, guards were expected to help protect society. Because of this obligation to *guard*, to maintain peaceful routines and to utilize inmate work-crews efficiently, guards could not behave like archetypical treatment agents. They could relax and enter into informal relations with inmates but they could not give unqualified support to meeting individual inmate needs for a relaxed "therapeutic climate." To do this would jeopardize their effectiveness as protectors of society. At the same time, to give unqualified support to a formal system of custodial control at the expense of therapeutic climate would jeopardize their effectiveness as treatment agents.

The dual role of the inmate—as patient in need of treatment and as a prisoner in need of control—thus brought into being a treatment-*oriented* organization in which it was extremely difficult for the guard to behave ideally in respect to the institution's official goal. The presence of the subsidiary goal, repression of inmates, meant that the discretion granted employees so that the organization would be therapeutic was not always used for therapeutic purposes. Rather, official decentralization of decision-making, introduced so that individualized treatment could be effected, had as one of its consequences the decentralization of *punishment*. In this institution, guards and other employees could not routinely refer inmates to a central court for disciplinary action because this would be evidence of "rigidity" and poor treatment practices. Faced, then, with the perceived need for stimulating conformity in a situation in which use of formal control mechanisms was denied them, guards used unofficial rewards and punishments to get the conformity they needed. Inmates occasionally were given duty which was dirty or unpleasant, deprived of recreational privileges or demoted from higher status jobs without ever going to a professional treatment specialist or to a disciplinary court. Probably there were few guards who did not informally use punishments in order to protect the institution and society, even if they subscribed to the notion that inmates should be understood rather than punished.

These variations in the structures of the two prisons were reflected in differences in the degree to which the unstated goal—protection of inmates—was achieved. In contradiction to the direction of the difference in protecting inmates from curious outsiders, protection from ridicule, humiliation and even physical contact by staff members was more complete at the custodially oriented prison than at the treatment-oriented institution.

While some employees in both prisons probably ridiculed and attempted to humiliate some inmates, this practice was very rare at the custodially-oriented prison but occurred occasionally at the treatment-oriented institution. At the former but not the latter all guards were frequently and carefully warned by the chief custodian against "needling" inmates. Further, at the custodially oriented prison guards were discouraged from holding any but very short conversations with inmates. Although they were permitted to talk briefly to inmates who came to them with questions about their work or who came to them for advice on some problem, they were not to engage in friendly or relaxed chats or to "joke" with inmates. One stated rationale for this rule was that friendly conversations and "joking" would lead to ridiculing inmates and this, in turn, might be misunderstood and lead to security problems. The investigator never heard an employee of the custodially oriented prison call an inmate names or otherwise deliberately ridicule him about his presumed low status in either the outside community or the prison.

At the treatment-oriented prison, on the other hand, guards were encouraged to engage in conversations with inmates, and the investigator occasionally heard inmates called "no good punks," "bums" and other names to their faces. One important employee always referred to inmates he didn't like as "rum dumbs," even when they were present. Ordinarily, however, such ridicule as occurred was in the form of "joking" with the youthful inmates about their presumed inability to hold a job or earn a living outside the institution.

It may be concluded that the lower degree of protection of inmates from ridicule by employees in the treatment-oriented institution was a function of the kind of controls guards were expected to exert. In the custodially oriented prison it was the duty of guards to maximize use of a formal system of control in order to protect society and this formal system operated in such a way that the unstated goal was efficiently achieved. In the treatment-oriented prison decision-making was decentralized so guards could contribute to inmate rehabilitation, but the consequent informal control mechanisms were sometimes used for the nontherapeutic purpose of protecting the institution and society. The informal control mechanisms included unofficially administered rewards and punishments. Among these were ridicule and humiliation and, generally, the granting or withholding of friendship, affection and esteem as reward or punishment. . . .

CONCLUSION

Historical trends and the concern of staff members in the two institutions studied for protecting inmates from the public, from each other and from the staff indicate that an unstated goal of prisons is the protection of inmates. This unstated goal was efficiently achieved in both institutions but two principal differences were present. Inmates of the treatment-oriented prison were more carefully protected from the stares of organized groups of tourists than were inmates of the other prison, and inmates of the custodially oriented prison were more carefully protected from ridicule by employees than was the case in the treatment-oriented prison. Analysis of these differences suggests: (1) that an organization's official, formal, policy has important effects even on achievement of unstated, informal, goals, (2) that an organization's arrangements with the larger social system maintaining it both determine and affect the accomplishment of unstated as well as official goals, and (3) that official substitution of informal for formal control mechanisms in an organization does not necessarily produce increased efficiency in accomplishing informal, unstated, goals.

James D. Thompson
and
William J. McEwen

Organizational Goals and Environment

In the analysis of complex organizations the definition of organizational goals is commonly utilized as a standard for appraising organizational performance. In many such analyses the goals of the organization are often viewed as a constant. Thus a wide variety of data, such as official documents, work activity records, organizational output, or statements by organizational spokesmen, may provide the basis for the definition of goals. Once this definition has been accomplished, interest in goals as a dynamic aspect of organizational activity frequently ends.

It is possible, however, to view the setting of goals (i.e., major organizational purposes), not as a static element but as a necessary and recurring problem facing any organization, whether it is governmental, military, business, educational, medical, religious, or other type. The goal-setting problem as discussed here is essentially determining a relationship of the organization to the larger society, which in turn becomes a question of what the society (or elements within it) wants done or can be persuaded to support.

GOALS AS DYNAMIC VARIABLES

Because the setting of goals is essentially a problem of defining desired relationships between an organization and its environment, change in either requires review and perhaps alteration of goals. Even where the most abstract statement of goals remains constant, application requires redefinition or interpretation as changes occur in the organization, the environment, or both.

Reprinted in part from James D. Thompson and William J. McEwen, *American Sociological Review*, 23 (1958), 23–31, by permission of the authors and the publishers, The American Sociological Association.

The corporation, for example, faces changing markets and develops staff specialists with responsibility for continuous study and projection of market changes and product appeal. The governmental agency, its legislative mandate notwithstanding, has need to reformulate or reinterpret its goals as other agencies are created and dissolved, as the population changes, or as non-governmental organizations appear to do the same job or to compete. The school and the university may have unchanging abstract goals, but the clientele, the needs of pupils or students, and the techniques of teaching change and bring with them redefinition and reinterpretation of those objectives. The hospital has been faced with problems requiring an expansion of goals to include consideration of preventive medicine, public health practices, and the degree to which the hospital should extend its activities out into the community. The mental hospital and the prison are changing their objectives from primary emphasis on custody to a stress on therapy. Even the church alters its pragmatic objectives as changes in the society call for new forms of social ethics, and as government and organized philanthropy take over some of the activities formerly left to organized religion.

Reappraisal of goals thus appears to be a recurrent problem for large organization, albeit a more constant problem in an unstable environment than in a stable one. Reappraisal of goals likewise appears to be more difficult as the "product" of the enterprise becomes less tangible and more difficult to measure objectively. The manufacturing firm has a relatively ready index of the acceptability of its product in sales figures; while poor sales may indicate inferior quality rather than public distaste for the commodity itself, sales totals frequently are supplemented by trade association statistics indicating the firm's "share of the market." Thus within a matter of weeks, a manufacturing firm may be able to reappraise its decision to enter the "widget" market and may therefore begin deciding how it can get out of that market with the least cost.

The governmental enterprise may have similar indicators of the acceptability of its goals if it is involved in producing an item such as electricity, but where its activity is oriented to a less tangible purpose such as maintaining favorable relations with foreign nations, the indices of effective operation are likely to be less precise and the vagaries more numerous. The degree to which a government satisfies its clientele may be reflected periodically in elections, but despite the claims of party officials, it seldom is clear just what the mandate of the people is with reference to any particular governmental enterprise. In addition, the public is not always steadfast in its mandate.

The university perhaps has even greater difficulties in evaluating its environmental situation through response to its output. Its range of "products" is enormous, extending from astronomers to zoologists. The test of a competent specialist is not always standardized and may be changing, and the university's success in turning out "educated" people is judged by many and often conflicting standards. The university's product is in process for four or more years and when it is placed on the "market" it can be only imperfectly judged. Vocational placement statistics may give some indication of the university's success in its objectives, but initial placement is no guarantee of performance at a later date. Furthermore, performance in an occupation is only one of several abilities that the university is supposed to produce in its students. Finally, any particular department of the university may find that its reputation lags far behind its performance. A "good" department may work for years before its reputation becomes "good" and a downhill department may coast for several years before the fact is realized by the professional world.

In sum, the goals of an organization, which determine the kinds of goods or services it produces and offers to the environment, often are subject to peculiar difficulties of reappraisal. Where the purpose calls for an easily identified, readily measured product, reappraisal and readjustment of goals may be accomplished rapidly. But as goals call for increasingly intangible, difficult-to-measure products, society finds it more difficult to determine and reflect its acceptability of that product, and the signals that indicate unacceptable goals are less effective and perhaps longer in coming.

ENVIRONMENTAL CONTROLS OVER GOALS

A continuing situation of necessary interaction between an organization and its environment introduces an element of environmental control into the organization. While the motives of personnel, including goal-setting officers, may be profits, prestige, votes, or the salvation of souls, their efforts must produce something useful or acceptable to at least a part of the organizational environment to win continued support.[1]

[1] This statement would seem to exclude anti-social organizations, such as crime syndicates. A detailed analysis of such organizations would be useful for many

In the simpler society social control over productive activities may be exercised rather informally and directly through such means as gossip and ridicule. As a society becomes more complex and its productive activities more deliberately organized, social controls are increasingly exercised through such formal devices as contracts, legal codes, and governmental regulations. The stability of expectations provided by these devices is arrived at through interaction, and often through the exercise of power in interaction.

It is possible to conceive of a continuum of organizational power in environmental relations, ranging from the organization that dominates its environmental relations to one completely dominated by its environment. Few organizations approach either extreme. Certain gigantic industrial enterprises, such as the *Zaibatsu* in Japan or the old Standard Oil Trust in America, have approached the dominance-over-environment position at one time, but this position eventually brought about "countervailing powers." [2] Perhaps the nearest approximation to the completely powerless organization is the commuter transit system, which may be unable to cover its costs but nevertheless is regarded as a necessary utility and cannot get permission to quit business. Most complex organizations, falling somewhere between the extremes of the power continuum, must adopt strategies for coming to terms with their environments. This is not to imply that such strategies are necessarily chosen by rational or deliberate processes. An organization can survive so long as it adjusts to its situation; whether the process of adjustment is awkward or nimble becomes important in determining the organization's degree of prosperity.

However arrived at, strategies for dealing with the organizational environment may be broadly classified as either *competitive* or *cooperative*. Both appear to be important in a complex society—of the "free enterprise" type or other.[3] Both provide a measure of environmental control over organizations by providing for "outsiders" to enter into or limit organizational decision process.

---

purposes; meanwhile it would appear necessary for them to acquire a clientele, suppliers, and others, in spite of the fact that their methods at times may be somewhat unique.

[2] For the *Zaibatsu* case see Japan Council, *The Control of Industry in Japan*, Tokyo: Institute of Political and Economic Research, 1953; and Edwin O. Reischauer, *The United States and Japan*, Cambridge: Harvard University Press, 1954, pp. 87–97.

[3] For evidence on Russia see David Granick, *Management of the Industrial Firm in the U. S. S. R.*, New York: Columbia University Press, 1954; and Joseph S. Berliner, "Informal Organization of the Soviet Firm," *Quarterly Journal of Economics*, 66 (August, 1952), pp. 353–365.

The decision process may be viewed as a series of activities, conscious or not, culminating in a choice among alternatives. For purposes of this paper we view the decision-making process as consisting of the following activities:

1. Recognizing an occasion for decision, i.e., a need or an opportunity.
2. Analysis of the existing situation.
3. Identification of alternative courses of action.
4. Assessment of the probable consequences of each alternative.
5. Choice from among alternatives.[4]

The following discussion suggests that the potential power of an outsider increases the earlier he enters into the decision process,[5] and that competition and three sub-types of cooperative strategy—*bargaining, co-optation,* and *coalition*—differ in this respect. It is therefore possible to order these forms of interaction in terms of the degree to which they provide for environmental control over organizational goal-setting decisions.

Competition

The term "competition" implies an element of rivalry. For present purposes competition refers to that form of rivalry between two or more organizations which is mediated by a third party. In the case of the manufacturing firm the third party may be the customer, the supplier, the potential or present member of the labor force, or others. In the case of the governmental bureau, the third party through whom competition takes place may be the legislative committee, the budget bureau, or the chief executive, as well as potential clientele and potential members of the bureau.

The complexity of competition in a heterogeneous society is much greater than customary usage (with economic overtones) often suggests. Society judges the enterprise not only by the finished product

[4] This particular breakdown is taken from Edward H. Litchfield, "Notes on a General Theory of Administration," *Administrative Science Quarterly,* 1 (June, 1956), pp. 3–29. We are also indebted to Robert Tannenbaum and Fred Massarik who, by breaking the decision-making process into three steps, show that subordinates can take part in the "manager's decision" even when the manager makes the final choice. See "Participation by Subordinates in the Managerial Decision-Making Process," *Canadian Journal of Economics and Political Science,* 16 (August, 1949), pp. 410–418.

[5] Robert K. Merton makes a similar point regarding the role of the intellectual in public bureaucracy. See his *Social Theory and Social Structure,* Glencoe: The Free Press, 1949, Chapter VI.

but also in terms of the desirability of applying resources to that purpose. Even the organization that enjoys a product monopoly must compete for society's support. From the society it must obtain resources—personnel, finances, and materials—as well as customers or clientele. In the business sphere of a "free enterprise" economy this competition for resources and customers usually takes place in the market, but in times of crisis the society may exercise more direct controls, such as rationing or the establishment of priorities during a war. The monopoly competes with enterprises having different purposes or goals but using similar raw materials; it competes with many other enterprises, for human skills and loyalties, and it competes with many other activities for support in the money markets.

The university, customarily a non-profit organization, competes as eagerly as any business firm, although perhaps more subtly.[6] Virtually every university seeks, if not more students, better-qualified students. Publicly supported universities compete at annual budget sessions with other governmental enterprises for shares in tax revenues. Endowed universities must compete for gifts and bequests, not only with other universities but also with museums, charities, zoos, and similar non-profit enterprises. The American university is only one of many organizations competing for foundation support, and it competes with other universities and with other types of organizations for faculty.

The public school system, perhaps one of our most pervasive forms of near-monopoly, not only competes with other governmental units for funds and with different types of organizations for teachers, but current programs espoused by professional educators often compete in a very real way with a public conception of the nature of education, e.g., as the three R's, devoid of "frills."

The hospital may compete with the midwife, the faith-healer, the "quack" and the patent-medicine manufacturer, as well as with neighboring hospitals, despite the fact that general hospitals do not "advertise" and are not usually recognized as competitive.

Competition is thus a complicated network of relationships. It includes scrambling for resources as well as for customers or clients, and in a complex society it includes rivalry for potential members and their loyalties. In each case a third party makes a choice among alternatives, two or more organizations attempt to influence that

[6] See Logan Wilson, *The Academic Man,* New York: Oxford University Press, 1942, especially Chapter IX. Also see Warren G. Bennis, "The Effect on Academic Goods of Their Market," *American Journal of Sociology,* 62 (July, 1956), pp. 28–33.

choice through some type of "appeal" or offering, and choice by the third party is a "vote" of support for one of the competing organizations and a denial of support to the others involved.

Competition, then, is one process whereby the organization's choice of goals is partially controlled by the environment. It tends to prevent unilateral or arbitrary choice of organizational goals, or to correct such a choice if one is made. Competition for society's support is an important means of eliminating not only inefficient organizations but also those that seek to provide goods or services the environment is not willing to accept.

Bargaining

The term bargaining, as used here, refers to the negotiation of an agreement for the exchange of goods or services between two or more organizations. Even where fairly stable and dependable expectations have been built up with important elements of the organizational environment—with suppliers, distributors, legislators, workers and so on—the organization cannot assume that these relationships will continue. Periodic review of these relationships must be accomplished, and an important means for this is bargaining, whereby each organization, through negotiation, arrives at a decision about future behavior satisfactory to the others involved.

The need for periodic adjustment of relationships is demonstrated most dramatically in collective bargaining between labor and industrial management, in which the bases for continued support by organization members are reviewed. But bargaining occurs in other important, if less dramatic, areas of organizational endeavor. The business firm must bargain with its agents or distributors, and while this may appear at times to be one-sided and hence not much of a bargain, still even a long-standing agency agreement may be severed by competitive offers unless the agent's level of satisfaction is maintained through periodic review. Where suppliers are required to install new equipment to handle the peculiar demands of an organization, bargaining between the two is not unusual.

The university likewise must bargain. It may compete for free or unrestricted funds, but often it must compromise that ideal by bargaining away the name of a building or of a library collection, or by the conferring of an honorary degree. Graduate students and faculty members may be given financial or other concessions through bargaining, in order to prevent their loss to other institutions.

The governmental organization may also find bargaining expedient. The police department, for example, may overlook certain violations of statutes in order to gain the support of minor violators who have channels of information not otherwise open to department members. Concessions to those who "turn state's evidence" are not unusual. Similarly, a department of state may forego or postpone recognition of a foreign power in order to gain support for other aspects of its policy, and a governmental agency may relinquish certain activities in order to gain budget bureau approval of more important goals.

While bargaining may focus on resources rather than explicitly on goals, the fact remains that it is improbable that a goal can be effective unless it is at least partially implemented. To the extent that bargaining sets limits on the amount of resources available or the ways they may be employed, it effectively sets limits on choice of goals. Hence bargaining, like competition, results in environmental control over organizational goals and reduces the probability of arbitrary, unilateral goal-setting.

Unlike competition, however, bargaining involves direct interaction with other organizations in the environment, rather than with a third party. Bargaining appears, therefore, to invade the actual decision process. To the extent that the second party's support is necessary he is in a position to exercise a veto over final choice of alternative goals, and hence takes part in the decision.

Co-optation

Co-optation has been defined as the process of absorbing new elements into the leadership or policy-determining structure of an organization as a means of averting threats to its stability or existence.[7] Co-optation makes still further inroads on the process of deciding goals; not only must the final choice be acceptable to the co-opted party or organization, but to the extent that co-optation is effective it places the representative of an "outsider" in a position to determine the occasion for a goal decision, to participate in analyzing the existing situation, to suggest alternatives, and to take part in the deliberation of consequences.

The term "co-optation" has only recently been given currency in this country, but the phenomenon it describes is neither new nor un-

[7] Philip Selznick, *TVA and the Grass Roots,* Berkeley and Los Angeles: University of California Press, 1949.

important. The acceptance on a corporation's board of directors of representatives of banks or other financial institutions is a time-honored custom among firms that have large financial obligations or that may in the future want access to financial resources. The state university may find it expedient (if not mandatory) to place legislators on its board of trustees, and the endowed college may find that whereas the honorary degree brings forth a token gift, membership on the board may result in a more substantial bequest. The local medical society often plays a decisive role in hospital goal-setting, since the support of professional medical practitioners is urgently necessary for the hospital.

From the standpoint of society, however, co-optation is more than an expediency. By giving a potential supporter a position of power and often of responsibility in the organization, the organization gains his awareness and understanding of the problems it faces. A business advisory council may be an effective educational device for a government, and a White House conference on education may mobilize "grass roots" support in a thousand localities, both by focussing attention on the problem area and by giving key people a sense of participation in goal deliberation.

Moreover, by providing overlapping memberships, co-optation is an important social device for increasing the likelihood that organizations related to one another in complicated ways will in fact find compatible goals. By thus reducing the possibilities of antithetical actions by two or more organizations, co-optation aids in the integration of the heterogeneous parts of a complex society. By the same token, co-optation further limits the opportunity for one organization to choose its goals arbitrarily or unilaterally.

Coalition

As used here, the term coalition refers to a combination of two or more organizations for a common purpose. Coalition appears to be the ultimate or extreme form of environmental conditioning of organizational goals.[8] A coalition may be unstable, but to the extent that it is

[8] Coalition may involve joint action toward only limited aspects of the goals of each member. It may involve the complete commitment of each member for a specific period of time or indefinitely. In either case the ultimate power to withdraw is retained by the members. We thus distinguish coalition from merger, in which two or more organizations are fused permanently. In merger one or all of the original parts may lose their identity. Goal-setting in such a situation, of course, is no longer subject to inter-organizational constraints among the components.

operative, two or more organizations act as one with respect to certain goals. Coalition is a means widely used when two or more enterprises wish to pursue a goal calling for more support, especially for more resources, than any one of them is able to marshall unaided. American business firms frequently resort to coalition for purposes of research or product promotion and for the construction of such gigantic facilities as dams or atomic reactors.

Coalition is not uncommon among educational organizations. Universities have established joint operations in such areas as nuclear research, archaeological research, and even social science research. Many smaller colleges have banded together for fund-raising purposes. The consolidation of public school districts is another form of coalition (if not merger), and the fact that it does represent a sharing or "invasion" of goal-setting power is reflected in some of the bitter resistance to consolidation in tradition-oriented localities.

Coalition requires a commitment for joint decision of future activities and thus places limits on unilateral or arbitrary decisions. Furthermore, inability of an organization to find partners in a coalition venture automatically prevents pursuit of that objective, and is therefore also a form of social control. If the collective judgment is that a proposal is unworkable, a possible disaster may be escaped and unproductive allocation of resources avoided.

DEVELOPMENT OF ENVIRONMENTAL SUPPORT

Environmental control is not a one-way process limited to consequences for the organization of action in its environment. Those subject to control are also part of the larger society and hence are also agents of social control. The enterprise that competes is not only influenced in its goal-setting by what the competitor and the third party may do, but also exerts influence over both. Bargaining likewise is a form of mutual, two-way influence; co-optation affects the co-opted as well as the co-opting party; and coalition clearly sets limits on both parties.

Goals appear to grow out of interaction, both within the organization and between the organization and its environment. While every enterprise must find sufficient support for its goals, it may wield initiative in this. The difference between effective and ineffective organizations may well lie in the initiative exercised by those in the organization who are responsible for goal-setting. . . .

4. Organizational Structures

»»

Of all the areas of organizational study, perhaps the most neglected is that of comparative study, in particular among organizations in the same culture and society. Most studies of organizations are case studies of a single organization, surveys of participants in a single organization, or abstract theories which presumably apply to all organizations. A careful examination of many so-called generalizations would show that they in fact apply only to certain types of organizations, frequently economic and governmental bureaucracies, but not to the many others.

The following section presents seven articles dealing with seven different organizations. It is hoped that this panorama will suffice to show that whereas these organizations are bureaucracies in one way or another there are interesting and significant differences among them, and that a comparative analysis of organizations will undoubtedly yield new insights into various functional problems of organizations and the ways in which these problems are met.

The organizations discussed in this section are presented in an order which reflects their position on a continuum. The continuum represents the increasing degree of *commitment required from lower participants for the effective operation of the organization.* It is lowest for inmates in *prisons;* somewhat higher for enlisted men in peacetime *military* organizations; even higher for workers in *industries,* but on the average not as high as for members of *trade-unions.* Still higher involvement, or identification, is a vital condition for effective education in *schools* as well as for therapy in *mental hospitals.* Religious commitments are generally regarded as the deepest. Therefore a discussion of *religious organizations* concludes the survey.*

* The editor hopes to spell out the significance of this continuum for comparative study of organizations in a future publication.

Each author, while depicting some of the characteristics of "his" organization, also illuminates some functional problems which, although not necessarily generic, are relevant to understanding the operation and structure of a number of different types of organizations. This fact, in itself, ought to demonstrate the bonuses attained by a comparative, as opposed to a case, approach.

Sykes points out that guards in prisons tend to accept the viewpoint of the inmates and to neglect that of society and the prison. Some of the factors which make for this "corruption of authority" lie in the close, intimate, and constant contact guards have with inmates; in the limited interaction among guards and between guards and their superiors; and in the need to win the cooperation of inmates in order to function effectively. Most of these factors can be found in other organizations in which supervision plays an important role, although usually they are more powerful in the prison, and therefore "corruption of authority" is probably highest there.

Janowitz, who examines the authority structure of military organizations, finds that it is becoming more like that of civilian organizations. The increased utilization of experts and complex technology, as well as the emphasis on positive relations between superiors and subordinates, are some of the factors making for this trend. It is quite possible that such changes can be discovered in many other organizations as well: more professionalization and stronger interests in democratic or persuasive controls can be ascertained in industries, mental hospitals, prisons, schools, and other organizations.

Increase in professionalization means more staff personnel and this, in turn, puts more strains on the relations between line and staff officers. Janowitz examines this problem in the military establishment.

Dalton studies the strain between staff and line in three modern corporations. The strain follows from the different functions the two organizational groups serve; it draws on differences in the social and cultural background of the two groups; it rests in part on differences in lines of communication with, and access to, top power positions in the organization. Adaptation through illegitimate deals between lower ranks of line and staff officers shows that "corruption of authority" is not limited to prisons and exists in horizontal as well as vertical relationships.

The problem Wilensky tackles in his book on staff experts in labor unions is the interplay of individuals and organizations in a large private association. He asks, "What types of experts doing what work with what outlook win high influence in the modern union—and how?" and "How do the experts respond to the pressures generated by both the organization and their own motives—what are the typical transformations in their role orientations?" This study, based on comparisons among twenty-eight unions, provides rich data on the structural context of union decisions. The excerpt printed here, although peripheral to the main analysis of expert functions, orientations, and influence, gives us "a picture of slowly growing, but as yet embryonic bureaucracy." On the one hand, there is some increase in professionalization, formalization of relationships, and systematic division of labor. On the other hand, the high emphasis on informal relations is a source of great frustration for the experts—many of whom, like the staff studied by Dalton—have a considerably different background from union leaders with whom they interact. Recruitment, training, promotion, and other aspects of the expert-union relations have undergone similar changes: they have become relatively more, but not highly, bureaucratized.

Hospitals and churches differ from these other types of organizations in that they employ professionals, not as advisers for performance carried out by others, under the direction of nonprofessionals (line), but rather as performers and controllers of performance. This distinction raises several problems which emerge in one way or another in both these organizations.

Howard S. Becker's study points to several variables which are of interest in the study of "professional" organizations in general. The degree of control by clients, by superiors, and by colleagues is one of them. The visibility of the performance is another. His examination of the teacher's authority in the school structure is of particular interest precisely because the teacher's professional authority is not fully acknowledged. The teacher demands full autonomy from client control but cannot deny the parents' right to have a say about the education of their children. The principal is expected to act on behalf of the teachers, to administer the school facilities, and not to interfere in the teaching process. But his superiors require that he shall exercise such control. The control of colleagues is minimized because neither the performance nor the "product" is readily visible to peers.

The effect of the psychological needs of participants on organizational activities has often been discussed. Studies of mental hospitals have brought into focus the reverse effect: that of the organizational structure and processes on the personalities of participants. Stanton and Schwartz bring forth several central themes in an analytical survey of studies relevant to this issue. First of all, the idea of a *therapeutic milieu* is discussed. Patients, we learn, are affected by their social environment as a whole, not only by the fifty minutes of psychoanalytical treatment. Organizational personnel are an important element of the milieu. To create a therapeutic community, the personnel must be treatment-oriented, share in efforts to cure the patients. The relations among various groups of personnel also seem to affect therapy. The lower the consensus among these groups, the higher the rate of disorder and other disturbances on the part of the inmates. Also discussed are processes of mobility in the mental hospital and the effect of "graduation" on the status system and leadership structure of the inmates' society. Other aspects of the interchange between the organizational community and its participants are discussed in Part V, in Goffman's contribution.

Religious establishments, one of the most interesting organizational types, are only rarely studied. After decades of extension, elaboration, and revision, the central approach is still the analysis and application of the church-sect continuum. Howard Becker examines the major characteristics of the ecclesia (or church), the sect, the denomination, and the cult. Several dimensions emerge from the analysis. Among them are the ways in which members are recruited (ascription as against achievement); the relative emphasis on education as it affects the forms of recruitment; individual in contrast to familial membership; scope of membership in terms of spheres of life permeated by the organization; the degree of formalization of the religious structure.

The extension of comparative study from these four types of religious establishments to the study of organizations in general will show that theorems developed here have interesting implications for any general organizational theory. Thus each of these presentations enhances our understanding of a single type, and at the same time contributes to the comparative study of organizations, a study which as yet has barely begun.

Gresham M. Sykes

The Corruption of Authority and Rehabilitation

I

The prison community has been well described as a social group made up of "custodial and professional employees, habitual petty thieves, one-time offenders, gangsters, professional racketeers, psychotics, pre-psychotics, neurotics, and psychopaths, all living under extreme conditions of physical and psychological compression."[1] The prison officials represent a custodial force charged with the primary function of preventing escapes and maintaining internal order. Standing in opposition to the official system of control there exists an inmate social system—a more or less organized criminal group.[2] . . .

The proliferation of prison regulations and the officials' emphasis on internal discipline is often attributed to institutional inertia of the bureaucratic mind. This viewpoint overlooks the potential danger which may lie in the most innocent appearing action when large groups of criminals are confined for long periods of time under condi-

Reprinted in part from *Social Forces,* 34 (1956), 257–262, with the permission of the author and the publisher, The University of North Carolina Press.

[1] L. W. McCorkle and R. Korn, "Resocialization Within Walls," *The Annals of the American Academy of Political and Social Science,* 293 (May 1954), pp. 88–98.

[2] Cf. D. Clemmer, *The Prison Community* (Boston: Christopher, 1940); N. Hayner and E. Ash, "The Prison Community as a Social Group," *American Sociological Review,* 4 (June 1939), pp. 362–369; F. E. Haynes, "The Sociological Study of the Prison Community," *Journal of Criminal Law and Criminology,* 39 (November–December 1948), pp. 432–440; S. K. Weinberg, "Aspects of the Prison's Social Structure," *American Journal of Sociology,* XLVII (March 1942), pp. 717–726; C. Schrag, "Leadership among Prison Inmates," *American Sociological Review,* 19 (February 1954), pp. 37–42.

tions of deprivation. Gambling, stealing, note-writing, quarrelling, or loitering may appear as trivial offenses to the casual observer. The difficulty is that such offenses can be symptomatic of, or prepare the ground for, far more serious situations. The unpaid gambling debt can lead to a knifing; stealing food, clothing, or objects to decorate a cell can provide a route of exchange which can be used for the transmission of weapons, drugs, or the materials necessary for an escape attempt; the illegal communication can establish a rendezvous for a homosexual relationship which may in turn lead to a vicious fight; a minor argument can easily flare into a dangerous battle under conditions of enforced, prolonged intimacy and this may touch off an uncontrollable riot; and loitering or "being out of place" may provide the momentary escape from supervision needed to perform a variety of illegal acts.

But the crisis is usually potential, not actual. Many infractions of the rules are in fact minor, not indicative of serious offenses, and only some of the inmates, not all, present major problems of discipline and security. The guard in the cellblock may rigidly enforce all rules on the grounds that a trivial violation of prison regulations *may* be the first symptom of a serious breach in the institution's defenses; or—and this is probably the more frequent case—he may be lulled into forgetting the possible dangers of his position. Like many social roles organized around the theme of potential crisis, the guard's position demands a fine edge of readiness which is difficult to maintain. The correctional officer is called on to make decisions in the daily flux of human affairs in which he must weigh the consequences of treating a possibly serious offense as actually minor against the consequences of treating a possibly minor offense as actually serious; and in such decisions (although this implies, perhaps, too great a degree of conscious rationality) he is under great pressure to take into account the reaction of the men he controls as well as the institution's requirements of security.

II

The guard in charge of a cellblock is required to perform a number of routine tasks during his tour of duty which have as their major aim the prison's function of custody and internal order. Counting inmates, periodically reporting to the center of communications, signing passes, checking mass movements of inmates, inspecting bars, windows, gratings, and other possible escape routes, searching cells for contraband material—these make up the minutiae of the eight-hour shift. In addition, the cellblock officer is supposed to be constantly alert for violations of prison rules which fall outside of his sphere of routine supervision and control.

In the exercise of authority, the deep and pervasive schism which is supposed to separate the captors and captives is actually bridged at innumerable points in the maximum security prison. Guards frequently fail to report infractions of the regulations; guards transmit forbidden information to inmates, neglect elementary security requirements, and join inmates in outspoken criticisms of higher officials. This "corruption" of the guard's authority is apparently seldom to be attributed to bribery—bribery is usually unnecessary, for far more subtle influences are at work which tend to destroy the authority of the cellblock guard.

Corruption through Friendship

The correctional officer is in close and intimate association with his prisoners throughout the course of the working day. He can remain aloof only with difficulty, for he possesses few of those devices which normally serve to separate rulers and the ruled. He cannot withdraw physically in symbolic affirmation of social distance; he has no intermediaries to bear the brunt of resentment springing from orders which are disliked; he cannot fall back on the dignity adhering to his office—he is a "hack" or "screw" in the eyes of those he controls, and an unwelcome display of officiousness evokes that great destroyer of respect, the ribald humor of the dispossessed.

There are many pressures in American culture to "be nice," to "be a good Joe," and the guard in the maximum security prison is not immune.[3] The guard is constantly exposed to a sort of moral blackmail in which the first signs of condemnation or estrangement are immediately countered by the inmates with the threat of ridicule or hostility. In this complex interplay, the guard does not always start from a position of determined opposition to "being friendly." The cellblock officer holds an intermediate post in a bureaucratic structure between top prison officials—his captains, lieutenants, and sergeants—and the prisoners in his charge. Like many "unlucky" Pierres always in the middle, the guard is caught in a conflict of loyalties. He resents many of the actions of his superiors—the reprimands, the lack of ready ap-

[3] For an incisive analysis of this theme in more general terms, see D. Riesman, *The Lonely Crowd* (New Haven: Yale University Press, 1950).

preciation, the incomprehensible order—and in the inmates he finds willing sympathizers: they too claim to suffer from the unreasonable caprice of power.

Furthermore, the guard in many cases is marked by a basic ambivalence towards the criminals under his supervision. Although condemned by society through its instrument the law, many criminals are a "success" in terms of a mundane system of values which places a high degree of prestige on notoriety and wealth even though won by devious means. The poorly paid guard may be gratified to associate with a famous racketeer. This ambivalence in the correctional officer's attitudes toward his captives cuts deeper than a discrepancy between the inmate's position in the power structure of the prison and his possible status in a *sub rosa* stratification system. There may also be a discrepancy between the judgments of society and the guard's work-a-day values as far as the "criminality" of the inmate is concerned. The bookie, the man convicted of deserting his wife, the inmate who stridently proclaims his innocence and is believed—the guard often holds that these men are not seriously to be viewed as criminals, as desperate prisoners to be rigidly suppressed.

Corruption through Reciprocity

To a large extent the guard is dependent on inmates for the satisfactory performance of his duties and like many figures of authority, the guard is evaluated in terms of the conduct of the men he controls—a troublesome, noisy, dirty cellblock reflects on the guard's ability to "handle prisoners," and this forms an important component of the merit rating which is used as the basis for pay raises and promotions. A guard cannot rely on the direct application of force to achieve compliance, for he is one man against hundreds; and if he continually calls for additional help he becomes a major problem for the short-handed prison administration. A guard cannot easily rely on threats of punishment, for he is dealing with men who are already being punished near the limits permitted by society, and if the guard insists on constantly using the last few negative sanctions available to the institution—the withdrawal of recreation facilities and other privileges, solitary confinement, or loss of good time—he again becomes burdensome to the prison administration which realizes that its apparent dominance rests on some degree of uncoerced cooperation. The guard, then, is under pressure to achieve a smoothly running cellblock not with the stick but with the carrot, but here again his stock of rewards is limited. One of the best "offers" he can make is ignoring minor offenses or making sure that he never places himself in a position to discover infractions of the rules.

Aside from winning routine and superficial compliance, the guard has another favor to be secured from inmates which makes him willing to forego strict enforcement of prison regulations. Many prisons have experienced a riot in which the tables are momentarily turned and the captives hold sway over their *quondam* captors. The guard knows that he may some day be a hostage and that his life may turn on the settling of old accounts. A fund of good will becomes a valuable form of insurance.[4]

Corruption through Default

Finally, much of the guard's authority tends to be destroyed by the innocuous encroachment of inmates on the guard's duties. Making out reports, checking cells at the periodic count, locking and unlocking doors—in short, all the minor chores which the guard is called on to perform during the course of the day—may gradually be transferred to the hands of the inmates whom the guard has come to trust. The cellblock "runner," formally assigned the tasks of delivering mail, housekeeping duties, and similar jobs, is of particular importance in this respect. Inmates in this position function in a manner analogous to that of the company clerk in the armed forces, and at times they may wield great power and influence in the life of the cellblock. For reasons of indifference, laziness, or naivete, the guard may find much of his authority whittled away; nonfeasance, rather than malfeasance, has corrupted the theoretical guard-inmate relationship.

Authority, like a woman's virtue, once lost is hard to regain. The measures to break up an established pattern of abdication need to be much more severe than those required to stop the first steps in the corruption of authority. In the first place, a guard assigned to a cellblock in which a large portion of control has been transferred in the past from the correctional officer to the inmates is faced with the weight of precedent. It requires a good deal of moral courage on his part to face the gibes and aggression of inmates who fiercely defend the legitimacy of the *status quo* established by custom. In the second place, if the guard himself has allowed his authority to be subverted,

[4] This fear for personal safety in an uprising is rarely voiced by the guards themselves, perhaps because it represents an explicit capitulation to the inmate social system. Conversations with the wives of guards are, however, much more revealing.

he may find his attempts to rectify his error checked by a threat from the inmates to send a "snitch-kite"—an anonymous note—to the guard's superior officers explaining his past derelictions in detail. This simple form of blackmail may on occasion be sufficient to maintain the existing balance of power.

III

The corruption of authority in the maximum security prison provides an illuminating example of the limits of totalitarian power.[5] To view the inmate social system of an American prison as an organized expression of rebellion against totalitarianism is undoubtedly misleading in a number of ways. We must take into account the matrix of the democratic community in which the prison is embedded, the lack of a well-developed political ideology which serves as a focus of resistance, the lack of cohesiveness in the inmate population itself, the prison administrators' adherence to democratic beliefs and practices, etc. Nonetheless, the maximum security prison is confronted with many of the problems of a system of total, or almost total, power; and foremost among these problems is the transmutation of orders and standard operating procedures in the process of their execution, particularly at the point where authority flows across the line separating the rulers from the ruled.

We do not know the extent of the corruption or destruction of the guard's authority and for rather obvious reasons such information would be difficult to obtain.[6] There is enough evidence, however, to suggest that it is a chronic problem of prison administration.[7] The

[5] David Riesman has noted that "resistance movements" are not simply heroic acts of individual defiance but also turn on the social organization of those who are subject to extremes of social control. Cf. D. Riesman, "Some Observations on the Limits of Totalitarian Power," *Antioch Review,* 12 (1952), pp. 155–168. For a further discussion, see K. W. Deutsch, "Cracks in the Monolith: Possibilities and Patterns of Disintegration in Totalitarian Systems," in C. F. Friedrich (ed.), *Totalitarianism* (Cambridge, Mass.: Harvard University Press, 1954).

[6] It should be noted here that the accumulation of data for this study has been made possible only because of the extraordinary cooperation of the prison officials in the institution being investigated. Not only has this made possible a marked frankness on the part of the guards and other prison employees—it has also made possible the interviewing of inmates under conditions which have led to a high degree of rapport.

[7] See C. McKendrick, "Custody and Discipline," in P. W. Tappan (ed.), *Contemporary Correction* (New York: McGraw-Hill Book Company, 1951), pp. 157–171.

pressures which tend to shift power from the hands of the guard to the hands of the inmates are often realized in fact and this raises a critical question: What are the implications of such a shift for the rehabilitation of the adult criminal? If we are correct in assuming that reformation depends on modifying those attitudes which neutralize the sanctions of society and its surrogates, it would appear that the corruption of the guard's authority makes the criminal still more unresponsive to legitimate social controls by encouraging the criminal in patterns of conniving, deception, and counterattacks against the normative order.

Insofar as the prison inmates manage to destroy the guard's role as an impersonal enforcer of the rules, the path is opened for a host of beliefs and attitudes which negate the approval or disapproval of legitimate society. When guards and inmates are enmeshed in a pattern of quasi-friendship and reciprocity, punishments by prison officials easily come to be interpreted as personal, vindictive attacks and thus lose their moral force. Similarly, rewards tend to be redefined as a "pay-off," and expedient product of a "deal," rather than social approval for conforming behavior.[8] The guard, the dominant symbol of law-abiding society in the daily life of the prison inmate, becomes a figure to be manipulated, coerced, and hoodwinked. It seems likely, therefore, that a major barrier to the rehabilitation of the adult criminal in a maximum security prison is to be attributed not only to the "unnaturalness" of his social environment and the lack of scientifically tested therapeutic devices but also to the corruption of the guard's authority in maintaining custody and discipline. Since these functions have long been held to be opposed to the aim of reformation, it would appear that a profound re-evaluation of the importance of these functions for the rehabilitation of the adult criminal is needed.

[8] The line here is a fine one, but legitimate rewards appear to be distinguishable from the "pay-off" on the following basis: if the individual views rewards as a necessary condition for the performance of a prescribed act, we are approaching the idea of the "deal"; if the individual views rewards as lagniappe, as a fortunate concomitant of duty, we are approaching legitimate positive sanctions. The important point is that when normative conformity is based on the principle of a favor for a favor, the individual is not subject to the critical social control of an internalized moral imperative. Cf. K. Davis, *Human Society* (New York: The Macmillan Company, 1949), chap. 3.

Morris Janowitz

Hierarchy and Authority in the Military Establishment

BUREAUCRACY: CIVILIAN OR MILITARY

As a social organization, the contemporary military establishment has for some time tended to display more and more of the characteristics typical of any large-scale nonmilitary bureaucracy. The decreasing difference is a result of continuous technological change which vastly expands the size of the military establishment, increases its interdependence with civilian society, and alters its internal social structure. These technological developments in war-making require more and more professionalization. At the same time, the impact of military technology during the past half-century can be described in a series of propositions about social change. Each of the conditions symbolized by these propositions has had the effect of "civilianizing" military institutions and of blurring the distinction between the civilian and the military.

1. An increasing percentage of the national income of a modern nation is spent for the preparation, execution, and repair of the consequences of war. Thus, there is a trend toward total popular involvement in the consequences of war and war policy, since the military establishment is responsible for the distribution of a progressively larger share of the available economic values.

2. Military technology both vastly increases the destructiveness of warfare and widens the scope of automation in new weapons. It is a commonplace that both of these trends tend to weaken the distinc-

Reprinted in part from Morris Janowitz, *Sociology and the Military Establishment*, pp. 15–24, 28–39, by permission of the author and the publisher, The Russell Sage Foundation. Copyright 1959.

tion between military roles and civilian roles as the destructiveness of war has increased. Weapons of mass destruction socialize danger to the point of equalizing the risks of warfare for both soldier and civilian. As long as the armed forces must rely on large numbers of drafted personnel, powerful influences toward civilianization are at work.

3. The revolution in military technology means that the military mission of deterring violence becomes more and more central as compared with preparing to apply violence. This shift in mission tends to civilianize military thought and organization as military leaders concern themselves with broad ranges of political, social, and economic policies.

4. The previous periodic character of the military establishment (rapid expansion, rapid dismantlement) has given way to a more permanent maintenance or expansion. The permanent character of the military establishment has removed one important source of civilian-military conflict, namely, the civilian tendency to abandon the military establishment after a war. Instead, because of the high rate of technological change, internal conflicts between the military services have been multiplied.

5. The complexity of the machinery of warfare and the requirements for research, development, and technical maintenance tend to weaken the organizational boundary between the military and the nonmilitary, since the maintenance and manning of new weapons require a greater reliance on civilian-oriented technicians.

6. Given the "permanent" threat of war, it is well recognized that the tasks which military leaders perform tend to widen. Their technological knowledge, their direct and indirect power, and their heightened prestige result in their entrance, of necessity, into arenas that in the recent past have been reserved for civilian and professional politicians. The need that political and civilian leaders have for expert advice from professional soldiers about the strategic implications of technological change serves to mix the roles of the military and the civilian.

Nevertheless, the typical sociological analysis of military organization does not take into account the consequences of these trends and instead continues to emphasize authoritarian, stratified-hierarchical, and traditional dimensions as a basis for distinguishing the military from the nonmilitary bureaucracy.[1]

[1] Stouffer, Samuel A., and others, *The American Soldier*, vol. 1, p. 55; Davis, Arthur K., "Bureaucratic Patterns in the Navy Officer Corps," *Social Forces*, vol.

Combat Goals

These observations do not deny the crucial differences that exist between military and nonmilitary bureaucracies. The goals of an organization supply a meaningful basis for understanding differences in organizational behavior. The military establishment as a social system has unique characteristics because the possibility of hostilities is a permanent reality to its leadership. The fact that thermonuclear weapons alter the role of force in international relations does not deny this proposition. The consequences of preparation for future combat and the results of previous combat pervade the entire organization. The unique character of the military establishment derives from the requirement that its members are specialists in making use of violence and mass destruction. In the language of the soldier, this is recognized on a common sense basis: military mission is the key to military organization.

Changing technology creates new patterns of combat, and thereby modifies organizational behavior and authority in the military establishment. The narrowing distinction between military and nonmilitary bureaucracies can never result in the elimination of fundamental organizational differences. Three pervasive requirements for combat set limits to these civilianizing tendencies.

First, while it is true that modern warfare exposes the civilian and the soldier to more equal risks, the distinction between military roles and civilian roles has not been eliminated. Traditional combat-ready military formations need to be maintained for limited warfare. The necessity for naval and air units to carry on the hazardous tasks of continuous and long-range reconnaissance and detection, demand organizational forms that will bear the stamp of conventional formations. In the future, even with fully automated missile systems, conventional units must be maintained as auxiliary forces for the delivery of new types of weapons.

More important, no military system can rely on expectation of

---

27, December, 1948, pp. 143–153; Rose, Arnold M., "The Social Structure of the Army," *American Journal of Sociology*, vol. 51, March, 1946, pp. 361–364; Freeman, Felton D., "The Army as a Social Structure," *Social Forces*, vol. 27, October, 1948, pp. 78–83; Brotz, Howard, and Everett Wilson, "Characteristics of Military Society," *American Journal of Sociology*, vol. 51, March, 1946, pp. 371–375; Spindler, G. Dearborn, "The Military—A Systematic Analysis," *Social Forces*, vol. 27, October, 1948, pp. 83–88; Page, Charles H., "Bureaucracy's Other Face," *Social Forces*, vol. 25, October, 1946, pp. 88–94.

victory based on the initial exchange of firepower—whatever the form of the initial exchange may be. Subsequent exchanges will involve military personnel—again regardless of their armament—who are prepared to carry on the struggle as soldiers, that is, subject themselves to military authority and to continue to fight. The automation of war civilianizes wide sectors of the military establishment; yet the need to maintain combat readiness and to develop centers of resistance after initial hostilities ensures the continued importance of military organization and authority.

Second, what about the consequences of the increased importance of deterrence as a military mission? Should one not expect that such a shift also would result in civilianizing the military establishment? If the military is forced to think about deterring wars rather than fighting wars, the traditions of the "military mind," based on the inevitability of hostilities, must change and military authority must undergo transformation as well. There can be no doubt that this shift in mission is having important effects on military thought and organization. In fact, military pacifism is a growing and important trend in modern society as the horrors of war force military leaders to concern themselves with the political consequences of violence.

Again, there are limits to the consequences of this civilianizing trend. The role of deterrence is not a uniquely new mission for the military establishment. Historically, the contribution of the military to the balance of power has not been made because of the civilian character of the military establishment. To the contrary, the balance of power formula operates, when it does, because the military establishment is prepared to fight effectively and immediately.

With the increase in the importance of deterrence, military elites become more and more involved in diplomatic and political warfare, regardless of their preparation for such tasks. Yet the specific and unique contribution of the military to deterrence is the threat of violence which has currency; that is, it can be taken seriously because of the real possibility of violence. Old or new types of weapons do not alter this basic formula. In short, deterrence still requires organization prepared for combat.

Third, the assumption that military institutions, as compared with economic and industrial institutions, are resistant to technological change is considerably undermined as the process of innovation in the military establishment itself has become routinized. Nevertheless, as long as imponderables weigh heavy in estimating military outcomes and as long as the "fighter" spirit is required to face combat, the military rejects the civilian engineer as its professional model. Of course, the engineer is held in high esteem, but the ideal image of the military continues to be the strategic commander, not the military technician. It is the image of a leader, motivated by national patriotism and not by personal monetary gain, who is capable of organizing the talents of specialists for all types of contingencies.

The question of relative resistance to technological innovation by the military, as compared with civilian economic and industrial organization, has produced volumes of historical writing. In his broad historical survey John U. Nef argues that military organization and the requirements of war-making were not crucial factors in Western technological development and, therefore, were not mechanisms for stimulating economic development.[2]

In all probability, military organization as late as the middle of the nineteenth century was strongly resistant to technological innovation. Until that time the military establishments of Western Europe were dominated by aristocratic elements that were concerned with a traditional way of life. These elements stood in opposition to social change and technological innovation, and accepted new developments in military organization with great reluctance.

However, in the middle of the twentieth century, military institutions can no longer be thought of as merely reacting to external pressures and resisting technological innovation. For the sociologists studying the military establishment, it is important to emphasize that the armed forces now create their own requirements for technological innovation, which in turn influence industrial organization. The classical view of the military standing in opposition to technological innovation is inapplicable as the present cycle of the arms race converts the armed forces into centers of support for the development of new weapons systems. The military establishment hardly presents the ideal conditions for the professional scientist or the research engineer. Yet military leaders, regardless of the validity of their professional judgments about technological matters, are not characterized by traditional thinking about technological requirements.

Likewise, the procedures of innovation in industry and in the military tend to converge; increasing specialization involves the replacement of individual entrepreneurship by staff work and group

[2] Nef, John U., *War and Human Progress.* Harvard University Press, Cambridge, Mass., 1950.

research. In the contemporary military establishment with its continuous rotation of persons through official roles, the process of assessment of needs and prospects of technological innovation is as routinized and automatic as in civilian industry.

Leadership based on traditional military customs must share power with experts not only in technical matters but also in matters of organizational and human relations. Specific organizational adaptations of the military even foreshadow developments in civilian society, since the military must press hard for innovation and respond more rapidly to social change. For example, the continued need for retraining personnel from operational to managerial positions and from older to newer techniques has led to a more rational spreading of higher education throughout the career of the military officer, rather than the concentrated dosage typical of the civilian in graduate or professional school.

No bureaucracy ever conforms to the ideal model of the rational organization and certainly the military establishment cannot be thought of in purely engineering terms. As long as "the battle is the pay off"—as long as there are dangerous and irksome tasks to be performed—an engineering philosophy cannot suffice as the organizational basis of the armed forces. Especially in a free enterprise, profit-motivated society, the military establishment is oriented to duty and honor. S. L. A. Marshall's observations touch directly on this essential theme of military life:

> A note of smugness was not missing from the remark all too frequently heard during World War II: "We go at this thing just like it was a great engineering job." What was usually overlooked was that to the men who were present at the pay off, it wasn't an engineering job, and had they gone about their duty in that spirit, there would have been no victory for our side.[3]

In a period of fantastic technological change, military leadership is confronted with an almost perpetual crisis of organization. The sociological analyst is concerned with understanding the organizational consequences of these technological changes. Yet it can be assumed that neither the increased automation of military technology, nor the military shift in mission from war-making to deterrence, nor the decline in the traditional military opposition to innovation can

[3] Marshall, S. L. A., *Men against Fire.* William Morrow and Co., New York, 1947, p. 210.

produce a complete civilianization of the military establishment. The structure of military authority—the key to military organization—is an expression of the unique goals of the military, namely, combat and combat preparation.

In terms of manpower and mass destruction, air power is the ascendant arm, while ground and sea power remain the essential components of a system of graduated deterrence. The diversification and specialization of military technology lengthen the formal training required to gain mastery of military technology. The temporary citizen soldier, sailor, and aviator will become less important and a completely professional armed force more vital. The need to fight limited wars or strategic wars instantly, with the available mobilized forces, tends to increase reliance on a professional military establishment. But these contemporary trends do not produce a professional army isolated and remote from civilian society, but a military establishment that is an integral part of the larger society on which its technological resources depend.

STAFF AND LINE IN THE MILITARY ESTABLISHMENT

Skill Structure

In all types of organizations the dilemma of ascriptive versus achievement authority is ever present. But it is a recurrent civilian perspective that the military establishment underemphasizes achievement in order to maintain traditional forms and the privileges of seniority. Thus, for example, the close link between age and rank in the military profession, particularly in naval organization, sets narrow limits within which skill is accorded positions of authority. In short, the hierarchical features of the military establishment strengthen the ascriptive sources of authority and compound the tasks of incorporating new skill groups.

First, there exists a deep source of organizational strain in all three services—ground, air, and naval—because the military staff-command structure does not articulate with its skill structure. In all three services the increased number and complexity of technical roles and specialists operate under the formally prescribed lines of authority developed for the simpler units of the past century. The basic dilemma centers about the staff officer who, despite his expanded functions and specialized skills, is defined as being subservient to the commanding officer. Originally, the role of the staff officer was defined as that of adviser to the commanding officer. Authority was vested solely in the commander. The supremacy of the commander appeared essential in order that specialists may operate within their competence and that they be effectively coordinated. This type of organizational structure in which the staff officer is limited to the role of adviser may have worked adequately as long as the technology of warfare developed slowly, but it presents continuing strain, given current complex technology.

As the division of labor becomes more complex and more specialized, the commander's dilemma becomes more pressing. He is not equipped with sufficient technical knowledge to supervise or assess adequately the performance of his technical subordinates. Nevertheless, the commander is held responsible for their performance by the formal hierarchy and the formal rules of the organization. The military establishment seeks to prepare him for this dilemma by increased schooling, by rotational assignments, and by specialized instruction in the techniques of administration.

Yet the military commander is forced to increase his reliance on staff officers to ensure that technical functions are efficiently performed in his own units and at lower echelons under his responsibility. The technical complexities of command force the commander to use his staff officers in supervisory as well as advisory roles. Authority conflicts are created for (a) the staff officer charged with "producing" efficient performance of those lower-echelon functions falling within his technical competence, and (b) for the commander in the lower-echelon units under such supervision. If the staff officer, in his capacity as technical specialist (and employing his achieved authority), attempts to exercise authority over a technical function in a lower echelon, he is vulnerable to the allegation that he is using authority which is specifically denied him by the formal rules of the military establishment. But if he fails to exercise his supervisory control, he risks the charge of failing to assist his commander in executing his responsibilities. If the lower-echelon commander permits direct intervention for efficiency, he does so in the face of formal regulations. He thereby weakens his ascribed authority over his unit, and often his own staff officers refuse to act on the "suggestion" of the higher-staff officer. But if he resists direct higher-staff intervention, he is confronted with the reality that higher-echelon commanders may not share his emphasis on formal regulations. Or by preventing higher staff from exercising technical authority, he is forced to exercise supervision himself, although often he lack the technical competence for this supervision. . . .

In the military establishment organizational strains exist which center about the continuous effort to develop a hierarchy of ranks appropriate to the new complex skill structure. In theory, in tradition, and in image the military rank system is a continuous pyramid with direct and clear-cut lines of authority and command channels from the top to the very bottom. In actuality, it has been transformed into a diamond-shaped hierarchy.

When armies became mass organizations through the introduction of the rifle, the assumption developed that a rank distribution of a single broadly based pyramid was the appropriate hierarchical form. The greatest number of men were privates, all of whom performed a relatively standardized task—infantrymen directly engaging the enemy. The task of the infantryman required only limited specialization, but it was a specialization without transferable skill to civilian employment. The officer of the line with his specialized training likewise had limited employment opportunities in the larger society. The number of officers at the higher levels of command and coordination dropped off progressively and sharply, but the concentration of technical specialists increased. In such a hierarchy the number of ranks could be small and the lines of authority could extend directly from the top to the very bottom. Traditionally, the Navy had a similar rank system.

However, the new skill structure of the military establishment is one in which specialization penetrates down the hierarchy into the formations assigned to combat. The concentration of persons engaged in purely military occupations is now a minority and even the combat occupations involve technical specialization. The transferability of skill to civilian occupations is extremely widespread. Top-ranking generals and admirals particularly have many nonmilitary functions to perform which involve general managerial skills. These long-term changes in the military establishment can be seen from an occupational analysis of enlisted personnel since the Civil War. Military type of occupations accounted for 93.2 per cent of the personnel in the Civil War, but after the Spanish-American War the civilian type of occupations began to predominate. By 1954 only 28.8 per cent of Army personnel were engaged in purely military occupations. The percentages are undoubtedly lower for both Navy and Air Force personnel.

OCCUPATIONAL SPECIALIZATION IN ARMY ENLISTED PERSONNEL, CIVIL WAR TO 1954

Occupational group	Civil War	Spanish American War	World War I	World War II	Korean War	Year 1954
Civilian type						
Technical, scientific	0.2	0.5	3.7	10.1	10.7	14.5
Administrative, clerical	0.7	3.1	8.0	14.6	19.2	17.5
Skilled mechanics, maintenance, etc.	0.6	1.1	21.5	15.8	16.9	20.3
Service workers	2.4	6.5	12.5	9.7	11.5	10.4
Operative, laborers	2.9	2.2	20.2	13.6	8.6	8.4
Military type	93.2	86.6	34.1	36.2	33.1	28.8

SOURCE: *Report on Conditions of Military Service for the President's Commission on Veterans' Pensions,* Question IV (Nature of Military Duties), December 28, 1955.

As already indicated, to meet the organizational requirements of this proliferation of skills, the military hierarchy has had to be adjusted, so that the allocation of ranks is no longer a pyramid, but is closer to a diamond in shape. More accurately, two diamond-shaped hierarchies—one for the enlisted men and one for the officers corps—have emerged. . . .

This proliferation of the middle-officer ranks also creates the image of a weakening of authority, since officers hold their rank not merely on the basis of the number of subordinates they command but because of their technical skills. In reality, authority has not been so much weakened as transformed. The tasks of military authority now more often relate to lateral coordination and cooperation than to the exercise of responsibility of the highest echelons over the lowest echelons. The task of the highest echelons is to create the conditions for the middle strata of specialists to coordinate their efforts. Consider a typical operation in the Korean conflict where an infantry combat team required air support from carrier-based planes, and it is abundantly clear that direct orders of a hierarchical variety are being supplemented by complex lateral coordination.

Military leadership is continuously seeking to offset the apparent weakening of authority by attempting to create a separate hierarchy of technical specialists and a separate hierarchy of commanders. The object is to re-establish something approaching a pyramid type of structure with clear lines of authority from the top to the very bottom. But fundamentally the new skill structure does not permit or allow for so simple a hierarchy. As the military establishment becomes more enmeshed in engineering and development, it is more difficult to maintain the distinction between the commander and the technical specialist. In the Air Force, which is an organization of combat flyers and former combat flyers, the organizational crisis is the deepest, since displacement of the "fighter" is proceeding more rapidly and more completely than in the ground or naval forces.

Traditional hierarchical authority is the basis on which the military establishment maintains its organizational boundaries. Such authority comes to be shared with the authority of skill and achievement, despite formal channels of command and the official hierarchy of rank.

Status Systems

Sociological analysis has long recognized that status systems are required to regulate and control the tensions and conflicts generated by competition among differing systems of authority. Authority, ascribed or achieved, is not operative because of the ultimate sanctions that an officer can mobilize. Rather, in any organization, civilian or military, authority systems operate on a day-to-day basis or fail to operate because of the status—that is, the prestige and the respect—the officers have. If authority is traditional and ascribed, status systems are likely to be fixed and clear-cut. But with the extension of achievement and skill criteria for allocating authority, status systems become fluid and are not clear-cut. Skilled specialists or men with outstanding combat records, despite low rank, may be accorded higher prestige than officers with higher rank. When status and prestige are in sharp variation to the contributions a person renders to an organization, authority systems are certain to be subject to strain and tension.

The effectiveness of military authority is deeply conditioned by the status and prestige which civilian society accords the military profession. It is generally recognized that, despite public acclaim of individual military heroes, officership is a low-status profession. The results of a national sampling of opinion placed the prestige of the officer in the armed services not only below the physician, scientist, college professor, and minister, but even below that of the public schoolteacher.[4] In this study, the relative prestige of the Air Force and Navy was above that of the Army and the Marine Corps, as measured by adult opinion as to which service they preferred for their

[4] Public Opinion Surveys, Inc., Princeton, N.J., *Attitudes of Adult Civilians Toward the Military Services as a Career.* Prepared for the Office of Armed Forces Information and Education, Department of Defense, Washington, 1955.

sons. Yet one adult civilian in two felt that he would be pleased if his son took up a career in the military services. Interestingly enough, the less educated civilian holds both the military officer and the public servant in higher esteem than does the better educated.[5]

An adequate level of prestige, difficult though that may be to define, is required to maintain organizational effectiveness and to inhibit excessive personnel turnover. In addition, the relatively low prestige of the military in the eyes of civilians conditions the conception that the military profession holds of itself. The military takes over this civilian image, with the result that the military exhibits extreme status sensitivity. The concern with status of the military professional is to be traced not only to the hierarchical organization of the armed forces. The military behaves very much like any other minority or low-status group.

It is, therefore, not surprising that the military establishment has evolved an elaborate basis for according its limited supply of status and prestige to its own members. Most pervasive is the criterion which is applied universally through the services, the distinction between the officers and the enlisted men. The other universal distinctions are between regulars and reservists, line versus staff, combat versus noncombat, and the like. There are also more particular designations, such as veteran status of a particular campaign, membership in a high-status formation, or graduation from a service academy. . . .

CHANGING MILITARY DISCIPLINE

The new skill structure modifies military discipline as well as status. At first glance, the military establishment is a vast organization for technical and logistical operations, and a preponderance of its personnel are engaged in administrative and housekeeping functions. But military authority, if it is to be effective, must strive to make combat units its organizational prototype, and the character of military organization can best be seen in combat units. In combat the maintenance of initiative has become a requirement of greater importance than the rigid enforcement of discipline. In the succinct formulation of S. L. A. Marshall,

> The philosophy of discipline has adjusted to changing conditions. As more and more impact has gone into the hitting power of weapons,

[5] Janowitz, Morris, and Deil S. Wright, "The Prestige of Public Employment," *Public Administration Review*, vol. 16, Winter, 1956, pp. 15–21.

necessitating ever-widening deployments in the forces of battle, the quality of the initiative in the individual has become the most praised of the military virtues.[6]

In a sense, the military ideology of authoritarian discipline has always been tempered by the necessities of human nature. But the close order formations based on relatively low firepower could be dominated and controlled by direct and rigid discipline. However, since the development of the rifle bullet of more than a century ago, the social organization of combat units has been changing continuously so as to throw the individual fighter on his own and his primary group's resources. Despite the proliferation of military technology, all three services are dependent on the initiative of a very small percentage of the fighting personnel, who are willing to press the attack under all circumstances. The Air Force discovered that less than one per cent of its military pilots became aces—five victories in air battle; yet this one per cent accounted roughly for 30 to 40 per cent of the enemy aircraft destroyed in the air.

In World War II and again in the Korean conflict, the command problem in the ground forces centered on developing the ability of the infantry soldier to make the fullest use of his weapons. The infantry squad, the air crew, and the submarine complement, all have wide latitude for making decisions requiring energy and initiative. The increased firepower of modern weapons causes military forces—land, sea, and air—to be more dispersed, in order to reduce exposure to danger. Each unit becomes increasingly dependent on its own organizational impetus, once the battle has started. Thus, the military establishment with its hierarchical structure, with its exacting requirements for coordination, and with its apparently high centralization of organizational power, must strive contrariwise to develop the broadest decentralization of initiative at the point of contact with the enemy. As the destructiveness of weapons systems increases, short of total destruction, the importance of initiative increases for the military formations that survive the initial exchange of hostilities.

The combat soldier, regardless of military arm, when committed to battle, is hardly the model of Max Weber's ideal bureaucrat following rigid rules and regulations. In certain respects he is the antithesis. The combat fighter is not routinized and self-contained. Rather, his rôle is one of constant improvisation, regardless of his service or weapon. Improvisation is the keynote of the individual fighter or

[6] Marshall, *op. cit.*, p. 22.

combat group. The impact of battle destroys men, equipment, and organization that need constantly to be brought back into some form of unity through on-the-spot improvisation. In battle the planned division of labor breaks down.

The technology of warfare is so complex that the coordination of a group of specialists cannot be guaranteed simply by authoritarian discipline. Members of a military group recognize their greater mutual dependence on the technical proficiency of their team members than on the formal authority structure. The military organization dedicated to victory is forced to alter its techniques of training and indoctrination. Rather than developing automatic reaction to combat dangers, it requires a training program designed to teach men not only to count on instruction from superiors but also to exercise their own judgment about the best response to make when confronted with given types of danger. The very designation "combat team" exemplifies the goals of such indoctrination, since it emphasizes the positive contributions of each person regardless of rank. Thus, the operational code of the Israeli forces in the Sinai campaign was, in effect, "when in doubt, attack"—an expression of sheer initiative.

Obviously, technology conditions these changing internal social relations in the military establishment. The morale and coordination of a complex group of specialists cannot be guaranteed simply by authoritarian discipline. The complexity of the machinery and the resultant social interdependence produce an important residue of organizational power for each participating member. All the members of a military group recognize their mutual dependence on the technical proficiency and level of performance of others, as well as on the formal authority structure.

Thus, the impact of technology has forced a shift in the practices of military authority. Military authority must shift from reliance on practices based on *domination* to a wider utilization of *manipulation.* Traditional or ascriptive authority relies heavily on domination, while manipulation is more appropriate for authority based on achievement. By domination we mean influencing a person's behavior, by giving explicit instruction as to desired behavior without reference to the goals sought. Domination involves threats and negative sanctions rather than positive incentives. It tends to produce mechanical compliance. Manipulation involves influencing an individual's behavior less by giving explicit instructions and more by indirect techniques of group persuasion and by an emphasis on group goals. While the term "manipulation" has come to be thought of as morally reprehensible, it describes the efforts of leadership when orders are issued and the reasons for them are given. It is impossible to analyze modern institutions without reference to a concept such as manipulation, or some more socially acceptable equivalent. Manipulation involves positive incentives rather than physical threats; manipulation does retain the threat of exclusion from the group as a control. The indirect techniques of manipulation are designed to take into account the individual soldier's predispositions.

The goal of military authority, in ideal terms, is to create stable and purposeful involvement at each level in the hierarchy of ranks. When military leaders operate successfully, they make use of their organizational skills to produce effective participation. So it can be said, as older forms of domination become outmoded, effective participation becomes a new criterion for judging military authority.

Melville Dalton

Conflict between Staff and Line Managerial Officers

Industrial staff organizations are relatively new. Their appearance is a response to many complex interrelated forces, such as economic competition, scientific advance, industrial expansion, growth of the labor movement, and so on. During the last four or five decades these rapid changes and resulting unstable conditions have caused top industrial officials more and more to call in "specialists" to aid them toward the goal of greater production and efficiency. These specialists are of many kinds, including chemists, statisticians, public and industrial relations officers, personnel officers, accountants, and a great variety of engineers, such as

Reprinted in part from Melville Dalton, *American Sociological Review,* 15 (1950), 342–351, by permission of the author and the publisher, The American Sociological Association.

mechanical, draughting, electrical, chemical, fuel, lubricating, and industrial engineers. In industry these individuals are usually known as "staff people." Their functions, again, for the most part are to increase and apply their specialized knowledge in problem areas, and to advise those officers who make up the "line" organization and have authority [1] over production processes.

This theoretically satisfying industrial structure of specialized experts advising busy administrators has in a number of significant cases failed to function as expected. The assumptions that (a) the staff specialists would be reasonably content to function without a measure of formal authority [2] over production, and that (b) their suggestions regarding improvement of processes and techniques for control over personnel and production would be welcomed by line officers and be applied, require closer examination. In practice there is often much conflict between industrial staff and line organizations and in varying degrees the members of these organizations oppose each other.

The aim of this paper is, therefore, to present and analyze data dealing with staff-line tensions.

Data were drawn from three industrial plants [3] in which the writer had been either a participating member of one or both of the groups or was intimate with reliable informants among the officers who were. . . .

For analytical convenience, staff-line friction may be examined apart from the reciprocal effects of the general conflict system. Regarded in this way, the data indicated that three conditions were basic to staff-line struggles: (1) the conspicuous ambition and "individualistic" behavior among staff officers; (2) the complication arising from staff efforts to justify its existence and get acceptance of its contributions; and, related to point two, (3) the fact that incumbency of the higher staff offices was dependent on line approval. The significance of these conditions will be discussed in order.

[1] *Inside* their particular staff organization, staff officers also may have authority over their subordinates, but not over production personnel.

[2] To the extent that staff officers influence line policy they do, of course, have a certain *informal* authority.

[3] These plants were in related industries and ranged in size from 4,500 to 20,000 employees, with the managerial groups numbering from 200 to nearly 1,000. Details concerning the plants and their location are confidential. Methodological details concerning an intensive study embracing staff-line relations and several other areas of behavior in one of the plants are given in the writer's unpublished

MOBILE BEHAVIOR OF STAFF PERSONNEL

As a group, staff personnel in the three plants were markedly ambitious, restless, and individualistic. There was much concern to win rapid promotion, to make the "right impressions," and to receive individual recognition. Data showed that the desire among staff members for personal distinctions often over-rode their sentiments of group consciousness and caused intra-staff tensions.

The relatively high turnover of staff personnel [4] quite possibly reflected the dissatisfactions and frustrations of members over inability to achieve the distinction and status they hoped for. Several factors appeared to be of importance in this restlessness of staff personnel. Among these were age and social differences between line and staff officers, structural differences in the hierarchy of the two groups, and the staff group's lack of authority over production.

With respect to age, the staff officers were significantly younger than line officers. This would account to some extent for their restlessness. Being presumably less well-established in life in terms of material accumulations, occupational status, and security, while having greater expectations (see below), and more energy, as well as more life ahead in which to make new starts elsewhere if necessary, the staff groups were understandably more dynamic and driving.[5]

Age-conflict [6] was also significant in staff-line antagonisms. The older line officers disliked receiving what they regarded as instruction from men so much younger than themselves, and staff personnel clearly were conscious of this attitude among line officers. In staff-line meetings staff officers frequently had their ideas slighted or even

---

doctoral thesis, "A Study of Informal Organization Among the Managers of an Industrial Plant" (Department of Sociology, University of Chicago, 1949).

[4] During the period between 1944 and 1950 turnover of staff personnel in these plants was between two and four times as great as that of line personnel.

[5] One might also hypothesize that the drive of staff officers was reflected in the fact that the staff heads and specialists gained their positions (those held when the data were collected) in less time than did members of the line groups. E.g., the 36 staff officers discussed above had spent a median of 10 years attaining their positions, as against a median of 11 years for the first-line foremen, 17 years for the general foremen, and 19 years for the superintendents. But one must consider that some of the staff groups were relatively new (13–15 years old) and had grown rapidly, which probably accelerated their rate of promotions as compared with that of the older line organization.

[6] E. A. Ross, in *Principles of Sociology* (New York: D. Appleton–Century Co., 1938), pp. 238–248, has some pertinent comments on age conflict.

treated with amusement by line incumbents. Whether such treatment was warranted or not, the effects were disillusioning to the younger, less experienced staff officers. Often selected by the organization because of their outstanding academic records, they had entered industry with the belief that they had much to contribute, and that their efforts would win early recognition and rapid advancement. Certainly they had no thought that their contributions would be in any degree unwelcome. This naiveté was apparently due to lack of earlier first-hand experience in industry (or acquaintance with those who had such experience), and to omission of realistic instruction in the social sciences from their academic training. The unsophisticated staff officer's initial contacts with the shifting, covert, expedient arrangements between members of staff and line usually gave him a severe shock. He had entered industry prepared to engage in logical, well-formulated relations with members of the managerial hierarchy, and to carry out precise, methodical functions for which his training had equipped him. Now he learned that (1) his freedom to function was snared in a web of informal commitments; (2) his academic specialty (on which he leaned for support in his new position) was often not relevant [7] for carrying out his formal assignments; and that (3) the important thing to do was to learn who the informally powerful line officers were and what ideas they would welcome which at the same time would be acceptable to his superiors.

Usually the staff officer's reaction to these conditions is to look elsewhere for a job or make an accommodation in the direction of protecting himself and finding a niche where he can make his existence in the plant tolerable and safe. If he chooses the latter course, he is likely to be less concerned with creative effort for his employer than with attempts to develop reliable social relations that will aid his personal advancement. The staff officer's recourse to this behavior and his use of other status-increasing devices will be discussed below in another connection.

The formal structure, or hierarchy of statuses, of the two larger plants from which data were drawn, offered a frustration to the ambitious staff officer. That is, in these plants the strata, or levels of authority, in the staff organizations ranged from three to five as against

[7] Among the staff heads and assistants referred to earlier, only 50 per cent of those with college training (32 of the 36 officers) were occupied with duties related to their specialized training. Among the college-trained of 190 line officers in the same plant, the gap between training and function was still greater, with 61 per cent in positions not related to the specialized part of their college work.

from five to ten in the line organization. Consequently there were fewer possible positions for exercise of authority into which staff personnel could move. This condition may have been an irritant to expansion among the staff groups. Unable to move vertically to the degree possible in the line organization, the ambitious staff officer could enlarge his area of authority in a given position only by lateral expansion—by increasing his personnel. Whether or not aspiring staff incumbents revolted against the relatively low hierarchy through which they could move, the fact remains that (1) they appeared eager to increase the number of personnel under their authority, (2) the personnel of staff groups *did* increase disproportionately to those of the line, and (3) there was a trend of personnel movement from staff to line, rather than the reverse, presumably (reflecting the drive and ambition of staff members) because there were more positions of authority, as well as more authority to be exercised, more prestige, and usually more income in the line.

Behavior in the plants indicated that line and staff personnel belonged to different social status groups and that line and staff antipathies were at least in part related to these social distinctions. For example, with respect to the item of formal education, the staff group stood on a higher level than members of the line. In the plant from which the age data were taken, the 36 staff officers had a mean of 14.6 years of schooling as compared with 13.1 years for 35 line superintendents, 11.2 years for 60 general foremen, and 10.5 years for 93 first-line foremen. The difference between the mean education of the staff group and that of the highest line group (14.6–13.1) was statistically significant at better than the one per cent level. The 270 nonsupervisory staff personnel had a mean of 13.1 years—the same as that of the line superintendents. Consciousness of this difference probably contributed to a feeling of superiority among staff members, while the sentiment of line officers toward staff personnel was reflected in name-calling.

Staff members were also much concerned about their dress, a daily shave, and a weekly hair-cut. On the other hand, line officers, especially below the level of departmental superintendent, were relatively indifferent to such matters. Usually they were in such intimate contact with production processes that dirt and grime prevented the concern with meticulous dress shown by staff members. The latter also used better English in speaking and in writing reports, and were more suave and poised in social intercourse. These factors, and the recreational preferences of staff officers for night clubs and "hot parties," assisted in raising a barrier between them and most line officers.

COMPLICATIONS OF STAFF NEED TO PROVE ITS WORTH

To the thinking of many line officers, the staff functioned as an agent on trial rather than as a managerial division that might be of equal importance with the line organization in achieving production goals. Staff members were very conscious of this sentiment toward them and of their need to prove themselves. They strained to develop new techniques and to get them accepted by the line. But in doing this they frequently became impatient, and gave already suspicious line officers the impression of reaching for authority over production.

Since the line officer regards his authority over production as something sacred, and resents the implication that after many years in the line he needs the guidance of a newcomer who lacks such experience, an obstacle to staff-line cooperation develops the moment this sore spot is touched. On the other hand, the staff officer's ideology of his function leads him to precipitate a power struggle with the line organization. By and large he considers himself as an agent of top management. He feels bound to contribute something significant in the form of research or ideas helpful to management. By virtue of his greater education and intimacy with the latest theories of production, he regards himself as a managerial consultant and an expert, and feels that he must be, or appear to be, almost infallible once he has committed himself to top management on some point. With this orientation, he is usually disposed to approach middle and lower line with an attitude of condescension that often reveals itself in the heat of discussion. Consequently, many staff officers involve themselves in trouble and report their failures as due to "ignorance" and "bull-headedness" among these line officers.

On this point, relations between staff and line in all three of the plants were further irritated by a rift inside the line organization. First-line foremen were inclined to feel that top management had brought in the production planning, industrial relations, and industrial engineering staffs as clubs with which to control the lower line. Hence they frequently regarded the projects of staff personnel as manipulative devices, and reacted by cooperating with production workers and/or general foremen (whichever course was the more expedient) in order to defeat insistent and uncompromising members of the staff. Also, on occasion (see below), the lower line could cooperate evasively with lower staff personnel who were in trouble with staff superiors.

EFFECT OF LINE AUTHORITY OVER STAFF PROMOTION

The fact that entry to the higher staff offices in the three plants was dependent on approval of top line officers had a profound effect on the behavior of staff personnel. Every member of the staff knew that if he aspired to higher office he must make a record for himself, a good part of which would be a reputation among upper line officers of ability to "understand" their informal problems without being told. This knowledge worked in varying degrees to pervert the theory of staff-line relations. Ideally the two organizations cooperate to improve existing methods of output, to introduce new methods, to plan the work, and to solve problems of production and the scheduling of orders that might arise. But when the line offers resistance to the findings and recommendations of the staff, the latter is reduced to evasive practices of getting some degree of acceptance of its programs, and at the same time of convincing top management that "good relations" exist with officers down the line. This necessity becomes even more acute when the staff officer aspires (for some of the reasons given above) to move over to the line organization, for then he must convince powerful line officers that he is worthy.

Staff personnel, particularly in the middle and lower levels, carried on expedient relations with the line that daily evaded formal rules. Even those officers most devoted to rules found that, in order not to arouse enmity in the line on a scale sufficient to be communicated *up* the line, compromising devices were frequently helpful and sometimes almost unavoidable both for organizational and career aims. The usual practice was to tolerate minor breaking of staff rules by line personnel, or even to cooperate with the line in evading rules, and in exchange lay a claim on the line for cooperation on critical issues. In some cases line aid was enlisted to conceal lower staff blunders from the upper staff and the upper line.[8]

[8] Failure of middle and lower staff personnel to "cooperate" with line officers might cause the latter to "stand pat" in observance of line rules at a time when the pressures of a dynamic situation would make the former eager to welcome line cooperation in rule-breaking.

While the staff organizations gave much time to developing new techniques, they were simultaneously thinking about how their plans would be received by the line. They knew from experience that middle and lower line officers could always give a "black eye" to staff contributions by deliberate mal-practices. Repeatedly top management had approved, and incorporated, staff proposals that had been verbally accepted down the line. Often the latter officers had privately opposed the changes, but had feared that saying so would incur the resentment of powerful superiors who could informally hurt them. Later they would seek to discredit the change by deliberate mal-practice and hope to bring a return to the former arrangement. For this reason there was a tendency for staff members to withhold improved production schemes or other plans when they knew that an attempt to introduce them might fail or even bring personal disrepute.

Line officers fear staff innovations for a number of reasons. In view of their longer experience, presumably intimate knowledge of the work, and their greater remuneration, they fear [9] being "shown up" before their line superiors for not having thought of the processual refinements themselves. They fear that changes in methods may bring personnel changes which will threaten the break-up of cliques and existing informal arrangements and quite possibly reduce their area of authority. Finally, changes in techniques may expose forbidden practices and departmental inefficiency. In some cases these fears have stimulated line officers to compromise staff men to the point where the latter will agree to postpone the initiation of new practices for specific periods.

In one such case an assistant staff head agreed with a line superintendent to delay the application of a bonus plan for nearly three months so that the superintendent could live up to the expedient agreement he had made earlier with his grievance committeeman to avoid a "wildcat" strike by a group of production workmen.[10] The lower engineers who had devised the plan were suspicious of the formal reasons given to them for withholding it, so the assistant staff head prevented them (by means of "busy work") from attending staff-

[9] Though there was little evidence that top management expected line officers to refine production techniques, the fear of such an expectation existed nevertheless. As noted earlier, however, some of the top executives *were* thinking that development of a "higher type" of first-line foreman might enable most of the staff groups to be eliminated.

[10] This case indicates the over-lapping of conflict areas referred to earlier. A later paper will deal with the area of informal union-management relations.

line meetings lest they inadvertently reveal to top management that the plan was ready.

The third area of staff-line accommodations growing out of authority relations revolved around staff use of funds granted it by top management. Middle and lower line charged that staff research and experimentation was little more than "money wasted on blunders," and that various departments of the line could have "accomplished much more with less money." According to staff officers, those of their plans that failed usually did so because line personnel "sabotaged" them and refused to "cooperate." Specific costs of "crack-pot experimentation" in certain staff groups were pointed to by line officers. Whatever the truth of the charges and counter-charges, evidence indicated (confidants in both groups supported this) that pressures from the line organization (below the top level) forced some of the staff groups to "kick over" parts of the funds appropriated for staff use [11] by top management. These compromises were of course hidden from top management, but the relations described were carried on to such an extent that by means of them—and line pressures for manipulation of accounts in the presumably impersonal auditing departments—certain line officers were able to show impressively low operating costs and thus win favor [12] with top management that would relieve pressures and be useful in personal advancement. In their turn the staff officers involved would receive more "cooperation" from the line and/or recommendation for transfer to the line. The data indicated that in a few such cases men from accounting and auditing staffs were given general foremanships (without previous line experience) as a reward for their understanding behavior.

SUMMARY

Research in three industrial plants showed conflict between the managerial staff and line groups that hindered the attainment of organizational goals. Privately expressed attitudes among some of the higher line executives revealed their hope that greater control of staff groups could be achieved, or that the groups might be eliminated and

[11] In two of the plants a somewhat similar relation, rising from different causes, existed *inside* the line organization with the *operating* branch of the line successfully applying pressures for a share in funds assigned to the *maintenance* division of the line.

[12] The reader must appreciate the fact that constant demands are made by top management to maintain low operating costs.

their functions taken over in great part by carefully selected and highly remunerated lower-line officers. On their side, staff members wanted more recognition and a greater voice in control of the plants.

All of the various functioning groups of the plants were caught up in a general conflict system; but apart from the effects of involvement in this complex, the struggles between line and staff organizations were attributable mainly to (1) functional differences between the two groups; (2) differentials in the ages, formal education, potential occupational ceilings, and status group affiliations of members of the two groups (the staff officers being younger, having more education but lower occupational potential, and forming a prestige-oriented group with distinctive dress and recreational tastes); (3) need of the staff groups to justify their existence; (4) fear in the line that staff bodies by their expansion, and well-financed research activities, would undermine line authority; and (5) the fact that aspirants to higher staff offices could gain promotion only through approval of influential line executives.

Harold L. Wilensky

The Trade Union as a Bureaucracy

The emergence of the staff expert in large-scale organizations, public and private, has been seen as the epitome of the bureaucratic trend in the modern world. Weber's classic account of the ideal-type bureaucracy emphasized these characteristics:

1. Minute division of labor and a clear-cut hierarchy of authority: the offices are clearly defined, have regular activities governed by impersonal rules, and are set off by fixed, official jurisdictional areas.
2. The offices are filled by full-time, appointed officials. The officials are recruited on the basis of technical qualifications ascertained through formal, impersonal procedures (e.g., tests).

Reprinted in part from *Intellectuals in Labor Unions,* pp. 243–258, by permission of the author and the publisher, The Free Press. Copyright 1956.

3. The technical specialists who fill the offices are autonomous within their sphere of competence.

4. They are politically neutral professionals whose performance of duty is independent of personal sentiments and opinions.

5. Such faithful performance of duty is assured by the rewards of stable careers: regular salary, expectation of promotion, more responsibility, salary advance, secure tenure, and a pension.

To what extent does the modern union—as seen from the perspective of its staff experts—share these characteristics of bureaucracy? In what direction do typical patterns of union administration move?

Both from the objective side (the patterns of headquarters organization, the decision-making procedures) and from the subjective side (the work experience and role orientations of the experts), the data present a picture of slowly growing, but as yet embryonic bureaucracy.

BUREAUCRACY: HEADQUARTERS ORGANIZATION

The Formal Channels

The fact that unions are big does not mean that unions are bureaucratized. The frequent reiteration of the old cliché that "the union is a political institution" attests to the fact that the forms of control and the bases of legitimation of leadership authority do not always conform to the Weberian model. There may be a world-wide trend toward rationalization of the means of administration; but the union leader is slow and sometimes reluctant to join. Still, he does join; some signs of embryonic bureaucracy are there. This section examines some of these signs in so far as they are relevant to a description of the channels of influence available to the staff expert.

The bureaucratization process goes forward most clearly in the national headquarters of a few large unions. One clue to it is the frequent, sometimes nostalgic, recollections of functionaries who have been around since the early days. "The functions have been more clearly defined," says one. "More and accurate records are kept of the work of the Department." (Questionnaire.) An old-timer in another union: "In the old days . . . I'd get into everything. Now things are different. We're really big business—specialized. I wouldn't dare try to interpret a contract today—except my section of it!"

Scattered throughout my interview data is talk of problems of "clearance," "jurisdiction," "good departmentalization" (or bad), "overlapping activity," the need for "joint staff meetings," etc. "The union is no longer run on a Saturday night supper basis," says one expert in a big organization.

> The [President] is beginning to recognize bailiwicks and refers letters for drafting replies to appropriate department heads. It's no longer a group of stray people who meet at a bar or at a house party and decide on what the next move is. We're beginning to shake down organizationally.

Even experts in unions only a few years old describe a process of routinization and specialization of their work.

Policy Meetings.—The increasing formalization of administrative behavior in these few large unions makes the formal channels of communication somewhat more prominent in the work of their staff experts. Regular department head meetings, executive board meetings, policy committee meetings, meetings of the "Braintrust," formal negotiation sessions, three-way phone conversations, "progress meetings," progress reports, inter-office memoranda—in a few unions these are places where the expert's voice is heard.

The Pressure Screener.—Aside from direct contact with policy-making boards, committees, and officials via memo or conference, there is in some unions a relatively new formal channel—or block, as the case may be. In large unions with highly developed departmentalization, the staff expert must cope with a series of functionaries assigned to watch over him and his expenditures: administrative assistants to the President, who channel important mail, pass out assignments, screen out the pressures (including those from the experts), do the follow-through work, the trouble-shooting, etc. They "smooth the situation over" when the situation gets out of hand; they apply the policy when the policy doesn't apply itself. They "try to make the job of the boss as easy as possible." They protect him from pressures and at the same time try to keep him from losing touch.

These men have more to do than watch the experts, but they constitute one of the principal formal channels for reaching the boss.[1] The expert may have a proposal he wants to put over. He can

[1] Sometimes they are officials from the line organization who are given department head titles, and assigned to act as liaison between the top officer and the staff people who do the work of the departments.

ask the boss' right-hand man what the boss would think of his proposal and get an accurate preview of his chances. For the administrative assistant works very closely with the top officer, knows his problems and moods, understudies his administrative style. "In fact," comments one expert, "it's hard to tell where X [Administrative Assistant] begins and Y [top officer] ends. I sometimes find myself wondering 'Shall I take it to X or Y?' "

In a few unions, the "Secretary-Treasurer" or the "Executive Secretary" or the "Executive Vice President" or the "Executive Assistant to the President" combines the duties of administrative assistant and the duties of chief financial officer—in which case he constitutes a formidable check on the discretion of the expert, for "Housekeeping" plainly overlaps "Policy-making." For example, the Internal Communications Specialist wants to set up a program that requires staff work in the field. This costs money—per diem expense, travel allowance, etc. The financial functionary calculates the cost. He says, "You'll run way over." "So"—as the expert involved in this little drama states —"we sit down with him and discuss questions of the duration of field work, the kind of program possible—policy questions."

"Clearance."—Whether through an administrative assistant or directly, the mechanism of "clearance" is often a channel of influence and support for the expert. "Having decided on a policy," says one expert, "I wanted them to be identified with it. So I cleared." Several respondents report the conviction that some officer "doesn't give a damn for the program," but tolerates it because of careful "clearance" and a previous involvement in the planning stage.

The Ecology of "Experting."—Communication requires access; and personal accessibility is often a matter of physical proximity. In the big unions the floor layout, the simple office location, may be an important factor in (1) the expert's degree of influence; (2) his ability to keep in touch, and hence to know the channels and possibilities of influence. Several experts are convinced that their sheer physical distance from the boss is a limiting factor on their influence. One traced the changes wrought by expansion of the union's headquarters:

> Because it was small, we ["professionals"] were involved in everything. . . . Now you can't possibly know everything that's going on—just the physical arrangements alone would prevent it. We have a standard joke around here: When we were [in a smaller] building you met [the top officer] in the john and could learn what's going on. Here

> we have a john on each floor! Actually it's more serious than funny. . . . There tends to be a tendency towards close contact by floors. The [nth] floor lunches together more and more.

Of course, physical distance, when coupled with a long and close personal association, high prestige and indispensability, may not lessen the expert's influence on important matters, but it does stack the cards against the kind of sustained, day-to-day influence achieved by some experts lodged in that office next door.

The Informal Channels

The beginnings of bureaucratization are there. But, as we have said, it is a process that comes to the trade unions only slowly. The examples above emphasize more what is in store for the unions than what is dominant now. Typically, the division of labor in the national headquarters is still not sharp, the hierarchy of authority not clear-cut. Jobs are loosely defined; jurisdictional areas, even if official, are blurred and shifting. It tries the patience of the participants to figure out the office hierarchy. I use the word "typically" advisedly—for whatever the size of the union, its age, its politics, or the length of time it has used experts, and whatever the role orientation of the expert, the picture seems to apply. Fifty-six staff experts of all types—over 43 per cent of our Main Sample—reported frustrations due to the absence of clear-cut or uniform administrative procedures, policies, hierarchy of authority or jurisdictional areas; or complained of clogged lines of communication.[2] Many more described a lack of rational, efficient, impersonal bureaucratic organization, but did not find it distasteful. This picture of "administrative chaos" is given emphasis by the fact that it applies in every respect—ambiguous and loose definition of job, division of labor, hierarchy of authority—to the union with the most thoroughly developed departmentalization.[3] "It's a very loose arrangement," says one functionary in this union.

> It depends on . . . an inexplicit mutual understanding which is thoroughly ambiguous. Some [union functionaries we can't deal with]

[2] All comments were either unelicited or in response to general open-ended questions on "what gets in your hair"—so this response is impressive. The comments were so distributed among role orientation types and unions that they may be assumed to reflect typical patterns of union administration.

[3] For example, all department heads in this union were asked for the kinds of things they clear with X. Everyone felt he had to clear expenditures with X, but no two respondents agreed on "expenditures above what figure" and several named a top figure beyond which they would go to someone else.

> without explicit instructions . . . others we can deal with without checking with anybody. A guy like Y will know which are which. You have to live in it, get absorbed by it, know it inside and out. . . . It's a labyrinth with respect to the chain of command. So many traditions have grown up—so many shared experiences—that ways of working together have evolved that can't be pinned down.

In the absence of clear-cut job duties, fixed jurisdictional areas and neat lines of authority, a premium is put upon skill in the use of the informal channels of communication and influence. "Guys in the national office in this organization," one expert observed, "have to make their own way. . . . You carve out what you can and reach who you can reach."

The Personal Relationship and Direct Access.—There is no more widely and strongly held conviction among the union staff experts than the idea that their personal relationship with the boss—the "confidence" the line officials have in them, their informal contacts with key officers on and off the job—is the crucial determinant of their influence. Typical comments from functionaries in a variety of unions, new and old, large and small, indicate this. . . . Whether they find the process comfortable or not, the experts recognize the importance of the thousands of casual deliverances of opinion in sustained, direct, informal contact with the boss and other line officials.

Indirect Informal Channels: The Use of a Third Party.—Some of the most effective informal channels of expert influence are indirect. If you can't reach the boss with a memo or through direct conversation, reach him through a third party.

The first channel is obvious:

> You plant your ideas with one officer rather than another—and expect him to carry the ball for you. [Officer no. 2] is less harrassed by broader union problems than [officer no. 1]. He's also less conservative on some things. . . . There are times where it's best [no. 2] instead of [staff expert] present the case to [no. 1].

The use of a more influential staff expert—e.g., one who is temporarily in favor, or has not recently bothered the boss—is also common. When the expert has much contact with the local activists and lower line officials, he is also in a position to build up pressure from below if he encounters resistance in headquarters. "I get what I want, anyway," says an Internal Communications Specialist, "by nurturing a demand from the field. . . ."

Less obvious are the expert-fostered pressures from the outside. Plant the idea with a government bureaucrat, a college professor, a politician who sees the boss in his more receptive moods. In return, feed him a little harmless "inside dope" that will help him in his work or prompt him to bring up the problem when he sees the boss.

Another *sub rosa* area of influence stems from the demands the third party may put on the expert. How often this occurs is an open question, but these two examples illustrate the point.

> Someone in the White House wanted a real feel as to what's going on; they called in [union staff experts] informally. . . . The way they figured [in the White House] is why take it up with the officers—the kid is going to write it anyway. There are situations where the office boy is a more efficient source!

The second example concerns an arbitrator who similarly used the staff expert to feel out the union's position. Reams of data had been submitted, lengthy written testimony and argument concluded. "Nobody could go through this tremendous pile . . . nobody," reports a participant. So——

> Two or three days after the hearings were concluded, the arbitrator came to me [expert] and said, "I want to ask you to clarify this table for me" (it was the critical table—one on productivity). "Would it be right if I said you had an increase of productivity of 15 per cent?" Then, I happen to know, he went to the employer and asked if he would clarify this table. "Would it be right if I said there's been a 10 per cent increase?" After having felt us both out he gets the difference between 10 and 15 and he splits it, awards 12.5 per cent. Is that economic interpretation I made a matter of research or of policy? The fact is, it's a policy matter! . . . That's an area of decision on the part of the [staff expert] that never appears in the record. He'd never admit he's feeling us out. He's not going to [the union officer] and say what will you take; he goes to the [staff expert]. He's an honest man. I knew he wouldn't betray the fact that I didn't read the table for him but on the basis of what observations I could make, interpreted the officers' limits for him. In that brief moment and within those narrow limits, I as [staff expert] had an effect on the outcome.

Another third-party channel of influence—more important and more pervasive than the friendly outsider—is the female contingent in the headquarters building and around the boss. The well-known "office wife" who protects the busy executive from unimportant people, picks up after him, shares his secrets, knows his weaknesses—this figure is not confined to the business world.

> His secretary was one of my principal problems when I came on—creating a good relationship with her. She figured like most private secretaries, "If you don't tell 'em anything you can't get in any trouble." I had a helluva time finding out what was going on. It took her and me two years before she became convinced I could be trusted.

The union leader's private secretary can be a source of much grief for the staff expert, or she can be a powerful support. For it is her job to decide whom the boss will see, whose memo gets on top of the pile, whose problem gets mentioned at the most propitious moment. The secretary is a key point of transmission on the grapevine, and can slant the content of the rumors that pass along it. But the crucial facts that make her a force for the expert to contend with are these: (1) the white-collar girls in the union are typically among the few females on an almost all-male payroll; and (2) unions often recruit the wives and relatives of loyal unionists for the clerical jobs. These white-collar girls easily establish liaisons of friendship or marriage—if they don't already have relations of blood—with visiting line officials. They sometimes acquire a better "base" than the staff expert can build. In fact, there are cases in which the office girls have been able to invoke the ultimate sanction against a staff expert, i.e., get him fired.

Not only the office wife, but the wife at home—the expert's wife and the officers' wives and the wives of one's colleagues—may play a role as a channel of influence. This occurs where the off-the-job social life of the inner staff and line officials is close-knit. The expert's position may be much affected by the performance of his wife in these off-the-job cliques.[4]

Smooth channel or rock-like blockade, the females with steady access to the boss must be counted as an important part of the communication system in the modern union; they often comprise for the expert an important indirect way to reach the top man.

In sum: the formal channels of influence are increasingly prominent in the work of staff experts in the larger unions. But typically,

[4] Compare the role of the business executive's wife as reported by William H. Whyte, *Is Anybody Listening* (New York: Simon and Schuster, 1952), pp. 146–205. Though the dilemmas posed by the social correlates of career climbing in industry are absent in the smaller staff hierarchies of the union world, the "union widow" must have many of the qualities Whyte finds in the business wife: adaptability, discretion, gregariousness and corporation [labor] identification. For a penetrating essay on the private secretary's relations with the union officer, see Kermit Eby, "In a Man's Shadow," *Mademoiselle,* 35 (Sept., 1952), 100–1, 161–163.

the aspects of bureaucracy we have discussed are not yet well developed: the division of labor, the definition of the job, the jurisdictional areas, and the hierarchy of authority remain fluid and loose.

As for autonomy within his sphere of competence, this is the exception, not the rule. In fact, the expert who moves out of his sphere of competence is more likely to acquire maximum leeway and autonomy. Hence the great load on the informal channels and ways of influence. To reach the boss, you cultivate his confidence in informal, direct contacts on and off the job; or you work indirectly through a third party who has his ear—other labor functionaries, local union activists, prestigeful outsiders, the female contingent at headquarters or in the inner-circle social clique.

BUREAUCRACY: RECRUITMENT AND TRAINING

A similar picture of slowly growing, but still embryonic, bureaucracy emerges from analysis of recruitment and other personnel practices. Data on how the experts got their jobs suggest that, in a substantial proportion of the cases, the method of selection involved no necessary demonstration of competence in a "technical" specialty (broadly defined).[5] However, the trend seems to be toward less casual recruitment. This is reflected, for example, in the fact that the Facts and Figures Men hired in the postwar period have more previous training and relevant occupational experience than those hired before 1945. The emergence of the synthetic rank-and-filer and the increased number of officers with "sea lawyer" inclinations or college background parallel this development.

Similar, too, is the picture of changes in the outlook of the experts recruited. The data suggest broadly that the rising labor movement attracted both Party Missionary and Rank-and-File Careerist types from the beginning; the Legislative-Liberals and Outsider-Careerists came along a bit later (over half in World War II or later); the Professional Service types were recruited when the movement had matured and organizational stability had been achieved.

The trend in recruitment is also seen in (1) the comments of

[5] Of 156 cases, some previous demonstration of competence was indicated in 51.2%; no such demonstration in 30.9%; no information in 17.9%. The most frequent ways to get a staff expert job are (1) general activity in local union or radical party politics (excluding specialized work); (2) contact through a government labor agency; (3) demonstration of "technical" skill in union work, usually at the local level; (4) contact as an independent consultant serving labor.

union leaders and other union people, and (2) scattered instances where hiring and training practices are approaching the bureaucratic model.

Several top officials note the drying up of some old sources of union staff people—the labor schools such as Brookwood Labor College (which in its dozen years turned out scores of men who moved into union jobs, both elective and appointive), the Rand School, Commonwealth College, etc.; the radical youth groups or political parties (ex-YPSL's for instance, constitute a large number of my sample of staff experts); various units of the workers' education movement on the periphery of the labor movement (American Labor Education Service, the WPA Workers' Education Service, the Wisconsin School for Workers, Hudson Shore Labor School, etc.). Fifteen years ago young men drawn from these sources would go to work for a union with much enthusiasm and little pay. Today the top officers say they are not so sure they can depend on "idealism" to attract and keep either their staff experts or their line officials. A hint of things to come, perhaps, is seen in advertisements recently run by the ILGWU-AFL: "*TRADE UNION CAREER* with *POSITION GUARANTEED.* Free Tuition. The International Ladies Garment Workers' Union Training Institute offers an opportunity to men and women interested in making service to the trade-union movement their life work. . . . Applicants must be in the 21–35 age group. All students completing the year's work are guaranteed a position with the ILGWU. . . . *ACT NOW!*" [6] This training Institute, established in its fiftieth year by a union once staffed largely from the ranks of the socialist movement, aims to train future organizers, business agents, managers, officers as well as staff experts.[7] . . .

The young man who wanted a starting job as a Facts and Figures Man a few years ago was told to go into the shop, get some union experience, volunteer on a picket line. Today, though the probabilities are still high that he would get that advice, in at least two unions he might be given a formal written examination as a preliminary screening. A few years ago no union would think of using the want ad columns for recruitment purposes. But recently, the ILGWU offers of "union careers" with "position guaranteed" have been matched by

[6] Advertisement in *ADA World,* Vol. 8, No. 1 (Jan., 1953), 4.

[7] International Ladies' Garment Workers' Union, *Report of the General Executive Board to the 27th Convention,* May 23–June 1, 1950, pp. 226–27. For general description of the Institute see Arthur Elder, "The ILGWU Training Institute," *Industrial and Labor Relations Review,* 3 (July, 1950), 627–29.

other unions: the TWUA-CIO has advertised in commercial papers for auditors, the Airline Pilots-AFL for a statistician and research director ("University graduate. Must be an aggressive, capable, responsible individual. Steady employment with progressive organization."[8]); the UAW-CIO, anticipating expansion of its negotiated health and disability insurance programs, circularized for "Group Insurance Consultant" and "Health and Welfare Program Administrators"—with the accent on persons with "transferable training and experience" who seek "advancement and professional growth." One union executive has even used a regular employment agency to recruit staff representatives.

While these attitudes and practices presage a new look in recruitment patterns, there are very strong resistances to bureaucratic ways, and the less systematic, less formal methods are still dominant, though the criteria of selection are clearly changing. In brief, the resistances include: (1) favorable union views of nepotism; (2) traditional requirements that union payrollers have shop-experience—and the attitudes these reflect; (3) traditional political criteria for selection of all staff; (4) the problem of what to do with incumbent old-timers when union needs change. The weight of their past character as a protest movement is very much with the unions. The barriers to bureaucratic ways of recruitment are similar to the resistances to bureaucratic behavior in other aspects of union administration and have a common root in the institutional pressures to which all union functionaries are sensitive.

THE BUREAUCRATS: ROLE ORIENTATION, CAREER PROSPECTS AND INFLUENCE

If bureaucratic tendencies are growing but slowly in headquarters organization and recruitment, what of the subjective side of bureaucracy—the mentality and outlook of the bureaucrats themselves?

The central tendency, as was evident in the discussion of role orientation, is toward the Professional Service type. But this professionalization process, pointing toward a future where most union experts will fit the image of the politically neutral, technically equipped bureaucrat, should not obscure the fact that as yet most of the incumbents deviate significantly from the Weberian model. Of the 126 typed by role orientation, only thirty-one are Technician

[8] *Chicago Tribune,* November 16, 1947.

Professionals and share neatly the characteristics of the professional bureaucratic type. The twelve Politicos and thirty-two Careerists are also means-centered, easily adaptable to shifting organizational goals, but they lack any dedication to the professional norms of objectivity and independence. Most important, however, are the fifty-one cases—twenty-nine Missionaries and twenty-two Program Professionals—who see the union as a vehicle for the promotion of some strongly held ideas; though the focus of the latter's interest in program impact is relatively narrow, both groups are policy-oriented. Moreover, when we examine the influence ratings of the staff experts, the relatively high influence of the Missionaries and Politicos suggests a low degree of bureaucratization—on the assumption that the character of a social group is reflected in the orientations of its successful men. Thus, on the subjective side, the bureaucratization process has begun, but its progress is still slow.

What about the rewards of bureaucratic compliance—can the union employee look forward to a stable career? What are the practices and expectations on promotion and tenure? Here is one of the sharpest deviations from rationalized bureaucratic procedures. A change in top union leadership typically brings a shake-up all the way down the line. The personal loyalty imperative makes the staff man's tenure dependent largely on the tenure of the man who hired him.

As for incremental salaries and regularized promotion procedures—these are typically missing. For one thing, the staff-expert hierarchies in unions using many experts are flat—with little possibility for the assistants to move into the departmental directorship, and nowhere else for the department director to go. Many of those interviewed in the lower positions called attention to the relatively high turnover among professionals below department head in several unions and attribute it to low morale among them. Not only are they confined to the less challenging work, but they typically see little chance of moving up within the union. Mobility for the subordinate, as for the department chief, tends to be horizontal—with "promotion" taking the form of a move to a more desirable union. And both the top expert and his subordinates are, with some exceptions, limited to a salary ceiling set by the top officer's Convention-determined level, which seldom matches the corporation counterpart. The distance between top and bottom salaries for professionals in unions tends to be slim, with good starting salaries but small prospects for salary advance and no system for increases.

This does not mean that there are no exceptions to the rule of unstable tenure or that no unit in the labor movement has a civil service mentality on the matter of promotions. One staff expert got himself a four-year contract with an arbitration clause attached to protect against an impending shift in leadership. Some of the older stable unions with no factionalism on a national level provide reasonable expectation of lifetime tenure for their staff—and in some cases, never fire anyone who has long service (new positions may be created to take care of the loyal aged).[9] If we include consideration of non-expert staff and line employees, the exceptions grow numerous—and the trend is clearly toward more bureaucratic administration. The large clerical and subprofessional staffs are typically organized into unions and operate under contracts comparable to those in corporate bureaucracies, with formalized salary structures, promotion systems, pension and insurance arrangements, etc. Lines of promotion for the administrative and organizing personnel may also be fairly clear. Unofficial organizations among the international representatives sometimes exist to regularize employment relations with the union. In one union, the spokesmen of such a group actually bargain on key issues with the top officer and present demands at union conventions. At a recent convention they demanded an increase in their home base per diem in return for a decrease in their out-of-town per diem, and got it.

Whatever the trend, and despite the exceptions noted, the career outlook of the staff expert—his expectations on promotions, salary advance, security of tenure and the other marks of bureaucratic reward—is still typically uncertain, and his role orientation in most cases deviates significantly from that of the bureaucratic professional. And the role orientations of the most successful experts do not reflect a bureaucratic mentality.

In sum: whether we consider objective patterns of organization, recruitment, and reward (tenure, promotion and salary practices), or the subjective orientations and career expectations of the staff experts, or the characteristics of those who are selected for high influence, the picture is one of slowly growing, but as yet embryonic bureaucracy. Much of the explanation for this picture lies in the social psychological content of the trade union leader's role as it develops through time, and the kind of working climate the pres-

[9] Yet—even in these stable unions—some of the staff experts are convinced they'd be the first to go if the union faced hard times.

sures on him foster. This working climate cross-cuts all functional and role orientation types, all influence positions.

Alfred H. Stanton
and
Morris S. Schwartz

The Mental Hospital and the Patient

The systematic study of *personality functioning as a part of institutional functioning* in the mental hospital began perhaps with the work of Harry Stack Sullivan at Sheppard and Enoch Pratt Hospital, in Towson, Maryland, 1929–1931 [1] Sullivan organized there an admission ward designed about the problems of the care and treatment of young male schizophrenic patients in an acute state. Unfortunately, Sullivan did not publish the organizational details of this remarkably successful ward; rather, his experiences on the ward led him to reformulate the problems of psychiatry as a whole. The resultant publications represent his first attempts to formulate psychiatry as a study of interpersonal relations, to treat "personality" and the "dynamisms" which form it as relatively enduring patterns of interpersonal relations, a point of view which he later developed more fully. However, interspersed among the more general statements, these papers do contain some comments on the nature of the ward organization. In particular, mention is made of the fact that the results were not obtained by special tricks, but rather by the functional organization as a whole.

Sullivan spent much of his time talking to, working with, the ward

Reprinted in part from *The Mental Hospital: A Study of Institutional Participation in Psychiatric Illness and Treatment,* pp. 13–24, by Alfred H. Stanton, M.D., and Morris S. Schwartz, Ph.D.

[1] Harry Stack Sullivan, "Socio-psychiatric Research: Its Implication for the Schizophrenia Problem and for Mental Hygiene," *Am. J. Psychiat.,* X (1931), 977–991; "The Modified Psychoanalytic Treatment of Schizophrenia," *ibid.,* XI (1931), 519–540.

staff. By implication, some of his remarks are bitterly critical of current hospital organization. In almost all possible aspects the ward was, or seemed to be, carefully insulated from the rest of the hospital. Later Sullivan reviewed those aspects of the more usual mental hospital that are probably helpful to its patients.[2]

> . . . the severity of any mental disorder is to an important degree a result of insecurity about one's status. . . . This part of the problem would be solved by removing the patient to a society in which vertical mobility is not possible. Just this, in effect, is achieved by his admission to the custodial institution.

Hospitalization often removes the patient from increasingly unfortunate interpersonal situations, and, if classification of patients is adequate (this may be impossible in smaller hospitals), surrounds him with other patients who act very much as he does. Sullivan finds the more or less rigidly enforced ordering of life by the clock rather beneficial than otherwise. But he goes on to stress the therapeutic potentialities of special communities to avoid such a drastic change in social situation as admission to a hospital. Throughout his practice and descriptions, he seems to speak primarily of the patient in an acute state, and to give only marginal consideration to the structure of the patient community within the hospital.

The next important work is reported in two studies by Rowland,[3] who was the first to describe clearly the fact that patients in a mental hospital organize themselves in an informal way for learning about events in the hospital, for mutual instruction on how to deal with physicians in staff conferences, on how to keep up appearances before physicians, and for other purposes related to their course in the hospital and in all likelihood to their illness. Rowland also describes the formal staff hierarchy and the fact that it breaks down into (or is supplemented by, depending on one's viewpoint) a series of informal, often clandestine, friendship patterns, dating, influence pulling, and other "unrecognized" aspects of the hospital. His study is of a state hospital; his descriptions permit the reader to contrast the informal organization of a large state hospital ward with that described here.

[2] Harry Stack Sullivan, *Conceptions of Modern Psychiatry* (Washington, D.C.: William Alanson White Psychiatric Foundation, 1947), pp. 111–115.

[3] Howard Rowland, "Interaction Processes in the State Mental Hospital," *Psychiatry*, I (1938), 323–337; and "Friendship Patterns in the State Mental Hospital," *ibid.*, II (1939), 363–373.

But he fails to describe in detail the relation between this informal organization and the clinical course of patients; his study was of a survey nature which may not have permitted the relatively microscopic observation which would bring such matters clearly to light.

Aside from a few brief studies on social interaction in the mental hospital the next important observations came from institutions for children. Anna Freud and Dorothy Burlingham reported on the Hampstead Nursery and its attempt to create "artificial families."[4] They noted that when all the children were cared for by all the attendants, the children showed signs of retarded development and some were slow in overcoming reverses in maturation caused by their separation from home. It was noticed that certain children showed strong preference for certain workers, and, since the workers felt that no favoritism should be shown, this led to many disappointments for the children. To meet these problems a change in the formal organization of the ward was prescribed:

> The step taken was the subdivision of the large nursery group into six small "family groups" of about four children. In assigning the children to their new substitute mothers, we followed the signs of preference shown on the one hand by the children, and on the other hand by the young workers. Each "mother" now has more or less complete charge of her family. She alone bathes and dresses her group, is responsible for their clothes and offers them protection against all the current mishaps of nursery life. There is no necessity any longer to refuse a child special attention of a motherly kind.
>
> The result of this arrangement was astonishing in its force and immediacy. The need for individual attachment for the feelings which had been lying dormant, came out in a rush. In the course of one week all six families were completely and firmly established.
>
> With the realization that their new mother substitute really belonged to them, reappeared as often as she disappeared and had no intention to desert them altogether, the state of frenzy subsided and gave way to a quieter, more stable and comforting attachment. At the same time, the children began to develop in leaps and bounds. The most gratifying effect was that several children who had seemed hopeless as far as the training for cleanliness was concerned, suddenly started to use the pot regularly and effectively.

Clearly, here is an experiment in formal organization of institutions which is a classic.

[4] Anna Freud and Dorothy Burlingham, *War and Children* (New York: International Universities Press, 1943), pp. 156–161.

Further clarification of the relation between the arrangement of an institution and the personality reactions of the children composing it was presented by Bettelheim and Sylvester, who discussed the concept of the therapeutic milieu, with supporting clinical data.[5] They described a syndrome of psychological institutionalism as an emotional deficiency disease occurring in children who have been in a certain kind of institution for a period of time, or who have been shifted from one home to another; its cause they believe to be the "absence of interpersonal relationships" particularly with adults, who have become shadowy figures rather than intimate ones. Determination of his behavior by external rules prevents the child from developing his own controls, deprives him of adequate parental images around which integration may center, and leads to passive submission, without spontaneity or the growth of reality testing in diversified conditions of life.

The authors go on to say that pleasure and tension were felt almost wholly in relation to the children's own bodies and were only very loosely associated with the adults responsible for their care. In contrast, when these children were placed in another milieu where consistency was not primarily represented by impersonal rules but by one person who supervised all of each child's activities, who personified consistency rather than enforcing or preaching it, the children showed a spontaneous growth in tolerating and then enjoying a relationship with an adult; internalization of controls appeared, along with some flexibility and spontaneity. For these children a therapeutic milieu was a *personal* one, where questions of schedule and routine were subservient to highly individualized and spontaneous interpersonal relationships. The picture of "psychological institutionalism," as described by these authors in relation to children, resembles a frequent picture of chronic schizophrenia. The similarity is suggestive to the student of the mental hospital. . . .

An outstanding further development is made by Szurek and his co-workers in two papers which illustrate how problems occurring among staff members are related to the clinical condition of patients.[6] Szurek's manner of working with his staff is in significant contrast to

[5] Bruno Bettelheim and Emmy Sylvester, "A Therapeutic Milieu," *Am. J. Orthopsychiat.*, XVIII (1948), 191–206.

[6] S. A. Szurek, "Dynamics of Staff Interaction in Hospital Psychiatric Treatment of Children," *Am. J. Orthopsychiat.*, XVII (1947), 652–664. S. L. Sheimo, J. Paynter and S. A. Szurek, "Problems of Staff Interaction with Spontaneous Group Formations on a Children's Psychiatric Ward," *ibid.*, XIX (1949), 599–611.

attitudes implicit in many other studies. He first describes systematic staff discussion of all patients. The staff are asked to describe in full detail *and also to interpret* observations not only of the children but of all persons involved in any particular incident. The reasons for this are that frequently the source of the difficulty is revealed through observing all possible details, including the emotional reaction of the nurse or attendant, who is not only the eyes and ears of the doctor, but may be the only person able to understand and deal effectively with a child's attitude at the moment. The most important clue as to treatment may appear in these accounts. After all reports were in, the psychiatrist would then make his own comments, feeling free to express approval or, by implication, disapproval and to admit ignorance frankly. When necessary as a last resort, the psychiatrist explicitly assumed responsibility for difficult chores and management, but, whenever possible, suggestions or clues for dealing with the problems were sought from the nursing staff. Often a decision was the joint achievement of the entire group, and required only the approval of the psychiatrist. Szurek gives case illustrations showing how these conferences sometimes formed turning-points in the patient's course and exerted a cumulative effect toward increased freedom and spontaneity.

The later paper discloses that these conferences also brought new light upon the troublesome phenomenon of spontaneously formed destructive groups in a children's psychiatric ward. Sheimo, Paynter, and Szurek here give a running account of such a group and its concomitants: disagreement between two nurses concerning general policies of management, mounting staff tension, and finally, difficulty between ward personnel on the one side and the superintendents of the hospital and of the power plant on the other. The problem seemed to the authors a result of a plan of the senior psychiatrist, not thoroughly thought out, which implied that the psychiatrist sided with one nurse against the other. They concluded that "no study of the dynamics of a group or of an individual patient on such a ward is complete without the study of the dynamics of staff interaction as well."

Szurek later outlined a point of view toward treatment which takes fully into account the child-staff-family matrix as the unit of study.[7]

[7] S. A. Szurek, "The Family and the Staff in Hospital Psychiatric Therapy of Children," *Am. J. Orthopsychiat.*, XXI (1951), 597–611.

> If hospitalization for the child . . . is considered only as an incident in the course of the total psychotherapeutic work of the staff with the members of the family, in which both sides continuously participate, many practices and attitudes of the hospital staff follow naturally. Contact between parents and the child is not dictated by the staff as to its timing, frequency or duration. . . . The interpersonal milieu in which each psychotherapist of a hospital staff works is composed of all the other members of the staff, who not only in some measure participate in his work with the child and his family, but are also constantly aware of the results of the work at a given stage, both from direct contact with all members of the family and from staff discussions. For this reason, his and their mutual attitudes become another field of influence and of interaction which often acquires considerable importance in the outcome of therapy.

There follows a general discussion of the integration of the team, with its problems of size and consequent social distance between staff members, their varying levels of prestige and responsibility, and the difficulties of communication among them. Szurek emphasizes the importance of intra-staff communication and the integration of open expression and discussion of differences in attitude and opinion which invariably arise among supervisory staff members.

An entirely different and invaluable set of observations was supplied by a study of a mental hospital by Caudill and his colleagues.[8] They used the technique of concealed participant observation, the anthropologist playing the role of patient. They were thus enabled to describe with unapproached detail and vividness the ways in which patients indoctrinated new patients in the role of patient. A listing of these highly complicated expectations of behavior illuminates many psychiatric concepts such as "insight into the fact of illness." For example, patients taught others that

> a patient should not deny the reality of being in the hospital for therapeutic purposes, should give up his defenses and try to bring himself to a middle ground where he neither engaged in extreme regressive behavior nor attempted to carry on life as if the hospital did not exist. Toward other patients, a patient should suspend judgment and attempt to see all sides of a person, sustain and support others, and if requested, try actively to help them with their problems by doing a sort of therapy

[8] William Caudill, Frederick C. Redlich, Helen R. Gilmore, and E. B. Brody, "Social Structure and Interaction Processes on a Psychiatric Ward," *Am. J. Orthopsychiat.*, XXII (1952), 314–334.

with them. . . . A patient should try to believe in the ability and competence of his doctor, cooperate in working with him, and feel that treatment on a "twenty-four-hour a day" basis in the hospital was better than therapy received in the outside world.

The degree of successful adaptation of personal characteristics to the new role of patient, thus actively and continuously defined among the patients themselves, varied considerably; it was related to the degree of personal comfort and to the occasional necessity of going to other wards. The authors emphasize the fact that subtle but extremely important misinterpretations are almost unavoidable because of the hierarchical organization of the hospital. For instance, the snacks organized by the patients for their own enjoyment were of vital significance for them in providing ways of establishing themselves in ordinary adult roles; for the staff, these were often considered mere fads. The findings make perfectly clear that upon a less disturbed ward the patients are highly organized, even though the organization is informal. Among the patients there is considerable pressure toward conformity with the rites and values of this informal group. The staff know little of this set of rites and values, just as the patients know little of the informal organization of the staff. The effect was, according to the authors, that the patient and the staff, as also noted by Rowland, lived "in two entirely separate social worlds, yet . . . in the closest proximity."

This study succeeds in establishing firmly the very great importance of the informal group-living of patients in a relatively undisturbed ward of a mental hospital as one factor determining clinical course.

As increasing sophistication has brought with it greater awareness of the degree to which patients can and do influence each other's behavior as well as that of the staff, practical attempts have been made to formalize this patient organization. "Self-government" has been tried not only in a hospital caring primarily for neurotic patients [9] but the findings of Hyde and Solomon show that it may be much more practical for psychotic patients than it would seem at first glance.[10] Indeed, Zinberg's experience in a large hospital led him to the opinion that under the conditions of a single psychiatrist for a large ward, the

[9] At the Cassell Hospital, Ham Common, Richmond, Surrey; personal communication from T. F. Main.

[10] R. W. Hyde and H. C. Solomon, "Patient Government; a New Form of Group Therapy," *Digest Neurol. and Psychiat.*, XVIII (1950), 207–218.

patients exercised better judgment in deciding which patients should go off the grounds than the psychiatrist had been able to do before a patient organization was set up.[11]

As compared with older articles dealing with hospital administration, recent literature shows a refreshing new point of view. There is an awareness of the fact of interaction, of the importance of the group of which the patient and personnel are parts (in contrast with older attitudes that people "should" become a part of a group), but even more important is a simpler change. Older articles usually speak of patients as if they were the passive objects of treatment, not as active participants in it. In contrast, the newer literature speaks of the patient as one of the whole group; he is included in the traditional "team." Not only does the staff affect him, he also affects it. He is alive, has opinions and has at least a partial ability to regulate himself—and the ability of the staff to regulate themselves is also partial.

This new spirit is nowhere stated more concisely and clearly than by Main in describing the pioneering Northfield Experiment.[12]

> By tradition, a hospital is a place wherein sick people may receive shelter from the stormy blasts of life, the care and attention of nursing and medical auxiliaries, and the individual attention of a skilled doctor. The concept of a hospital as a refuge too often means, however, that patients are robbed of their status as responsible human beings. Too often they are called "good" or "bad" only according to the degree of their passivity in the face of the hospital demand for their obedience, dependency, and gratitude. The fine traditional mixture of charity and discipline they receive is a practiced technique for removing their initiative as adult beings and making them "patients." They are less trouble for the staff. . . .
>
> Within such a setting, health and stability are too often bought at the excessive price of desocialization. . . . Sooner or later the patient, alone and unsupported, must face the difficult task of returning to the society in which he became unstable, and there regain social integration, and a daily sense of values and purpose. This task is no light one for a desocialized man, however healthy he may have become. . . .
>
> Certain matters appear to be plain. The daily life of [the hospital] community must be related to real tasks, truly relevant to the needs and aspirations of the small society of the hospital, and the larger

[11] Personal communication from Norman Zinberg. For a further discussion of self-government, see also Joan Thurston, "The Patients Rule Themselves," *Smith Coll. Stud. Soc. Work,* XXII (1951), 27–51.

[12] T. F. Main, "The Hospital as a Therapeutic Institution," *Bull. Menninger Clin.,* X (1946), 66–70.

society in which it is set; there must be no barriers between the hospital and the rest of society; full opportunity must be available for identifying and analyzing the interpersonal barriers which stand in the way of participation in a full community life.

For Main, the new function of the psychiatrist in such a hospital is that of a "technician among, rather than a superintendent of, his patients." And for the hospital as a whole, "It is doubtful whether the hospital can usefully remain a building within which individual treatment is practiced. Perhaps it should become a therapeutic institution."

Maxwell Jones reports upon experiments in designing institutions about the particular interpersonal handicaps of the patients, a vigorous and imaginative approach to the goal of the therapeutic institution.[13] He describes the social structure of an industrial neurosis unit in a hospital and the treatment program which was founded on the concept of the therapeutic effect of the activity of the group as a whole, together with psychotherapy, special group functions, and the closest possible integration into the neighboring community. Particularly important was the use of local industries for part of the scheduled activities of the patients from the very beginning of their stay, a technique prompted by the occupational handicaps of the patients selected for treatment at the unit. A follow-up study of the discharged patients indicated a very impressive success. Such genuinely appropriate planning of a treatment program, from the broadest strategic point of view to the smallest detail, must surely be a long step toward effective treatment.

[13] Maxwell Jones, *The Therapeutic Community* (New York: Basic Books, 1953).

Howard S. Becker

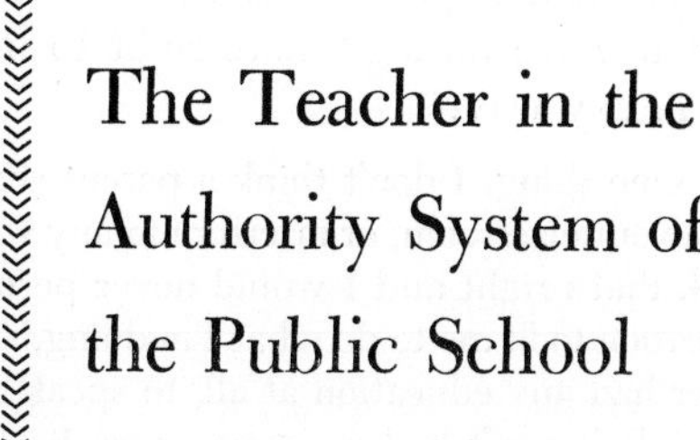

The Teacher in the Authority System of the Public School

This paper deals with the authority problems of the metropolitan public school teacher. I have elsewhere described the problems of the teacher in her relations with her pupils,[1] and will here continue that discussion to include the teacher's relations with parents, principals, and other teachers. The following points will be considered in connection with each of these relationships: the teacher's conception of her rights and prerogatives, her problems in getting and maintaining acceptance of this conception on the part of others, and the methods used to handle such problems. The picture one should get is that of the teacher striving to maintain what she regards as her legitimate sphere of authority in the face of possible challenge by others. This analysis of the working authority system of the public school is followed by a discussion which attempts to point up its more general relevance. The description presented here is based on sixty long and detailed interviews with teachers in the Chicago public schools.[2]

TEACHER AND PARENT

The teacher conceives of herself as a professional with specialized training and knowledge in the field of her school activity: teaching

Reprinted in part from *Journal of Educational Psychology*, 27 (1953), 128–141, by permission of the author and the publisher, Payne Educational Sociology Foundation, Inc.

[1] Howard S. Becker, "Social-Class Variations in the Teacher-Pupil Relationship," *Journal of Educational Sociology*, XXV (April, 1952), 451–465.

[2] Details of method are reported in Howard S. Becker, "Role and Career Problems of the Chicago Public School Teacher" (unpublished Ph.D. dissertation, University of Chicago, 1951).

and taking care of children. To her, the parent is a person who lacks such background and is therefore unable to understand her problems properly. Such a person, as the following quotation shows, is considered to have no legitimate right to interfere with the work of the school in any way:

> One thing, I don't think a parent should try and tell you what to do in your classroom, or interfere in any way with your teaching. I don't think that's right and I would never permit it. After all, I've a special education to fit me to do what I'm doing, and a great many of them have never had any education at all, to speak of, and even if they did, they certainly haven't had my experience. So I would never let a parent interfere with my teaching.

Hers is the legitimate authority in the classroom and the parent should not interfere with it.

Problems of authority appear whenever parents challenge this conception, and are potentially present whenever parents become involved in the school's operation. They become so involved because the teacher attempts to make use of them to bolster her authority over the child, or because they become aware of some event about which they wish to complain. In either case the teacher fears a possible challenge of her basic assumption that the parent has no legitimate voice with regard to what is done to her child in school.

In the first instance, the teacher may send for the parent to secure her help in dealing with a "problem child." But this is always done with an eye to possible consequences for her authority. . . .

Parents may also become involved in the school's operation on their own initiative, when they come to complain about some action of the school's functionaries. Teachers recognize that there are kinds of activity about which parents have a legitimate right to complain, for which they may legitimately be held responsible, although the consequences of the exercise of this right are greatly feared. They recognize, that is, that the community, in giving them a mandate to teach, reserves the right to interfere when that mandate is not acted on in the "proper" manner. Teachers fear that the exercise of this latent authority by parents will be dangerous to them.

One form of this fear is a fear that one will be held responsible for any physical harm that befalls the child:

> As far as the worst thing that could happen to me here in school, I'd say it would be if something awful happened someplace where I was supposed to be and wasn't. That would be terrible.

This, it is obvious, is more than a concern for the child's welfare. It is also a concern that the teacher not be held responsible for that welfare in such a way as to give the parents cause for complaint.

> I've never had any trouble like that when the children were in my care. Of course, if it happens on the playground or someplace where I'm not there to watch, then it's not my responsibility, you see. . . .

Another area in which a similar fear that the parents will exercise their legitimate latent authority arises is that of teaching competence; the following incident is the kind that provokes such fears:

> There was a French teacher—well, there's no question about it, the old man was senile. He was getting near retirement. I think he was sixty-four and had one year to go to retire. The parents began to complain that he couldn't teach. That was true, of course, he couldn't teach any more. He'd just get up in front of his classes and sort of mumble along. Well, the parents came to school and put so much pressure on that they had to get rid of him.

The teachers' fear in these and similar situations is that intrusion by the parents, even on legitimate grounds, will damage their authority position and make them subject to forms of control that are, for them, illegitimate—control by outsiders. . . .

The school is for the teacher, then, a place in which the entrance of the parent on the scene is always potentially dangerous. People faced with chronic potential danger ordinarily develop some means of handling it should it become "real" rather than "potential," some kind of defense. The more elaborate defenses will be considered below. Here I want to point to the existence of devices which teachers develop or grow into which allow them some means of defense in face-to-face interaction with the parent.

These devices operate by building up in the parent's mind an image of herself and of her relation to the teacher which leads her to respect the teacher's authority and subordinate herself to it:

> Quite often the offense is a matter of sassiness or back talk. . . . So I'll explain to the parent, and tell him that the child has been sassy and disrespectful. And I ask them if they would like to be treated like that if they came to a group of children. . . . I say, "Now I can tell just by looking at you, though I've never met you before, that you're not the kind of a person who wants this child to grow up to be disrespectful like that. You want that child to grow up mannerly and polite." Well, when I put it to them that way, there's never any argu-

ment about it. . . . Of course, I don't mean that I'm not sincere when I say those things, because I most certainly am. But still, they have that effect on those people.

In short, the teacher wishes to avoid any dispute over her authority with parents and feels that this can be accomplished best when the parent does not get involved in the school's operation any more than absolutely necessary. The devices described are used to handle the "parent problem" when it arises, but none of them are foolproof and every teacher is aware of the ever-present possibility of a parent intruding and endangering her authority. This constant danger creates a need for defenses and the relations of teacher and principal and of teachers to one another are shaped by this need. The internal organization of the school may be seen as a system of defenses against parental intrusion.

TEACHER AND PRINCIPAL

The principal is accepted as the supreme authority in the school:

> After all, he's the principal, he is the boss, what he says should go, you know what I mean. . . . He's the principal and he's the authority, and you have to follow his orders. That's all there is to it.

This is true no matter how poorly he fills the position. The office contains the authority, which is legitimated in terms of the same principles of professional education and experience which the teacher uses to legitimate her authority over parents.

But this acceptance of superiority has limits. Teachers have a well-developed conception of just how and toward what ends the principal's authority should be used, and conflict arises when it is used without regard for the teachers' expectations. These expectations are especially clear with regard to the teacher's relationships with parents and pupils, where the principal is expected to act to uphold the teacher's authority regardless of circumstances. Failure to do this produces dissatisfaction and conflict, for such action by the principal is considered one of the most efficient defenses against attack on authority, whether from parents or pupils.

The principal is expected to "back the teacher up"—support her authority—in all cases of parental "interference." This is, for teachers, one of the major criteria of a "good" principal. . . .

This necessity for support is independent of the legitimacy of the teacher's action; she can be punished later, but without parents knowing about it. And the principal should use any means necessary to preserve authority, lying himself or supporting the teacher's lies:

> You could always count on him to back you up. If a parent came to school hollering that a teacher had struck her child, Mr. D—— would handle it. He'd say, "Why, Mrs. So-and-So, I'm sure you must be mistaken. I can't believe that any of our teachers would do a thing like that. Of course, I'll look into the matter and do what's necessary but I'm sure you've made a mistake. You know how children are." And he'd go on like that until he had talked them out of the whole thing.
>
> Of course the teacher would certainly catch it later. He'd call them down to the office and really give them a tongue lashing that they wouldn't forget. But he never failed them when it came to parents.

Not all principals live up to this expectation. Their failure to support the teacher is attributed to cowardice, "liberalism," or an unfortunate ability to see both sides of a question. The withholding of support may also, however, be a deliberate gesture of disapproval and punishment. This undermining of the teacher's authority is one of the most extreme and effective sanctions at the principal's command. . . .

Teachers expect the same kind of support and defense in their dealings with pupils, again without regard for the justice of any particular student complaint. If the students find the principal a friendly court of appeal, it is much harder for the teacher to maintain control over them.[3]

The amount of threat to authority, in the form of challenges to classroom control, appears to teachers to be directly related to the principal's strictness. Where he fails to act impressively "tough" the school has a restless atmosphere and control over pupils is difficult to attain. The opposite is true where the children know that the principal will support any action of a teacher.

> The children are scared to death of her [the principal]. All she has to do is walk down the hall and let the children hear her footsteps and right away the children would perk up and get very attentive. They're really afraid of her. But it's better that way than the other.

[3] Cf. *The Sociology of Georg Simmel*, trans. Kurt Wolff (Glencoe: Free Press, 1950), p. 235: "The position of the subordinate in regard to his super-ordinate is favorable if the latter, in his turn, is subordinate to a still higher authority in which the former finds support."

Such a principal can materially minimize the discipline problem, and is especially prized in the lower-class school, where this problem is greatest. . . .

Conflict arises when the principal ignores his teachers' need for professional independence and defense against attacks on authority. Both principal and teachers command sanctions which may be used to win such a conflict and establish their definition of the situation: i.e., they have available means for controlling each other's behavior. The principal has, as noted above, the powerful weapon of refusing to support the teacher in crucial situations; but this has the drawback of antagonizing other teachers and, also, is not available to a principal whose trouble with teachers stems from his initial failure to do this.

The principal's administrative functions provide him with his most commonly used sanctions. As administrator he allocates extra work of various kinds, equipment, rooms, and (in the elementary school) pupils to his teachers. In each category, some things are desired by teachers while others are disliked—some rooms are better than others, some equipment newer, etc. By distributing the desired things to a given teacher's disadvantage, the principal can effectively discipline her. A subtle use of such sanctions is seen in this statement:

> TEACHER: That woman really used to run the school, too. You had to do just what she said.
>
> INTERVIEWER: What did she do if you "disobeyed"?
>
> TEACHER: There were lots of things she could do. She had charge of assigning children to their new rooms when they passed. If she didn't like you she could really make it tough for you. You'd get all the slow children and all the behavior problems—the dregs of the school. After six months of that you'd really know what work meant. She had methods like that.

Such sanctions are ineffective against those few teachers who are either eccentric or determined enough to ignore them. They may also fail in lower-class schools where the teacher does not intend to stay.[4]

The sanctions teachers can apply to a principal who respect or protect their authority are somewhat less direct. They may just ignore him: "After all if the principal gets to be too big a bother, all you have to do is walk in your room and shut the door, and he

[4] See Becker, "The Career of the Chicago Public School Teacher," *op. cit.*, 472–3.

can't bother you." Another weapon is hardly a weapon at all—making use of the power to request transfer to another school in the system. It achieves its force when many teachers use it, presumably causing higher authorities to question the principal's ability:

> I know of one instance, a principle of that type, practically every teacher in her school asked to leave. Well, you might think that was because of a group that just didn't get along with the new principal. But when three or four sets of teachers go through a school like that, then you know something's wrong.

Finally, the teachers may collectively agree on a line of passive resistance, and just do things their way, without any reference to the principal's desires.

In some cases of extreme conflict, the teachers (some of whom may have been located in the school for a longer period than the principal) may use their connections in the community to create sentiment against the principal. Cooperative action of parents and teachers directed toward the principal's superiors is the teachers' ultimate sanction.

The principal, then, is expected to provide a defense against parental interference and student revolt, by supporting and protecting the teacher whenever her authority is challenged. He is expected, in his supervisory role, to respect the teacher's independence. When he does not do these things a conflict may arise. Both parties to the conflict have at their disposal effective means of controlling the other's behavior, so that the ordinary situation is one of compromise (if there is a dispute at all), with sanctions being used only when the agreed-on boundaries are overstepped.

COLLEAGUE RELATIONS

It is considered that teachers ought to cooperate to defend themselves against authority attacks and to refrain from directly endangering the authority of another teacher. Teachers, like other work groups, develop a sense that they share a similar position and common dangers, and this provides them with a feeling of colleagueship that makes them amenable to influence in these directions by fellow teachers.

Challenging of another teacher so as to diminish her authority is the basic crime:

> For one thing, you must never question another teacher's grade, no matter if you know it's unjustified. That just wouldn't do. There are some teachers that mark unfairly. A girl, or say a boy, will have a four "S" report book and this woman will mark it a "G." . . . Well, I hate to see them get a deal like that, but there's nothing you can do.

Another teacher put it more generally: "For one thing, no teacher should ever disagree with another teacher or contradict her, in front of a pupil." The result in terms of authority vis-à-vis students is feared: "Just let another teacher raise her eyebrow funny, just so they [the children] know, and they don't miss a thing, and their respect for you goes down right away." With regard to authority threats by parents it is felt that teachers should not try to cast responsibility for actions which may provoke parental interference on another teacher.

Since teachers work in separate rooms and deal with their own groups of parents and pupils, it is hard for another teacher to get the opportunity to break these rules, even if she were so inclined. This difficulty is increased by an informal rule against entering another teacher's room while she is teaching. Breaches of these rules are rare and, when they do occur, are usually a kind of punishment aimed at a colleague disliked for exceeding the group work quotas or for more personal reasons. However, the danger inherent in such an action—that it may affect your own authority in some way or be employed against you—is so feared that it is seldom used.

In short, teachers can depend on each other to "act right" in authority situations, because of colleague feeling, lack of opportunity to act "wrong," and fear of the consequences of such action.

DISCUSSION

I have presented the teacher as a person who is concerned (among other things) with maintaining what she considers to be her legitimate authority over pupils and parents, with avoiding and defending against challenges from these sources. In her view, the principal and other teachers should help her in building a system of defenses against such challenges. Through feelings of colleagueship and the use of various kinds of sanctions, a system of defenses and secrecy (oriented toward preventing the intrusion of parents and children into the authority system) is organized.

This picture discloses certain points of general relevance for the study of institutional authority systems. In the first place, an institution like the school can be seen as a small, self-contained system of social control. Its functionaries (principal and teachers) are able to control one another; each has some power to influence the others' conduct. This creates a stable and predictable work setting, in which the limits of behavior for every individual are known, and in which one can build a satisfactory authority position of which he can be sure, knowing that he has certain methods of controlling those who ignore his authority.

In contrast, the activities of those who are outside the professional group are not involved in such a network of mutual understanding and control. Parents do not necessarily share the values by which the teacher legitimates her authority. And while parents can apply sanctions to the teacher, the teacher has no means of control which she can use in return, in direct retaliation.

To the teacher, then, the parent appears as an unpredictable and uncontrollable element, as a force which endangers and may even destroy the existing authority system over which she has some measure of control. For this reason, teachers (and principals who abide by their expectations) carry on an essentially secretive relationship vis-à-vis parents and the community, trying to prevent any event which will give these groups a permanent place of authority in the school situation. The emphasis on never admitting mistakes of school personnel to parents is an attempt to prevent these outsiders (who would not be subject to teacher control) from getting any excuse which might justify their intrusion into and possible destruction of the existing authority system.

This suggests the general proposition that the relations of institutional functionaries to one another are relations of mutual influence and control, and that outsiders are systematically prevented from exerting any authority over the institution's operations because they are not involved in this web of control and would literally be uncontrollable, and destructive of the institutional organization, as the functionaries desire it to be preserved, if they were allowed such authority.

Howard Becker

Four Types of Religious Organizations

1. The social structure known as the ecclesia is a predominantly conservative body, not in open conflict with the secular aspects of social life, and professedly universal in its aims. The phrase "Come out from among them and be ye separate" has no place in the ideology of the genuine ecclesiastic; "Force them to come in" is likely to characterize his thinking. The fully developed ecclesia attempts to amalgamate itself with the state and the dominant classes, and strives to exercise control over every person in the population. Members are *born into* the ecclesia; they do not have to *join* it. It is therefore a social structure somewhat, although remotely, akin to the nation or the state, and is in no sense elective. Membership in an ecclesia is a necessary consequence of birth into a family, folk, or similar structure, and no special requirements condition its privileges.

The ecclesia naturally attaches a high importance to the means of grace which it administers, to the system of doctrine which it has formulated, and to the official administration of sacraments and teaching by official clergy. It is in a very real sense an educational institution which, when functioning properly, trains its youthful members to conformity in thought and practice, and thus fits them for the exercise of the religious "rights" they have automatically inherited.

The ecclesia as an inclusive social structure is closely allied with national and economic interests; as a plurality pattern its very nature commits it to adjustment of its ethics to the ethics of the secular world; it must represent the morality of the respectable majority.

Reprinted in part from Howard Becker, *Systematic Sociology on the Basis of the* Beziehungslehre *and* Gebildelehre *of Leopold von Wiese* (New York: Wiley, 1932), pp. 624–628; reissued with the 1950 preface, Norman Paul Press, 1148 St. Joseph St., Gary, Ind., 1950. This section is, however, of the pen of Mr. Becker only. Reprinted by permission of the author and copyright holder.

Two main varieties of the ecclesia may be distinguished: international and national. The Catholic Church is the most outstanding example of the first, whereas the Lutheran and Anglican varieties illustrate the second.

It should not be supposed, however, that a sharp line can be drawn between the two. Catholicism, nominally international, as a matter of fact is pervaded by a great many minor nationalistic rivalries that sometimes flare out in controversy. French Catholicism, for example, sometimes maintains an attitude of marked aloofness toward the Vatican; just before the Reformation it was so thoroughly detached from the papacy that one could justifiably speak of two Catholicisms: French and "other." When all the necessary qualifications are made, however, there is no doubt that the Catholic ecclesia is much more international in character than is any other.

Lutheranism and Anglicanism, to mention but two varieties of the national ecclesia, are and have been extremely nationalistic; they are types which began to flourish when the isolated sacred structure of the Middle Ages began to give way to the new ethnic cultures born in the Renaissance, soon after the Commercial Revolution shattered the agrarian basis of medieval life.

2. The sect is in marked contrast to the ecclesia. In the first place, it is a relatively small plurality pattern that has abandoned the attempt to win the whole world over to its doctrines; the phrase "Come ye out from among them and be ye separate" is followed literally. It is readily seen that the sect is an elective body which one must join in order to become a member. At bottom, the sect is exclusive in character, appeals to strictly personal trends, and emphasizes ethical demands; it frequently requires some definite type of religious experience as a prerequisite of acceptance. It therefore attaches primary importance to the religious experience of its members prior to their fellowship with the plurality pattern, to the so-called "priesthood of all believers." It frequently rejects an official clergy, preferring to trust for guidance to lay inspiration rather than to theological or liturgical expertness.

In many instances sects are persecuted, but this persecution only reinforces the separatist and semi-ascetic attitude toward the world inherent in the sect as a social structure. At times it refuses participation in the government, at times rejects war and other resort to force, and at times seeks to sever as much as possible the bonds which tie it to the common life of the larger plurality pattern within which it develops. In general, the sect prefers isolation to compromise.

Sects exist in great variety at the present time, but they were to be found even before the period of the Reformation, as evidenced by the Cathari, the Waldensians, the Wyckliffites, and others. Since the Reformation, of course, many such bodies have come into being: Anabaptists, Mennonites, Huguenots, Presbyterians, Baptists, and scores of others dot the pages of history.

3. Denominations are simply sects in an advanced stage of development and adjustment to each other and the secular world. The early fervor of the self-conscious sect has disappeared, as a general thing, by the second or third generation, and the problem of training the children of the believers almost inevitably causes some compromise to be made in the rigid requirements for membership characteristic of the early phases of sectarian development. Thus, for example, the Presbyterians inaugurated the Half-Way Covenant in order that children whose "calling and election" was not yet sure could be held within the fold, with the consequence that in time the greater proportion of professing Presbyterians were those who had gone no further than the Half-Way Covenant. Similarly, the Baptists have gradually lowered the age of "adult baptism" so that at the present time, in some branches of the denomination, it is possible for children only twelve years old to be baptized. Similar instances can be gleaned from the history of almost any sect one cares to name; age inevitably brings compromise.

A further factor in mitigating the mutually exclusive tendency of the sect in Western Christendom is the common opposition of all genuinely Protestant bodies to Roman Catholicism. In the early phases of the Reformation members of rival Protestant sects detested each other just as thoroughly as they detested adherents of "Babylon the Mighty"; the burning of Servetus by Calvin is a case in point. With the passage of time, however, opposition to the common foe has gradually drawn the Protestant sects, especially of the evangelical variety, into a vague sort of mutual adjustment; it is tacitly agreed that Protestants should engage in polemics with Rome rather than with each other. It should not be forgotten, however, that any denomination is a sect in historical origin and doctrine, and only failure or unwillingness on the part of the clergy to emphasize the grounds of division can obscure this fundamental fact.

4. Tendencies toward religion of a strictly private, personal character—tendencies fairly well marked in the sect—come to full fruition

in the cult as here defined. The goal of the adherent of this very amorphous, loose-textured, uncondensed type of social structure is not the maintenance of the structure itself, as in the case of the church and sect, but is that of purely personal ecstatic experience, salvation, comfort, and mental or physical healing. Instead of *joining* a cult, an act which implies the consent of others, one simply chooses to believe particular theories or follow certain practices, and the consent of other members of the cult is not necessary. It therefore verges on the abstract crowd, although its well-marked ideology probably entitles it to a place among the abstract collectivities. The religious mystic of the Catholic or Protestant varieties has marked leanings toward the cult, although his mystical practices may be incorporated in the general body of sanctioned behavior.

The sources of emotional satisfaction for the cult believer lie wholly within himself; the injustices or good fortune which others may suffer affect him, to be sure, but the center of his cosmos is his "I."

Only a highly atomized and essentially secular social order gives rise to extensive cult belief. The frontier cities of Ionia, Athens in the famous fifth century, the cities of the Italian Renaissance, and the urban centers of the modern world have been and are the fertile soil from which new cults arise in rank profusion. The cult is the most ephemeral of all types of religious structure—indeed, it is usually so loosely integrated and so transitory that the term "structure" is almost a misnomer.

Cults frequently are much like sects, and it is extremely difficult to draw a line between the two—just as it is difficult to draw a line between the sect and the denomination. At the same time, the following cults are fairly well marked types: Spiritualism, Theosophy, New Thought, Christian Science, Unity, Buchmanism, and the various pseudo-Hinduism associated with Swamis and Yogis who consent, for a consideration, to carry their message to the materialistic Western World.

5. Organization and Society

»»

Modern society is to a large degree a bureaucratic society; that is, many of its functional requirements—such as allocation of means and social integration—are carried out and controlled by complex organizations. But not only does modern society as a whole tend to be bureaucratic. The most powerful social units which make up modern society are bureaucracies. In addition to big business and big labor, which are often cited in this context, political parties, military organizations, school systems, voluntary associations, and many others make up a good part of the societal web. Finally, some organizations develop into social monsters, which embrace more and more social activities and control so many aspects of the life of their members that they are almost societies in themselves.

The most important organizations, from the viewpoint of the integration of society, are probably the governmental bureaucracies. Both Lipset and Janowitz and his associates study these organizations. Lipset analyzes the effect of the Civil Service on the political stability and changeability of society. Janowitz, Wright, and Delany examine the conditions for administration by consent, i.e., the conditions under which the operation of a governmental bureaucracy maintains rather than decreases social and political integration. Eisenstadt examines the conditions under which societies keep control of bureaucracies, in contrast to conditions under which bureaucracies overwhelm societies. Given the interaction that occurs among large organizations, Dubin and Rossi study the effect of this interaction on the wider social unit in which it takes place. Dubin deals with the effect of union-management relations on society; Rossi, with the effect of interaction of business corporations and voluntary associations on the political structure of a community. Goffman examines organizations which extend the scope of their activities and controls to such a degree that they become societies of a sort in themselves.

Lipset studies the effect of the political orientation of a country's Civil Service on the balance of its social and political powers. Supposedly, the Civil Service maintains a neutral position and serves as a tool in the hands of whoever gains political power. But, Lipset points out, the neutrality of the Civil Service seems to be limited. It is willing to play an instrumental and passive role as long as the change of powers in office is confined to what the leading bureaucrats consider politically and ideologically legitimate. When a new social power, such as the Social Democrats in Western societies, gains political power and ruling position, the Civil Service tends to undermine the effectiveness of the government, and to divert or distort its policies. Such subversion generates an imbalance between the social and political power, which blocks reforms and endangers social stability.

Janowitz, Wright, and Delany study the ways in which the public sees the local public administration. To what degree are the conditions present which enable rule by consent? Four criteria are developed: Does the public have sufficient knowledge about the administration? Does the public feel that its self-interest is preserved? Does the public regard the bureaucracy as guided by principles? And is the prestige of the Civil Service high enough, yet not too high? Forms of imbalance are discussed which arise between the public and the administration, when one or more of these bases of consent are lacking.

The studies of Lipset and Janowitz *et al.* thus complement each other. Lipset studies national public bureaucracies; Janowitz, local public bureaucracies. Lipset traces the effect of the Civil Service on the balance between society and polity; Janowitz, the effect of the orientation of social groups to the Civil Service, on the balance between the polity and society.

Eisenstadt examines the social context in which the bureaucratic sector of society emerges, develops, and expands. The major conditions seem to be a development of *Gesellschaft* orientations (universalistic, specific, etc.) and high differentiation of social systems from one another. Once the bureaucratic sector is fairly established, three forms of relationships between it and society may develop: one, in which the bureaucracy maintains its distinct characteristics, so that it is the reliable servant of social goals and political powers; second, in which the bureaucracy penetrates into more and more spheres of life, and becomes the omnipotent organ of society; third, in which particularistic pressures of various social groups become so intense that the conditions for effective bureaucratic activities are undermined, and its value as an instrumental unit is to a large degree lost. The conditions are specified under which each of the three types of relationships is likely to emerge.

Dubin examines the effect on society of the interaction of two large organizations, and the repercussions of societal changes on the interaction between the two organizations. The interaction of management and labor unions reveals a general tendency toward more and more institutionalized conflict, i.e., conflict taking place in the framework of shared values, accepted procedures, and established traditions. The conflicting parties affect society not only through the outcomes of their conflicts but also through their efforts to influence political processes in order to change the setting in which collective bargaining takes place (e.g., legislation such as the Taft-Hartley Act), and through participation in governmental processes (e.g., control of votes which elect judges).

Rossi finds that two major local branches of national organizations—business corporations and voluntary associations—are the main centers of power in the local community. Their positions and interaction determine to a considerable degree the policy of the community's political bodies. The local municipality reflects the power relations between these organizations and their interests, rather than a power and a policy of its own.

Rossi casts new light on the sources of participation of business leaders in community activities. Business leaders seem to be less concerned with creating an attractive image of their corporation in the eyes of their clients, workers, and the citizens of the community than the public relations ideology would have it, and more motivated by their own political, social, and prestige needs. Here, as on the national level, interaction among organizations makes up much of the web which constitutes the sociopolitical structure. This structure, in turn, takes part in molding more specific relations among the various organizations.

Goffman presents a descriptive characterization and careful analysis of "a social hybrid which is part residential community and part formal organization." The inmates live in such social establishments; in other words, many aspects of their behavior, considered "private" on the outside, are here controlled and supervised by the staff. Inmates, as a rule, do not engage in paid work; they are "taken care of." Having a family is incompatible with the organizational needs and structure. Entrance or exit are usually not voluntary.

The interests in total organizations are many: they have intense effects on the moral orientation of their inmates; they constitute miniature totalitarian societies and as such may enhance research into the mentality and structure of totalitarian regimes. Total organizations tend, even more than other organizations, to divert means from their goals—such as therapy, rehabilitation, education, and religious service—for the purpose of promoting the fulfillment of needs of the staff and organization. Awareness of the special problems involved in these structures may lead to a reconsideration of their use in some situations, and in others to a search for mechanisms which will reduce their negative effects. Thus, while the other writers are interested in the balance between organizations and the society in which they operate, Goffman informs us about the balance between organizations and "societies" which develop in them, a problem which is common to all organizations but which comes into sharp relief in total organizations.

Symour M. Lipset

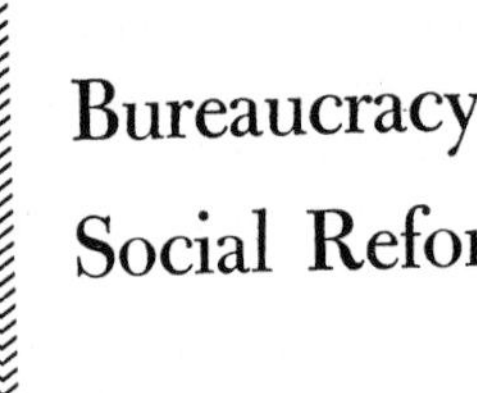

Bureaucracy and Social Reform

Various writers and social scientists have long called attention to the fact that, in large-scale social organizations, administrative functions cannot be separated from policy-making power.[1] It is impossible to understand the operation of a government purely by analyzing the goals of the politicians in power,

Reprinted from *Research Studies, State College of Washington*, 17 (1949), 11–17, by permission of the author and editor.

[1] See Harold Laski, *Democracy in Crisis* (London: George Allen and Unwin, Ltd., 1933), pp. 99–104; Max Weber, *Essays in Sociology*, ed. by H. Gerth and

and the nongovernmental pressures on them. The members of the administrative bureaucracy, the Civil Service, constitute one of the major "Houses" of government, and as such have the power to initiate, amend, and veto actions proposed by other branches. The goals and values of the Civil Service are at least as important a part of the total complex of forces responsible for state policy as those of the ruling political party.

The political problem of the power and influence of a permanent Civil Service is not important as long as the social and economic values of the bureaucracy and the governing politicians do not seriously conflict. The problem becomes crucial, however, when a new political movement takes office and proposes to enact reforms which go beyond the traditional frame of reference of previous government activity. It is especially important today, when the explicit formal goals of many democratic states are changing from the *laissez-faire* policeman regulation of society to those of the social-welfare-planning state.[2]

The tradition and concept of a merit nonpatronage Civil Service developed in many countries as a result of the needs of the dominant business groups which demanded cheap, efficient, and predictable service from the state. Kingsley has shown how in Great Britain, the policy of the impartial Civil Service grew with the increase in political power of the business class.[3] Business men desired an efficient state which would facilitate and protect the development of commerce. Permanent, nonpolitical officials insured continuity of government regulations and practices and made for stable relations with the state, regardless of party fortunes. The policy of the merit Civil Service was not challenged as long as party politics remained contests between groups which accepted the basic orientation and activities of the state and society.[4]

The establishment of reform and socialist governments, which propose radical changes in the functions of the state, necessarily raises the problem of whether the reforms that these governments are pledged to carry out can successfully be initiated and administered by

---

C. W. Mills (New York: Oxford University Press, 1946), pp. 232–233; Herman Finer, *The Future of Government* (London: Methuen and Co., 1946), pp. 12–13.

[2] See J. Donald Kingsley, *Representative Bureaucracy* (Yellow Springs: The Antioch Press, 1944), pp. 287–305.

[3] *Ibid.*, pp. 42–72.

[4] See L. D. White and T. V. Smith, *Politics and Public Service* (New York: Harper and Brothers, 1939), pp. 132–33.

a bureaucratic structure, which is organized to regulate a different set of norms, and whose members possess different values from those of the "radical" politicians.

Since the days of Karl Marx, some socialists have maintained that a successful socialist state "must destroy the old state apparatus," that is, erect a new administrative organization. In recent times, various individuals who have served in or studied socialist or "social welfare" governments have suggested that one crucial reason for their failure to proceed more vigorously toward the attainment of their goals has been the "bureaucratic conservative" influence of permanent Civil Servants. This point has been made about the Social-Democratic governments in Weimar (Germany), the various Labor governments in Great Britain, Australia, and New Zealand, the Popular Front governments in France, and the New Deal in the United States.[5]

The validity of the hypothesis about the "conservative" role of a permanent Civil Service was tested by the author in the course of a research study of a social-democratic movement which secured power towards the end of the last war.

The Cabinet Ministers in this government anticipated "sabotage" and resistance to their plans by the permanent Civil Service. In a pre-election speech, the head of the government stated his belief that the Civil Service must be sympathetic to the objectives of the government:

> It is most necessary for any government that those in charge of various departments shall be competent and capable of absorbing new ideas and techniques. No matter how good legislation is, if those in charge of administering it are unsympathetic or incapable of a new approach, little good will come of it.

The government ministers entered office ready to change key Civil Servants as soon as they showed any signs of opposition to government proposals. The ministers, however, envisaged opposition as deliberate "sabotage" and explicit defiance of government proposals. The key Civil Servants, on the other hand, expected to be discharged

[5] See Arnold Brecht, "Bureaucratic Sabotage," *Annals of American Academy of Political and Social Science* (January, 1937), p. 5; Edgar Lansbury, *George Lansbury, My Father* (London: Sampson Low Masston and Co., Ltd., no date), p. 197; Charles Aiken, "The British Bureaucracy and the Origin of Parliamentary Policy," *American Political Science Review,* XXXIII (Feb., 1939), pp. 40–41; V. G. Childe, *How [Australian] Labour Governs* (London: Labour Publishing Co. Ltd., 1923), p. 16; J. Donald Kingsley, *op. cit.,* p. 274; and Leon Blum, *For All Mankind* (London: Victor Gollanz, 1946), p. 59.

or demoted soon after the socialists took office. A number of them, therefore, had begun to look for other jobs or planned to retire. In the hope of maintaining their positions, however, many of these Civil Servants began to ingratiate themselves with their ministers.

Almost all of the leading Civil Servants were outwardly obsequious, flattered their ministers, and in general did everything they could to convince the Cabinet that they were cooperative. In many departments, during the early period of the new government, the best "socialists" were in the top ranks of the government bureaucracy. The administratively insecure Cabinet ministers were overjoyed at the response which they secured from the Civil Servants. They were happy to find people in their departments who were friendly and helpful. To avoid making administrative blunders which would injure them in the eyes of the public and the party, the ministers gradually began to depend on the Civil Servants, who never criticized and knew the internal operations of the department.

The failure to change key members of the Civil Service had important consequences for the future work of the government, as it was interpreted by many of the officials as revealing personal weakness on the part of their ministers and a lack of political strength on the part of the movement. The Civil Servants, soon realizing that there was no danger of being discharged, fell back into the bureaucratic pattern of maintaining the traditional practices and the equilibrium of their departments. Some Civil Servants succeeded in convincing their ministers that various proposed changes were administratively infeasible, or that they would incur too much opposition from important groups in the community. Top-ranking Civil Servants exchanged information with each other on their techniques of "controlling" their ministers. It is difficult to demonstrate concretely, and it would be revealing confidential information to do so, but it is a fact that in conversations with others, key officials have boasted of "running my department completely," and of "stopping hair-brained radical schemes."

The resistance of top-level Civil Servants to proposed new reforms was not necessarily a result of their conscious anti-socialist sympathies. Though there were probably instances in which direct partisan sabotage of the government took place, the most significant "bureaucratic conservative" influence on the government does not appear to be a result of attempts to injure the government. Many of the leading officials appeared to be honestly concerned with doing their jobs.

These Civil Servants would probably have attempted to modify schemes of conservative governments which appeared unworkable to them. The bureaucracy, however, had become institutionalized under conservative governments. Its pattern of reacting to problems had been routinized. New methods of administration were often considered difficult or "impossible" to the incumbent bureaucrat, either because they had never been tried before, or because they would require the revamping of the work of a department. By opposing such changes, the Civil Servant was only taking the easy way out of preserving the *status quo* in his own area of working and living.

> In all large scale enterprise men who are desirous of avoiding great responsibility (and the majority of men is so desirous) are necessarily tempted to avoid great experiments. In a political democracy this obviously becomes an official habit where there is a . . . bureaucratic system. . . .
>
> The tendency accordingly has been a certain suspicion of experimentalism, a benevolence toward the "safe" man. . . . Administrative codes . . . are applied simply from the conservatism of habit.[6]

Civil Service modification of government goals took three major forms: (1) the continuation by government departments of traditional and, from the socialist point of view, "reactionary" modes of procedure; (2) changes in the intent of new laws and regulations through administrative practices; and (3) direct and indirect methods of influencing Cabinet members to adopt policies advocated by top-level Civil Servants. Each of the above statements will be documented in a larger study of the work of this government.[7]

The sources of Civil Service action cannot be found in an unidimensional analysis. Civil Servants, like all individuals, do not operate in a social vacuum (though one suspects that some advocates of the "impartial" Civil Service believe that they do). Their opinions about relative "right" and "wrong" on a particular issue are determined by various pressures existing in their social milieu. A department official is not only interested in whether a minister's proposals can be effectively put into operation, but must also be concerned with the effect of such policies on the traditional practices of the department, and of the long-term relations of the department with other groups in the

[6] Harold Laski, "Bureaucracy," in *Encyclopedia of the Social Sciences,* Volume III, ed. by Edwin R. A. Seligman (New York: The Macmillan Company, 1935), p. 72.

[7] S. M. Lipset, *Agrarian Socialism* (University of California Press, 1950).—Ed.

government and in the community. A reform which may be socially desirable, but which disrupts the continuity of practices, and interpersonal relations within the department, will often be resisted by a top-ranking Civil Servant. He is obligated to protect those beneath him in the administrative hierarchy from the negative consequences of a change in policy.

Second, and as important in influencing the decisions of government officials, is the fact that their opinion of the feasibility of any proposal is necessarily colored by their social and political outlook and by the climate of opinion in the social group in which they move. Many of the top-ranking Civil Servants are members of the upper class socially in the capital city in which they live. Their social contacts are largely with people who believe that they will be adversely affected by many socialist policies. Civil Servants cannot avoid being influenced by the predicament of their own social group. Those government officials who belong to professional or economic groups, whose power or privileges are threatened by government policies, tend to accept the opinion of their group that reforms which adversely affect the group are wrong and will not work.[8] There are a number of examples of Civil Servants reducing the significance of reforms directed against their own groups.

The failure of this government to change the character of the top-level Civil Service precipitated a major conflict within the party between the Cabinet ministers and the majority of the non-office holding leaders of the movement. The majority of the members of the party's legislative group, the party executive, and annual convention delegates have demanded that the government replace old administrators by more sympathetic personnel. The members of these groups usually cite many examples of actions by the Civil Service which they consider to be "administrative sabotage." The attacks on the Cabinet by the rest of the party has gradually forced the Cabinet to modify its public position on the question, and in the last two years it has accepted the principle of a partially politicized bureaucracy and has appointed a number of sympathetic experts to leading positions in the administrative apparatus.

Many of the new "radical" Civil Servants have suggested new policies or specific means of carrying out over-all government policy which would probably never have been proposed if policy formation had been left to the Cabinet and the permanent Civil Service. The

[8] See Max Weber, *op. cit.*, p. 234.

ministers did not have the technical knowledge to suggest needed changes in their own field, and the old Civil Servants were not imbued with the social-democratic values of finding means to reduce the wealth and power of private-interest groups and of using the agencies of the government to increase the standards of living of the people. In at least two departments the differences in orientation of the new and old Civil Service resulted in the two groups engaging in a covert struggle to determine department policy. The permanent Civil Servants in these departments repeatedly brought their ministers into contact with representatives of the more conservative groups in their field, whereas the new Civil Servants encouraged supporters of reform to visit the minister and impress him with the widespread public support for changes. Examination of the work of many government departments makes it apparent that there is a direct relationship between the extent and vigor of reform, and the degree to which the key administrative positions in a department are staffed by persons who adhered to the formal goals of the government.

In recent years many individuals have become concerned with the problem of "bureaucratic domination" in large-scale society. The justified concern with the dangers of oligarchic or "bureaucratic" domination of social organization has, however, led many persons to ignore the fact that it does make a difference to society which set of "bureaucrats" controls its destiny. To suggest, as many social scientists have, that trade unions, cooperatives, corporations, political parties, and states are large social organizations which must develop a bureaucratic structure in order to operate efficiently still leaves a large area of indeterminate social action for a bureaucratically organized society. No matter how structured a situation, every individual and group acts somewhat differently within it, as determined by his past background and present social pressures.

The emphasis on a single theory of bureaucracy has been encouraged by the lack of a sociological approach on the part of political scientists working in the field of governmental bureaucracies. For the most part, they have not raised questions about the social origins and values of government administrators and about the relationship of such factors to government policy.[9] The determinants of the role

[9] For two studies by sociologists which deal with this problem, see Reinhard Bendix, *Higher Civil Servants in American Society* (Boulder: University of Colorado Press, 1949), and Philip Selznick, *T.V.A. and the Grass Roots* (Berkeley: University of California Press, 1949).

played by the Civil Servant in affecting government policy are analyzed largely on the bureaucratic level; that is, the actions of the bureaucracy are explained in terms of the self-preservation and efficiency goals of the Civil Service. These interests may be defined in terms of prestige and privilege, preservation of existent patterns of organization or relationships within a department, or maintenance of department traditions and policies. There is as yet little formal recognition that the behavior of a governmental bureaucracy also varies with the nongovernmental social background and interests of those inhabiting the bureaucratic structure. Members of a Civil Service—like members of the judiciary, trade-unions, or business corporations—are also members of other nongovernmental social groups and classes. Social pressures from the multi-group affiliations and loyalties of individuals will determine their behavior. The behavior of an individual or group in a given situation cannot be considered as if the individual or group members had no other life outside of the given situation one is analyzing.

A permanent governmental bureaucracy which is part of or loyal to a minority social group can be an effective check against social reforms desired by the majority in a period of changing social values such as the present. There is no simple solution to the dilemma of keeping government administration efficient, as well as responsive to the will of the electorate. The increase in the power, functions, and sheer size of modern government necessitates the search for some means of controlling the bureaucracy. It is utopian to think that the electorate's changing the inexpert politician who formally heads the bureaucracy will by itself change the course of the activities of the government. As Max Weber stated:

> The question is always who controls the existing bureaucratic machinery. And such control is possible only in a very limited degree to persons who are not technical specialists. Generally speaking, the trained permanent official is more likely to get his way in the long run than his nominal supervisor, the Cabinet Minister, who is not a specialist.[10]

[10] *The Theory of Social and Economic Organization*, translated by Talcott Parsons and A. R. Henderson (New York: Oxford University Press, 1947), p. 128.

S. N. Eisenstadt

Bureaucracy, Bureaucratization, and Debureaucratization

CONDITIONS OF DEVELOPMENT OF BUREAUCRATIC ORGANIZATIONS

We shall start with an analysis of the conditions of development of bureaucratic organizations and see to what extent these conditions can explain the existence of different inherent tendencies in their development and their patterns of activities. . . .

The available material suggests that bureaucratic organizations tend to develop in societies when

1. There develops extensive differentiation between major types of roles and institutional (economic, political, religious, and so forth) spheres.

2. The most important social roles are allocated not according to criteria of membership in the basic particularistic (kinship or territorial) groups, but rather according to universalistic and achievement criteria, or criteria of membership in more flexibly constituted groups such as professional, religious, vocational, or "national" groups.

3. There evolve many functionally specific groups (economic, cultural, religious, social-integrative) that are not embedded in basic particularistic groups, as, for example, economic and professional organizations, various types of voluntary associations, clubs, and so forth.

4. The definition of the total community is not identical with, and consequently is wider than, any such basic particularistic group, as can be seen, for instance, in the definition of the Hellenic culture in Byzantium or of the Confucian cultural order.

Reprinted in part from S. N. Eisenstadt, *Administrative Science Quarterly*, 4 (1959), 302–320, by permission of the author and the publisher, Cornell University.

5. The major groups and strata in the society develop, uphold, and attempt to implement numerous discrete, political, economic, and social-service goals which cannot be implemented within the limited framework of the basic particularistic groups.

6. The growing differentiation in the social structure makes for complexity in many spheres of life, such as increasing interdependence between far-off groups and growing difficulty in the assurance of supply of resources and services.

7. These developments result to some extent in "free-floating" resources, i.e., manpower and economic resources as well as commitments for political support which are neither embedded in nor assured to any primary ascriptive-particularistic groups, as, for example, monetary resources, a relatively free labor force, and a free political vote. Consequently, the various institutional units in the society have to compete for resources, manpower, and support for the implementation of their goals and provision of services; and the major social units are faced with many regulative and administrative problems.

The available material suggests that bureaucratic organizations develop in relation to such differentiation in the social system. Bureaucratic organizations can help in coping with some of the problems arising out of such differentiation, and they perform important functions in the organization of adequate services and coordination of large-scale activities, in the implementation of different goals, in the provision of resources to different groups and in the regulation of various intergroup relations and conflicts. Such bureaucratic organizations are usually created by certain elites (rulers, economic entrepreneurs, etc.) to deal with the problems outlined and to assure for these elites both the provision of such services and strategic power positions in the society.

Thus in many historical societies bureaucratic administrations were created by kings who wanted to establish their rule over feudal-aristocratic forces and who wanted, through their administration, to control the resources created by various economic and social groups and to provide these groups with political, economic, and administrative services that would make them dependent on the rulers.

In many modern societies bureaucratic organizations are created when the holders of political or economic power are faced with problems that arise because of external (war, etc.) or internal (economic development, political demands, etc.) developments. For the solution of such problems they have to mobilize adequate resources from different groups and spheres of life.

Obviously, these conclusions have to be tested and amplified. . . .

BUREAUCRATIZATION AND DEBUREAUCRATIZATION

It is through continuous interaction with its environment that a bureaucratic organization may succeed in maintaining those characteristics that distinguish it from other social groups. The most important of these characteristics, common to most bureaucratic organizations and often stressed in the literature, are specialization of roles and tasks; the prevalence of autonomous, rational, nonpersonal rules in the organization; and the general orientation to rational, efficient implementation of specific goals.[1]

These structural characteristics do not, however, develop in a social vacuum but are closely related to the functions and activities of the bureaucratic organization in its environment. The extent to which they can develop and persist in any bureaucratic organization is dependent on the type of dynamic equilibrium that the organization develops in relation to its environment. Basically, three main outcomes of such interaction or types of such dynamic equilibrium can be distinguished, although probably each of them can be further subdivided and some overlapping occurs between them.

The first type of equilibrium is one in which any given bureaucratic organization maintains its autonomy and distinctiveness. The basic structural characteristics that differentiate it from other social groups and in which it implements its goal or goals (whether its initial goals or goals added later) are retained and it is supervised by those who are legitimately entitled to do this (holders of political power, "owners," or boards of trustees).

The second main possibility is that of bureaucratization. This is the extension of the bureaucracy's spheres of activities and power either in its own interest or those of some of its elite. It tends toward growing regimentation of different areas of social life and some extent of displacement of its service goals in favor of various power interests and orientations. Examples are military organizations that tend to impose their rule on civilian life, or political parties that exert pressure on their potential supporters in an effort to monopolize their private and

[1] See, for instance, P. M. Blau, *Bureaucracy in Modern Society* (New York, 1956). Blau summarizes much of the available literature on this problem.

occupational life and make them entirely dependent on the political party.

The third main outcome is debureaucratization. Here there is subversion of the goals and activities of the bureaucracy in the interests of different groups with which it is in close interaction (clients, patrons, interested parties). In debureaucratization the specific characteristics of the bureaucracy in terms both of its autonomy and its specific rules and goals are minimized, even up to the point where its very functions and activities are taken over by other groups or organizations. Examples of this can be found in cases when some organization (i.e., a parents' association or a religious or political group) attempts to divert the rules and working of a bureaucratic organization (school, economic agency, and so forth) for its own use or according to its own values and goals. It makes demands on the members of bureaucratic organizations to perform tasks that are obviously outside the specific scope of these organizations. . . .

Many overlappings between these various tendencies and possibilities may, of course, develop. The tendencies toward bureaucratization and debureaucratization may, in fact, develop side by side. Thus, for instance, a growing use of the bureaucratic organization and the extension of its scope of activities for purposes of political control might be accompanied by deviation from its rules for the sake of political expediency. The possibility of these tendencies occurring in the same case may be explained by the fact that a stable service-oriented bureaucracy (the type of bureaucracy depicted in the Weberian ideal type of bureaucracy) is based on the existence of some equilibrium or *modus vivendi* between professional autonomy and societal (or political) control. Once this equilibrium is severely disrupted, the outcome with respect to the bureaucracy's organization and activity may be the simultaneous development of bureaucratization and debureaucratization in different spheres of its activities, although usually one of these tendencies is more pronounced. . . .

SOME VARIABLES IN THE STUDY OF BUREAUCRACY

It is as yet very difficult to propose any definite and systematic hypothesis about this problem since very little research is available that is specifically related to it.[2]

[2] Thus, for instance, in existing literature there is but little distinction between

What can be done at this stage is, first, to point out some variables that, on the basis of available material and the preceding discussion, seem central to this problem, and then to propose some preliminary hypotheses, which may suggest directions in which research work on this problem may be attempted.

On the basis of those discussions we would like to propose that (a) the major goals of the bureaucratic organization, (b) the place of these goals in the social structure of the society, and (c) the type of dependence of the bureaucracy on external forces (clients, holders of political power, or other prominent groups) are of great importance in influencing both its internal structure and its relation with its environment. These different variables, while to some extent interdependent, are not identical. Each brings into relief the interdependence of the bureaucratic organization with its social setting from a different point of view.

The bureaucracy's goals, as has been lately shown in great detail by Parsons,[3] are of strategic importance, because they constitute one of the most important connecting links between the given organization and the total social structure in which it is placed. That which from the point of view of the organization is the major goal is very often from the point of view of the total society the function of the organization. Hence the various interrelations between a bureaucratic organization, other groups, and the total society are largely mediated by the nature of its goals. This applies both to the resources needed by the organization and to the products it gives to the society.[4]

But it is not merely the contents of the goals, i.e., whether they are mainly political, economic, cultural, and so forth, that influence the relation of the organization with its environment, but the place of the goals in the institutional structure of the society as well. By the relative place of the specific goals of any given bureaucratic organization within the society we mean the centrality (or

---

conditions which make for the growth of bureaucracy and those conducive to increasing bureaucratization. Gouldner's polemics against those who foresee the inevitability of bureaucratization are to some extent due to the lack of this distinction in the available literature. See his Metaphysical Pathos and the Theory of Bureaucracy. *American Political Science Review,* 49 (1955), 496–507.

[3] See T. Parsons, Suggestions for a Sociological Approach to the Theory of Organization, I and II, *Administrative Science Quarterly,* 1 (June and Sept. 1956), 63–85, 225–239.

[4] See Trend Report. *Current Sociology,* Vol. 7 (1958), 99–163.

marginality) of these goals with respect to the society's value and power system and the extent of legitimation it affords them. Thus there would obviously be many differences between a large corporation with critical products and a small economic organization with marginal products; between a political party close to the existing government performing the functions of a "loyal opposition" and a revolutionary group; between established churches and minority or militant sects; between fully established educational institutions and sectarian study or propaganda groups.

A third variable which seems to influence the bureaucracy's structural characteristics and activities is the extent and nature of its dependence on external resources and power. This dependence or relation may be defined in terms of

1. The chief function of the organization, i.e., whether it is a service, market, or membership recruitment agency. (This definition is closely related to, but not necessarily identical with, its goals.)

2. The extent to which its clientele is entirely dependent upon its products, or conversely, the type and extent of competition between it and parallel agencies.

3. The nature and extent of the internal (ownership) and external control.

4. The criteria used to measure the success of the organization as such and its members' performance, especially the extent of changes in the behavior and membership affiliation of its clients (as, for instance, in the case of a political party).

5. The spheres of life of its personnel that the activities of a given bureaucratic organization encompass.

It is not claimed that this list is exhaustive, but it seems to provide some preliminary clues as to the possible direction of further research on the problem.

All these variables indicate the great interdependence existing between the bureaucratic organization and its social environment. Each variable points to some ways in which a bureaucratic organization attempts to control different parts of its environment and to adapt its goals to changing environment or to different ways in which groups outside the bureaucracy control it and direct its activities. The outcome of this continuous interaction varies continuously according to the constellation of these different variables.

CONDITIONS OF BUREAUCRATIZATION AND DEBUREAUCRATIZATION

On the basis of the foregoing considerations and of current research like that of Janowitz,[5] of historical research on which we have reported already, and research in progress on the relations between bureaucratic organization and new immigrants in Israel,[6] we propose several general hypotheses concerning the conditions that promote autonomy or, conversely, bureaucratization or debureaucratization. . . .

The first of these hypotheses proposes that the development of any given bureaucratic organization as a relatively autonomous service agency is contingent upon the following conditions obtaining in its social setting:

1. Relative predominance of universalistic elements in the orientations and goals of the groups most closely related to the bureaucracy.

2. Relatively wide distribution of power and values in the economic, cultural, and political spheres among many groups and the maintenance of continuous struggle and competition among them or, in other words, no monopoly of the major power positions by any one group.

3. A wide range of differentiation among different types of goals.

4. The continuous specialization and competition among different bureaucratic organizations and between them and other types of groups about their relative places with regard to implementation of different goals.

5. The existence of strongly articulated political groups and the maintenance of control over the implementation of the goals by the legitimate holders of political, communal, or economic power.

Thus a service bureaucracy, one that maintains both some meas-

[5] See M. Janowitz, D. Wright, and W. Delany, *Public Administration and the Public—Perspectives towards Government in a Metropolitan Community* (Ann Arbor, 1958), which is one of the few available works that have a bearing on this problem. We would also like to mention the work of J. A. Slesinger, who has worked with Janowitz, and who has recently proposed several hypotheses concerning some of the factors that might influence aspects of the development of bureaucracy that are of interest to us. See Slesinger, "A Model for the Comparative Study of Public Bureaucracies," Institute of Public Administration, University of Michigan, 1957 (mimeo.).

[6] See E. Katz and S. N. Eisenstadt, Some Sociological Observations on the Response of Israeli Organizations to New Immigrants, *Administrative Science Quarterly*, Vol. 5 (1960), pp. 113–33.

ure of autonomy and of service orientation, tends to develop either in a society, such as the "classical" Chinese Empire or the Byzantine Empire from the sixth to the tenth century, in which there exist strong political rulers and some politically active groups, such as the urban groups, aristocracy, and the church in the Byzantine Empire, or the literati and gentry in China, whose aspirations are considered by the rulers.[7] It also tends to develop in a democratic society in which effective political power is vested in an efficient, strong, representative executive. In both cases it is the combination of relatively strong political leadership with some political articulation and activity of different strata and groups (an articulation which necessarily tends to be entirely different in expression in historical empires from modern democracies) that facilitates the maintenance of a service bureaucracy.

In some societies a group may establish a power monopoly over parts of its environment and over the definition and establishment of the society's goals and the appropriation of its resources. This group may use the bureaucracy as in instrument of power and manipulation, distort its autonomous function and service orientation, and subvert some of its echelons through various threats or inducements for personal gratification. Historically the most extreme example of such developments can be found in those societies in which the rulers developed political goals that were strongly opposed by various active groups that they tried to suppress, such as in Prussia in the seventeenth and eighteenth centuries, in many conquest empires such as the Ottoman, or in the periods of artistocratization of the Byzantine Empire.[8] Modern examples of this tendency can be found in totalitarian societies or movements. Less extreme illustrations can also be found in other societies, and it should be a major task of comparative research to specify the different possible combinations of the conditions enumerated above and their influence on the possible development of bureaucratic organizations.

The development of a bureaucratic organization in the direction of debureaucratization seems to be connected mainly with the growth

[7] For a more complete discussion of some of the problems of these societies see the references in note 4.

[8] Hans Rosenberg, *Bureaucracy, Aristocracy and Autocracy: The Prussian Experience, 1660–1815* (Cambridge, Mass., 1958); A. Lybyer, *The Government of the Ottoman Empire in the Time of Suleiman the Magnificent* (Cambridge, Mass., 1913); and Eisenstadt, Internal Contradictions.

of different types of *direct* dependence of the bureaucratic organization on parts of its clientele. At this stage we may propose the following preliminary hypotheses about the influence that the type of dependency of the bureaucracy on its clients has on some of its patterns of activity. First, the greater its dependence on its clientele in terms of their being able to go to a competing agency, the more it will have to develop techniques of communication and additional services to retain its clientele and the more it will be influenced by different types of demands by the clientele for services in spheres that are not directly relevant to its main goals. Second, insofar as its dependence on its clients is due to the fact that its criteria of successful organizational performance are based on the number and behavior pattern of the organization's members or clients (as is often the case in semipolitical movements, educational organizations, and so forth), it will have to take an interest in numerous spheres of its clients' activities and either establish its control over them or be subjected to their influence and direction. Finally, the greater its *direct* dependence on different participants in the political arena, and the smaller the basic economic facilities and political assurance given by the holders of political power—as is the case in some public organizations in the United States and to some extent also in different organizations in Israel [9]—the greater will be its tendency to succumb to the demands of different political and economic pressure groups and to develop its activities and distort its own rules accordingly.

As already indicated, in concrete cases some overlapping between the tendencies to bureaucratization and debureaucratization may occur. Thus, for instance, when a politically monopolistic group gains control over a bureaucratic organization, it may distort the rules of this organization in order to give special benefits to the holders of political power or to maintain its hold over different segments of the population. On the other hand, when a process of debureaucratization sets in because of the growing pressure of different groups on a bureaucracy, there may also develop within the bureaucratic organization, as a sort of defense against these pressures, a tendency toward formalization and bureaucratization. This shows that the distinctive characteristics of a specific bureaucratic organization and role have been impinged upon in different directions, and one may usually discern which of these tendencies is

[9] See Janowitz *et al.*, *op. cit.*, pp. 107–114, and Katz and Eisenstadt, *op. cit.*

predominant in different spheres of activity of the bureaucracy. It is the task of further research to analyze these different constellations in greater detail.

Morris Janowitz,
Deil Wright,
and
William Delany

Public Administration and the Public

Our objectives were two-fold. First, we sought to describe public contact with government agencies in the metropolis and to investigate public knowledge and evaluations of the administrative process. We tried to uncover the correlates of these basic perspectives toward administrative authority. By analyzing the public's image of the administrative process we were studying by inference administrative "public relations" in its broadest context. Second, we sought to evalute the extent to which these public perspectives were creating a political climate appropriate for administration based on consent. To this end we developed and applied four criteria with the hope that our analysis might be made relevant to the traditional interests of political theorists.

Our attention was on those administrative agencies which penetrate the daily routines of the metropolitan community. This arbitrarily neglects some crucial and controversial aspects of governmental administration. We believe, however, that the metropolitan community is the initial locus for the analysis of public administration and the public. The willingness and ability of the public to support the more remote aspects of administration depend in good measure on its more direct experiences with the organs of government.

Reprinted in part from Morris Janowitz, Deil Wright, and William Delany, *Public Administration and the Public: Perspectives toward Government in a Metropolitan Community*, pp. 101–114, by permission of the authors and the publisher, The University of Michigan, Institute of Public Administration.

OVERVIEW OF THE FINDINGS

It became apparent from our findings in the Detroit metropolitan community that political party affiliation was not a good index to fundamental differences in public perspectives toward the administrative process. Our assumption that these perspectives would not be sharply linked to partisan party politics was repeatedly confirmed. . . .

These empirical data provide documentation of the rather pervasive acceptance of the current scope and performance of metropolitan-based administration. This is not to overlook either the small minority who object or the fact that specific operations of government may produce intense and outspoken criticism or rejection. Nor is this acceptance incompatible with the desire or even the demand for improvement. But our study did not probe willingness to support improvement. To some degree, the essential services of government are accepted simply because there is no alternative or because the public sees no possibility of alternatives. Our findings, however, underline the extent to which the new integrative functions of government, especially those connected with "service" government, have an impact on all strata throughout the social structure. All the various strata, not just the lower social groups in the metropolitan community, have developed a stake in and a reliance on these new functions of government. As a consequence, they contribute a basis for social and political consensus. For example, it should be recalled that only seven per cent of the population thought the scope of government welfare service was too broad or extensive.

These findings do not deny widespread ambivalent feelings toward the symbols of administrative authority. Ambivalence and reservation could be quickly mobilized by probing perspectives about the worth of government services and lack of principle mindedness among public servants. The fact that such negativism was less concentrated among young people may indicate a long-term trend. Generations which are growing up under the broadened scope of government are perhaps not so likely to hold the more negative orientations toward government authority historically attributed to the American public.

Also noteworthy was the finding that persons display a generalized syndrome of a tendency to accept or a tendency to reject the performance of administrative agencies. In other words, each member of the public seemed to address himself to the diffuse functions and organizations of metropolitan-based administration with some degree of self-consistency in his evaluation of its performance. Here our findings are merely compatible with the current assumptions of political behavior research which see political perspectives as being conditioned by underlying and persistent motivations. Along with the complex of perspectives concerning political partisanship we have identified another complex—that dealing with administrative authority.

For our second objective, that of evaluating the extent to which public perspectives were appropriate for administrative behavior based on consent, four categories—knowledge, self-interest redefined, principle mindedness, and prestige—formed the core of our analysis. A meaningful application of these categories would require trend data in order to establish the direction of social change. A meaningful application would also require comparative data on other nation states, such as Great Britain, to establish how much information, self-interest, principle mindedness, and prestige are required for democratic consent. For each perspective there is some optimum level, so that these four categories could be formulated into evaluative criteria and thereby constitute a bench mark for research.

First, the public failed to display extensive information about the practices of administration. The tests of the desired level of knowledge were indeed minimal. To avoid an over-intellectualized approach, a distinction was made between generalized knowledge and instrumental knowledge. *Generalized* knowledge deals with the understanding of the over-all working of an agency or a system of administration. *Instrumental* knowledge deals with the information essential to an individual about his rights and obligations concerning a specific agency. Clearly, instrumental knowledge was the crucial test, and the level of instrumental knowledge was somewhat higher than that of generalized knowledge. Contact—personal or familial—with a particular agency supplied a pragmatic means for overcoming social class and educational limitations on instrumental knowledge about that agency. But even contact did not necessarily produce a very well-informed citizenry.

The heart of the matter rests in the levels of ignorance that persist even after personal and family contact. Public administrators, public affairs leaders, and communications specialists must face the reality of a relatively uninformed citizenry. The majority of the population finds it difficult to translate its self-interest into an adequate level of understanding of key social welfare programs, such as social security. This is not a matter of lower class ignorance, for lack of knowledge penetrates deeply into the middle class. Our data revealed that widespread ignorance exists about other basic functions of government enterprise. But ignorance about key social welfare benefits is likely to have greater disruptive consequences for social stability than ignorance of other governmental activity since these programs are designed to deal directly with the sources of mass insecurity in the modern metropolitan community.

Nevertheless, lack of knowledge was not associated with a pervasive feeling that the public bureaucracy was thwarting personal self-interest. To the contrary, our second criterion—that the public bureaucracy must be seen as serving personal self-interest—was operative to a considerable degree. Self-interest must operate with built-in limitations. Therefore, as a check on the disruptive consequences of self-interested demands on the bureaucracy, the public must simultaneously acknowledge the bureaucracy's capacity to act as a neutral agent in resolving social conflicts.

In applying the criterion of self-interest, three different dimensions were investigated. One dimension assumed that for self-interest to be realized there would have to be a basic and essential acceptance, rather than rejection, of the current performance of the metropolitan-based bureaucracy. A pervasive or deep-seated antagonism against the organs of government—a crude anti-bureaucratic outlook—emerged as the orientation of only a small minority. The quantitative findings, although preliminary and perhaps arbitrary, fix the size of this group at between 10 and 15 per cent of the population.

A second dimension of self-interest assumed that agreement about the desired scope of government would be a manifestation of realized, rather than thwarted, self-interest. As pointed out above, opposition to the present scope of government, in social welfare for example, was also very limited; the transformation of government over the past two decades is now an accepted event. But this consensus should not be overinterpreted. Feelings of thwarted self-interest about the scope of government bureaucracy were lodged in varying degree among those persons who demanded an expansion of government administration at the metropolitan community level. About 40 per cent of the population has such an orientation. The demand for the expansion of governmental services was most concentrated in the lower class and less prestigeful social groups.

But it was on our third dimension of self-interest—the person's estimate of the economic worth of government—that disaffection emerged most sharply. No doubt it is a chronic and perhaps superficial popular reaction to decry high taxes and red tape in public administration. But the results of our probing of these topics are too convincing to dismiss the findings that a near majority feel hostile when these standards of administrative behavior are brought into question. These negative and hostile feelings were concentrated at the bottom of the social pyramid, where simultaneously the demands for more government administration predominate. It may well be that, in our mixed economy, the cost accounting and capital funding systems that public administration is developing as techniques of internal management control may assume new functions. These techniques may produce essential material by which public information programs can demonstrate to clients and public the economic worth of government operations.

The third criterion—that the public view the bureaucracy as being guided by principles—permits no simple evaluation since beliefs about morality in government emerged as more complex than we had anticipated. We did not uncover widespread belief in active corruption among public servants. The public, however, accepted without a sense of moral indignation the perceived importance of political pull in securing aid from administrative agencies. Political pull seemed to connote little more than those advantages of personal contact and acquaintanceships which were useful in dealing with the complexity and impersonality of large organizations. This seemed to be true of both public and private organizations. It was human, so to speak, to feel defensive in dealings with an impersonal government agency. Therefore, those persons who had intimate contacts with the public bureaucracy merely had desirable advantages. The growth and persistence of such a perspective, however, cannot be viewed as compatible with administration based on consent.

The fourth criterion, or requirement, dealt with the prestige of public employment. While we were not able to study in particular the prestige of the higher civil servants, there was a marked general improvement in public attitudes toward the civil servant since 1930. The trend emerged from a comparison of our data with those of Professor L. D. White collected over a quarter of a century ago. It seems hardly likely, however, that this enhanced prestige will rise to a level at which the prestige of the civil servant would endanger administration based on consent. Certainly, impressionistic observations about the higher civil servants' prestige seem to indicate that desired levels have not yet been reached. In the particular case of the military elite, leaving aside the role of the military hero as president, this key elite continues to have relatively limited prestige.

In summary, we believe that the categories of knowledge, self-interest, principle mindedness, and prestige describe consensus about the administrative process as it actually operates in the metropolitan community setting. Thus, to point out by means of these four public perspectives the extent to which administrative behavior rests on essential consent is not to ignore more precise specification of the vulnerabilities confronting our administrative system. With insufficient information, incomplete feelings of self-interest, and considerable indifference about principle mindedness consensus remains inadequate.

IMPLICATIONS FOR BALANCED ADMINISTRATION

. . . Foreign observers have repeatedly commented on the uneasiness with which government administrative authority is exercised in the United States. This is the result not only of the organization of public administration in the United States, but also of the ambivalent public perspectives toward administrative authority in our culture and society.

Analyzing administrative behavior from the point of view of public perspectives—from the external standpoint—is almost certain to result in policy considerations pointing to the need for public informational programs. The application of our four criteria clarify, perhaps, the goals for such efforts. It is not merely a task of disseminating more information. Present efforts to increase the level of public knowledge, to project a clear image of the worth of government, and to raise the prestige of public service seem inadequate. They seem to be without focus as well. . . .

Scarcity of administrative resources is the limiting factor. Government agencies are not permitted to develop informational staffs to fill the gaps between hierarchical levels and between agency personnel and the public. Civil service managerial personnel and facilities in the agencies studied impressed us as generally inadequate for effective "community relations" programs. Given their limited resources, we were impressed however with the ingenuity used by personnel to solve these problems. The upper levels of the agencies were aware of their enforced neutrality among the competing power groups in the metropolitan community. They knew that as community-based agencies they had to make use of the imperfect, though extensive, social consensus in the community to develop their informational activities. This meant that, in large part, the task of disseminating information about their programs was assigned to voluntary associations and economic groups —business, labor, and special interest. The administrators were fully aware of the local community press and utilized it because of its emphasis on consensus in residential and suburban communities. The solutions they had to find were obviously inadequate but, just as noteworthy here, they were realistic. The problems of governmental communications with the metropolitan community will remain unsolved until organizational resources are placed at the disposal of administrative agencies.

Only by thinking in such long-range terms can progress be hoped for in the presentation of metropolitan-based government in the mass media. Perhaps the findings of this study will supply to the policy makers of the mass media a reasoned argument that a positive rather than a negative approach to the public information requirement of metropolitan-based government is very much in order. In short, leadership from the mass media is possible since the public is already prepared for leadership. . . .

To speak of the need for positive public information programs does not mean that planning and development should exclusively be preoccupied with the mass media and with mass channels. Our findings emphasize the pervasive character of "over-the-counter" activities and of the face-to-face contacts with administrative personnel. Scarcity of resources is at work here just as in the case of the bureaucracy's utilization of mass media. In a sense, the scarcity of resources is even more disruptive since inadequate mass media programs represent administrative limitations, but poorly trained and overworked contact personnel are a positive liability. To be concerned with the improvement here is not to overlook the observation that, as of the present time, a person's contact with public agencies is less important in fashioning perspectives than is his position in the social structure. Thus, we are saying that a person's perspective toward an agency is more a function of what he judges the agency contributes to his self-interest and less a function of the way in which the agency presents itself to him.

Yet it would be most misleading and incomplete if the policy implications of this research were exclusively directed to public relations and public information. This study sought to extend beyond concerns with direct internal management of public administration. It was a basic assumption that administrative behavior needs to be analyzed in the context of politics and the political process. The development of the public bureaucracy is in the last resort "politic" in the common sense meaning of the word. In planning the strategy of legislative reform, in developing and recruiting a civil service and in guaranteeing its accountability political issues are at stake.

It is fashionable to decry administrative reliance on voluntary associations as private co-optation of public functions. One just cannot overlook the findings of social science research in the field of communication which highlight the advantages of voluntary associations as more efficient and effective means of communication to their members than are the generalized mass vehicles. There are undoubtedly dangers when public information programs of governmental enterprise must rest exclusively on voluntary associations. But without a multiplicity of voluntary association outlets and resources a pluralistic society is impossible. The alternative would be co-optation of information activities by the political parties; and there seems to be no reasons why such an arrangement would necessarily be advantageous.

In any case, an important share of the task of informing the public will continue to fall on the general mass media over which the processes of government have no direct control. . . .

The justification of the legitimate goals of administration is a political task. It involves the election process and the deliberation of the legislature. It is not the primary or ultimate task of the public administrator to justify his own activities; this is the task of the politician and the public affairs leader—both on the national and on the metropolitan community level.

Robert Dubin

Society and Union-Management Relations

The social structure of complex industrial societies is continuously changing. This general conclusion raises important questions about the sources of change in social structure. In particular, we want to examine the linkages between a changing society and industrial conflict.

Four major historical developments are central in the general features of American social structure pertinent to industrial relations: technology of production has been, and is, undergoing profound changes, size as well as organization of business firms has changed radically, and with the changes have come important modifications of the employment relationship, social controls of our society have been modified in recent decades, and ideological positions have changed as the balance of social power has shifted among groups.

These four features of our changing American social structure are particularly crucial for understanding industrial relations and industrial conflict. They are by no means the only areas of significant change in our society. . . .

Sources of Change

Sources of social change may lie outside the areas affected by it. No area of human behavior is a closed system. In particular, industrial relations, as an area of group interaction, are affected by changing features of the culture not directly a part of the collective relations between unions and management. We will examine changes

Reprinted in part from Robert Dubin, *Working Union-Management Relations: The Sociology of Industrial Relations*, pp. 232–234, 236–255.

in technology, business organization, social control, and ideology as causes of social change having important consequences for industrial relations.

The technology of industrial production and business operations is a consequence of scientific and engineering developments. The first Industrial Revolution is reaching its climactic stage. Continuous production lines with their subdivision of tasks to be performed by individual workers or specialized power driven machines, coupled with transfer equipment to move work in process between work stations, are the climax scheme for organizing production in the first Industrial Revolution.

Automation, permitting prior programing of operations and feedback for their self-control, is the basis for the new era of the second Industrial Revolution. Automation of production operations will be sustained by the new sources of power generated in atomic powerhouses. Consequences for workers and work organizations of the technological developments are far-reaching. Vast obsolescence of old skills and need for entirely new skills are only the more obvious results. Technology, which was not developed to change work *per se,* has modified the nature of work as one of its major consequences.[1]

Management has developed new techniques and administrative inventions for directing work forces operating with the new technologies. Workers do things differently now than they did in the past in producing goods and services. The rapidity with which technology changes, and the vast transformations wrought by the changes, have introduced important modifications in worker-management relations. The sources of the changes lie in the technology, outside the worker-management relationship, but their consequences are central to the relationship.

Bureaucratization of industry has moved apace with technological advance. Large scale, complex industrial firms have developed. Bureaucratic administration has been invented to provide the necessary linkage between top management decision makers and workers at the operating levels.[2] This is a relatively new form of administration developed to solve internal problems of command. The need for the new administrative form derives from the size and complexity of organizations. One impact of bureaucratic administration is charge in the nature of the employment relationship.

[1] An analysis of the impact of technology on work behavior is in Chapters 10 and 11 of Dubin, *The World of Work,* N.J., Prentice Hall, Inc., 1958.

[2] See *ibid.,* especially Chapter 20, "Management as Bureaucracy."

Two major trends can be observed in American society in the development of social control. The delicate balance of the economic system, requiring continuous flow of goods and services to consumers, has placed powers in the hands of the state for limiting the disruptive consequences of conflict. Legislative control of industrial relations and industrial conflict, social security programs, economic planning directed toward stability, and directed production in wartime are examples of centralization of social control in government. At the same time, private associations, businesses and unions, have developed important self-policing mechanisms for controlling the consequences of their own interactions.

Social control has tended to polarize into the legislative and administrative actions of government, and into the private agreements of corporate and organized groups.[3] This, too, has had important consequences for work and industrial conflict. Businesses and unions focus on influencing government action to maximize their respective chances in collective bargaining. These groups also enter into detailed and rigid agreements in union contracts specifying the rights and obligations of each, and establishing enforcement methods. The polarization of social control has had significant consequences for the welfare of workers and the methods by which this welfare is pursued.[4]

The ideological climate has also been transformed. The welfare state, the welfare corporation, and the welfare union have replaced the laissez-faire state and its citizens' Horatio Alger self-image. Man is increasingly viewed as being entitled to a "fair shake" from life. The social system now has built-in ideological positions leading to social practices providing individual opportunities as a matter of right, irrespective of competence or contribution.[5] Here again, changes have taken place outside the employment relationship that have important bearing upon it. . . .

[3] Other locations of social control, effective in simpler societies and in sectors of our own, include social controls lodged in the local community, the neighborhood, and kinship groups.

[4] We have suggested the polarization of social control in Chapter 8, "Industrial Disputes and Strikes."

[5] All American social security legislation, together with "health and welfare" provisions of union agreements, is based upon declared rights to their benefits, not selective qualifications or "means tests" for their application. The "dynamic conservatism" of the Eisenhower administration explicitly emphasizes protection of opportunities as a matter of right. . . .

CONFLICT—A FUNDAMENTAL SOCIAL PROCESS

Conflict between groups is a fundamental social process. Social theorists have been fascinated by the analysis of conflict. In a moralistic framework, conflict is viewed as undesirable, even though it may be inevitable. From such a standpoint, conflict is considered a "last resort" social process, a poor substitute for more civilized and less destructive modes of determining social policy. This value position prefers to consider conflict as essentially immoral, because some of its more violent forms, like war, lead to vast destruction of human life and cultural products.

From the standpoint of social order, conflict is viewed from two positions. It may be destructive of social stability, and therefore bad because stability is good. It may be evidence of the breakdown of social control and therefore symptomatic of an underlying instability in the social order. Both positions express a value preference for stability. . . .

Conflict is a fundamental social process. Various social theorists have accorded it different positions in their theoretical schemes. Marx viewed conflict, in the form of the class struggle, as an historical imperative of evolving capitalism. Simmel and other German theorists have looked at social systems and concluded that conflict is an empirical reality which must be taken into account in building models about social behavior.[6] The American sociologists, Park and Burgess, principally influenced by their German sociological predecessors, gave conflict a coordinate position with cooperation, accommodation, and assimilation as basic social processes of group interaction.[7] More recent formulations, like Blumer's,[8] identify conflict as the consequence of power relations, and make it a fundamental category of social inter-

[6] Georg Simmel's chapter on conflict from his *Soziologie* has been given its first translation into English in Georg Simmel, *Conflict and the Web of Group-Affiliations* (Glencoe: The Free Press, 1955). A brilliant analysis of conflict as a fundamental social process, functional for social life, is contained in Lewis Coser, *The Functions of Social Conflict* (Glencoe: The Free Press, 1956). The general thesis of this chapter is parallel to Coser's analysis, as are a number of specific points.

[7] Robert E. Park and Ernest W. Burgess, *Introduction to the Science of Sociology* (Chicago: University of Chicago Press, 1921). This was probably the most influential single textbook in the history of American sociology.

[8] Herbert Blumer, "Social Structure and Power Conflict," Chapter 17 in Arthur Kornhauser, Robert Dubin, and Arthur M. Ross (eds.), *Industrial Conflict* (New York: McGraw-Hill Book Company, 1954).

action along with codified relations and sympathetic relations. Those sociological theorists concerned with consensus have always made a place for conflict as an unstabilizing process inimical to existing social agreements.[9] Group conflict cannot be wished out of existence. It is a reality with which social theorists must deal in constructing their general models of social behavior.

Social Power and Social Policy

Social power is the control of decision making about social policy. Social power can be measured by the exclusiveness with which essential social functions are performed.[10] We have already suggested that social policy embodies the decisions governing changing aspects of the society.

Groups pursuing given goals or means of social change ultimately have to direct their tactics at controlling the decision making functions with respect to social policy supportive of their aims. . . .

The polarization of decision making in American society, which we have already examined, suggests that union-management relations are carried out in two arenas. Unions and business firms seek to influence governmental decision making on social policy by direct action. The phenomenon of pressure groups in the governmental process is a familiar one. Union and management pressure groups operate to gain dominance in the legal social policy decisions directly by control of governments or parties, or indirectly, as organized voting blocs influencing individual legislators, executives, and judges.

Collective bargaining centers social policy making in the private sector of the society. Here the continuing struggles between unions and companies, in the past sometimes bitter and violent, center on the ways in which decision making will be allocated in arriving at collective agreements. The tactical goals may be "more, more, more," for workers, or protection of the manager's prerogatives to manage.[11] The

[9] See, for example, the presidential address made before the annual meeting of the American Sociological Society by the late Louis Wirth, "Consensus and Mass Communication," *American Sociological Review*, 13:1–15 (February, 1948).

[10] Cf. Robert Dubin, "Power and Union-Management Relations," *Administrative Science Quarterly*, 2:60–81 (June, 1957), where the analysis of power in union-management relations is elaborated.

[11] Samuel Gompers, long time influential president of the American Federation of Labor, when asked what labor was after, replied, "More, more, more." It has remained to this day a much used aphorism. An excellent analysis of management prerogatives is contained in Neil W. Chamberlain, *Union Challenge to Management Control* (New York: McGraw-Hill Book Company, 1948).

strategic goal, however, is amassing sufficient social power to dominate decision making about social policy in the private sector of the economy. . . .

Conflict and Change

Amount, kind, and direction of social change is the central issue around which group conflict develops. Social conflicts are concerned with "where do we go from here?" This leads to two general types of group value orientation.

Most special interest groups are concerned with policies modifying present arrangements. These groups see current social arrangements as requiring change in directions they propose. Some groups may have only limited objectives requiring minor changes in social policy for their achievement. Other groups may call for far-reaching changes whose enactment may require revolutionary steps to achieve them.

A conservative stance may also be the value outlook around which power seeking groups organize. Conservatism may be of a backward-orienting character, with some previous position of social policy being favored over its present state. Such groups may also be organized to conserve present social policy and protect it from decisions that will change it.

In union-management relations there is no guarantee that unions will be found exclusively on the side favoring change toward a future which they describe as better. Nor is there any guarantee that management groups will be exclusively oriented toward conserving or conservative positions. For example, management spokesmen are the most vigorous advocates of very rapid technological development through automation. They view this fundamental development in technology as desirable and necessary. They are pressing hard for social policies supporting rapid introduction of automation. Indeed, management's business decisions, lying outside the area in which decisions are shared with unions, press forward with the policy of hastening automation. Clearly management is in a future-oriented posture regarding technology. Labor tends to support a conserving policy regarding automation, fearing for the destiny of displaced workers and the huge problems of organizing entirely new kinds of automation technicians and specialists.

Another example of the reversal of the folk picture of union and management policy stances is the recent history of national labor legislation. Management has pressed vigorously and successfully for modification of the Wagner Act as now embodied in the Taft-Hartley Law. Unions have, with equal vigor over the past decade, attempted to return federal legislation to the Wagner Act social policies. In this instance unions have clearly adopted a conservative position in the face of admittedly important gains made through collective bargaining by unions, in spite of the Taft-Hartley Law, not because of it.

In the arena of private social control—collective bargaining—unions have generally adopted a forward-oriented social policy. Management, on the other hand, has tended toward a conserving social policy with occasional wistful glances backward toward a conservative position embodied in the image of earlier days when management was truly free to manage. Such conservative nostalgia is probably symptomatic of cultural lag in social values rather than a forthright appraisal of current realities.

CONFLICT IS INSTITUTIONALIZED

Conflict between groups becomes institutionalized. Conflict between groups is not random; neither does conflict occur over chance subjects that happen to be the fleeting concern of a group.

Conflict between groups has form and exhibits order. The very orderliness of conflict provides the basis on which we can view conflict as institutionalized. Institutionalized behavior is systematic social relations.

Relations between groups become institutionalized when they are continuous. This is true regardless of the mode of interaction. Conflict can be institutionalized as well as cooperation. The measure of an institutionalized relationship is the orderliness of the actions in it.

Industrial relations have five principal standardized features. They are the principal components of institutionalized labor relations.[12]

Evolution of Ends

Continuous conflict between groups leads to evolution of the ends sought by each group. Historical views of the evolution of collective bargaining issues from epoch to epoch reveal a developmental process in two senses. Bargaining claims and demands of a period are logical outgrowths of those dealt with in prior periods. At any given

[12] Discussed in more detail in Dubin, "Power and Union-Management Relations."

time new goals are established whose realistic accomplishment is expected in the future.

There is uneven development of collective bargaining in the economy, with some unions able to win more and better concessions than other unions. Successful unions pioneer the goals for which their less successful sister unions later strive. Pioneering advances made by leading unions become the landmarks, guiding the labor movement's evolving policy from epoch to epoch.

The evolutionary character of the ends of collective bargaining is also revealed in the logic connecting present gains with future anticipations. It has been suggested, for example, that unions have largely won the right of individual worker protection *in* a given job. Seniority clauses and grievance procedures buttress this protection. The next step in evolving union goals appears to be the protection of workers in their right *to* a job for their entire productive life.[13] This new goal necessitates a broad welfare program designed to insure that all citizens capable of work and willing to work, will have employment opportunities somewhere in the economy.

One consequence of this logical tie between past gains and future goals is that preparatory planning is carefully done to lay the groundwork for achieving future goals. Such forward planning often takes the form of making demands repeatedly, adjusting opposing groups to their anticipation, and perhaps ultimately winning a grudging acceptance. For example, Reuther does not really claim he has won a guaranteed annual wage from the automobile industry. However, the present supplementation of unemployment compensation is clearly a current compromise between the annual wage demand and straight unemployment compensation during layoffs. The Auto Workers continue to press for the annual wage and have obviously moved one step toward it.

There is a connection between the bargaining demands of succeeding epochs. This evolution features the diffusion of an idea from its point of original success to the far reaches of the collective bargaining arena. This evolution also features commitments to a course of development of ends sought, that evolves logically from a key success. Finally, the evolution of the ends of collective bargaining exhibits a characteristic forward planning by successful groups, anticipating a considerable lag between the initiation of a demand and its eventual achievement.

[13] Developed in Solomon Barkin, "Labor Unions and Workers' Rights in Jobs," Chapter 8 in Kornhauser *et al.*, *Industrial Conflict*.

It seems clear that the subject matter of industrial conflict is not random. Past resolutions of industrial conflicts, and commitments to the solutions of past issues, become the background out of which new issues are brought to the fore. The evolution of the ends of collective bargaining takes on a systematic character. In this sense, we can label the processes by which new goals are developed by unions and managements in their continuing relationship, the institutionalization of the ends of group conflict.

Shared Values

Continuous conflict between groups leads to shared values about formerly conflicting ends. Under some circumstances there may be agreement in principle regarding desirable ends. However, the abstract goal agreed on requires methods by which it can be achieved.

Some illustrations of abstract goals agreed on in industrial relations follow:

> An individual worker should not be subjected to arbitrary, discriminatory action by a supervisor.
>
> Wages should bear some logical relationship to an objective standard like locality or industry levels, or movements in the cost of living.
>
> Unions are permanent institutions for carrying out collective bargaining.
>
> Objective methods should be used to determine work loads and pay rates for individual jobs.

These illustrations of goals now generally shared by management and unions also accurately catalog some of the principal areas of industrial conflict.

Agreement on broad goals carries the parties halfway down the road toward resolution of their conflicts. The parties have a mutual commitment to a general outcome. They are caught up in this mutual commitment and bound together by consensus regarding it.

Sharing of values about ends produces a commitment to each other by the parties to the conflict. It also turns attention to finding some operational means for achieving the agreed-on goals. This brings order into the relationship. The parties are no longer free to move away from their points of mutual commitment. This shared commitment to an outcome is important to systematic relations between union and company. It is another point in union-management relations that is institutionalized.

Search for Means

Continuous conflict between groups leads to a focus on disputes over means to a shared end. A high percentage of the actual disputes in collective bargaining are concerned with hammering out satisfactory means for achieving shared ends. There are two general types of disputes over means: procedural disputes, and disputes over power structure.

A procedural dispute over means to an end has to do with the actual operating steps for satisfying the acceptable goal. For example, there are various procedures for measuring output, and various degrees of involvement of a union in this measurement.

There are many procedural disputes. They tend, however, to be minor causes of dispute. They are the kinds of issues typically traded in collective bargaining on a "you take one, we'll take one" basis. An important feature of procedural disputes is that the alternate solutions lie very close together. Procedural disputes over means are very rapidly handled through collective bargaining.

Structural disputes over means are much more serious because they involve the power positions of the parties. Structural disputes have to do with control of decision making. For example, there may be agreement that declines in work opportunities should be shared by all workers through a reduction in working hours for all employees. Company and union may agree to this end. A union, however, may insist that the reasons for any cutback in hours of work must be examined and explained satisfactorily before hours are reduced. The union may even claim the right to challenge the company justifications. In the extreme case, the union might even claim a voice in planning company policies so as to avoid the need for such cutbacks in output. This example clearly illustrates the various ways in which decision making on the cutback could be shared with the union. It is exceedingly important to management and to the union, for different reasons, to want to control decisions about levels of operations. A very bitter conflict can result from such structural disputes because they involve the central reason for union-management conflict—control over decisions about company-union policies.

Systematic interaction between union and company in solving disputes about means depends on the distance between alternatives. In procedural disputes, choices are very close together and their differences may actually be inconsequential. In disputes over power positions, differences may be more widely separated and distinctive. They are still differences over a relatively limited range, and are not polarized as are choices about ends. Consequently, union-management relations take on a systematic character in the narrower ranges over which choices about means towards ends are typically made, and made in a horse-trading manner.

Standard Forms of Conflict

Continuous conflict between groups leads to standardized modes of conflict. Industrial conflict follows typical patterns in its action phases. Negotiation usually establishes the existence of a dispute. Failure, through negotiation, to solve the dispute typically leads to intervention by a government agency to conciliate or mediate the differences. . . . Should peaceful means for resolving the conflict fail, a strike or lockout may result. The recent history of strikes indicates a remarkable standardization of this form of emotionally toned group behavior. The conduct of a strike has largely been reduced to a routine. In industries that have continuous operations, like steel, the union is very careful to help the company bank furnaces and protect continuous processes during the strike. Pickets are posted as symbolic rather than physical barriers to entry into the plant. Members of management may be given passes to facilitate crossing picket lines. Management usually does not attempt to operate during the strike, and may even provide comforts to pickets during inclement weather.

The strike itself has taken on a largely symbolic character as a signal to government or plant management that some action has to be taken to resolve a dispute.

The modes of industrial conflict are being increasingly institutionalized. Surprise is no longer a significant tactic in carrying out industrial conflict. There is no advantage in secretly calling a strike and then springing it on management. Indeed the opposite seems to be true, namely, that the deliberate planning of a strike for the future proves more threatening to the parties than its actual occurrence. Similarly, there is no special advantage to overt violence in industrial disputes, or to the use of novel tactics like the sit-down strike and mass picketing. These devices once had important functions as tactics of conflict, when unions had not yet established continuing relations with management, and strikes for simple recognition had to be dramatic.

With continuing relations between companies and unions has come standardization of the modes of overt conflict. Overt conflict has become systematic—it has been institutionalized.

Routine Relations

Continuous conflict between groups leads to routinized interactions. The conflicts of union-management relations lead to the development of: functionaries on both sides whose permanent assignments are to be experts in conflict; and a constitution composed of rules for carrying out conflict.

Both unions and managements develop permanent functionaries whose sole responsibilities are to carry out industrial relations. These functionaries are skilled in conflict tactics and effective conflict resolution. In a sense, these functionaries become professional antagonists facing each other across the bargaining table. They operate with precepts about strategy and tactics, shared with like-professionals. They view their professional activities as respectable, legitimate, and functional in the social structure. In short, there is no animus attached to being a professional in conflict.

The common law of the plant is the body of past decisions on settled disputes. This common law of the plant is a sociological framework of norms, standards, and procedures into which most future dispute settlements can be fitted. Present positions of union and management, and current decisions in collective bargaining, are made relevant to the common law deriving from precedent settlements in the union-management relationship. Precedence becomes an important criterion for future action.

Permanent functionaries who carry out conflict, and the common law upon which settlements are made in disputes, are the two main strands of evidence pointing to the routinization of continuing relations between unions and companies. This routine of day-to-day living with each other and having common guide points for predicting each other's behavior and stance is further evidence of the institutionalization of industrial conflict.

Disputes Are Settled

Continuous conflicts between groups are eventually resolved. The resolution of disputes is central to understanding collective bargaining and union-management relations. However stringent and violent particular conflicts appear to be, the parties to them always follow tactics that explicitly or implicitly assume some solution will result. The parties to industrial conflict are bound up in systematic ways of interacting that create a strain on them to resolve conflicts. However unsatisfactory a particular solution may be, it is always better than no solution; better, that is, in the sense that union and management can continue to deal with each other only if there is sure expectation that present and future conflicts will be settled.[14] . . .

RESOLVED CONFLICT DIRECTS CHANGE

Culture Contains Settled Issues

Issues permanently resolved through conflict become part of the culture. When permanent solutions are achieved to issues in conflict, these issues eventually fade from the picture, and solutions to them become part of the culture. The social policies permanently settled become part of the broadly accepted notions of "right and proper" among the populace as a whole. These social policies become part of what is taken for granted, rather than what is fought over.

For example, during the period of mass organization of American workers in the late '30's, unions placed among their first demands the inclusion of union protection clauses in contracts. Union recognition clauses now tend to become ceremonial affirmations rather than active social policy, as unions have become permanent features of the industrial landscape. Indeed, there is even some tendency to drop such clauses altogether from union contracts. More frequently, such clauses take on a new function of granting bargaining rights to one union rather than another—management is committed to bargaining with some union and does not need to affirm this intent. The permanency of unions and the legitimacy of their functions are now generally accepted. Unions are part of the social beliefs of the society and their

[14] It is one of the interesting paradoxes of group conflict that complete destruction of the opponent is not the most desired goal. For example, the viciousness with which World War II was pursued, even against civilians on both sides, must be viewed in the perspective of the rebuilding aid and succor of the victors for the vanquished. In continuous collective bargaining, neither party seeks destruction of the other. Indeed, this phenomenon of combat stopping short of annihilation has been emphasized by the title of E. Wight Bakke's treatment of union-management relations: *Mutual Survival: The Goals of Unions and Management* (New York: Harper & Brothers, 1947).

very existence is largely taken for granted. Unionism no longer needs the support of specific social policy. It is now supported by values embedded in the culture.

It would not be meaningful to say that issues permanently resolved are settled forever. By permanent solution of conflict issues we mean that the parties to the conflict eventually recognize that they need not continually incorporate the solution into enacted social policy. The solution becomes part of cultural values or cultural practices. . . .

Group Values and Social Well Being

Successful power seeking groups identify their values with social well being. The old adage that "might makes right" is modified by the persistent efforts of power seeking groups to provide self-justifications. Might does not make right without the support of a continuous "selling" program.

The publicly exposed, moral self-images of power seeking groups are intended to convince the whole of the society that its well being depends upon the social policies of the power group.

For management there are two central moral positions in its proclaimed images of itself.[15] The first is the broad assertion that the stability of the society is dependent upon management's stout defense of the principles of free enterprise. The second moral foundation of management's self-image is the belief that managerial techniques are designed to maximize the material and psychological security of the individual worker.

Management's free enterprise argument is particularly enticing because it views society as regulated, not by power relations, but by impersonal market mechanisms independent of individuals or groups. The market mechanisms regulating competition give no recognition to group power. Indeed, the massing of such power, in the form of monopoly in a market, is viewed as deviant behavior, at least nominally to be discouraged. Thus, management's insistence upon the defense of a free enterprise system relieves managerial spokesmen of having to speak as power bloc representatives. They are defending a system which they declare to be self-regulatory. The management power bloc does not propose to police the free enterprise system. It simply proposes to defend it against abnormal accumulations of power in the hands of

[15] This analysis is drawn from a more detailed treatment in Kornhauser *et al.*, *Industrial Conflict*, pp. 18–20. I have added here a comparison of the union and management self-images as to their impact on public opinion.

labor. The managerial defense of the free enterprise system gets turned into a "selling campaign" against labor monopoly.

The moral self-images of organized labor also rest on two foundations. Labor unions view themselves as instruments of social justice. They also view themselves as providing material and psychological security for individual workers, protecting them from exploitation by employers.

Unions as instruments of social justice see themselves as a power bloc. Indeed, their self-conception is built upon the fact that they consider themselves the only effective power bloc in the society capable of combating managerial dominance in social policy making. Labor unions are locked in direct battle with the managerial class at the only point in the social structure where the battle has meaningful outcome—in the industrial arena. Organized labor considers itself the only group capable of challenging and defeating management in its own stronghold—the control of decision making about the industrial foundations of our society.

At the plant level, the union sees itself as the champion of individual workers immersed in a bureaucratic structure over which individually they exercise no control. The union protects workers from individual exploitation by defending their collective rights, established in union contracts, and policed through the grievance procedure.

It seems clear that at the plant level, concerned with individual worker security, the differences between management and unions are over the means by which security can be achieved. Management has recourse to "scientific" methods of fitting workers to jobs, and jobs to people. Unions generally concede the personnel functions to management, seeking only to protect individuals against malfunctioning personnel practices. The union and company means for maximizing individual worker security actually turn out to be complementary rather than competitive.

At the level of the society, the moral self-images of management and unions are based upon fundamentally different views of societal mechanisms. Management has an effective "selling point" for its own value orientation because it can disguise its position as a power seeking and power holding group. Management contends that the free enterprise system is self-regulating and that common devotion to the system is sufficient to perpetuate it.

The union position clearly envisions the social system as an interplay of power seeking groups. Unionism's self-justification freely admits that it is a power bloc. It must be a power bloc because management is a power holding group whose control of social policy can be changed only in group power struggles.

Social Policy Differences

Industrial conflict defines areas of divergent social policies. The outcome of industrial conflict determines the life history of competing social policies underlying the conflict.

Unions and management are not really concerned, in facing each other, with value positions regarding the nature of society and its functioning. They have much more limited objectives in dealing with each other. They struggle for opportunities to make decisions about the destiny of the industrial foundations of the society. Specific and concrete policies must be hammered out to guide work and the output of goods and services.

The value positions expressed by union and management spokesmen are stances taken for purposes of legitimation in the eyes of the citizens of the society. The value positions are, in a concrete sense, rationalizations for the existence of power seeking groups as legitimate in the social structure. The public value positions do not directly guide group social policy. The policy takes its shape from the strategy and tactics of group conflict, and the amount of power amassed for carrying it out.

Industrial conflict, by constantly changing social policy as one group or the other becomes the current victor, permits continual tests of the effectiveness of given policies. . . .

Where the balance of power is fairly even, as it certainly seems to be in modern American industrial relations, we would expect that the temporary ascendency of either labor or management would not result in material departures from past policy decisions. The notion of countervailing power has precise relevance here.[16] It is out of the balancing of social power between groups that continuity of social policy comes. Only when one group suddenly has a material accretion of power will it be able to introduce revolutionary social policies that depart radically from past policies. Where the balance of power is fairly even, neither labor nor management feels strong enough to provoke a prolonged open conflict by major departures from past policy decisions. The resolution of particular industrial struggles usually represents small modifications

[16] Cf. John K. Galbraith, *American Capitalism: The Concept of Countervailing Power* (Boston: Houghton Mifflin Company, 1952).

of social policy. It is only through a period of time that the accumulated small changes sometimes add up to major shifts in direction for social policy.

Peter H. Rossi

The Organizational Structure of an American Community

PART I. LOCAL GOVERNMENT, VOLUNTARY ASSOCIATIONS, AND COMMUNITY STRUCTURE

The most striking characteristic of contemporary cities, compared with the American community in the nineteenth century, is the relative drop in the importance of local government, not only in its relation to state and federal governments but also in its relation to local voluntary associations. To understand what is happening within a contemporary community an investigator cannot confine himself to the official table of organization for municipal government but must add to it a host of voluntary associations which act on behalf of the community and which together with the formal structure of local government form the basic organizational framework of the local community.

There is no doubt that this is the age of the "community project." Significant community enterprises are often initiated outside the framework of local government, and are aided and abetted by a proliferation of civic associations and citizen committees.

In many communities the mayor and city council often appear to

This paper is published for the first time in this volume. Its first part is taken from an address delivered to the Institute of Community Development and Services, Michigan State University, April 28, 1959. The second part is excerpted, with permission, from "Industry and Community: A Pilot Study of the Community Relations of Local Telephone Companies and Other Businesses," Report No. 64, National Opinion Research Center, University of Chicago, October 1957 (Mimeo.). James A. Davis of the University of Chicago assisted the author in the research reported in Part II.

be dragging their heels while organized "prominent" citizens exhort the community to push toward progress. The voluntary associations, ranging from the more permanent varieties—the Community Chest, Chamber of Commerce, and service clubs—to the *ad hoc* Citizens' Committees, have taken over many of the functions of initiating social change and marshaling community support for changes that are formally allocated to local government and to political parties. Although it is often true that voluntary associations eventually must move local authorities, the initial spark and a great part of the task of mobilizing public opinion have been performed for these authorities in advance.

Another striking characteristic of the American community of today, in contrast to that of the past, is the status gap between the personnel of local government and the local elites of wealth, intellect, and status. The local echelons of the party organizations and the elective offices of municipal, county, and even state governments are manned by persons whose social positions are often many levels below the denizens of the Country Club, Rotary Club, and the Chamber of Commerce. The City Fathers and the county commissioners are recruited, at best, from among local lawyers of somewhat uncertain income and miscellaneous clientele, and more likely from among small proprietors or professional politicians. Money, status, and intellect seem to be in one place and political control in another. Such anomalies lead to the hypothesis that somewhere there are strings by means of which local government is guided from without.

How things "get done" has therefore become more and more problematical as the lack of articulation grows between the political elite and the industrial, commercial, and professional elites. It is hard to believe that the corner grocer who is elected mayor can govern in his own right in a community with branch factories of several national firms, a local elite of considerable wealth, and several large commercial establishments.

As a consequence of this separation in status and resources, the organizational structure of the American community consists of the formally constituted local government and its agencies, supplemented by a number of organizations which are concerned with the local community but which have no standing in the official table of organization. The number of such supplementary organizations and their vigor vary from community to community, but they all share several characteristics in common. First, such community organizations are the focus of the community activities of the elite of wealth and status. Second, such organizations are not responsible to a constituency broadly defined, as is local government, but are run as private preserves. Finally, these unofficial community organizations serve to redress the local imbalance of power by giving to the elite of status and wealth important sectors of community life to control.

PART II. BUSINESS, VOLUNTARY ASSOCIATIONS, AND COMMUNITY STRUCTURE [1]

A. A Functional Analysis of the Community Participation Activities of Businesses

The rationale advanced by Mediana's businessmen for participating in community activities is the impact of such activities on workers and customers. Typically, a manager of the local branch of a large corporation would state that his workers expected him to play an important role in the community and that they rewarded such participation by loyalty to the firm. However, as we shall see later on, industrial workers scarcely knew of the participation of managers and concentrated their expectations of business firms primarily on the bread-and-butter topics of wages and layoffs. The incongruity between managerial rationale and workers' concerns raises the question anew why there is such a strong drive toward participation among the businessmen of this community.

A fruitful way of looking at participation in the community by business is to examine it from the perspective of what functions it serves for business. In this connection, we must look beyond the manifest or surface motivations to view the community organizations as a system performing various types of functions for the participating organizations and individuals.

Perhaps the most obvious function served by clubs and other community organizations is to provide a framework for social life, opportunities for interaction and for gregarious pleasures. Many respondents, particularly those who had experienced mobility from community to community, remarked how the clubs provided opportuni-

[1] The research reported was designed as an exploratory study of the roles played by business enterprises in the local community. It was requested and paid for by the American Telephone and Telegraph Company.

Mediana is a pseudonym for a Midwest industrial city of about 45,000 population. The data were collected through personal interviews with about fifty businessmen and community leaders, supplemented by fifteen interviews with a "sample" of the general population.

ties to meet and become acquainted with persons on roughly the same status level.

Secondly, participation provides a context in which businessmen may build up the right of access to one another and to community leaders. At the same time, community leaders can have easy access to those who control the economic institutions of the community. Most business managers are on a first-name basis with one another and with city and county officials. The number of times these "contacts" are employed is considerable. During many of the interviews, telephone calls were received by respondents from other businessmen and community leaders concerning "favors" or other actions facilitating the conduct of business. As one city official put it,

> If a new firm comes in and remains completely aloof (from civic affairs) there would be no effort from the city to make their load lighter.

Asked how the city might make a firm's load lighter, he replied,

> Of course, for a firm coming in, the city can do a hell of a lot. There is one firm in this town that is only paying a dollar a year for water. Or, you might rent them city property at a nominal rate. Now, Power Parts and American Ceramics: we helped them out on their parking problem. (City Solicitor)

Mediana Bell commercial managers have excellent access to officials of the city government and to the local newspaper. The number of items on Bell activities appearing in the newspaper is quite large, a function, we believe, of the excellent relationships between the local manager and the editor of the newspaper.[2]

Although the traffic in favors among businessmen and between businessmen and community leaders is not a traffic in heavy goods, it does constitute a steady flow of a considerable magnitude. The stream of favors is a lubricant, making the conduct of business in Mediana much easier than it would be if every request had to go through official channels and be subject to bureaucratic scrutiny.

Community participation also builds a bridge between the locals and the itinerant managers of business enterprises. The locals, who can command popular support by virtue of their personal reputations and higher degrees of notoriety, occupy the posts of leadership in the local government and in whatever civic organizations rest on mass support.

[2] Most of the items were personal or social items relating to employees of the company, such as promotions, safety awards, and the like.

It is in the civic organizations that the business-manager outsiders establish contact with the local leaders and obtain their support in actions involving the general population.

Finally, the community participation system provides a means of ordering firms and individuals who have no intrinsic ordering relationships among themselves. Most of the firms in Mediana are not competing with one another but with firms located elsewhere. Business managers do not compete with one another in their career lines, which are located primarily within the industries of which their firms are parts. In the absence of any enduring economic traffic among firms and individuals, the status of units within both groups is quite ambiguous. The community participation activities provide a means of ordering firms according to a unitary criterion. Indeed, the reputation of a firm in Mediana among members of the business community—an important reference group for businessmen—is to a large part determined by the extent to which its managers participate in community affairs. Note that this explanation also provides an understanding of why firms and their managers are not allowed to participate beyond what is their proper level—or, at least, they are not given credit for such participation. This is an ordering device for separating firms which are alike in size and wealth, not for producing anomalies.

As a device for allocating prestige among businessmen, community participation furnishes the major outside-of-plant method of cashing in on one's success and achievements. It is particularly important for the top men in each of the industrial plants, the remainder of whose firms are located at some distance. For these persons success in community organizations represents on-the-spot prestige returns. It is significant that for the telephone company, especially the plant and traffic departments, where company loyalty is much greater on the managerial level, and where career opportunities within the company are so plentiful, community participation does not seem to be as important a source of gratification.

One consequence of the development of community participation as a ranking device is to give to the professional community organization manager (e.g., the Chamber of Commerce manager or the United Fund manager) the function of prestige broker. He serves as the information center, relaying to each businessman how he stands vis-à-vis the others. Indeed, the Mediana United Fund manager has managed thoroughly to convince the telephone company personnel that they are much lower on the totem pole of United Fund contributions than they actually are. Since the success of the managers of community organizations depend on the extent to which they are able to rally the financial and manpower support of the business community to their organizations, a clever man has a powerful weapon at his command.

This analysis implies that the primary audience in front of whom the roles of community participation are played consists of the members of the business community. This, of course, is not the only audience. To some degree what a firm's management does becomes known to the workers in the plant and to the public at large. A firm which has a good reputation in this respect probably benefits by being able to recruit workers and to obtain a favorable acceptance, generally. But the process by which the activity of a firm becomes known is slow and somewhat tricky. The things which are best known about firms by the general public are not those which necessarily mean the most to the business community. For example, the outstanding company in public esteem is Ajax Steel, whose employees' park (an impressive place indeed) was often referred to as its major contribution to the community. The busy committee life of the Chamber or the clubs receives some mention in the newspaper, but, like announcements of birth, deaths, and marriages, such notices seem to be read mainly by those most closely concerned. Indeed, it would almost appear that the general public is about a decade behind in its perception of various firms' activities.

The analysis of community participation presented here receives additional support when we consider the types of activities in which businessmen prefer to participate. The desirable forms of participation in the eyes of Mediana's business community are those which are clearly acceptable to the community as disinterested and which meet with no overt opposition. Participating in political affairs is acceptable only when the element of hostility and possible opposition are moved from the scene, preferably in advance. Hence, the preference is for the "citizens' committee" form of organization, a citizens' committee being ordinarily composed of representatives from all segments of the community which might possibly raise some opposition. Thus, in Mediana, the citizens' committee which sponsored the school bond issue drives was headed by a Protestant, a Catholic, and a Jew.

Because the business community entertains such a strong negative evaluation of the political area, it is worth while to spend some time here in trying to understand this point of view and to seek for its sources.

It should be noted that there are a number of paradoxes involved in this viewpoint. First of all, a good proportion of the civic activities which businessmen prize so highly are directly political in character. The bond issue drives, the move to change the city charter, to get the expressway bypass, all involve some sort of governmental action. The main social problems of Mediana are political, but there is a deprecation of politics and a definite reluctance to get into this area.

Secondly, although all these men expressed their unwillingness to get into politics in terms of the adverse effects such participation would have on their businesses, this rationale does not ring very true. Most of the persons presently holding political office in Mediana, as well as a large proportion of the leaders of both political parties, are businessmen. (For example, only one member of the City Council is an industrial worker; the others are all either the owners of small businesses or on the supervisory levels of some industrial plant.) Those who are in the thick of political life claim that there is no resultant noticeable effect on their businesses. It is almost as though the business community fears hostility and is unable to sustain it. In fact, one of the clear characteristics of the business community is its uncertainty about how to handle both opposition and hostility.

Finally, although there is widespread recognition of the need for "better" (i.e., businessmen) public officials, at the same time there is a definite and firm rejection of the possibility of personal participation in this sphere. The politician in Mediana is viewed by the businessman as a pariah: a man who does necessary and even essential work but who contaminates himself in the process of so doing. Just as the pariah is dangerous because of his contamination, so politics is dangerous because of the possibility of achieving pariah status. Politics, say the respondents, forces a man to be untrue to himself: he must compromise principle, associate with undesirables (i.e., across class lines), and be prepared to be assaulted unfairly and to retaliate in kind.

Note that the activities which receive approval in the business community are those in which the possibility of failure is minimized. It is this maximization of success which is the key to the rejection of "politics." The failure of a high-level manager to "put across" his project would cast too much doubt on his position within the business community. Hence projects are carefully scouted out in advance and those for which there is no guarantee of success are carefully avoided. Projects which respect the proper order and which will not be attacked are the appropriate form of participation for Mediana's businessmen.

B. Business and Community Leadership

The managers of the "average" business enterprise are at least members of the Chamber and one or more of the clubs. The firm contributes to the various fund drives and allows the solicitation of contributions from its employees. Some of the firms provide "leadership" —this is to say, its managers take on more than rank-and-file duties, perhaps setting up drives or becoming members of the various boards of the civic organizations. Even more important is the type of leadership which goes beyond office holding to supply some kind of initiative and momentum to community projects.

The leaders of Mediana—both officeholders and "hot rods"—come from two sources. Locals provide a good proportion of the leadership. Particularly political office, which involves popular appeal, is almost the exclusive province of this group. For a local it often does not matter what his occupation is as long as he is in business. A local, in other words, can rise to leadership position on his personal merits, whatever they might be.

Not so for the recent arrival, however. His rise to leadership seems more dependent on his job and his firm. The new manager of a large plant can find himself a place in the local firmament much more easily than the new manager of a small enterprise. All he need do is give in to the invitations he will receive.

While leadership is open to the larger outsider firms, it is not expected that leadership necessarily is forthcoming. However, for the managers of locally owned [3] large enterprises, leadership is definitely expected. Hence the common complaint in our interviews concerning the failure of the owners of American Ceramics to provide leadership for the community.

These considerations all lead to the conclusion that it is difficult for the manager of a small branch of an outside firm to make any significant impact on Mediana's civic life. Mediana Bell, which fits into this category, can rise only to the second level of leadership, because it is neither local nor large. Indeed, the personnel of Mediana Bell tie in most closely with the second level of command in large industries (e.g., personnel director, general foreman, and the like), or on the level of the small retail merchants.

Among the various management levels within a particular firm, each finds its own niche in the organizational structure. In Mediana,

[3] A local industry is one which has its home office in Mediana.

all persons on the top two or three levels within a firm are in the Chamber of Commerce: usually it is mainly the top man who is active enough to get on the Board of Directors.

There is a rank order to the service clubs as well. The personnel of Mediana Bell demonstrate this rather nicely: the District Commercial Manager is in Rotary, the Local Commercial Manager is in Kiwanis, and the Plant and Traffic Chiefs are in lower-ranking clubs like Sertoma and Optimists. There is a saying in Mediana to the effect that Rotary owns the town, Kiwanis runs it, and the Jaycees do all the leg work. . . .

C. Community Expectations and Enterprises

If the participation of business in community affairs is as we have interpreted it, a matter of conforming to company policy and to the prevailing patterns of life in the business community, then we should be able to detect the existence of commonly agreed-upon expectations concerning the roles to be played by business. Such is indeed the case.

1. *Expectations by Nonbusiness Leaders*

Perhaps the main expectation concerns financial contributions to the organization. Here expectations vary according to the size and prosperity of the business operation. The larger and more prosperous the operation, the more it is expected to give, and to help the civic organization to obtain funds from other businesses.

In addition, businesses are expected to supply personnel to man committees, and to do all the work that constitutes a "project." A "cooperating" firm is defined as one which is liberal in assigning one or another from its staff to do community "duties." . . .

Community leaders hope that each firm lives up to the expectations they hold of it. However, the highest rewards do not go to firms which fulfill only these expectations. Additional credit goes to firms whose participation is performed in proper *style*. Grudging and reluctant fulfillment of expectations, even if it is complete, is not regarded as highly as partial fulfillment accomplished in a spontaneous and generous mood.

Perhaps the best way to define this style element is to give a few examples: the two companies which received especially commendatory remarks from the United Fund manager were Mediana Power and Power Parts. Mediana Power's manager was praised because he had worked out a method, by cooperating with the Utility Workers' Union, of getting around the Power Company's stricture against pay-roll deductions for the United Fund. Union representatives and company personnel men stationed themselves at the pay office on pay day and solicited contributions from the Power Company employees.

Power Parts received special praise because of its policy of permitting its workers to work up to four hours overtime at time-and-a-half, the wages so earned to be contributed to the United Fund. The overtime is worked on a particular day each year, specially designated as "Good Neighbor Day." Power Parts gives to its participating workers special stickers for their cars and for the windows of their homes as visible indicators of contributions as "Good Neighbors."

2. *Business Community Expectations*

The business managers in Mediana have somewhat less firm expectations concerning the participation of other business enterprises in the community. Perhaps the common theme which ran through all the interviews was that these men expected other business managers to "do their share." In fact, this attitude came out quite clearly in the way in which they talked about their own companies. Perhaps the most frequent response was, "We do our share."

Specifically, a "proper share" means participating in the following activities: a company should have a number of memberships on the Chamber of Commerce, the number being proportionate to the size of the company's operations in Mediana. The company should make a reasonable corporate contribution to the United Fund and to the special drives. It should allow the fund solicitors to have access to its workers, and to allow a pay-roll deduction plan for United Fund gifts and pledges to other fund drives. The company should send some of its managerial personnel into the various service clubs and its younger executives into the Jaycees. Some member of the firm should be in the Country Club. It is not expected that a company should strive for leadership in the civic organizations or in other community activities. However, if some member of the company does provide leadership, it redounds to the benefit of the company. . . .

3. *Expectations Held by the General Public*

Perhaps the weakest expectations concerning participation along the lines desired by the business community in Mediana are held by the few members of the general public whom we interviewed. For the general public, the world of community organization is a newspaper phenomenon—that is, something about which the newspaper generally prints articles but which has relatively little connection with their everyday life. The typical respondent was more concerned with the community problems amenable to political treatment than with those amenable to treatment through the voluntary organizations. Typically, the average citizen was concerned with community problems like parking, street conditions, the pollution of Mediana's rivers, and the provision of adequate recreation for children. Business community projects are usually on a "higher" plane, concerned with less "concrete" matters.

When asked what should be the obligations of a business to the city where it is located, twelve of the fifteen respondents indicated that a primary obligation of a business was to pay "adequate" or "just" or "decent" wages. This obligation to maintain a reasonable wage policy was the most important one in the minds of our respondents. Another nine referred to "working conditions," indicating that it is the obligation of an industry to provide conditions of work which are not dangerous to life or limb and have some amenities. The typical respondent would refer both to wages and working conditions as areas in which businesses had their primary obligations. Four indicated that businesses should not be "anti-labor"—that is, they should have an accommodative attitude toward labor unions. Three referred to the permanency of the plant, indicating that the industry should "stay in Mediana." Another three spoke of contributions to fund drives. Two referred to "contributions to community progress," meaning largely aiding the town to obtain additional industries. Finally, one each referred to "becoming part of the town" and to keeping their plants looking well.

Note that the major emphasis given by the general population sample concerns obligations to offer and maintain high labor standards, referring to wages, working conditions, and attitudes toward unions. A minority of respondents referred to the typical activities of the civic organizations of the community. Significantly, the three respondents who referred to this sort of obligation were members of the business community themselves: a medical doctor, the owner of a business equipment and stationery store, and an engineer in one of the industrial plants.

Whether or not these expectations would also be found to characterize the same groups in other communities is, of course, impossible to say. In Mediana, the business community is well-organized around the Chamber of Commerce and the service clubs. In another community whose civic life was less well developed, expectations are likely to be weaker. Similarly, in a community in which employment is not a problem, the general public might focus its attention on other types of business activities.

Erving Goffman

The Characteristics of Total Institutions

Social establishments—institutions in the everyday sense of that term—are buildings or plants in which activity of a particular kind regularly goes on. . . . Each captures something of the time and interest of its members and provides something of a world for them; in brief, every institution has encompassing tendencies. When we review the different institutions in our Western society we find a class of them which seems to be encompassing to a degree discontinuously greater than the ones next in line. Their encompassing or total character is symbolized by the barrier to social intercourse with the outside that is often built right into the physical plant: locked doors, high walls, barbed wire, cliffs and water, open terrain, and so forth. These I am calling total institutions, and it is their general characteristics I want to explore.[1] This exploration will be phrased as if securely based on findings but will in fact be speculative.

Reprinted in part from Erving Goffman, "The Characteristics of Total Institutions," in *Symposium on Preventive and Social Psychiatry,* 15–17, April 1957, Walter Reed Army Institute of Research, Washington, D.C., by permission of the author and publisher.

[1] The category of total institutions has been pointed out from time to time in the sociological literature under a variety of names, and some of the characteristics of the class have been suggested, most notably perhaps in Howard Roland's neglected paper, "Segregated Communities and Mental Health," in *Mental Health Publication of the American Association for the Advancement of Science,* No. 9, edited by F. R. Moulton, 1939. A preliminary statement of the present paper is reported in the *Third Group Processes Proceedings,* Josiah Macy Foundation, edited by Bertram Schaffner, 1957.

The total institutions of our society can be listed for convenience in five rough groupings. *First,* there are institutions established to care for persons thought to be both incapable and harmless; these are the homes for the blind, the aged, the orphaned, and the indigent. *Second,* there are places established to care for persons thought to be at once incapable of looking after themselves and a threat to the community, albeit an unintended one: TB sanitariums, mental hospitals, and leprosoriums. *Third,* another type of total institution is organized to protect the community against what are thought to be intentional dangers to it; here the welfare of the persons thus sequestered is not the immediate issue. Examples are: Jails, penitentiaries, POW camps, and concentration camps. *Fourth,* we find institutions purportedly established the better to pursue some technical task and justifying themselves only on these instrumental grounds: Army barracks, ships, boarding schools, work camps, colonial compounds, large mansions from the point of view of those who live in the servants' quarters, and so forth. *Finally,* there are those establishments designed as retreats from the world or as training stations for the religious: Abbeys, monasteries, convents, and other cloisters. This sublisting of total institutions is neither neat nor exhaustive, but the listing itself provides an empirical starting point for a purely denotative definition of the category. By anchoring the initial definition of total institutions in this way, I hope to be able to discuss the general characteristics of the type without becoming tautological.

Before attempting to extract a general profile from this list of establishments, one conceptual peculiarity must be mentioned. None of the elements I will extract seems entirely exclusive to total institutions, and none seems shared by every one of them. What is shared and unique about total institutions is that each exhibits many items in this family of attributes to an intense degree. In speaking of "common characteristics," then, I will be using this phrase in a weakened, but I think logically defensible, way.

Totalistic Features

A basic social arrangement in modern society is that we tend to sleep, play and work in different places, in each case with a different set of coparticipants, under a different authority, and without an over-all rational plan. The central feature of total institutions can be described as a breakdown of the kinds of barriers ordinarily separating these three spheres of life. *First,* all aspects of life are conducted in the same place and under the same single authority. *Second,* each phase of the member's daily activity will be carried out in the immediate company of a large batch of others, all of whom are treated alike and required to do the same thing together. *Third,* all phases of the day's activities are tightly scheduled, with one activity leading at a prearranged time into the next, the whole circle of activities being imposed from above through a system of explicit formal rulings and a body of officials. *Finally,* the contents of the various enforced activities are brought together as parts of a single over-all rational plan purportedly designed to fulfill the official aims of the institution.

Individually, these totalistic features are found, of course, in places other than total institutions. Increasingly, for example, our large commercial, industrial and educational establishments provide cafeterias, minor services and off-hour recreation for their members. But while this is a tendency in the direction of total institutions, these extended facilities remain voluntary in many particulars of their use, and special care is taken to see that the ordinary line of authority does not extend to these situations. Similarly, housewives or farm families can find all their major spheres of life within the same fenced-in area, but these persons are not collectively regimented and do not march through the day's steps in the immediate company of a batch of similar others.

The handling of many human needs by the bureaucratic organization of whole blocks of people—whether or not this is a necessary or effective means of social organization in the circumstances—can be taken, then, as the key fact of total institutions. From this, certain important implications can be drawn.

Given the fact that blocks of people are caused to move in time, it becomes possible to use a relatively small number of supervisory personnel where the central relationship is not guidance or periodic checking, as in many employer-employee relations, but rather surveillance—a seeing to it that everyone does what he has been clearly told is required of him, and this under conditions where one person's infraction is likely to stand out in relief against the visible, constantly examined, compliance of the others. Which comes first, the large block of managed people or the small supervisory staff, is not here at issue; the point is that each is made for the other.

In total institutions, as we would then suspect, there is a basic split between a large class of individuals who live in and who have restricted contact with the world outside the walls, conveniently called *inmates*, and the small class that supervises them, conveniently called *staff*, who often operate on an 8-hour day and are socially integrated into the outside world.[2] Each grouping tends to conceive of members of the other in terms of narrow hostile stereotypes, staff often seeing inmates as bitter, secretive and untrustworthy, while inmates often see staff as condescending, high-handed and mean. Staff tends to feel superior and righteous; inmates tend, in some ways at least, to feel inferior, weak, blameworthy and guilty.[3] Social mobility between the two strata is grossly restricted; social distance is typically great and often formally prescribed; even talk across the boundaries may be conducted in a special tone of voice. These restrictions on contact presumably help to maintain the antagonistic stereotypes.[4] In any case, two different social and cultural worlds develop, tending to jog along beside each other, with points of official contact but little mutual penetration. It is important to add that the institutional plant and name comes to be identified by both staff and inmates as somehow belonging to staff, so that when either grouping refers to the views or interests of "the institution," by implication they are referring (as I shall also) to the views and concerns of the staff.

The staff-inmate split is one major implication of the central features of total institutions; a second one pertains to work. In the ordinary arrangements of living in our society, the authority of the workplace stops with the worker's receipt of a money payment; the spending of this in a domestic and recreational setting is at the discretion of the worker and is the mechanism through which the authority of the workplace is kept within strict bounds. However, to say that inmates in total institutions have their full day scheduled for them is to say that some version of all basic needs will have to be planned for, too. In other words, total institutions take over "responsibility" for the inmate and must guarantee to have everything that is defined as essential "layed on." It follows, then, that whatever incentive is given

[2] The binary character of total institutions was pointed out to me by Gregory Bateson, and proves to be noted in the literature. See, for example, Lloyd E. Ohlin, *Sociology and the Field of Corrections*, Russell Sage Foundation, New York; 1956, pp. 14, 20. In those special situations where staff too is required to live in, we may expect staff members to feel they are suffering from special hardships and to have brought home to them a status-dependency on life on the inside which they did not expect. See Jane Cassels Record, "The Marine Radioman's Struggle for Status," *American Journal of Sociology*, Vol. LXII, 1957, p. 359.

[3] For the prison version, see S. Kirson Weinburg, "Aspects of the Prison's Social Structure," *American Journal of Sociology*, Vol. 47, 1942, pp. 717–726.

[4] Suggested in Ohlin, *op. cit.*, p. 20.

for work, this will not have the structural significance it has on the outside. Different attitudes and incentives regarding this central feature of our life will have to prevail.

Here, then, is one basic adjustment required of those who work in total institutions and of those who must induce these people to work. In some cases, no work or little is required, and inmates, untrained often in leisurely ways of life, suffer extremes of boredom. In other cases, some work is required but is carried on at an extremely slow pace, being geared into a system of minor, often ceremonial payments, as in the case of weekly tobacco ration and annual Christmas presents, which cause some mental patients to stay on their job. In some total institutions, such as logging camps and merchant ships, something of the usual relation to the world that money can buy is obtained through the practice of "forced saving"; all needs are organized by the institution, and payment is given only after a work season is over and the men leave the premises. And in some total institutions, of course, more than a full day's work is required and is induced not by reward, but by threat of dire punishment. In all such cases, the work-oriented individual may tend to become somewhat demoralized by the system.

In addition to the fact that total institutions are incompatible with the basic work-payment structure of our society, it must be seen that these establishments are also incompatible with another crucial element of our society, the family. The family is sometimes contrasted to solitary living, but in fact the more pertinent contrast to family life might be with batch living. For it seems that those who eat and sleep at work, with a group of fellow workers, can hardly sustain a meaningful domestic existence. Correspondingly, the extent to which a staff retains its integration in the outside community and escapes the encompassing tendencies of total institutions is often linked up with the maintenance of a family off the grounds. . . .

Total institutions, then, are social hybrids, part residential community, part formal organization, and therein lies their special sociological interest. There are other reasons, alas, for being interested in them, too. These establishments are the forcing houses for changing persons in our society. Each is a natural experiment, typically harsh, on what can be done to the self.

Having suggested some of the key features of total institutions, we can move on now to consider them from the special perspectives of the inmate world and the staff world.

THE INMATE WORLD

Mortification Processes

It is characteristic of inmates that they come to the institution as members, already full-fledged, of a *home world,* that is, a way of life and a round of activities taken for granted up to the point of admission to the institution.[5] It is useful to look at this culture that the recruit brings with him to the institution's door—his *presenting culture,* to modify a psychiatric phrase—in terms especially designed to highlight what it is the total institution will do to him. Whatever the stability of his personal organization, we can assume it was part of a wider supporting framework lodged in his current social environment, a round of experience that somewhat confirms a conception of self that is somewhat acceptable to him and a set of defensive maneuvers exercisable at his own discretion as a means of coping with conflicts, discreditings and failures.

Now it appears that total institutions do not substitute their own unique culture for something already formed. We do not deal with acculturation or assimilation but with something more restricted than these. In a sense, total institutions do not look for cultural victory. They effectively create and sustain a particular kind of tension between the home world and the institutional world and use this persistent tension as strategic leverage in the management of men. The full meaning for the inmate of being "in" or "on the inside" does not exist apart from the special meaning to him of "getting out" or "getting on the outside."

The recruit comes into the institution with a self and with attachments to supports which had allowed this self to survive. Upon entrance, he is immediately stripped of his wonted supports, and his self is systematically, if often unintentionally, mortified. In the accurate language of some of our oldest total institutions, he is led into a series of abasements, degradations, humiliations, and profanations of self. He begins, in other words, some radical shifts in his *moral career,* a career laying out the progressive changes that occur in the beliefs that he has concerning himself and significant others.

[5] There is reason then to exclude orphanages and foundling homes from the list of total institutions, except insofar as the orphan comes to be socialized into the outside world by some process of cultural osmosis, even while this world is being systematically denied him.

The *stripping processes* through which *mortification of the self* occurs are fairly standard in our total institutions. Personal identity equipment is removed, as well as other possessions with which the inmate may have identified himself, there typically being a system of nonaccessible storage from which the inmate can only reobtain his effects should he leave the institution. As a substitute for what has been taken away, institutional issue is provided, but this will be the same for large categories of inmates and will be regularly repossessed by the institution. In brief, standardized defacement will occur. In addition, ego-invested separateness from fellow inmates is significantly diminished in many areas of activity, and tasks are prescribed that are *infra dignitatem*. Family, occupational, and educational career lines are chopped off, and a stigmatized status is submitted. Sources of fantasy materials which had meant momentary releases from stress in the home world are denied. Areas of autonomous decision are eliminated through the process of collective scheduling of daily activity. Many channels of communication with the outside are restricted or closed off completely. Verbal discreditings occur in many forms as a matter of course. Expressive signs of respect for the staff are coercively and continuously demanded. And the effect of each of these conditions is multiplied by having to witness the mortification of one's fellow inmates.

We must expect to find different official reasons given for these assaults upon the self. In mental hospitals there is the matter of protecting the patient from himself and from other patients. In jails there is the issue of "security" and frank punishment. In religious institutions we may find sociologically sophisticated theories about the soul's need for purification and penance through disciplining of the flesh. What all of these rationales share is the extent to which they are merely rationalizations, for the underlying force in many cases is unwittingly generated by efforts to manage the daily activity of a large number of persons in a small space with a small expenditure of resources.

In the background of the sociological stripping process, we find a characteristic authority system with three distinctive elements, each basic to total institutions.

First, to a degree, authority is of the *echelon* kind. Any member of the staff class has certain rights to discipline any member of the inmate class. This arrangement, it may be noted, is similar to the one which gives any adult in some small American towns certain rights to correct and demand small services from any child not in the immediate presence of his parents. In our society, the adult himself, however, is typically under the authority of a *single* immediate superior in connection with his work or under authority of one spouse in connection with domestic duties. The only echelon authority he must face—the police—typically are neither constantly nor relevantly present, except perhaps in the case of traffic-law enforcement.

Second, the authority of corrective sanctions is directed to a great multitude of items of conduct of the kind that are constantly occurring and constantly coming up for judgment; [6] in brief, authority is directed to matters of dress, deportment, social intercourse, manners and the like. In prisons these regulations regarding situational proprieties may even extend to a point where silence during mealtime is enforced, while in some convents explicit demands may be made concerning the custody of the eyes during prayer.

The third feature of authority in total institutions is that misbehaviors in one sphere of life are held against one's standing in other spheres. Thus, an individual who fails to participate with proper enthusiasm in sports may be brought to the attention of the person who determines where he will sleep and what kind of work task will be accorded to him.

When we combine these three aspects of authority in total institutions, we see that the inmate cannot easily escape from the press of judgmental officials and from the enveloping tissue of constraint. The system of authority undermines the basis for control that adults in our society expect to exert over their interpersonal environment and may produce the terror of feeling that one is being radically demoted in the age-grading system. On the outside, rules are sufficiently lax and the individual sufficiently agreeable to required self-discipline to insure that others will rarely have cause for pouncing on him. He need not constantly look over his shoulder to see if criticism and other sanctions are coming. On the inside, however, rulings are abundant, novel, and closely enforced so that, quite characteristically, inmates live with chronic anxiety about breaking the rules and chronic worry about the consequences of breaking them. The desire to "stay out of trouble" in a total institution is likely to require persistent conscious

[6] The span of time over which an employee works at his own discretion without supervision can in fact be taken as a measure of his pay and status in an organization. See Elliot Jacques, *The Measurement of Responsibility: A Study of Work, Payment, and Individual Capacity,* Harvard University Press, Cambridge, 1956. And just as "time-span of responsibility" is an index of position, so a long span of freedom from inspection is a reward of position.

effort and may lead the inmate to abjure certain levels of sociability with his fellows in order to avoid the incidents that may occur in these circumstances.[7]

It should be noted finally that the mortifications to be suffered by the inmate may be purposely brought home to him in an exaggerated way during the first few days after entrance, in a form of initiation that has been called *the welcome.* Both staff and fellow inmates may go out of their way to give the neophyte a clear notion of where he stands.[8] As part of this *rite de passage,* he may find himself called by a term such as "fish," "swab," etc., through which older inmates tell him that he is not only merely an inmate but that even within this lowly group he has a low status.

Privilege System

While the process of mortification is in progress, the inmate begins to receive formal and informal instruction in what will here be called the *privilege system.* Insofar as the inmate's self has been unsettled a little by the stripping action of the institution, it is largely around this framework that pressures are exerted, making for a reorganization of self. Three basic elements of the system may be mentioned.

First, there are the *house rules,* a relatively explicit and formal set of prescriptions and proscriptions which lay out the main requirements of inmate conduct. These regulations spell out the austere round of life in which the inmate will operate. Thus, the admission procedures through which the recruit is initially stripped of his self-supporting context can be seen as the institution's way of getting him in the position to start living by the house rules.

Second, against the stark background, a small number of clearly defined *rewards or privileges* are held out in exchange for obedience to staff in action and spirit. It is important to see that these potential gratifications are not unique to the institution but rather are ones carved out of the flow of support that the inmate previously had quite

[7] Staff sometimes encourages this tendency for inmates to stand clear of one another, perhaps in order to limit the dangers of organized inmate resistance to institutional rule. Through an interesting phrase, inmates may be officially encouraged to "do their own time."

[8] For the version of this process in concentration camps, see Elie A. Cohen, *Human Behaviour in the Concentration Camp,* Jonathan Cape, n.p., 1954, p. 120. For a fictionalized treatment of the welcome in a girls' reformatory, see Sara Norris, *The Wayward Ones,* Signet Pocket Books, New York, 1952, pp. 31–34.

taken for granted. On the outside, for example, the inmate was likely to be able to unthinkingly exercise autonomy by deciding how much sugar and milk he wanted in his coffee, if any, or when to light up a cigarette; on the inside, this right may become quite problematic and a matter of a great deal of conscious concern. Held up to the inmate as possibilities, these few recapturings seem to have a reintegrative effect, re-establishing relationships with the whole lost world and assuaging withdrawal symptoms from it and from one's lost self.

The inmate's run of attention, then, especially at first, comes to be fixated on these supplies and obsessed with them. In the most fanatic way, he can spend the day in devoted thoughts concerning the possibility of acquiring these gratifications or the approach of the hour at which they are scheduled to be granted. The building of a world around these minor privileges is perhaps the most important feature of inmate culture and yet is something that cannot easily be appreciated by an outsider, even one who has lived through the experience himself. This situation sometimes leads to generous sharing and almost always to a willingness to beg for things such as cigarettes, candy and newspapers. It will be understandable, then, that a constant feature of inmate discussion is the *release binge fantasy,* namely, recitals of what one will do during leave or upon release from the institution.

House rules and privileges provide the functional requirements of the third element in the privilege system: *punishments.* These are designated as the consequence of breaking the rules. One set of these punishments consists of the temporary or permanent withdrawal of privileges or abrogation of the right to try to earn them. In general, the punishments meted out in total institutions are of an order more severe than anything encountered by the inmate in his home world. An institutional arrangement which causes a small number of easily controlled privileges to have a massive significance is the same arrangement which lends a terrible significance to their withdrawal.

There are some special features of the privilege system which should be noted.

First, punishments and privileges are themselves modes of organization peculiar to total institutions. Whatever their severity, punishments are largely known in the inmate's home world as something applied to animals and children. For adults this conditioning, behavioristic model is actually not widely applied, since failure to maintain required standards typically leads to indirect disadvantageous consequences and not to specific immediate punishment at all. And privileges, it should be emphasized, are not the same as prerequisites, indulgences or values, but merely the absence of deprivations one ordinarily expects one would not have to sustain. The very notions, then, of punishments and privileges are not ones that are cut from civilian cloth.

Second, it is important to see that the question of release from the total institution is elaborated into the privilege system. Some acts will become known as ones that mean an increase or no decrease in length of stay, while others become known as means for lessening the sentence.

Third, we should also note that punishments and privileges come to be geared into a residential work system. Places to work and places to sleep become clearly defined as places where certain kinds and levels of privilege obtain, and inmates are shifted very rapidly and visibly from one place to another as the mechanisms for giving them the punishment or privilege their cooperativeness has warranted. The inmates are moved, the system is not.

This, then, is the privilege system: a relatively few components put together with some rational intent and clearly proclaimed to the participants. The overall consequence is that cooperativeness is obtained from persons who often have cause to be uncooperative.[9]

Immediately associated with the privilege system we find some standard social processes important in the life of total institutions.

We find that an *institutional lingo* develops through which inmates express the events that are crucial in their particular world. Staff too, especially its lower levels, will know this language, using it when talking to inmates, while reverting to more standardized speech when talking to superiors and outsiders. Related to this special argot, inmates will possess knowledge of the various ranks and officials, an accumulation of lore about the establishment, and some comparative information about life in other similar total institutions.

Also found among staff and inmates will be a clear awareness of the phenomenon of *messing up,* so called in mental hospitals, prisons, and barracks. This involves a complex process of engaging in forbidden activity, getting caught doing so, and receiving something like the full punishment accorded this. An alteration in privilege status

[9] An excellent description of this model universe as found in a State mental Hospital may be found in Ivan Belknap, *Human Problems of a State Mental Hospital,* McGraw-Hill, New York, 1956, p. 164.

is usually implied and is categorized by a phrase such as "getting busted." Typical infractions which can eventuate in messing up are: fights, drunkenness, attempted suicide, failure at examinations, gambling, insubordination, homosexuality, improper taking of leave, and participation in collective riots. While these punished infractions are typically ascribed to the offender's cussedness, villainy, or "sickness," they do in fact constitute a vocabulary of institutionalized actions, limited in such a way that the same messing up may occur for quite different reasons. Informally, inmates and staff may understand, for example, that a given messing up is a way for inmates to show resentment against a current situation felt to be unjust in terms of the informal agreements between staff and inmates,[10] or a way of postponing release without having to admit to one's fellow inmates that one really does not want to go.[11]

In total institutions there will also be a system of what might be called *secondary adjustments,* namely, technics which do not directly challenge staff management but which allow inmates to obtain disallowed satisfactions or allowed ones by disallowed means. These practices are variously referred to as: the angles, knowing the ropes, conniving, gimmicks, deals, ins, etc. Such adaptations apparently reach their finest flower in prisons, but of course other total institutions are overrun with them too.[12] It seems apparent that an important aspect of secondary adjustments is that they provide the inmate with some evidence that he is still, as it were, his own man and still has some protective distance, under his own control, between himself and the institution. In some cases, then, a secondary adjustment becomes almost a kind of lodgment for the self, a churinga in which the soul is felt to reside.[13]

The occurrence of secondary adjustments correctly allows us to

[10] For example, see Morris G. Caldwell, "Group Dynamics in the Prison Community," *Journal of Criminal Law, Criminology and Police Science,* Vol. 46, 1956, p. 656.

[11] There are some interesting incidental social functions of messings up. First, they tend to limit rigidities which might occur were seniority the only means of mobility in the privilege system. Secondly, demotion through messing up brings old-time inmates in contact with new inmates in unprivileged positions, assuring a flow of information about the system and the people in it.

[12] See, for example, Norma S. Hayner and Ellis Ash, "The Prisoner Community as a Social Group," *American Sociological Review,* Vol. 4, 1939, pp. 364 ff. under "Conniving Processes"; also, Caldwell, *op. cit.,* pp. 650–651.

[13] See, for example, Melville's extended description of the fight his fellow seamen put up to prevent the clipping of their beards in full accordance with Navy regulations. Melville, *White Jacket* (New York: Grove Press, n.d.), pp. 333–347.

assume that the inmate group will have some kind of a *code* and some means of informal social control evolved to prevent one inmate from informing staff about the secondary adjustments of another. On the same grounds we can expect that one dimension of social typing among inmates will turn upon this question of security, leading to persons defined as "squealers," "finks," or "stoolies" on one hand, and persons defined as "right guys" on the other.[14] It should be added that where new inmates can play a role in the system of secondary adjustments, as in providing new faction members or new sexual objects, then their "welcome" may indeed be a sequence of initial indulgences and enticements, instead of exaggerated deprivations.[15] Because of secondary adjustments we also find *kitchen strata,* namely, a kind of rudimentary, largely informal, stratification of inmates on the basis of each one's differential access to disposable illicit commodities; so also we find social typing to designate the powerful persons in the informal market system.[16]

While the privilege system provides the chief framework within which reassembly of the self takes place, other factors characteristically lead by different routes in the same general direction. Relief from economic and social responsibilities—much touted as part of the therapy in mental hospitals—is one, although in many cases it would seem that the disorganizing effect of this moratorium is more significant than its organizing effect. More important as a reorganizing influence is the *fraternalization process,* namely, the process through which socially distant persons find themselves developing mutual support and common *counter-mores* in opposition to a system that has forced them into intimacy and into a single, equalitarian community of fate.[17] It seems that the new recruit frequently starts out with something like the staff's popular misconceptions of the character of the inmates and then comes to find that most of his fellows have all the

[14] See, for example, Donald Clemmer, "Leadership Phenomenon in a Prison Community," *Journal of Criminal Law, Criminology and Police Science,* Vol. 28, 1938, p. 868.

[15] See, for example, Ida Ann Harper, "The Role of the 'Fringer' in a State Prison for Women," *Social Forces,* Vol. 31, 1952, pp. 53–60.

[16] For concentration camps, see the discussion of "Prominents" throughout Cohen, *op. cit.;* for mental hospitals, see Belknap, *op. cit.,* p. 189. For prisons, see the discussion of "Politicos" in Donald Clemmer, *The Prison Community,* Christopher Publishing House, Boston, 1940, pp. 277–279, 298–309; also Hayner, *op. cit.,* p. 367; and Caldwell, *op. cit.,* pp. 651–653.

[17] For the version of this inmate solidarity to be found in military academies, see Sanford M. Dornbusch, "The Military Academy as an Assimilating Institution," *Social Forces,* Vol. 33, 1955, p. 318.

properties of ordinary decent human beings and that the stereotypes associated with their condition or offense are not a reasonable ground for judgment of inmates.[18]

If the inmates are persons who are accused by staff and society of having committed some kind of a crime against society, then the new inmate, even though sometimes in fact quite guiltless, may come to share the guilty feelings of his fellows and, thereafter, their well-elaborated defenses against these feelings. A sense of common injustice and a sense of bitterness against the outside world tends to develop, marking an important movement in the inmate's moral career.

Adaptation Alignments

The mortifying processes that have been discussed and the privilege system represent the conditions that the inmate must adapt to in some way, but however pressing, these conditions allow for different ways of meeting them. We find, in fact, that the same inmate will employ different lines of adaptation or tacks at different phases in his moral career and may even fluctuate between different tacks at the same time.

First, there is the process of *situational withdrawal.* The inmate withdraws apparent attention from everything except events immediately around his body and sees these in a perspective not employed by others present. This drastic curtailment of involvement in interactional events is best known, of course, in mental hospitals, under the title of "regression." Aspects of "prison psychosis" or "stir simpleness" represent the same adjustment, as do some forms of "acute depersonalization" described in concentration camps. I do not think it is known whether this line of adaptation forms a single continuum of varying degrees of withdrawal or whether there are standard discontinuous plateaus of disinvolvement. It does seem to be the case, however, that, given the pressures apparently required to dislodge an inmate from this status, as well as the currently limited facilities for doing so, we frequently find here, effectively speaking, an irreversible line of adaptation.

Second, there is the *rebellious line*. The inmate intentionally chal-

[18] An interesting example of this re-evaluation may be found in a conscientious objector's experience with nonpolitical prisoners, see Alfred Hassler, *Diary of a Self-Made Convict,* Henry Regnery, Chicago, 1954, pp. 74, 117. In mental hospitals, of course, the patient's antagonism to staff obtains one of its supports from the discovery that, like himself, many other patients are more like ordinary persons than like anything else.

lenges the institution by flagrantly refusing to cooperate with staff in almost any way.[19] The result is a constantly communicated intransigency and sometimes high rebel-morale. Most large mental hospitals, for example, seem to have wards where this spirit strongly prevails. Interestingly enough, there are many circumstances in which sustained rejection of a total institution requires sustained orientation to its formal organization and hence, paradoxically, a deep kind of commitment to the establishment. Similarly, when total institutions take the line (as they sometimes do in the case of mental hospitals prescribing lobotomy [20] or army barracks prescribing the stockade) that the recalcitrant inmate must be broken, then, in their way, they must show as much special devotion to the rebel as he has shown to them. It should be added, finally, that while prisoners of war have been known staunchly to take a rebellious stance throughout their incarceration, this stance is typically a temporary and initial phase of reaction, emerging from this to situational withdrawal or some other line of adaptation.

Third, another standard alignment in the institutional world takes the form of a kind of *colonization*. The sampling of the outside world provided by the establishment is taken by the inmate as the whole, and a stable, relatively contented existence is built up out of the maximum satisfactions procurable within the institution.[21] Experience of the outside world is used as a point of reference to demonstrate the desirability of life on the inside; and the usual tension between the two worlds collapses, thwarting the social arrangements based upon this felt discrepancy. Characteristically, the individual who too obviously takes this line may be accused by his fellow inmates of "having found a home" or of "never having had it so good." Staff itself may become vaguely embarrassed by this use that is being made of the institution, sensing that the benign possibilities in the situation are somehow being misused. Colonizers themselves may feel obliged to deny their satisfaction with the institution, if only in the interest of sustaining the counter-mores supporting inmate solidarity. They may find it necessary to mess up just prior to their slated discharge, thereby allowing themselves to present involuntary reasons for continued incarceration. It should be incidentally noted that any humanistic

[19] See, for example, the discussion of "The Resisters," in Edgar H. Schein, "The Chinese Indoctrination Program for Prisoners of War," *Psychiatry*, Vol. 19 (1956), pp. 160–61.

[20] See, for example, Belknap, *op. cit.*, p. 192.

[21] In the case of mental hospitals, those who take this line are sometimes called "institutional cures" or are said to suffer from "hospitalitis."

effort to make life in total institutions more bearable must face the possibility that doing so may increase the attractiveness and likelihood of colonization.

Fourth, one mode of adaptation to the setting of a total institution is that of *conversion.* The inmate appears to take over completely the official or staff view of himself and tries to act out the role of the perfect inmate. While the colonized inmate builds as much of a free community as possible for himself by using the limited facilities available, the convert takes a more disciplined, moralistic, monochromatic line, presenting himself as someone whose institutional enthusiasm is always at the disposal of the staff. In Chinese POW camps, we find Americans who became "pros" and fully espoused the Communist view of the world.[22] In army barracks there are enlisted men who give the impression that they are always "sucking around" and always "bucking for promotion." In prisons there are "square johns." In German concentration camps, longtime prisoners sometimes came to adopt the vocabulary, recreation, posture, expressions of aggression, and clothing style of the Gestapo, executing their role of straw-boss with military strictness.[23] Some mental hospitals have the distinction of providing two quite different conversion possibilities—one for the new admission who can see the light after an appropriate struggle and adapt the psychiatric view of himself, and another for the chronic ward patient who adopts the manner and dress of attendants while helping them to manage the other ward patients with a stringency excelling that of the attendants themselves.

Here, it should be noted, is a significant way in which total institutions differ. Many, like progressive mental hospitals, merchant ships, TB sanitariums and brainwashing camps, offer the inmate an opportunity to live up to a model of conduct that is at once ideal and staff-sponsored—a model felt by its advocates to be in the supreme interests of the very persons to whom it is applied. Other total institutions, like some concentration camps and some prisons, do not officially sponsor an ideal that the inmate is expected to incorporate as a means of judging himself.

While the alignments that have been mentioned represent co-

[22] Schein, *op. cit.*, pp. 167–169.

[23] See Bruno Bettelheim, "Individual and Mass Behavior in Extreme Situations," *Journal of Abnormal and Social Psychology,* Vol. 38, 1943, pp. 447–451. It should be added that in concentration camps, colonization and conversion often seemed to go together. See Cohen, *op. cit.*, pp. 200–203, where the role of the "Kapo" is discussed.

herent courses to pursue, few inmates, it seems, carry these pursuits very far. In most total institutions, what we seem to find is that most inmates take the tack of what they call *playing it cool.* This involves a somewhat opportunistic combination of secondary adjustments, conversion, colonization and loyalty to the inmate group, so that in the particular circumstances the inmate will have a maximum chance of eventually getting out physically and psychically undamaged.[24] Typically, the inmate will support the counter-mores when with fellow inmates and be silent to them on how tractably he acts when alone in the presence of staff.[25] Inmates taking this line tend to subordinate contacts with their fellows to the higher claim of "keeping out of trouble." They tend to volunteer for nothing, and they may even learn to cut their ties to the outside world sufficiently to give cultural reality to the world inside but not enough to lead to colonization.

I have suggested some of the lines of adaptation that inmates can take to the pressures that play in total institutions. Each represents a way of managing the tension between the home world and the institutional world. However, there are circumstances in which the home world of the inmate was such, in fact, as to *immunize* him against the bleak world on the inside, and for such persons no particular scheme of adaptation need be carried very far. Thus, some lower-class mental hospital patients who have lived all their previous life in orphanages, reformatories and jails, tend to see the hospital as just another total institution to which it is possible to apply the adaptive technics learned and perfected in other total institutions. "Playing it cool" represents for such persons, not a shift in their moral career, but an alignment that is already second nature.

The professional criminal element in the early periods of German concentration camps displayed something of the same immunity to

[24] See the discussion in Schein, *op. cit.*, pp. 165–166 of the "Get-Alongers," and Robert J. Lifton, "Home by Ship: Reaction Patterns of American Prisoners of War Repatriated from North Korea," *American Journal of Psychiatry*, Vol. 110, 1954, p. 734.

[25] This two-facedness, of course, is very commonly found in total institutions. In the state-type mental hospital studied by the writer, even the few elite patients selected for individual psychotherapy, and hence in the best position for espousal of the psychiatric approach to self, tended to present their favorable view of psychotherapy only to the members of their intimate cliques. For a report on the way in which Army prisoners concealed from fellow offenders their interest in "restoration" to the Army, see the comments by Richard Cloward in Session 4 of *New Perspectives for Research on Juvenile Delinquency*, ed. by Helen L. Witmer and Ruth Kotinsky, U. S. Department of Health, Education and Welfare, Children's Bureau Bulletin, 1955, especially p. 90.

their surroundings or even found new satisfactions through fraternization with middle-class political prisoners.[26] Similarly, Shetland youths recruited into the British merchant marine are not apparently threatened much by the cramped arduous life on board, because island life is even more stunted; they make uncomplaining sailors because from their point of view they have nothing much to complain about. Strong religious and political convictions may also serve perhaps to immunize the true believer against the assaults of a total institution, and even a failure to speak the language of the staff may cause the staff to give up its efforts at reformation, allowing the nonspeaker immunity to certain pressures.[27] . . .

Consequences

Total institutions frequently claim to be concerned with rehabilitation, that is, with resetting the inmate's self-regulatory mechanisms so that he will maintain the standards of the establishment of his own accord after he leaves the setting.[28] In fact, it seems this claim is seldom realized and even when permanent alteration occurs, these changes are often not of the kind intended by the staff. With the possible exception presented by the great resocialization efficiency of religious institutions, neither the stripping processes nor the reorganizing ones seem to have a lasting effect.[29] No doubt the availability of secondary adjustments helps to account for this, as do the presence of countermores and the tendency for inmates to combine all strategies and "play it cool." In any case, it seems that shortly after release, the ex-inmate will have forgotten a great deal of what life was like on the inside and will have once again begun to take for granted the privileges around which life in the institution was organized. The sense of injustice, bitterness and alienation, so typically engendered by the inmate's experience and so definitely marking a stage in his moral career,

[26] Bettelheim, *op. cit.*, p. 425.

[27] Thus, Schein, *op. cit.*, p. 165 fn., suggests that Puerto Ricans and other non-English-speaking prisoners of war in China were given up on and allowed to work out a viable routine of menial chores.

[28] Interestingly enough, staff is expected to be properly self-regulating upon first coming to the total institution, sharing with members of other kinds of establishments the ideal of needing merely to learn procedure.

[29] The strongest evidence for this, perhaps, comes from our knowledge of the readjustment of repatriated brain-washed prisoners of war. See, for example, Lawrence E. Hinkle, Jr., and Harold G. Wolff, "Communist Interrogation and Indoctrination of 'Enemies of the State,'" *Archives of Neurology and Psychiatry*, Vol. 76, 1956, p. 174.

seems to weaken upon graduation, even in those cases where a permanent stigma has resulted.

But what the ex-inmate does retain of his institutional experience tells us important things about total institutions. Often entrance will mean for the recruit that he has taken on what might be called a *proactive status*. Not only is his relative social position within the walls radically different from what it was on the outside, but, as he comes to learn, if and when he gets out, his social position on the outside will never again be quite what it was prior to entrance. Where the proactive status is a relatively favorable one, as it is for those who graduate from officers' training schools, elite boarding schools, ranking monasteries, etc., then the permanent alteration will be favorable, and jubilant official reunions announcing pride in one's "school" can be expected. When, as seems usually the case, the proactive status is unfavorable, as it is for those in prisons or mental hospitals, we popularly employ the term "stigmatization" and expect that the ex-inmate may make an effort to conceal his past and try to "pass." [30]

THE STAFF WORLD

Humane Standards

Most total institutions, most of the time, seem to function merely as storage dumps for inmates, but as previously suggested, they usually present themselves to the public as rational organizations designed consciously, through and through, as effective machines for producing a few officially avowed and officially approved ends. It was also suggested that one frequent official objective is the reformation of inmates in the direction of some ideal standard. This contradiction, then, between what the institution does and what its officials must say that it does, forms the central context of the staff's daily activity.

Within this context, perhaps the first thing to say about staff is that their work, and hence their world, has uniquely to do with people. This people-work is not quite like personnel work nor the work of those involved in service relationships. Staffs, after all, have objects

[30] As Cloward, *op. cit.*, pp. 80–83, implies, one important kind of leverage staff has in regard to inmates and one factor leading inmates to act convertible in presence of staff is that staff can give the kind of discharge that may appear to reduce stigmatization. Prison barracks officials can hold up the possibility of the inmate's "restoration" to active duty and, potentially, an honorable discharge; mental hospital administrators can hold up the possibility of a "clean bill of health" (discharged as cured) and personal recommendations.

and products to work upon, not relationships, but these objects and products are people.

As material upon which to work, people involve some of the considerations characteristic of inanimate objects. Just as an article being processed through an industrial plant must be followed by a paper shadow showing what has been done by whom, what is to be done, and who last had responsibility for it, so human objects moving, say, through a mental hospital system must be followed by a chain of informative receipts detailing what has been done to and by the patient and who has most recent responsibility for him. In his career from admission suite to burial plot, many different kinds of staff will add their official note to his case file as he temporarily passes under their jurisdiction, and long after he has died physically his marked remains will survive as an actionable entity in the hospital's bureaucratic system. Even the presence or absence of a particular patient at a given meal or for a given night may have to be recorded so that cost-accounting can be maintained and appropriate adjustments rendered in billing.

Other similarities between people-work and object-work are obvious. Just as tin mines or paint factories or chemical plants may involve special work hazards for employees, so (staffs believe at least) there are special dangers to some kinds of people-work. In mental hospitals, staffs believe that patients may strike out "for no reason" and injure an official. In army prisons, staff "is ever haunted by the spectre of riot, revolt or mutiny. . . ."[31] In TB sanitariums and in leprosoriums, staff feel they are being specially exposed to dangerous diseases.

While these similarities between people- and object-work exist, it is, I think, the unique aspects of people as material to work upon that we must look to for the crucial determinants of the work-world of staff.

Given the physiological characteristics of the human organism, it is obvious that certain requirements must be met if any continued use is to be made of people. But this, of course, is the case with inanimate objects, too; the temperature of any storehouse must be regulated, regardless of whether people or things are stored. However, persons are almost always considered to be ends in themselves, as reflected in the broad moral principles of a total institution's environing society. Almost always, then, we find that some technically

[31] Cloward, *op. cit.*, p. 82.

unnecessary standards of handling must be maintained with human materials. This maintenance of what we can call humane standards comes to be defined as one part of the "responsibility" of the institution and presumably is one of the things the institution guarantees the inmate in exchange for his liberty. Thus, prison officials are obliged to thwart suicidal efforts of the prisoner and to give him full medical attention even though in some cases this may require postponement of his date of execution. Something similar has been reported in German concentration camps, where inmates were sometimes given medical attention to tidy them up into a healthier shape for the gas chamber.

A second special contingency in the work-world of staff is the fact that inmates typically have statuses and relationships in the outside world that must be taken into consideration. (This consideration, of course, is related to the previously mentioned fact that the institution must respect some of the rights of inmates qua persons.) Even in the case of the committed mental patient whose civil rights are largely taken from him, a tremendous amount of mere paper work will be involved. Of course, the rights that are denied a mental patient are usually transferred to a relation, to a committee, or to the superintendent of the hospital itself, who then becomes the legal person whose authorization must be obtained for many matters. Many issues originating outside the institution will arise: Social Security benefits, income taxes, upkeep of properties, insurance payments, old age pension, stock dividends, dental bills, legal obligations incurred prior to commitment, permission to release psychiatric case records to insurance companies or attorneys, permission for special visits from persons other than next of kin, etc. All of these issues have to be dealt with by the institution, even if only to pass the decisions on to those legally empowered to make them.

It should be noted that staff is reminded of its obligations in these matters of standards and rights, not only by its own internal superordinates, by various watchdog agencies in the wider society, and by the material itself, but also by persons on the outside who have kin ties to inmates. The latter group present a special problem because, while inmates can be educated about the price they will pay for making demands on their own behalf, relations receive less tutoring in this regard and rush in with requests for inmates that inmates would blush to make for themselves.

The multiplicity of ways in which inmates must be considered ends in themselves and the multiplicity of inmates themselves forces upon staff some of the classic dilemmas that must be faced by those who govern men. Since a total institution functions somewhat as a State, its staff must suffer somewhat from the tribulations that beset governors.

In the case of any single inmate, the assurance that certain standards will be maintained in his own interests may require sacrifice of other standards, and implied in this is a difficult weighing of ends. For example, if a suicidal inmate is to be kept alive, staff may feel it necessary to keep him under constant deprivatizing surveillance or even tied to a chair in a small locked room. If a mental patient is to be kept from tearing at grossly irritated sores and repeating time and again a cycle of curing and disorder, staff may feel it necessary to curtail the freedom of his hands. Another patient who refuses to eat may have to be humiliated by forced feeding. If inmates of TB sanitariums are to be given an opportunity to recover, it will be necessary to curtail freedom of recreation.[32]

The standards of treatment that one inmate has a right to expect may conflict, of course, with the standards desired by another, giving rise to another set of governmental problems. Thus, in mental hospitals, if the grounds gate is to be kept open out of respect for those with town parole, then some other patients who otherwise could have been trusted on the grounds may have to be kept on locked wards. And if a canteen and mailbox are to be freely available to those on the grounds, then patients on a strict diet or those who write threatening and obscene letters will have to be denied liberty on the grounds.

The obligation of staff to maintain certain humane standards of treatment for inmates represents problems in itself, as suggested above, but a further set of characteristic problems is found in the constant conflict between humane standards on one hand and institutional efficiency on the other. I will cite only one main example. The personal possessions of an individual are an important part of the materials out of which he builds a self, but as an inmate, the ease with which he can be managed by staff is likely to increase with the degree to which he is dispossessed. Thus, the remarkable efficiency with which a men-

[32] Extremely useful material on TB sanitariums as total institutions will be available in the forthcoming work by Julius A. Roth, Committee on Human Development, University of Chicago. Preliminary statements may be found in his articles "What Is an Activity?" *Etc.*, Vol. XIV, Autumn 1956, pp. 54–56, and "Ritual and Magic in the Control of Contagion," *American Sociological Review*, Vol. 22, June 1957, pp. 310–314.

tal hospital ward can adjust to a daily shift in number of resident patients is related to the fact that the comers and leavers do not come or leave with any properties but themselves and do not have any right to choose where they will be located. Further, the efficiency with which the clothes of these patients can be kept clean and fresh is related to the fact that everyone's soiled clothing can be indiscriminately placed in one bundle, and laundered clothing can be redistributed not according to ownership but according to rough size. Similarly, the quickest assurance that patients going on the grounds will be warmly dressed is to march them in file past a pile of the ward's allotment of coats, requiring them for the same purposes of health to throw off these collectivized garments on returning to the ward.

Just as personal possessions may interfere with the smooth running of an institutional operation and be removed for this reason, so parts of the body itself may conflict with efficient management and the conflict resolved in favor of efficiency. If the heads of inmates are to be kept clean and the possessor easily identified, then a complete head shave is efficacious, regardless of the damage this does to appearance. On similar grounds, some mental hospitals have found it useful to extract the teeth of "biters," give hysterectomies to promiscuous female patients, and perform lobotomies on chronic fighters. Flogging on men-of-war as a form of punishment expressed the same conflict between organizational and humane interests: [33]

> One of the arguments advanced by officers of the Navy in favor of corporal punishment is this: it can be inflicted in a moment; it consumes no valuable time; and when the prisoner's shirt is put on, *that* is the last of it. Whereas, if another punishment were substituted, it would probably occasion a great waste of time and trouble, besides thereby begetting in the sailor an undue idea of his importance.

I have suggested that people-work differs from other kinds because of the tangle of statuses and relationships which each inmate brings with him to the institution and because of the humane standards that must be maintained with respect to him. Another difference occurs in cases where inmates have some rights to visit off the grounds, for then the mischief they may do in civil society becomes something for which the institution has some responsibility. Given this responsibility, it is understandable that total institutions tend not to view off-grounds

[33] Melville, *op. cit.*, p. 139.

leave favorably. Still another type of difference between people-work and other kinds, and perhaps the most important difference of all, is that by the exercise of threat, reward or persuasion human objects can be given instructions and relied upon to carry them out on their own. The span of time during which these objects can be trusted to carry out planned actions without supervision will vary of course a great deal, but, as the social organization of back wards in mental hospitals teaches us, even in the limiting case of catatonic schizophrenics, a considerable amount of such reliance is possible. Only the most complicated electronic equipment shares this capacity.

While human materials can never be as refractory as inanimate ones, their very capacity to perceive and to follow out the plans of staff insures that they can hinder the staff more effectively than inanimate objects can. Inanimate objects cannot purposely and intelligently thwart our plans, regardless of the fact that we may momentarily react to them as if they had this capacity. Hence, in prison and on "better" wards of mental hospitals, guards have to be ready for organized efforts at escape and must constantly deal with attempts to bait them, "frame" them, and otherwise get them into trouble. This leads to a state of anxiety in the guard that is not alleviated by knowledge that the inmate may be acting thusly merely as a means of gaining self-respect or relieving boredom.[34] Even an old, weak, mental patient has tremendous power in this regard; for example, by the simple expedient of locking his thumbs in his trouser pockets he can remarkably frustrate the efforts of an attendant to undress him.

A third general way in which human materials are different from other kinds and hence present unique problems is that, however distant staff manages to stay from them, they can become objects of fellow-feeling and even affection. Always there is the danger that an inmate will appear human. If what are felt to be hardships must be inflicted on the inmate, then sympathetic staff will suffer. And on the other hand, if an inmate breaks a rule, staff's conceiving of him as a human being may increase their sense that injury has been done to their moral world. Expecting a "reasonable" response from a reasonable creature, staff may feel incensed, affronted and challenged when this does not occur. Staff thus finds it must maintain face not only before those who examine the product of work but before these very products themselves.

[34] For comments on the very difficult role of guard, see McCorkle and Korn, *op. cit.*, pp. 93–94, and Gresham M. Sykes, "The Corruption of Authority and Rehabilitation," *Social Forces*, Vol. 34, 1956, pp. 257–262.

The capacity of inmates to become objects of staff's sympathetic concern is linked to what might be called an involvement cycle sometimes recorded in total institutions. Starting at a point of social distance from inmates, a point from which massive deprivation and institutional trouble cannot easily be seen, the staff person finds he has no reason not to build up a warm involvement in some inmates. The involvement, however, brings the staff members into a position to be hurt by what inmates do and by what they suffer, and also brings him to a position from which he is likely to threaten the distant stand from inmates taken by his fellow members of the staff. In response, the sympathizing staff member may feel he has been "burnt" and retreat into paper-work, committee work or other staff-enclosed routine. Once removed from the dangers of inmate contact, he may gradually cease to feel he has reason to remain so, and thus the cycle of contact and withdrawal may be repeated again and again.

When we combine together the fact that staff is obliged to maintain certain standards of humane treatment for inmates and may come to view inmates as reasonable, responsible creatures who are fitting objects for emotional involvement, we have the background for some of the quite special difficulties of people-work. In mental hospitals, for example, there always seem to be some patients who dramatically act against their own obvious self-interest. They drink water they have themselves first polluted; they rush against the wall with their heads; they tear out their own sutures after a minor operation; they flush false teeth down the toilet, without which they cannot eat and which take months to obtain; or smash glasses, without which they cannot see. In an effort to frustrate these visibly self-destructive acts, staff may find itself forced to manhandle these patients. Staff then is forced to create an image of itself as harsh and coercive, just at the moment that it is attempting to prevent someone from doing to himself what no human being is expected to do to anyone. At such times it is extremely difficult for staff members to keep their own emotions in control, and understandably so.

Moral Climate

The special requirements of people-work establish the day's job for staff, but this job must be carried out in a special moral climate. For the staff is charged with meeting the hostility and demands of the inmates, and what it has to meet the inmate with, in general, is the rational perspective espoused by the institution. It is the role of the staff to defend the institution in the name of its avowed rational aims —to the inmate as well as to outsiders of various kinds. Thus, when inmates are allowed to have incidental face-to-face contact with staff, the contact will often take the form of "gripes" or requests on the part of the inmate and of justification for prevailing restrictive treatment on the part of the staff. Such, for example, is the general structure of staff-patient interaction in mental hospitals. Further, the privileges and punishments meted out by staff will often be couched in a language that reflects the legitimated objectives of the institution, even though this may require that inmates or low-level members of staff translate these responses into the verbal language of the privilege system.

Given the inmates over whom it has charge and the processing that must be done to these objects, staff tends to evolve what may be thought of as a *theory of human nature.* This verbalized perspective rationalizes the scene, provides a subtle means of maintaining social distance from inmates and a stereotyped view of them, and gives sanction to the treatment accorded them.[35] Typically, the theory covers the "good" and "bad" possibilities of inmate conduct, the forms that messing up take, and the instructional value of privileges and punishments. In army barracks, officers will have a theory about the relation between discipline and obedience under fire, about the qualities proper to men, about the "breaking point" of men, and about the difference between mental sickness and malingering. In prisons, we find currently an interesting conflict between the psychiatric and the moral-weakness theory of crime. In convents, we find theories about the way in which the spirit can be weak and strong, and the ways its defects can be combatted. Mental hospitals, it should be noted, are especially interesting in this connection because staff members pointedly establish themselves as specialists in the knowledge of human nature who must diagnose and prescribe on the basis of this philosophy. Hence, in the standard psychiatric textbooks there are chapters on "psychodynamics" and "psychopathology" which provide charmingly explicit formulations of the "nature" of human nature.

Given the fact that the management of inmates is typically rationalized in terms of the ideal aims or functions of the establishment and that certain humane standards will form part of this ideal, we

[35] I derive this from Everett C. Hughes' review of Leopold von Wies's *Spätlese,* in *American Journal of Sociology,* Vol. LXI, 1955, p. 182. A similar area is covered under the current anthropological term "ethnopsychology," except that the unit to which it applies is a culture, not an institution.

can expect that professionals ostensibly hired to service these functions will likely become dissatisfied, feeling that they are being used as "captives" to add professional sanction to the privilege system and that they cannot here properly practice their calling. And this seems to be a classic cry. At the same time, the category of staff that must keep the institution going through continuous contact with inmates may feel that they too are being set a contradictory task, having to coerce inmates into obedience while at the same time giving the impression that humane standards are being maintained and that the rational goals of the institution are being realized. . . .

INSTITUTIONAL DIFFERENCES

One important difference among total institutions is found in the spirit in which recruits enter the establishment. At one extreme we find the quite involuntary entrance of those who are sentenced to prison, committed to a mental hospital, or impressed into the crew of a ship. It is perhaps in such cases that staff's version of the ideal inmate has least chance of taking hold among the inmates. At the other extreme, we find religious institutions which deal only with those who feel they have gotten the call and, of these volunteers, take only those who seem to be the most suitable and the most serious in their intentions. In such cases, conversion seems already to have taken place, and it only remains to show the neophyte along what lines he can best discipline himself. Midway between these two extremes we find institutions like the army barracks whose inmates are required to serve, but who are given much opportunity to feel that this service is a justifiable one required in their own ultimate interests. Obviously, significant differences in tone will appear in total institutions, depending on whether recruitment is voluntary, semivoluntary or involuntary.

Another dimension of variation among total institutions is found in what might be called their *permeability*, that is, the degree to which the social standards maintained within the institution and the social standards maintained in the environing society have influenced each other sufficiently to minimize differences.[36] This issue, incidentally, gives us an opportunity to consider some of the dynamic relations be-

[36] If the analogy were to be carried out strictly, we would have to say of course that every total institution had a semipermeable membrane about it, since there will always be some standard equally maintained on the inside and outside, the impermeable effects being restricted to certain specific values and practices.

tween a total institution and the wider society that supports it or tolerates it.

When we examine the admission procedures of total institutions, we tend to be struck with the impermeable aspects of the establishment, since the stripping and leveling processes which occur at this time directly cut across the various social distinctions with which the recruit entered. St. Benedict's advice [37] to the abbot tends to be followed:

> Let him make no distinction of persons in the monastery. Let not one be loved more than another, unless he be found to excel in good works or in obedience. Let not one of noble birth be raised above him who was formerly a slave, unless some other reasonable cause intervene.

Thus, the new cadet in a military school finds that discussions "of wealth and family background are taboo," and that, "Although the pay of the cadet is very low, he is not permitted to receive money from home." [38]

Even the age-grading system of the wider society may be stopped at the gates, as nicely suggested in a recent memoir [39] of an ex-nun:

> Gabrielle moved to the place that would ever be hers, third in line of forty postulants. She was third oldest in the group because she had been third to register on that day less than a week ago when the Order had opened its doors to new entrants. From that moment, her chronological age had ceased and the only age she would henceforth have, her age in the religious life, had started.

It is, of course, by suppressing outside distinctions that a total institution can build up an orientation to its own system of honor. There is a sense then in which the harshest total institution is the most democratic, and in fact the inmate's assurance of being treated no worse than any other of his fellows can be a source of support as well as a deprivation.

But regardless of how radical a total institution appears to be, there will always be some limits to its reshuffling tendencies and some use made of social distinctions already established in the environing society, if only so it can conduct necessary affairs with this society and be tolerated by it. Thus, there does not seem to be a total institution

[37] St. Benedict, *Holy Rule,* Ch. 2.

[38] Dornbusch, *op. cit.,* p. 317. The classic case of this kind of echelon leveling is found perhaps in the fagging system in British public schools.

[39] Kathryn C. Hulme, *The Nun's Story,* Little, Brown & Co., Boston, 1956, pp. 22–23.

in Western society which provides batch living completely independent of sex; and ones like convents that appear to be impervious to socio-economic gradings, in fact tend to apportion domestic roles to converts of rural peasant background, just as the patient garbage crews in our prize integrated mental hospitals tend to be wholly Negro.[40] More important, perhaps, than the fact that total institutions differ in overall permeability to outside standards, we find that each is permeable with respect to different social standards.

One of the most interesting differences among total institutions is to be found in the social fate of their graduates. Typically, these become geographically dispersed; the difference is found in the degree to which structural ties are maintained in spite of this distance. At one end of the scale we find the year's graduates of a particular Benedictine abbey, who not only keep in touch informally but find that for the rest of their life their occupation and location have been determined by their original membership. At the same end of the scale, we find ex-convicts whose stay in prison orients them to the calling and to the nationwide underworld community that will comprise their life thereafter. At the other end of the scale, we find enlisted men from the same barracks who melt into private life immediately upon demobilization and even refrain from congregating for regimental reunions. Here, too, are ex-mental patients who studiously avoid all persons and events that might connect them with the hospital. Midway between these extremes, we find "old-boy" systems in private schools and graduate universities, which function as optional communities for the distribution of life-chances among sets of fellow graduates.

[40] It seems to be true that within any given establishment the topmost and bottommost roles tend to be relatively permeable to wider community standards, while the impermeable tendencies seem to be focused in the middle ranges of the institution's hierarchy.

6. Organizational Change

»»»

If the concept of change is interpreted loosely, most studies in this volume deal with organizational change in one way or another. Since organizations are planned social units, oriented to specific goals under relatively rational and self-conscious leadership, they are probably more given to change than any other social unit is. Some studies discuss changes in goals; others, changes in structure; still others discuss changes in the relationship between organizations and their social environments. But if the term "change" is conceived more strictly as change in the organization as a unit rather than as change in this or that variable, if the term "study of change" means to determine the factors which further change, the conditions under which a state of equilibrium is maintained, in contrast to the conditions under which it is undermined or substituted, if it means to specify the alternative courses open to a changing structure and the conditions under which this or that path is chosen, the study of organizational change —as well as the study of change of other social units—is still a relatively undeveloped field. The following studies contribute, each in its own way, to the development of a systematic analysis of organizational change.

Bureaucracies are often considered to be conservative structures, oriented toward maintaining the external as well as internal status quo. This theorem is examined by both Merton and Lipset in earlier sections of this volume. Blau suggests that certain external and internal factors might turn a bureaucracy into an innovating organization, interested in social change as well as in changing itself. Changes are likely to be supported by the personnel if they are aimed at satisfying organizational "needs." Such changes may in turn raise new needs calling for additional adjustments. Blau specifies some conditions under which an organization is likely to be open to internal changes. These include actors' feeling of security, a professional orientation, and pressing organizational needs. Lack of basic conflict between management and personnel, and cohesion among staff members, are reported as factors which enhance organizational change.

Selznick analyzes the process by which an organization develops a form expressive of its purpose. He examines histories of organizations from this viewpoint. Three developmental problems are emphasized: (a) the selection of social bases for the organization in terms of clientele, market, allies, and others; (b) building an institutional core: selection of the staff's social bases, development of recruitment criteria; and (c) formalization of procedure. The higher the formalization, the lower the need for leadership decisions concerning routine issues.

Organizations change their character as they develop and become more institutionalized. Examining these changes, Selznick points out that they are associated with extensive personnel turnover, i.e., with a change of the institutional core. Such substitution of personnel takes place on both managerial and staff levels.

Change of personnel is also the subject of the presentation by Levenson. He studies personnel turnover, which is part of organizational routine, and its effect on the organization. Theoretically, the flow of personnel, like the flow of raw material, need not affect the organization. For each person who leaves, a new one can be recruited. Actually, Levenson shows, the ways in which people leave an organization, and the channels and media by which new employees are recruited, invariably exert an influence on the social structure of the organization.

In contrast to Levenson, who studies the effect of a routine process on the organizational structure, McCleery makes a major structural change the focus of his study. He studies the change of a prison's structure from authoritarian to liberal. He raises such cardinal questions as the nature of organizational structure and power (McCleery emphasizes communication processes), unanticipated consequences of managerial policy (e.g., decrease in the degree of arbitrariness led to a temporary increase in inmate disorder), the role of external agencies in internal changes (e.g., legislature had to support the liberalization of the prison), and other issues. *In toto,* McCleery supplies a full analysis of a change of organization from one structure to another, including a detailed analysis of the transition period and the mechanisms of transformation, such as turnover of personnel, redefinition of authority and power positions, rechanneling of communication processes, and change in the potency of various goals.

Barton and Anderson's examination of McCleery's study is one of the relatively rare instances in the literature of social science in which an empirical study is submitted to an intensive methodological analysis. Barton and Anderson contribute to the construction of a bridge between qualitative and quantitative study by showing how one would go about conducting the same study, applying a quantitative method. At the same time, the substantive theory developed by McCleery is formalized by the use of a mathematical model. This model, in turn, is utilized to supply a precise exposition of what is meant when one refers to the organization, or for that matter to any social unit, as a social system. Finally, an arithmetic model is presented, which allows one to study changes in systems.

Barton and Anderson's paper raises a question. If so much measurement is required to turn a qualitative study into a quantitative one, does this not mean that the price of additional precision is high, perhaps too high? The authors' answer is that, even if their rigorous procedure is not adopted, keeping their model in mind would make qualitative analysis more systematic.

Peter M. Blau

The Dynamics of Bureaucracy

"One cannot step twice into the same river," said Heraclitus, twenty-five centuries ago; and if one returns to the same river bed, it also has imperceptibly changed. The only

Reprinted in part from Peter M. Blau, *Dynamics of Bureaucracy*, pp. 201–214, 216–219, by permission of the author and publisher, the University of Chicago Press.

permanence in bureaucratic structures is the occurrence of change in predictable patterns, and even these are not unalterably fixed.

The two government agencies studied had been established by law to achieve designated purposes. One was responsible for providing employment service, the other for enforcing legal standards of employment. The external situation in which different segments of each organization found themselves differed, and this situation continually changed. Finding jobs for accountants and finding work for day laborers called for different procedures, and practices that sufficed for enforcing the law during a war might not do so in a period of recession. In order to discharge prescribed responsibilities under varying conditions, adjustments of the bureaucratic organization were necessary.

Changes in the external situation were not the only reason for making modifications in the structure. Most procedures, even if instituted for a specific purpose, had several unintended consequences. Statistical records of performance, for example, not only furnished a means for evaluating operations but also had a variety of other effects. Some of these—latent functions of record-keeping—furthered the achievement of organizational objectives, but others—dysfunctions—interfered with it and thus necessitated further innovations. Perfect adjustment is hardly possible, because the very practices instituted to enhance adjustment in some respects often disturb it in others. Hence the stable attainment of organizational objectives depends on perpetual change in the bureaucratic structure.

Indeed, the dynamics of bureaucratic development is not confined to the emergence of new instruments for the accomplishment of specified objectives, but in the process the objectives themselves change, too. Particularly in innovating organizations, although not only there, competent officials tend to become interested in assuming new responsibilities and in expanding the jurisdiction of the agency, since this would increase their work satisfaction and benefit their career.

EMERGENT ORGANIZATIONAL NEEDS AND STRUCTURAL CHANGE

Weber conceived of bureaucracy as the social mechanism that maximizes efficiency in administration and also as a form of social organization with specific characteristics. Both these criteria cannot be part of the definition, since the relationship between the attributes of a social institution and its consequences is a question for empirical verification and not a matter of definition. Weber's discussion may be interpreted in one of two ways. Either he defined bureaucracy by specifying formal characteristics and hypothesized its superior operating efficiency; or he intended to define it as any administrative apparatus that maximizes efficiency and advanced hypotheses about organizational attributes that would typically have this effect.

In terms of the second alternative, bureaucracies can be looked upon as institutionalized strategies for the achievement of administrative objectives by the concerted effort of many officials. They are methods of organizing social conduct in order to transform exceptional problems into routine duties of experts and to effect the co-ordination of specialized tasks. In different cultures, different social arrangements will prove most suitable for these purposes. When an authoritarian orientation toward social relationships prevails in the family and in the society generally and when lack of education limits the qualification of subaltern officials, as in Germany at Weber's time, strict hierarchical control may be the most efficient method of bureaucratic operation. However, when equality in social relationships is highly valued and when a much higher level of popular education has been reached, as in the United States today, permitting junior officials considerable discretion in discharging their responsibilities may be a more efficient system of administration. Similarly, in a culture where people are oriented toward century-old traditions, bureaucratic efficiency probably requires less change in organization than in a young culture where progress is a central value.

Internal as well as external forces made change a recurrent phenomenon in the two organizations studied, and efficient operations depended on such readiness to reorganize. The concept of organizational need has been helpful in the analysis of these processes of bureaucratic development, since it indicates the relationship between the consequences of established practices and the emergence of new ones. Many social patterns that served important functions for operations also had some dysfunctions, that is, they produced conditions that impeded the effective attainment of organizational objectives. These emergent needs often gave rise to new practices which met them. The introduction of statistical records in the employment agency, for instance, effected needed improvements in placement operations, but it also engendered competitiveness, which interfered with service to handicapped clients and with productivity in general. In response to these two organizational needs, social innovations developed that restored operating efficiency. First, special interviewers for handicapped clients assumed duties that obligated other interviewers to help them find jobs for their clients. Second, one group of regular interviewers devised methods for discouraging competitive tendencies, and this increased productivity, as indicated by the fact that this group was more productive than the other group of regular interviewers, where competitive practices prevailed.

Contacts with clients furnish another illustration of adjustments that had dysfunctions necessitating further adjustments. Interviewers concerned with making many placements were frustrated by refusals of benefit clients to accept low-paying jobs. They often tried, therefore, to discourage such refusals by the more or less implicit threat that unemployment benefits would be discontinued. This practice, although adequate for its purpose, created conflicts with clients, which were particularly disturbing for these service-oriented interviewers. The resulting tensions constituted new obstacles to the effective performance of duties. In response to this emergent need, a custom developed that restored equanimity, namely, complaining and joking about clients in conversations with colleagues. This new pattern, in turn, had a dysfunction. It facilitated the interviewer's work, not by eliminating conflicts with clients, but by immunizing him against their disturbing effects, and consequently made inconsiderate treatment of clients more likely. Since this dysfunction, which did not directly interfere with operations, did not give rise to an organizational need, it persisted, to the detriment of clients.

Consultations in the federal agency reveal a different aspect of the same process of change in the structure. Agents, anxious to assure the accuracy of their decisions without exposing their difficulties to the supervisor, were in need of advice from another source. The practice of consulting colleagues met this need. It reduced the anxiety about making decisions which interfered with operations, and it generated social cohesion. However, it also produced needs that led to new patterns of interpersonal relationships.

To consult peers was easier than to consult the superior in the department, but if they were approached for help too often, they ceased to be peers, and this made consulting them more difficult. As the advice of some agents was in constant demand, while others recurrently requested assistance with solving their problems, status differences emerged in the group. Agents hesitated to consult expert colleagues too frequently, lest their unofficial position suffer, just as they were reluctant to ask the supervisor too many questions for fear of endangering their official position. In either case, hierarchical relations prevented free access to consultants. The resurgent need for advice from actual peers induced most agents to establish partnerships of mutual consultation and to reserve consultations with experts for their most perplexing problems.

Peer relationships rest on reciprocity in social exchange. Unilateral services engender obligations which destroy equality of status and erect barriers to the free flow of communication. This interference with egalitarian social interaction is dysfunctional for work groups. The emerging status distinctions in Department Y not only restricted the choice of consultant but even threatened the integrated position of the less competent agents. As all were attracted to popular experts, the others felt left out of group life and experienced a need for better interpersonal relationships. This need was also met by new patterns of interaction. The less competent agents tended to cultivate extensive informal relations with colleagues during the lunch period. Since this improved their popularity, it constituted an equalizing force. Although some status differences persisted, alternative mechanisms for becoming integrated in this group re-created equivalence of status in fundamental respects.

Social cohesion depends on basic equality of status. Cooperative interaction, such as the pattern of consultation, therefore affects it in two opposite ways. Cooperation is a major source of cohesion in work groups, because it unites members in the voluntary exchange of valued assistance, but it simultaneously weakens cohesion by giving rise to status distinctions which inhibit social intercourse and thus limit feelings of fellowship. As a result of these conflicting forces, cohesiveness is not a stable condition. It requires constant effort to renew the fundamental equality that makes the members of the group fully accessible to one another and permits them to become interested in one another as distinctive persons. Treatment of associates as unique individuals rather than as social types develops primarily among peers, and such an approach is a prerequisite for social interaction that is intrinsically gratifying and thereby produces strong social ties. To perpetuate group cohesion, the orientation in interpersonal relations should disallow quantitative differentiation of status but stress qualitative differentiation of persons. This orientation toward equals whose particular qualities merit consideration is also likely to enhance identification with the purposes of the group and its standards of behavior, at least in a culture where submission to authoritarian commands is negatively valued.

The significance of an egalitarian approach is not restricted to the internal structure of the work group but extends to the larger bureaucratic organization. Rational operations require the expeditious removal of obstructions to efficient performance. Effective communication in the hierarchy of authority, without which needed official innovations would not be made, is a necessary condition for this adjustment, but not a sufficient one. No system of rules and supervision can be so finely spun that it anticipates all exigencies that may arise. Moreover, some impediments to efficiency, such as the feelings of anxiety and other emotional tensions which often develop in the course of operations, cannot be eradicated by official decree. Maximum rationality in the organization, therefore, depends on the ability of operating officials to assume the initiative in establishing informal relations and instituting unofficial practices that eliminate operational difficulties as they occur. This ability, in turn, presupposes the absence of acute feelings of inequality among the members of the bureaucracy.

To be sure, the status distinctions inherent in the exercise of authority are necessary for the effective administration of a large organization, where officials in central positions must be able to direct and coordinate the work of specialized groups. However, since bureaucratic authority rests on social consensus that issuing certain directives is just as much the duty of the superior as compliance with these directives is that of subordinates, such compliance is not experienced as subjugation, while obedience to arbitrary commands of a superior would be. Hence bureaucratic authority itself does not create profound feelings of inequality, although it involves some status differences, but it often gives rise to additional hierarchical distinctions, which are not essential for systematic administration and which destroy all feelings of equality. If subaltern officials are treated as inferiors whose sole duty is to obey detailed orders of their superior, they have neither sufficient security nor incentive to cope with problems of their work on their own initiative. To supply the confidence and motivation needed for such efforts, junior officials must be considered as collaborators of administrators in the pursuit of common professional objectives. This limited type of egalitarian treatment, which is not too dissimilar from that which actually prevailed in the federal agency, is not incompatible with the exercise of bureaucratic authority. Of course, the absence of fundamental inequalities is not the only bureaucratic condition that must be met for work groups to take the initiative in making improvements when obstructions to efficient operations arise.

SOME PREREQUISITES OF ADJUSTIVE DEVELOPMENT

Spontaneous adjustments often occurred in the two agencies under consideration, that is, practices which solved incipient operational problems emerged among officials in the course of their work without being deliberately instituted by superiors. At this point, a question on the next-higher level of abstraction should be raised: What were the bureaucratic conditions that accounted for this pattern of self-adjustment, which was essential for efficiency? The exceptional cases where organizational needs persisted without evoking innovations to meet them provide some indications of these prerequisites of adjustive development in bureaucratic organizations.

Receptionists in the employment agency, quite unconsciously, treated clients of their own skin color preferentially. Since this did not disturb the work of the members of Department X, impartial treatment of applicants was not restored. However, some organizational needs that were very disturbing also persisted. When special interviewers, fearful of risking disapproval of requests to discontinue service to psychotic clients, continued to interview these clients, they found this task most irritating. In this case a conflict between this group of officials and a top administrator prevented adjustment. Still a different factor accounts for the finding that reviewers were not relieved from cross-pressures that interfered with their work, even though they allowed agents to correct most mistakes unofficially. These temporary reviewers did not constitute a distinct group, since each one remained identified with his former departmental group, and consequently were not able effectively to defend themselves against pressure from other officials. Finally, the members of Section A in the state agency, a distinct group, did not suppress competitive practices, which were disruptive and lowered productivity. Two important differences between this situation and that in Section B, where cooperative adjustment occurred, were that no common professional orientation had developed in Section A and its members had felt insecure in their job.

These cases of enduring dysfunctions suggest five prerequisites of adjustive development: first, a minimum of employment security; second, a professional orientation toward the performance of duties; third, established work groups that command the allegiance of their members; fourth, the absence of basic conflict between work group and management; fifth, organizational needs that are experienced as disturbing. Without assuming this list to be exhaustive, the following discussion will be confined to these five conditions, the absence of which was observed to obstruct the process of adjustment.

The ability to originate new patterns of adjustment and to adapt to those officially introduced presupposes relative job security. To be sure, the unemployed worker who feels he has nothing to lose may become a revolutionary, but insecurity in the bureaucratic situation, where one's job hangs in the balance, breeds ritualistic adherence to the existing order. Interviewers in Section A, while on probation for their civil service appointment, were so anxious to comply with the demands of superiors that they could not afford to discourage competitive practices. The members of Section B, who already held permanent civil service positions, felt free to cooperate in disregard of official statistical records, and they thereby improved productivity. Factory workers, who can be fired any time, resist changes in the organization, and so did officials in the federal agency whose lesser competence made them insecure in a period of reductions in staff; but the majority of agents, secure in their job, preferred frequent change to a constant routine.

Employment security engenders the psychological freedom of action that enables individuals to initiate adjustments, but it does not guarantee that these will further the objectives of the agency. Indeed, tenure may lead to private adaptations that are detrimental to the interest of the organization. To preclude this possibility, a professional orientation must prevail among officials. This involves a common identification with professional values and norms, which makes the process of attaining professional objectives a source of satisfaction.

Civil service personnel policies enhance the chances that officials will have a professional orientation toward their work. Recruitment standards assure that only applicants with the technical training required for a job are appointed. The relative security of civil service positions and the consequent long tenure of most officials encourage loyalty to the organization and its values, particularly since the specialized qualifications acquired in many years of experience in government agencies often cannot be utilized in private industry. The expert customs inspector, for instance, can hardly find a job commensurate with his skills outside the government, and even the demand for expert employment interviewers in private industry is small. Promotions in civil service, moreover, follow explicit regulations, which enable the official to predict his promotion chances with relative accuracy, in contrast to the private employee, who is promoted at the pleasure of his employer [1] and can therefore hope for a promotion at all times.[2] The system that prevents civil servants from deriving satisfaction from hopes of spectacular advancements probably also constrains them to find gratification in their work and thus invites a professional attitude toward it.

Evaluation on the basis of results achieved rather than techniques used likewise fosters a professional orientation. If interviewers in the employment agency criticized statistical records as unprofessional, it was because they felt that the indices measured only superficial accomplishments, such as the number of placements. In the federal agency, more refined statistical criteria supplemented by qualitative evaluation of results compelled agents to strive to achieve specified objectives in their work and obviated the need for many operating rules and close supervision. This external compulsion was internalized. The periodic rating by the supervisor constrained agents to adapt to their dependent position by adopting the bureaucratic system of values and norms as their own orientation toward their tasks. Moreover, the supervisor, as a means of extending his authority over subordinates, rarely enforced operating rules but relied for control on the obligations he thereby created and on his evaluation of completed cases. This put agents under further pressure to identify with professional objectives and with self-imposed standards of workmanship.

[1] Except in private bureaucracies that have also adopted explicit promotion procedures.

[2] None of 69 officials interviewed *aspired* to high positions in civil service within the next ten years, but 30 aspired to high positions in private industry or self-employment, although only eight *expected* to leave the government. Whether an individual directed his aspirations outside or inside civil service was not related to his work satisfaction, but simply depended on whether he expressed *any high* aspirations or not. Hopeful aspirations are not necessarily realistic, but their attainment must be conceivable, not impossible. Since officials knew that it was legally impossible for them suddenly to be promoted to, say, assistant commissioner, they either ceased to entertain hopes of this type of success or, if they wanted to indulge in wishful thinking, directed their aspirations toward careers outside the government service. One of the merits of the civil service system is that it discourages occupational aspirations which, by their very nature, must be frustrated in the majority of cases.

A professional orientation makes officials concerned with impediments to efficient operations and directs them to attempt adjustments, but it also engenders anxiety. The greater their interest in professional objectives and the fewer the external restraints on their method of achieving them, the more likely it is that they will experience anxiety. The bureaucratic officials observed found themselves in this predicament, although perhaps not to the same extent as independent professionals. Anxieties that persevered, whether among interviewers or department heads, agents or reviewers, led to maladaptation, rigidity, and poor performance. Adaptation to the organization in general and the ability to reorganize procedures when necessary in particular depend on relatively cohesive work groups which relieve such anxiety.

Recurrent cooperative and congenial interaction with most co-workers, and not just with a few friends, gives officials a feeling of security in the work situation. This promotes assimilation in the bureaucratic structure and efficient performance of strenuous tasks, such as complex negotiations. The social support of the group also makes it easier for officials to adopt new practices, since it lessens their need to find emotional security in familiar routines. Social cohesion, therefore, paves the way for the development of new adjustments. In addition, it furnishes the group with instruments for instituting them.

To meet organizational needs requires group action. When agents found that reports of bribes by one of them endangered success in future negotiations of others, any single individual was helpless in the face of this difficulty, but the group could eliminate it by collectively discouraging every agent from making such reports. When competitive practices interfered with the work of interviewers, individual efforts to check them were ineffective, but the collective enforcement of cooperation in an entire group removed this obstacle to operations. Unofficial practices that met organizational needs were most prevalent in cohesive groups, because they alone could effectively enforce informal norms.

Most members of cohesive groups value their interpersonal relationships with one another, and this makes them subject to the control of the group. Unofficial sanctions are either indications by others that they have lost respect for a colleague and become less interested in associating with him or ostracism in miniature, signs of hostility in social situations that threaten an individual with ostracism. These sanctions, as well as the serious penalty of ostracism, are effective deterrents to deviant behavior only when an official's position in the group is important to him, and not otherwise. Social cohesion is the source of the group's power to exact obedience to its norms and thus of its ability to develop adjustive social patterns independent of official rules.

The process of enforcing norms affects the relative position of individuals within the group. Social differentiation develops, as the members of the group are especially attracted to some co-workers and seek to associate with them more than with others. Officials who received disproportionately many contacts in the course of integrative interaction occupied a superior unofficial status, which found expression in their assuming a dominant role in group situations. One major source of attraction was the possession of characteristics valued by the group, such as expert knowledge. Another basis of differential association was the degree of conformity with group norms. Deviants lost status in the group, because the others reacted, often inadvertently, to a violation of standards they valued by associating less with the offender.

Social differentiation endangered cohesiveness and optimum performance of duties, unless counterforces developed that minimized it again, as previously noted in this chapter. Continuous structural modifications, changes in relative positions as well as operating practices, occurred within the larger framework of comparatively stable hierarchical positions and specified objectives. Just as a solid body consists of moving molecules, so the bureaucratic structure is composed of constantly changing elements.

Although social cohesion cannot be officially created, conditions favorable for its development can be. Job security and the explicit promotion procedure in civil service have this function. They supply most officials with the knowledge that they will neither be promoted nor lose their job within the next few years and thus greatly lessen their need to compete with fellow-officials. Besides, the civil service system assures that most officials remain in the same group for years, usually under conditions that give rise to a common professional orientation. Daily associations between like-minded colleagues without serious conflicts for long periods of time stimulate the emergence of social cohesion.[3]

[3] Conditions that reduce social cohesion are, of course, dysfunctional for bureaucratic operations. This seems to be an unintended dysfunction of loyalty investigations. For example, two agents, both of whom were subsequently cleared, had

Social cohesion enables the members of a group to institute adjustments that further their interest. These adjustments will, however, not advance the objectives of the organization, if operating employees feel that their interest conflicts with that of management. This is a typical occurrence in private industry. Restriction of output among factory workers is an adjustment which is designed to protect the economic interest of workers against management and which is dysfunctional for operations. The comments and behavior of workers show that these practices are motivated by fear of losing their jobs or lowering their wages rather than by lack of professional concern with their work.[4] In contrast to those of factory workers, most unofficial practices observed in the two agencies, including some that violated official rules, contributed to operating efficiency. An important reason for this, in addition to job security, may well have been that the civil service system eliminates a basic source of conflict between operating officials and management.

Authority over personnel is split in government agencies. In private organizations, management controls employment conditions as well as operations. In government agencies, on the other hand, management controls operations, but not employment conditions. Salaries and the procedures that govern promotion and discharge are determined by the civil service commission in accordance with legal statutes. Since the rating influences advancement chances, an individual's economic interest may bring him into conflict with superiors. However, the conflict between the *collective* economic interest of operating officials and the budgetary considerations of their employer finds expres-

been investigated. This gave rise to serious dissension in the federal agency, involving many officials aside from the two directly concerned. It stirred up political differences, which had hardly been discussed before; it produced conflict between those who testified for an innocent colleague and those who strongly disapproved of testifying for somebody under suspicion of disloyalty; it created emotional conflicts for those who were afraid to testify for a colleague whom they considered innocent, and disputes between them and those who regarded a refusal to bear witness in such a situation a betrayal; and it alienated from one another those who testified in support of and those who testified against the charges.

[4] Roy indicates that the workers he observed were professionally oriented. They derived satisfaction from working efficiently but felt they must work slowly, although they did not like to do so for fear their piece rates would be cut. See Donald Roy, "Quota Restriction and Goldbricking in a Machine Shop," *American Journal of Sociology*, 57 (1952), 432. See also Mathewson, and Roethlisberger and Dickson, who observe the same phenomenon but interpret it differently; Stanley B. Mathewson, *Restriction of Output among Unorganized Workers* (New York: Viking Press, 1931), and F. J. Roethlisberger and W. J. Dickson, *Management and the Worker* (Cambridge: Harvard, 1939).

sion in their opposition to the civil service commission and the legislature, which set the conditions of their employment. It does not affect their relationship with the administration of the agency. On the contrary, operating officials and administrators are united by their interest in legislation that benefits civil servants.

The dominant concern of employees with their job and income may submerge a common professional interest in effective performance, but this was not characteristic of the civil servants studied. Their job was relatively secure, and they did not feel that improvements in operations would evoke managerial action detrimental to their economic welfare, as factory workers apparently do. This situation permitted officials to become and remain primarily interested in their professional responsibilities. Cohesive groups in which such a professional orientation prevailed readily initiated social practices that eliminated obstacles to efficient performance. This strain toward adjustive development in the organization greatly contributed to the achievement of its objectives.

Philip Selznick

Critical Decisions in Organizational Development

In the search for more general connections between policy and social structure, something may be gained from the study of organization histories. . . . Apparently similar events or practices should not be compared directly, but only as their relation to the organization's stage of development is determined. The design of forms and procedures will then be guided by this interpretation. Administrative issues will be decided only after a diagnosis that takes account of the historical context.

Reprinted in part from *Leadership in Administration,* pp. 102–112, by permission of the author and the publisher, Row, Peterson & Company. Copyright 1957.

The language of evolution or life-cycle can be misleading when applied to organizations, but at least a natural-history approach can call attention to the developmental problems that arise in organizational experience. In doing this, we must distinguish problems posed by the task at hand, which do not call for organizational changes, from problems that are set for an organization by the stage of growth in which it finds itself. Some of these are quite obvious, as when we anticipate the need for more regularized budgeting procedures as size increases. Less obvious are problems that emerge as changes occur in the roles and needs of the participants and of the organization as a whole. Although such changes may be consciously planned and directed, they are characteristically unplanned and responsive. Taken as a total experience, each such history is of course unique. Nevertheless, to the extent that similar situations summon like responses from similar groups, we may expect to find organizational evolutionary patterns. The hope is that this uniformity, once discovered, may provide tools for more adequate description and more perceptive diagnosis.

Certain types of problems seem to characterize phases of an organization's life-history. As these problems emerge, the organization is confronted with critical policy decisions. Examples of these developmental problems are:

1. The Selection of a Social Base

Among the critical decisions facing leadership, closely related to the definition of mission, is the selection of a clientele, market, target, allies, or other segment of the environment to which operations will be oriented. Personnel recruitment, public relations, and many other areas of decision will be affected by this key choice of an external "social base." The early phase of an institution's life is marked by a scrutiny of its own capabilities, and of its environment, to discover where its resources are and on whom it is dependent. The achievement of stability is influenced by this appraisal; and the future evolution of the institution is largely conditioned by the commitments generated in this basic decision. Of course, the "decision" is not always consciously made; and often the outcome is forced upon the organization by compelling circumstances which leave little freedom of choice.

When a merchant adapts his enterprise to a particular market, say for luxury goods; when a political organization bases itself on some special social force, say the labor movement or business interests; when a government agency adapts itself to the influential groups it must please in order to stay alive—there is created an effective and controlling environment of decision. As these commitments evolve, the organization loses its purity as an abstractly or ideally envisioned entity; it assumes a definite role in a living community; it becomes institutionalized. The *design* of that role, insofar as freedom to do so exists, is very largely a matter of choosing the social base upon which the organization will rest. Often this outcome is not designed but simply emerges in an unplanned way, as a precipitant of many short-run decisions.

2. Building the Institutional Core

Another developmental problem is that of creating an initial homogeneous staff. The members of this core group reflect the basic policies of the organization in their own outlooks. They can, when matured in this role, perform the essential task of indoctrinating newcomers along desired lines. They can provide some assurance that decision-making will conform, in spirit as well as letter, to policies that may have to be formulated abstractly or vaguely. The development of derivative policies and detailed applications of general rules will thus be guided by a shared general perspective. This is especially important, of course, where the assessment of tasks and results cannot be settled by routine formulae. As always, the "openness" of decision-making calls for leadership, in this case to build a social structure that will induce a spontaneous regularity of response. Where this regularity may be imposed formally, as a clear-cut technical matter, leadership is more readily dispensable.

The creation of an institutional core is partly a matter of selective recruiting, and to this extent overlaps with the task of selecting a social base. By choosing key personnel from a particular social group, the earlier conditioning of the individuals can become a valuable resource for the new organization. Conversely, of course, just such conditioning is in question when a particular source of personnel is *rejected.* But core-building involves more than selective recruiting. Indoctrination and the sharing of key experiences—especially internal conflicts and other crises—will help to create a unified group and give the organization a special identity.

The importance of core-building for institutional development is quite familiar. The recruitment of key personnel for the new CIO Steel Workers Organizing Committee from the United Mine Workers

Union decisively influenced the later evolution of the steelworkers' union, particularly in ensuring tight control from the top; the dependence of the new "action agencies" in the U.S. Department of Agriculture on a pool of agricultural personnel brought up in another tradition required special emphasis on "orientation," i.e., self-definition, in the new agencies; the emergence of communism from a socialist background entailed a very large effort to overcome earlier conditioning and create a new institutional core. Even in business, where self-definition may seem less important than in political and other community enterprises, there is a need to build a self-conscious group that fully understands "the kind of company this is."

While core-formation may be a conscious and designed process, it also develops naturally, as an indirect result of day-to-day interaction. Hence the general problem of leadership is *control* of core-formation, whether to build one congenial to desired policy or to restrain one that creates unwanted rigidities in organization and policy. This problem is developmental. It is associated with a special phase in the organization's life-history, and must be dealt with in some way if control over the long-run evolution of policy is to be maintained.

3. Formalization

A very familiar phase in the life-history of organizations is the formalization of procedure. The organization reduces its dependence on the personal attributes of the participants by making supervision more routine and by externalizing discipline and incentive. Formalization limits the open-endedness of organizations and thereby reduces the number of leadership decisions required.

While this process is well known, it is worth noting here that the transition from personal supervision to managerial control is developmental and brings with it characteristic growing pains, including shifts in top personnel. Formalization should be understood as an emergent problem, for in diagnosis we must ask whether a given instance of formalization is *premature,* as well as whether necessary adaptations to the new stage have been made. Premature formalization, sometimes reflecting an overemphasis on the quick achievement of clarity in communication and command channels, may seal off leadership during the early stages of organization building, when it is most needed. As a result, leadership decisions—such as those affecting the institutional core and the social base—may be left to uncontrolled adaptation.

A historical sensitivity will aid the planner to revamp organizational structure in the light of developmental changes that have created new risks and opportunities. These advantages will be illustrated in the following comments on (1) some characteristic personnel crises in organizational evolution, and (2) the relation of decentralization to social integration.

PERSONNEL CRISES AND GROWTH STAGES

Developmental changes are most sharply reflected in personnel turnover. This does not mean just any turnover, such as routine attrition and replacement, but that involving a shift from one type of person to another. As new problems emerge, individuals whose ways of thinking and responding served the organization well in an early stage may be ill-fitted for the new tasks. Characteristically, this is not so much a matter of technical knowledge as of attitudes and habits. These shape an individual's outlook and orientation to the job, resulting in a distinctive pattern of emphasis and judgment. The more firmly set the personal pattern—a condition that may be highly desirable during creative periods of organization development--the less adaptable is the individual.

A good example of personnel crisis associated with developmental change is found in the early history of many unions and in particular of the United Automobile Workers. This union was founded in 1935, in a situation of severe economic distress. Militance was the keynote during its early years. The problem of leadership was largely one of conducting a struggle for power and recognition, in which techniques of mobilization necessarily played a large role. The men who came to the fore reflected this emphasis on militancy. Successful office-seekers in the locals were those who could be counted on to deal roughly with management. Such men met the needs of a union more concerned with hewing out a place for itself, and surviving, than with responsible management of a stable organization.

After the union achieved its initial aims, the older methods of direct strike action, associated with a class-struggle outlook, became inappropriate and sometimes even harmful. Work stoppages were costly for both labor and management. While they might be thought indispensable as demonstrations of power by a group struggling for recognition, they could not be satisfactory as a permanent way of dealing with management. As this became clear, new leadership—locally and nationally—was indicated. While earlier shop stewards and local presidents were chosen for their strength in facing up to management, now it was necessary to choose men at the local level who could keep out of trouble and avoid unnecessary shutdowns. There began a movement away from militance, toward more astute negotiating techniques. To implement this change, a widespread turnover of personnel was required.[1]

Similar problems arise in industrial management. A characteristic crisis is the shift from a production orientation to an emphasis on sales and public relations. The Ford Motor Company, among others in the auto industry, went through a crisis of this sort. The organization that produced the famous "Model T" was dedicated to the goal of producing more cars per day at an ever lower cost per car. In this it was highly successful. But the organization that made this achievement possible failed to recognize or respond to changes in the market. Consumer preference was shifting to comfort, styling, and performance. By 1926, when sales were off disastrously, Ford permitted his company to engage in a national advertising campaign. He accepted this technique grudgingly, only under the pressure of a major crisis.

But much more than advertising was needed to permit sales an adequate role in the organization. Design and engineering had to be influenced as well. Finally, in 1927, production of the Model T was stopped, and Ford undertook the monumental task of retooling for a completely new automobile and rebuilding factory interiors so that it could be manufactured. It was now clear that the very techniques that brought about the great production achievement of the Model T were stumbling blocks when the need was speedy and efficient changeover. Huge, single-purpose machines had been built into production lines where more flexible machines were needed to keep up with periodic model changes. When the policy that "the customer could have any color he wanted as long as it was black" gave way to color styling, the old finishing process became completely obsolete.

> Nearly every piece of the company's monolithic equipment, laid out on the assumption that the Model T would linger on forever, had to be torn down and rebuilt. The staggering changeover necessitated the replacement of some 15,000 machine tools, the total rebuilding of another 25,000, as well as the redesigning and rearrangement of $5,000,000 worth of dies and fixtures.[2]

[1] Based on an unpublished analysis by Edward Boehm. For the experience in the steel industry, see Clinton S. Golden and Harold J. Ruttenberg, *Dynamics of Industrial Democracy* (New York: Harper, 1942), pp. 59 ff. [2] See next page.

Conversion to the Model A took eighteen months and cost $100,-000,000. Yet even this did not bring about the changes in orientation, with attendant upward revisions in the status of sales and public relations activities, that were required. Only after World War II was a reorganization in depth completed. The Ford enterprise paid a heavy price for a policy, valuable in the early state of development, that was not abandoned in good time. Given a deep initial commitment, so often required by pioneering ventures, such adaptations are likely to require correspondingly severe shifts in personnel.

An important caution is necessary at this point. Such terms as "early" and "late" can be misleading, if they are taken too literally, as referring to chronological periods in a *given* organization. In fact, of course, we must see an organization in its historical context, as an institution. When, for example, the production problems of an industry have been largely solved, it is not to be expected that a new firm will go through a stage of "production orientation." It begins at the level already reached by the industry (or branch of it) as a whole. This means that developmental analysis is most relevant where there is "openness," where the organization enters new paths. Every organization does this to some extent, and has some developmental problems, but it is safe to say that these problems will be more acute among ground-breaking enterprises or where there are few sure guides to decision and action.

It seems evident that the proper assignment of personnel and the diagnosis of administrative troubles will gain from a better understanding of the relation between personnel orientations and organization life-history. Consider, for example, the following administrative problem: In the case of a large research organization, what sort of men should be chosen as chiefs of the various research divisions? Should they be subject-matter specialists or administrators? This decision presumes an assessment of the stage of development in which the organization finds itself. If basic policy has not been worked out or not yet effectively communicated, if key staff members have not been chosen, there may well be a need for the research-oriented, creative person, whose job will be to give direction to the division and to build that orientation into its personnel structure and operating procedures. When these tasks have been accomplished, it may be in order for a person whose speciality is administrative skill to take over the reins. The selection of key personnel requires an understanding of the shift in problems that occurs as the organization moves from one stage of

[a] Keith Sward, *The Legend of Henry Ford* (New York: Rinehart, 1948), p. 199.

development to another. And for best results the participants should be able to recognize the phase through which they are passing.

Bernard Levenson

Bureaucratic Succession

For several centuries, the word succession has been used to refer to the process by which one religious or political leader replaces another. When the word was converted into a sociological concept, chiefly by Max Weber toward the beginning of this century, it retained the historically ingrained emphasis upon the replacement of men in the higher reaches of institutional life. So it was that Weber discussed succession as part of the routinization of charisma, centering upon the consequences that follow the death of a particular kind of leader. Later, when Alvin Gouldner studied succession in an industrial organization, the emphasis on change in top management was still there.[1]

When the focus of inquiry is only on changes in top leadership, succession tends to be viewed as sporadic, turbulent, often as disruptive. And it tends to emphasize cases in which organizations are largely ill-prepared to cope with succession, cases in which the successor learns his role only after he assumes the position. Thus the personalities of the aspirants, their informal relations, their manipulative prowess, and the process by which the new leader, once selected, stabilizes himself in power become the foci of analysis. Once the successor is secure in his position, the succession as a process is assumed to be completed.

This paper is published for the first time in this volume. It was written while on a fellowship granted by the Ford Foundation, whose support is gratefully acknowledged. The author is indebted to Robert K. Merton and David Caplovitz for their many stimulating suggestions.

---

[1] See *From Max Weber: Essays in Sociology*, H. H. Gerth and C. Wright Mills (trans. and eds.) (New York: Oxford, 1946), pp. 262 ff.; Alvin W. Gouldner, *Patterns of Industrial Bureaucracy* (Glencoe: Free Press, 1954).

Succession to office at the top, of course, is sometimes accompanied by explosive changes in organizational structure and policy. But the viability of an organization requires that vacancies be filled on *all* levels, not merely on the top level.[2] That succession is a normal and continuous feature of organizational life leads directly to the concept of *anticipatory succession.* By this, I refer simply to the circumstance that personnel are trained for higher-level jobs while those jobs are occupied by other people. The occasions contributing to anticipatory succession are familiar enough: the incumbent of a position is absent—because of illness, jury duty, vacation, or whatever—and one or another subordinate temporarily fills this position. Anticipatory succession is evidenced not only through this "pinch-hitting" role but also through the preparatory "coaching" of subordinates and through the informal delegation of tasks by the immediate supervisor.[3]

Moreover, the obvious fact that bureaucratic positions are hierarchically connected points up the artificiality of studying top positions apart from lower-level types. Replacement on a higher level necessarily sets off a chain reaction in the organization. When a successor is recruited from a lower level within the organization, the change at once creates the problem of filling the position which he vacates. Succession does not involve a single personnel transaction but rather a chain of transactions.

In the following discussion I shall try to work out the implications of a broader conception of bureaucratic succession. The first section examines anticipatory succession from the vantage point of middle-level supervisors. In particular, I shall argue that anticipatory succession decisively influences styles of supervision—and consequently affects the opportunities of subordinates. The second section views succession from the perspective of subordinates with the aim of showing how their differential opportunities pressure them to behave differently. The final section considers succession from the viewpoint of management and discusses some devices for dealing with obstructed channels of mobility.

[2] Sociologists refer to succession on lower levels by the negatively toned term "turnover," a conceptual distinction which this paper proposes to dispel.

[3] In this discussion, "supervisor" will refer to an employee who has authority over subordinates. "Superior" will refer to an employee who has authority over supervisors.

ANTICIPATORY SUCCESSION

A frequent approach to the analysis of supervisory practices starts with the *leadership traits* of individuals occupying supervisory positions. But these same supervisory practices can also be seen as consequences of anticipatory succession.

To clarify the important distinction, consider a hypothetical case. The manager of a company intends to retire soon and begins in earnest to appraise his lieutenants in order to select and train one as his successor.[4] On all social and technical criteria, his lieutenants are highly competent and not measurably different. The selection narrows to evaluating them on such leadership traits as the following: ability to deal informally with subordinates; willingness to delegate tasks to them and train them for higher-level positions; allowing them latitude and autonomy in their work instead of stifling them with supervision.

In such a case, the lieutenant who manifests these traits to the greatest extent may be selected as "next-in-line." There is evidence that the subordinates of such supervisors generally have relatively high morale and productivity.[5] In general, the "trait approach" to supervisory behavior searches for traits of leadership, such as those just mentioned, that make for promotability within an organization.

But supervisory behavior which appears to stem from deep-seated personality dispositions may sometimes be a consequence, not a cause, of promotability. Suppose, for example, that the lieutenants are equal in all respects. Nonetheless, to ensure the uninterrupted functioning of company activities and the orderly transfer of status the manager must select someone. By a feat of imagination, let us sup-

[4] Managers, particularly of small companies, often are too preoccupied with daily activities to think of their company's future management. External forces frequently exert pressure on them to lengthen their time perspectives. Banks and suppliers represent such forces. Before extending appreciable credit, they usually must be satisfied with a company's plans for succession. See C. Roland Christensen, *Management Succession in Small and Growing Enterprises* (Andover, Mass.: Andover Press, 1953), Chap. 5.

[5] For typical descriptions of the leadership traits associated with high morale and productivity, see, for example, Rensis Likert, "A Motivation Approach to a Modified Theory of Organization and Management," in Mason Haire (ed.), *Modern Organization Theory* (New York: Wiley, 1959); Robert L. Kahn and Daniel Katz, "Leadership Practices in Relation to Productivity and Morale," in D. Cartwright and A. Zander (eds.), *Group Dynamics: Research and Theory* (Evanston, Ill.: Row, Peterson, 1953).

pose that unable to choose among them in a more rational way, he makes his decision by the throw of a die.

This done, a particular lieutenant is signaled that he is the anticipatory successor. Thereupon his behavior toward subordinates may well undergo a change. Whatever his personality traits, the supervisor who knows himself to be next-in-line may become motivated to adopt leadership practices such as those described above. His structural situation makes it a matter of self-interest.

The promotable knows that after he is promoted the position he has vacated will have to be filled. Delay in filling it will mean more work for the people under him. Since the one who fills his job will be supervised by him, more than likely he will want to train one of his own subordinates: they already know what to expect of him and he of them. However little zeal a promotable may have for coaching, his failure to train a successor to his old position may later compel him to fill it with a subordinate who owes loyalty to another sponsor.

Furthermore, the anticipatory successor will be pressured to delegate many of his present duties, in order to have enough free time to learn the duties of his next job and to pinch-hit for *his* superior whenever his help is enlisted. But this, in turn, has consequences for the network of relationships in the company. Having less time to police his subordinates, he will be obliged to give them more information and autonomy.

An anticipatory successor need not worry that informing subordinates about the details of his current job will lessen his indispensability. Quite the contrary; if he is too "security-minded" and does not tell them just what they would need to know to fill his job someday, he might become indispensable, in a pyrrhic sense, by being regarded as essential in his *current* job. Anticipatory successors are, undoubtedly, apt to sense all this as a result of the exigencies of their situation.[6]

These observations suggest that morale and productivity of work units may *lessen* following the replacement of a supervisor who has himself just been promoted. Usually this is interpreted as resulting from the circumstance that the replacement has not yet "learned the ropes." This of course is often so—but it may also result from the replacement's

[6] Two studies which discuss the behavior of supervisors with discrepant chances of promotion are "Human Problems in U.S. Enterprises in Latin America," by William F. Whyte and Allen R. Holmberg, *Human Organization*, 15 (1956), 1–40; and Floyd Mann and James Dent, *Appraisals of Supervisors* (Ann Arbor: Univ. Michigan, Survey Research Center, 1954).

having no prospects for immediate promotion. Since he is not likely to be promoted again for some time, his style of supervision may be quite different from that of his predecessor. Consequently his subordinates may be less likely to cooperate as closely with him as with their previous supervisor. If this hypothesis has any merit, we should find that work units exhibit cycles of high and low productivity and morale depending upon the promotability status of the supervisor.

It cannot be assumed that supervisors uniformly know their prospects for advancement. The cues by which this information is ferreted out are important themes for organizational research. As I have implied, occasions of anticipatory succession in which people are called upon to substitute in performing the roles of absent or otherwise occupied higher-level personnel are apparently prime sources of such information. Whatever the sources, the awareness of the degree of promotability (whether accurate or imagined) may account for much of the difference in supervisory behavior among those occupying the same formal position.

Sometimes management may adopt the policy of obscuring the promotability of personnel in order to spur aspirants to competitive, and thereby presumably peak, effort. One way of implementing such a policy is to postpone the selection and training of successors until supervisors have vacated positions. To prevent anticipatory successors from emerging will require that pinch-hitters for temporarily absent supervisors be recruited from the *same* level rather than *below.*[7] In so far as there has been no opportunity to train or test replacements prior to promotion, organizations that adopt this policy run the risk of promoting the "wrong" people. (The final section of this paper discusses the difficulties of reversing such "mistakes.")

Management can also obscure promotability, not by failing to train anyone for a position, but by training many aspirants. Anticipatory succession, however, involves costs. There is, first, the time and effort expended by higher-level personnel in training. There is, second, the cost of the sometimes expensive errors made by neophytes before they have acquired a command of the higher-level job. And, third, there is the hidden cost resulting from the loss in productivity while trainees are absent from their usual jobs. Moreover, the time

[7] Instead of lateral pinch-hitters, higher-level personnel can substitute for lower-level absentees. *Downward substitution,* however, is often perceived as an indicator of unpromotability. Hence, while the action would serve to obscure promotability status on one level, it will reveal unpromotability on a higher level.

will come when someone must be selected to fill a vacancy. The successor may then experience difficulty in maintaining authority over a group of subordinates who have received virtually the same training and experience as he has. The company may discover that its resources had been spent in developing people for employment elsewhere—inasmuch as many of those trained for higher-level positions who turn out to be also-rans may seek higher-level employment in another company.

Thus dilemmas will confront every organization when it seeks to ensure continuity in succession to positions. In addition to its particular goals, every organization has the implicit goal of survival. If it over-ensures survival by having anticipatory successors two or three deep, it may, in effect, be operating a training school which services the needs of other organizations. Contrastingly, the organization which pays little heed to continuity of succession may become too unstable to achieve its principal objectives.

ADAPTATIONS OF SUBORDINATES TO UNPROMOTABLE SUPERVISORS

Whether promotability has its source in the leadership traits of a supervisor or whether promotability itself evokes the practices of leadership, it is evident that subordinates of highly promotable supervisors are in greatly different situations from those of subordinates of less promotable supervisors. Whatever their abilities, their structural location makes them either beneficiaries of their supervisor's success or depressed shareholders of their supervisor's immobility.

From the subordinate's viewpoint, the unpromotable supervisor [8] restricts his opportunities. As Merton has pointed out, marked discrepancy between culturally emphasized goals and socially structured opportunities for realizing those goals generates pressures toward deviance.[9] Merton's paradigm, though exemplified by a discussion of mobility in the larger social system, can, with appropriate modifications, be used to analyze mobility within a single organization. In fact, it would seem that the student of deviant behavior should find the organization a strategic site for investigating the social genesis of

[8] As used here, unpromotability refers to "dead-end" personnel occupying particular positions as distinct from the familiar notion of the "dead-end" position.

[9] Robert K. Merton, "Social Structure and Anomie," in *Social Theory and Social Structure* (rev. ed.; Glencoe, Ill.: Free Press, 1957), pp. 131–160.

deviance, its control, and structural rearrangements aimed at mitigating its effects.[10]

In the remaining part of this section, Merton's paradigm will be utilized to analyze the behavior of subordinates to unpromotables.

Withdrawal

One way in which the subordinate of an unpromotable supervisor can come to terms with his situation is by leaving. Viewing his opportunities as limited, he may decide that chances for success will be greater in another organization.[11] "Withdrawal" is analogous to Merton's category of "retreatism." The subordinate who quits a job does not withdraw from society, as Merton's retreatist does, but he does abandon the success goals and the means for realizing them held out to him by the organization he leaves behind.

Whether the subordinate of an unpromotable adapts in this way rather than another will depend in part on his status-set and on other aspects of his situation, outside the organization. It might be conjectured, for example, that the subordinates who are comparatively young, unmarried, or endowed with savings will to a greater extent than the rest choose to leave. The conjecture might also be advanced that although the subordinates of unpromotables will tend to leave an organization in greater proportion than the subordinates of promotables, the latter, when they do leave, are more likely to obtain higher-level positions, whereas the former are more likely to take positions at the same level as those they have quit. These observations may be enough to suggest how the conceptions under review could be fruitfully applied to problems of organizational turnover.

Ritualism

Employees who do not have the economic leverage or the physical vitality to start anew may resign themselves to the fact that they have reached a "point of no return." Aware that they must remain in their job despite blocked mobility, they may gradually lose interest

[10] For an elaboration of the concept of *strategic research site,* see Robert K. Merton, "Notes on Problem-Finding in Sociology," in Robert K. Merton, Leonard Broom, and Leonard S. Cottrell, Jr. (eds.), *Sociology Today* (New York: Basic Books, 1959), esp. pp. xxvi–xxix; Robert K. Merton, "Social Conflict Over Styles of Sociological Work," pp. 21–27 (paper presented at Fourth World Congress of Sociology, Milan, Italy, September 1959).

[11] Throughout the analysis, I shall consider only the cases of subordinates who are motivated to move upward in the organization. Whether or not they are in a particular organization is a matter for empirical investigation.

in their work and settle down to a minimum level of performance. In short, by abandoning ambition, their adaptation corresponds to Merton's "ritualism."

Innovation

Subordinates who neither withdraw nor slip into ritualism but persist in their efforts to advance are perhaps more interesting sociologically. They provide clues to a major source of organizational change. An employee may continue to conform to the organizational norm of seeking advancement, but in trying to overcome his relative deprivation he may be impelled to innovate.

The innovation may take the form of "public relations" to attract the notice of promotable supervisors, who may subsequently recruit him, and the notice of his supervisor's superiors so that they may come to know of his performance and abilities. The employee may become assertive at meetings; he may invent occasions for interacting with those who can facilitate his recognition; or he may write numerous memoranda proposing organizational improvements. As a way of accelerating advancement which might otherwise come slowly, if at all, public relations may be quite legitimate; often as it forwards the employee's personal goals, it also enhances his contribution to the organization.[12]

If the actions designed to by-pass the immediate unpromotable supervisor and to attract the favorable notice of higher officials are executed in a brash or ostentatious manner they will, of course, defeat their purpose. The immediate (unpromotable) supervisor and the promotable supervisors, as well as their superiors, will be alienated. For these actions deny, in effect, the legitimacy of the hierarchic structure. Subordinates of promotables do not have to engage in such attention-getting activities to the same extent; they already have access to a relative influential in the organization and through him have comparative opportunity for being observed by superiors. The structural context rather than personality traits may thus frequently account for "pushy" or aggressive behavior.

In the effort to impress superiors and focus attention upon himself, the subordinate of the unpromotable may take imprudent risks; if he seeks, for example, an overly lucrative contract, his company may lose

[12] For a succinct statement of this philosophy, see John W. Milford, "Can a Planned Personal PR Program Help You to Win Promotion?" *Sales Management* (June 21, 1957), pp. 29–31, 110–113.

a valued customer. In other cases, risk taking may be coupled with departures from organizationally prescribed behavior: duties or staff may be opportunistically inflated; functions may be "pirated" from other units; competent rivals may be eclipsed by dubious means.

Rebellion

When an organization makes a supervisor unpromotable, an unintended consequence may be to encourage his subordinates to scrutinize his assumptions and procedures of work. A subordinate who wants to advance would understandably try to discover what superiors expect. Knowledge that a supervisor is unpromotable may be interpreted to mean that he is not fulfilling the expectations of his superior. The subordinate may conclude that such a supervisor is not a model to be emulated and that advancement in the organization will presumably not be achieved by replicating his behavior. Re-examining a supervisor's mode of work in this way may generate new ideas which may provide the impetus for eliminating inefficient procedures.

Carried out extensively, however, this form of innovation may undermine a supervisor's authority. This situation will occur especially when a subordinate holds the supervisor responsible for his immobility and acts aggressively toward him. This typically results in "staging a showdown." An occasion is selected when the supervisor is demonstrably in error and the intervention of someone superior to them both is required to resolve the conflict. The superior, while he may conclude that the subordinate is indeed more clever and capable than his immediate supervisor, may have little taste for being thrust into such an explosive situation and regard the behavior as little more than rebelliousness.

Merton's rebel seeks to bring into being a new social structure; rebellion here is far more restricted, being directed mainly against the authority of the unpromotable supervisor.

In discussing adaptations of subordinates located behind unpromotable supervisors it has not only been taken for granted that the subordinate is motivated to achieve success in the organization but it has also been assumed that he knows the promotability status of his supervisor. This, of course, varies empirically. Adaptations of subordinates will be contingent upon the degree to which the promotability of supervisors is visible and the extent to which the perceptions of subordinates are accurate. There is ample room here for distorted perceptions.

The ways in which promotability status of supervisors is communicated to subordinates may be similar to the ways in which supervisors learn about their own chances. Of primary importance, I believe, is the phenomenon of anticipatory succession. Situations where one or another supervisor is called upon to substitute frequently for a superior—and in turn calls upon one of his subordinates to substitute for him—may heighten the observability of promotional prospects.

Another source may be supervisors who know themselves to be "next-in-line." They will often communicate their prospective advancement to subordinates, sensing that this will enlarge their capacity to elicit cooperation. Correspondingly, unpromotable supervisors will be motivated to obscure their dim prospects, although with time their unpromotability becomes increasingly difficult to hide.

And even where direct communication does not occur, ambitious subordinates will have their antennae out for indicators of promotability. By comparing the characteristics of those who have been promoted with those who have not, inferences are bound to be made concerning the technical capacities, interpersonal skills, and social characteristics essential for advancement in a particular organization. Those who have been with the organization for some time, for example, may observe that above a certain echelon no position is occupied by a woman; if their supervisor happens to be a woman, they may conclude (perhaps mistakenly) that organizational policy discourages her upgrading.

The literature on personnel and administration devotes considerable attention to assessment of employees by their supervisors. As the foregoing discussion suggests, important complementary processes are at work: lower-echelon employees continually assess the mobility chances of their supervisors. "Who is going where?" comprises a large share of employee conversation and thought, and research on these complementary evaluations would undoubtedly contribute much to organizational sociology.[13]

[13] David Caplovitz, in his study *Student-Faculty Relations in Medical School* (Monograph of the Bureau of Applied Social Research, Columbia University, 1960), finds that the faculty members judged by students to be most competent were more likely to be *subsequently* promoted. It is significant that lower echelons (i.e., medical students), though not even aspiring to displace faculty members, reliably ferret out the institutional criteria governing advancement.

MANAGERIAL ADAPTATIONS TO BLOCKED CHANNELS OF MOBILITY

The social unit analyzed by Merton in his theory of deviant behavior is the total society. When the theory is applied to smaller social structures such as a single bureaucracy, a difference soon becomes apparent: the structural sources of deviance are more visible and more modifiable. The political administrator may be persuaded that crime, suicide, or mental illness stems from limited access to legitimate means of achieving success. But changing structural conditions to make means and ends more congruent is a problem so complex that, except perhaps in monolithic societies, political action tends to be directed more toward the control of deviants than toward social change. In an organization, however, identifying and removing pressures toward deviance does not present as formidable a task. To the extent that the blocking of mobility channels by unpromotables generates deviance, there are numerous ways for management to come to terms with the problem. This last section considers a few of these.

Two classes of organizational devices for clearing blocked channels can be provisionally identified: (1) removing an unpromotable from his position, and (2) changing the nature of the position itself.

Removing the Unpromotable from His Position

It might seem that removing an unpromotable from his job is a simple managerial task. But the expense, effort, and subterfuge that frequently accompany attempts to dislodge presumably incompetent staff from their jobs show that it is anything but simple.

If the problem is defined as removing an unpromotable from his position, there are four types of "solution": he can be fired; he can be moved laterally within the organization; he can be demoted; or he can be promoted, to an innocuous and seemingly honorific position. Each of these solutions entails costs as well as gains for the organizations. The frequency with which one or another of these solutions is employed, as well as the conditions disposing management to use one rather than another, is a matter of no small interest for future investigation.[14]

[14] For material dealing with problems of managing organizational channels of mobility, see Norman Martin and Anselm Strauss, "Patterns of Mobility within Industrial Organization," *Journal of Business*, 29 (1956), 101–110; Howard S.

In discussing the strains involved in discharging personnel, Goffman has stressed the psychic damage to the people who are fired. He has noted that some managers, aware of these adverse effects, look for alternatives to this means of ridding themselves of a man judged unsuitable or incompetent. But other considerations—apart from altruism or compassion—make separation unsatisfactory as a solution. For one thing, the judgment that he is incompetent will embarrass not only the man being fired but also the superior who had sponsored his appointment or earlier promotion. To discharge a protégé is to administer a managerial rebuke to his sponsor; in effect, it proclaims to others within the organization his incapacity for judging ability. For this reason, we would expect that firing an unpromotable will less often be adopted when the sponsor is still with the organization—unless he himself is the actual target of the firing. Furthermore, if discharge or forced resignation is often used as a device for removing roadblocks to mobility, the system of succession may be damaged. Others in the organization might be made insecure, sufficiently so to be alert for positions in other organizations which do not rely on such harsh personnel techniques.

As has been noted, another technique for clearing blocked channels is to move the unpromotable to a job on the same level of status and authority, but with differing responsibilities. This technique, too, sometimes has not altogether intended consequences. If it is to be effective, presumably the reason for the transfer must be hidden; the alleged need to give the horizontally mobile man breadth of experience can at best veil the real aim. Since the veil is thin, the real reason can easily be discerned. If it is not, the danger arises that such horizontal movement will be perceived by others as a normal step in the organization's career line. When management blurs lateral "promotions" with horizontal shunting there is always the chance that promising personnel will be shunted into dead-end jobs.

The most difficult and perhaps the least satisfactory solution is demotion. Copeland has put the matter well, explaining why its secondary effects preclude widespread use:

Becker and Anselm Strauss, "Careers, Personality, and Adult Socialization," *American Journal of Sociology*, 62 (1956), 253–263; Erving Goffman, "On Cooling the Mark Out: Some Adaptations to Failure," *Psychiatry*, 15 (1953), 451–463.

So much is this a matter of common notoriety in business circles that the problem of firing has (it would seem inevitably) initiated a satirical book on the subject: Bill Longgood and Ed Wallace, *The Pink Slip* (New York: McGraw-Hill, 1959).

> . . . long before a mistake in promotion has become so apparent that corrective action is warranted, the misfit's former position ordinarily will have been filled, and a whole chain of promotions and shifts in personnel will have taken place. The misfit cannot be returned to his old job without upsetting these new arrangements, thereby causing disappointments, resentments, and even feelings that there has been a lack of good faith. It is almost axiomatic in business administration that a mistake in promotion, particularly in the higher administrative echelons, cannot be corrected by demotion. . . .[15]

In passing, it might be noted that the chain of consequences which Copeland ascribes to demotion probably parallels the consequences of filling a higher-echelon vacancy by an "outsider." The person within the organization who anticipated being the successor often experiences failure to move into the vacancy as being equivalent to demotion. Moreover, if knowledge of the vacancy is widely known throughout the organization, it is possible that a chain of anticipatory successors has crystallized, each member of which experiences the event as virtual demotion.

A fairly common solution to the problem of blocked channels of mobility is to install the unpromotable in a higher-level honorific position, often one created especially for him. The existence of quasi-functional positions to allow for the practice of "kicking a man upstairs" cannot be accounted for adequately without a general conception of succession as a social process. Weber, for example, maintains that bureaucracies require individuals to be qualified to fill the positions they hold. Creating a job to fit a particular individual—especially where he will contribute little to the organization—appears hardly rational. Although honorific jobs may seem nonrational in a short-run reckoning, they are probably functional in the long-run if by clearing blocked channels they facilitate the effective flow of personnel within the organization.

Clearing blocked channels by honorific promotion poses its own problems. If the position is manifestly functionless, it may not serve its purpose of providing a dignified resting place for an employee who has reached "executive menopause." Neither the employee himself nor others will be convinced that it is more than retirement on the job, a sinecure imposed upon the recipient. If, however, its true nature is screened, the honorific position might become imbedded permanently

[15] Melvin T. Copeland, *The Executive at Work* (Cambridge, Mass.: Harvard, 1955), p. 126.

in the organizational structure instead of being merely a transient arrangement to accommodate a single loyal employee. After the unpromotable retires, others might be sought to occupy the position; and unless appropriate functions are added to the position, the process of utilizing honorific positions may prove partly self-defeating.

Modification of Job Content

When it becomes apparent that a "job is too big for a man," a solution might be to tailor the job to fit the man rather than to remove him. Since mistakes in succession are not easily reversible by restoring the promoted man to his previous position, the blocked-channels situation sometimes signals management that the duties of the position are too demanding for the abilities of the typical occupant. By subdividing a job, the range of competence needed to perform it is reduced. And at the same time that the promotable is made more effective in this less demanding job, a new channel of mobility is created. In short, the existence of unpromotables in organizations can catalyze the process of bureaucratization and can result in the expansion of an organizational structure.[16]

CONCLUSION

In extending the concept of succession to cover replacements throughout organizations rather than only in high-echelon positions, I have tried to take seriously two characteristics of bureaucracies: continuity and the hierarchical interdependence of roles. The first requires that personnel be trained for higher-level positions *before* vacancies occur. This aspect of organizational life has been designated by the concept of anticipatory succession. The second directs attention to the effects upon subordinates of the differential promotability of their supervisors. The fruitfulness of this more general approach to succession is exemplified by the light it sheds upon such seemingly diverse organizational phenomena as styles of supervision, deviant behavior, and organizational change.

[16] It can also lead to contraction. By merging two units, a post occupied by an unpromotable can be eliminated. Reorganizations that seem dictated by market conditions or by efforts to increase efficiency sometimes have their source in the need to eliminate the organizational stasis produced by an unpromotable.

Richard H. McCleery

Policy Change in Prison Management

The Theoretical Context

The power of man over man is the brute fact of political experience. Much of political theory is devoted to a search for the real or ideal foundations on which power is based. Depending in large part on the time in which a philosopher writes, the basis of political power may be found in force, ownership of the means of production, natural law, or divine right. Each of these bases of power may seem dominant in a culture at some stage of its historical development. As a theory for our time, this paper will suggest the role of communication patterns as a basis for a system of authority and power.

Direct application of coercive force may be regarded as the most primitive basis of power in interpersonal relations. When social affairs approach a state of anarchy, a Thomas Hobbes may take that principle as the heart of his argument. The measure of stability or even civilization, however, is the development of alternative foundations for the social order. In stable societies, a pattern of communication appears in close connection with the power structure; and the "authoritative allocation of values" becomes a matter of definition and assignment rather than snatch and grab. While abstract political theory may find an ultimate basis of authority in force, empirical research in politics often equates interaction with influence and processes of definition with power.[1]

Excerpted from *Policy Change in Prison Management,* by permission of the author and the publisher, Governmental Research Bureau, Michigan State University, 1957.

---

[1] A review of the approach which identifies power structures in terms of patterns of contact and the communication of influence is found in Robert Agger, "Power Attributions in the Local Community: Theoretical and Research Considerations," *Social Forces,* 34 (May, 1956), pp. 322–31. For more general theoretical treatment, see Harold Lasswell and Abraham Kaplan, *Power and Society* (New Haven: Yale University Press, 1950).

The immediate focus of this study is on administration and the management of men in a situation which presents power relations with naked clarity—the prison. The bulk of administrative theory notwithstanding, the administrator is strictly limited in the sanctions which he can apply to sustain authority, and even the power of summary dismissal is a relic from a more primitive economic era. These limitations do not apply to prison management where force and fear stand ready as instruments of control. The task of analysis here is to weigh the role of force in comparison to the communication patterns as the basis of power. . . .

If we assume that communication patterns serve as one functional equivalent for force in sustaining the power structure of a stable society, these propositions would seem to follow:

1. Change in a formal power structure should be reflected in the patterns of communication and contact of the group.

2. Change in the patterns of communication, however instituted, should react on the system of formal power and authority, causing either its collapse or a resort to other means for its support.

3. A failure of the communication patterns to correspond to a given system of authority should result in anarchy and produce an increased resort to force.

The Research Context

The prison, as a distinctive system of power, provides a setting in which to examine the above propositions. The present discussion is drawn from the context of a broader study of prison management in transition which compared the processes of inmate society under authoritarian and more liberal prison administrations. . . .

The prison presents special advantages as a setting for the study of communications and power. In familiar communities, power is a complex which includes large elements of habit, tradition, loyalty and even affection. Customary deference is supported by a differentiation in status symbols and by class functions accumulated over centuries. The exercise of power in the prison, while not entirely independent of these elements, is clarified by its greater dependence on authority. The prison regime tends to suppress all class distinctions in dress and possessions and to reduce its subject to a uniform status of subordination. Hence in the relative absence of a symbolic basis of class distinction, the functional bases of those distinctions which do emerge and characterize inmate society to a marked degree become more evident. The commanding position of the "old con," his power to compel and coerce other inmates, may be traced to the process by which he creates the definitions accepted by his society.

Although the prison should not be taken uncritically as a society in microcosm, the comparative isolation of its social process from the impact of external variables provides a rare opportunity for systematic analysis. The vast majority of interaction patterns in inmate society begin and end within the walls and are subject to a measure of official control and manipulation. Finally, the identification of formal and informal systems of behavior is simplified by a sharp distinction between the ruling and subject class of the prison community.

The discussion to follow will consider the administrative and social characteristics of an authoritarian prison, certain liberal changes introduced and their consequences, and the basis of reconstruction in inmate and official societies.

THE AUTHORITARIAN PRISON

Organization and Communications

The formal organization and official policy of the traditional prison recognized industry as a goal and reform as a hope along with the objective of custodial control. However, one basic proposition emerging from this study is that formal organization is modified by the location and control of communication channels. Thus, while the prison had a work program, its inmates were sentenced to "hard labor," and the economic self-sufficiency of the institution was an ideal, the effective roles of industry and the industrial supervisor were institutionalized in their relations with the custodial force.

The Warden and his Deputy were the only policy-making officials of the institution. At the beginning of this study, the main divisions of the staff were the custodial force, organized in three watches under a Senior Captain, and the work line supervisors. Past attempts to vitalize a treatment program had atrophied by that time into a single position—an ex-guard supervised recreation. There were other functions performed within the walls—a kitchen, an admissions and records office, and a hospital—but these seemed to have no independent organizational status.

The entire staff accepted those implications for organizational structure which were institutionalized in the custodial force. The structure of that force was borrowed directly from military organization. The steps in its uniformed and disciplined hierarchy served as the measure by which those who performed non-custodial services determined their own status within the structure of formal organization. Hence the admissions officer insisted upon the rank of Captain which he had earned through many years of custodial service.

The nerve center for all institutional communication lay in the office of the Captain of the Yard. This location was dictated by the primary interest of custodial officials in the hour-by-hour reports on the location and movement of men. However, it was not just the report of counts and the time books of the work line supervisors but all orders, requests and reports which passed through this communications center. With the issuance of orders and the assignment of men channeled through a communication system controlled by custody, the perceived status of work line supervisors was below that of the guards from whom, in effect, they took their orders. . . .

Record items of costs, production, or the needs of the men might be ignored, but control information was never overlooked. The institutional pressures which dominated the office in which communication centered dictated its content and use. Custodial control of communications, and the interactional patterns thus established, imposed custodial attitudes, values and behaviors throughout the industrial program, negating its formal position and purpose.

Work supervisors had little contact with the Director of Industry but daily contact with the guards. Their ability to communicate their day-to-day needs depended on the influence involved in that contact. But contact normally involves effective communication only to the extent that shared attitudes and values are present.[2] As a result, supervisors came to think, act and dress like the guards. They justified labor in terms of disciplinary rather than productive or training results, maintained sharp class distinctions on the job, and repressed the rare examples of initiative which appeared among their inmate employees.

[2] There is no effective execution of orders in an agency except as some motive or sentiment appears in connection with and in support of the activity. In the absence of some more complex sentiment, the desire to earn wages may be enough to gain a tolerable level of activity, but the activity itself seems to produce sentiments in respect to the work among the employees. The manner in which the work is then carried on and the aspects of the work which gain emphasis in time are colored by the sentiments held about it and the manner of their communication. For a careful analysis of the relationships between activity, interaction and sentiment, note George Homans, *The Human Group* (New York: Harcourt, Brace and Co., 1950).

Accepting that definition of labor and the status of the supervisor, inmates opposed the industrial program and gave the minimum tolerable effort to it. Supervisors, in turn, borrowed custodial attitudes which explained failures of production on the basis of the malice and incompetence of the inmates. The institutionally shared belief in the limited possibilities of prison industry further reduced its role.

The status of other functions performed in the prison was subverted in a similar way, and this may be illustrated most clearly in respect to professional services. Psychological diagnosis and medical treatment were carried on in the institution. Referral to and reports from these services were passed through custodial channels which emphasized security considerations above all else. Psychological services seemed to the inmates to be an adjunct of disciplinary control, and medical treatment appeared to be geared to the detection of malingering. Consequently, inmates believed, with some justification, that these services were subordinated to custody, and the prison community in general regarded the professional with a contempt inconsistent with his formal status and the real motive of his work.[3] The "bug doctor" was considered lower than a "screw." That contempt, in turn, reduced the actual function of professional services to insignificance.

Thus, its control of communication permitted custody to co-opt the efforts of other institutional units to the support of its own function and status. . . .

Delegating a monopoly over communication controls has different and more dictatorial power implications for a society than simply delegating a monopoly over the instruments of force. Censorship goes beyond action to control over how men think. It goes beyond overt resistance to sap the very will to resist. It removes from the universe of discourse the premises on which criticism might be based. Thus, it gains a blind and fatalistic conformity not only while the eye of authority is on the subject but even while it sleeps. Inmates regarded the traditional structures of authority in the old prison as mean, abusive and unjust; but, most important, they regarded it as inevitable. . . .

There is an anarchic tendency in the principle of backing up the subordinate which would seem to maximize discretionary authority

[3] The contrast between the formal and the effective status of professionals in penal work has been generally noted. Harvey Powelson and Reinhard Bendix discuss the conflict with custodial forces and the attitudes of inmates which negate the work of the professional in prisons. "Psychiatry in Prison," *Psychiatry,* 14 (February, 1951), pp. 73–86.

throughout an organization. The absence of two-way communications controlled that tendency in the authoritarian prison. All communication flowed upward, leaving each superior better informed than his subordinate and limiting the information on lower levels on which discretion could be based. Official definitions alone are not enough to establish the legitimacy of senior officials and enforce discipline in a strict hierarchy of rank. The patterns of communication in the authoritarian institution established the official hierarchy as a relative intellectual elite and legitimized the assumption that the superior was correct on any question. The superior was always better informed. . . .

Decisions are influenced as much by withholding information as by injecting it into communication channels. However, subordinate officers hesitated to stop reports or deny requests where there was any possibility of being reversed later. Each superior reinforced his place in the hierarchy with a wider sphere of movement and access to personal contact than those of his subordinates. While the fundamental basis of status in both inmate and official societies was power to command others, prestige was closely related to freedom of movement. The power to exert influence was directly proportioned to one's access to communication channels and information. . . .

Procedures of Governing

The character of the prison as a system of power may be further illustrated in the procedures of decision, control and ordinary operation. The Warden was free to express the principle of having a constructive industrial policy. Given custodial control over operational decision, however, the practice of using inmate labor only in menial tasks of no value to the inmate and little use to the state contradicted formal declarations of institutional policy but illustrated a principle of wide application in this social system. Decision reflects the interests which are communicated most effectively on the administrative level at which decisions are made. The institutional autocrat is not responsible to his subordinates, but he is no less responsive than any other executive to those who define the premises of his discretion.

In the authoritarian prison, the exercise of coercive power based essentially on force constituted one foundation of social control. But this power was, perhaps, least effective when it took the form of punitive sanctions imposed on individuals. A high degree of discipline was maintained with the minimum of direct sanctions. A vital basis of social control lay in procedures of regimentation—frequent counts and assemblies—which imposed a psychology of domination and placed the subject in a posture of silence, respect and awe. Recognition of distinctions in rank was imposed in all inmate-official contacts by the requirements of a salute and special forms of address.

More punitive forms of control rested on summary procedure and a few rules as broad in their import as the officer's sense of insubordination. Control, rather than "justice" in the familiar sense, was the object. Hence, there was no place for a body of principles or "constitutional" rights to restrain disciplinary procedure. Secret accusation was the rule, and the accused had no notice, hearing, counsel or appeal. The resulting atmosphere of "terror," produced as much by secrecy as by the actual use of informers, was vital to formal control and a key to values and social structures in inmate society. . . .

The distinguishing characteristic of ordinary operations in the authoritarian prison was the absence of alternatives for behavior permitted to or provided for the inmates. Rewards went only for ritual conformity, and initiative was as suspect to the static inmate community as to the officials. This accent on conformity did not prevent—in fact, seemed to require—the emergence of a complex organization in inmate society. Silence was imposed wherever inmates congregated, but the patterns of inmate organization and communication could not be suppressed by even the most rigid silent system. They could only be controlled. . . .

The Inmate Social System

Reason would seem to indicate what official policy assumed in the old prison: that men stripped of all but the necessities of life would be equal and that they would be ready to attack the system which reduced them to that condition. However, analysis must deal with two predominant facts of the situation. Inmate society was structured in terms of striking inequalities, and, under normal circumstances, it was geared to adjustment rather than rebellion. Only under exceptional conditions, to be examined later, did violent and aggressive men emerge to a position of leadership in prison life.

Inmate society demanded and the officials asserted, as a basic premise of prison life, that all inmates be treated alike. In spite of this, the basic interpersonal relationship in inmate society was that of dominance and subordination. The highest personal value in that system was placed on the exercise of coercive power.[4] This suggests that a fundamental goal of control over men was uncritically borrowed by the inmates from the administration.[5] While there are striking parallel values expressed in dress and habit between inmate and official society, the pursuit of power was not simply an end in itself.

A goal of the inmates was to achieve integrity and independence from official sanctions—to gain deliverance from perils. To gain this type of freedom, the society enforced conformity on its members by sanctions more severe than those employed by officials. In defiance of formal premises of equality, inmate society was structured in a power hierarchy at least as sharply defined and static as that of the officials. It was defended in its independence by a basic imperative of the code: "Never talk to a screw."

The absence of published regulations or official orientation for new men, the secrecy and arbitrariness of disciplinary action, the shocking unfamiliarity of the prison world to men just arrived, and the demands imposed by regimentation—all these combined to make the new inmate dependent on the experienced prisoner.[6] The old inmate knew the uncertain limits of official tolerance in a system which, of necessity, prohibited far more than it punished. He could share on his own conditions the knowledge which made life tolerable for the new man.

Knowledge of prison operations made for physical adjustment,

[4] The apparent contradiction between the tight power hierarchy of inmate society and its constant demand for equality of treatment is discussed by Lloyd McCorkle and Richard Korn, "Resocialization Within Walls," *The Annals*, 293 (May, 1954), pp. 89 ff.

[5] Erich Fromm writes, in his study of authoritarian culture, "In any society the spirit of the whole culture is determined by the spirit of those groups that are most powerful in that society." *Escape from Freedom* (New York: Farrar and Rinehart, Inc., 1941), pp. 112 f. Only the most cynical approach could apply that proposition directly to the prison and claim that the spirit of the inmate population is taken directly from its rulers. This is too uncharitable to the rulers. However, a reformulation of the proposition in more behavioral terms permits its application to the prison. The effective pursuit of security by the ruling class of the prison imposes patterns of contact and social process upon the subjects which, in turn, dictate the dominant goals and values which can emerge in their society.

[6] The complex processes by which the new inmate becomes oriented or "prisonized" in his unfamiliar setting are outlined by Donald Clemmer, "Observations on Imprisonment as a Source of Criminality," *The Journal of Criminal Law and Criminology*, 41 (September–October, 1950), pp. 311–19. For those interested in intensive study of the prison as a setting for the management of men, the most substantial work on prison government is Clemmer's *The Prison Community* (Boston: The Christopher Publishing House, 1940).

but knowledge of explanations was required to make life psychologically tolerable. Inmates, no less than other men, needed rationalizations to give meaning to their daily lives. This was not provided by the authoritarian prison system. In the words of an old guard, "We don't have to make excuses to inmates." Senior officials dismissed the importance of the inmate grapevine because it was inaccurate, but its importance lay in its very inaccuracy. The myths and fantasies circulated by the grapevine performed vital adjustive functions for inmate society, explaining events in satisfying ways, holding officials in contempt, and attributing a certain dignity to the inmate class. Initiation into these mysteries of the inmate tribe was as important as the process of physical adjustment, and it was sharing in these myths of solidarity, more than physical association, which gave a certain unity to the inmate group. . . .

Inmate society protected itself from the betrayal of both its power structure and its myths by ostracizing such men from communication and the benefits of membership. At the same time, it regarded isolates as fair game for abuse, exploitation and domination. Constant emphasis on the idea of the "rat" supported a maximal valuation of power in inmate society and still restricted the most obvious recourse to power—an appeal by informers to official sanctions. The demand for equality was not a demand against the administration but an assertion among inmates that power gained by contacts outside inmate society had no legitimacy there. Denial of validity to outside contacts protected the inmate culture from criticism and assured the stability of its social order. . . .

Inmate leaders were men able to explain, predict, or control to some degree a situation in which others were helpless and confused. Lesser men gained security and protection by attaching themselves to those leaders and supplying them the petty tribute which conveyed status.[7] This type of dominance depended on access to informal communication, contacts on the grapevine and, also, contacts with official

[7] The significance of the constant exchange of food and goods in inmate society has led to conflicting interpretation. Norman Hayner and Ellis Ash believe that "the organization of this community is primarily an economic arrangement devoted to obtaining goods and services denied by the administration." "The Prison Community as a Social Group," *American Sociological Review* 4 (June, 1949), p. 369. The present study suggests that conspicuous display of goods and privileges among inmates serves only to symbolize status which must be earned by other means. The symbols declare an ability to manipulate power, and inmate society supplies these symbols to men undergoing punishment or in death row when the only function performed by such men is to resist power bravely.

sources. Because these men were expected to manipulate power and mediate between the forces of official action and their followers, they were given a license to talk with officials never permitted to men of unproven dependability. . . .

Under stable conditions, inmate culture supported custodial values. Its accent on conformity, on doing one's own time without fear or complaint, on avoiding behavior which would "bring on the heat," on never talking to a "screw," all these were ideally suited to custodial control. In a period of disorganization or challenge to inmate values, however, aggressiveness became the assertion of a moral independence and contempt for officials played a special, self-justifying role. The inmate whose rebellion was undeterred by the most violent official sanctions was elevated to the role of a Promethean hero.[8] The utter disregard of consequences, expressed by attacks on officials or repeated attempts to escape, assumed the stature of moral courage enhanced by the disproportionate weight of the punishment resulting. Under certain conditions, the ability to resist power bravely became the equivalent of an ability to manipulate power. With the collapse of a system by which adjustive definitions of the situation were applied throughout the inmate community, the hero was called on to give violent assertion to the values of the group.

Traditional inmate culture accented the values of adjustment within the walls and the rejection of outside contacts. It supported a social hierarchy, reduced new arrivals to subordination, and adjusted its own social conflicts with sanctions more severe than those available to the guards. As will be indicated by later developments in the prison, control of a disorganized mass of men was beyond the ability of the guard force. Control of a rigid social system in which the vast majority of definitions and sanctions were informally imposed was a far more simple matter. Hence the custodial goals of peace, order and adjustment dictated an alliance between senior officers and inmate leaders in the interests of stability and to the end of minimizing the role of the hero.

In some respects it could be said that the inmates ran the authoritarian prison. Senior inmates, at least, had a voice in the assignment of men and the distribution of privileges. Integrating contacts be-

[8] The elements of a hero-making situation are identified by Orrin Klapp, "The Creation of Popular Heroes," *The American Journal of Sociology*, 54 (September, 1948), pp. 135–41. In the prison setting, any collapse of the myths by which inmates justify themselves and their place in the world seems to demand some aggressive assertion of the idea that they are not defeated and helpless.

tween officials and high status inmates were conducted in a responsible way. Both groups shared a sincere contempt for "rats." Their exchanges were not moved by a desire to employ sanctions against individuals or to gain immediate private advantage so much as by a wish to maintain a condition of peace and order in which each senior group enjoyed the advantage of its position. Each group held power in its own sphere by means of ability to predict events and extended that power by intercommunication which violated the norms of both systems. In order to maintain these contacts with inmates which provided warning of danger, officials were willing to tolerate a considerable amount of rule evasion, pilfering, and petty exercises of power by inmate leaders. These privileges stabilized the inmate society. While the authoritarian prison is often accused of tolerating abuse, corruption, exploitation and inequality, such things were permitted in the interests of security and adjustment—the values most firmly institutionalized in the system.

Summary

The analysis so far has identified systems of communication intimately allied with the structure of power in both inmate and official societies. The unit of the official system which administered communications as a means of control imposed its values and assumed a commanding role in the institution as a whole. At the same time, a power hierarchy emerged in the presumptively egalitarian inmate community which seemed directly related to its communication and informational environment.

THE LIBERAL REVOLUTION

Three phases can be distinguished in the prison's period of transition. The first runs from the death of the old Warden in 1946 to the end of 1950. In that period, a liberal group appeared in the administration, gained formal authority, and revolutionized the policies of the institution. In the next phase, from 1950 through 1953, the liberal group engaged in a contest with the guards for control over operating procedures and, in effect, for control over the population. The present section will trace these developments. A following section will outline that contest, in which control was nearly lost, to its result in the defeat of the "old guard." The final period from 1954 through

1955 was one of reconstruction, adjustment, and, as stated by the officials, "tightening up the organization."

The seeds of revolution were contained in the appointment of five men from 1946 through 1949 who had no previous penal experience and who would not or could not adjust to traditional processes by which custody had become fixed as the dominant institutional goal. While these appointments were policy acts, they did not, in themselves, indicate a policy change, and the consequences which were to follow from altered patterns of behavior were not anticipated. The extent to which these new men injected inconsistent patterns of behavior from the free community into the prison, as much as their democratic policy statements later, marks the change as a liberal or democratic revolution. . . . The tactics of their revolt were little more than the habits of open communication, concern for "justice" as well as control, and performance as well as conformity, the rejection of status differentials in social contact, and the determination to be informed of their own responsibilities—all of which they imported from free society. Yet these simple behaviors, inconsistent with the authoritarian tradition, had a direct impact on policy and organization throughout the institution.

Reformulation of Policy

The disciplined traditions of the custodial force and the attitudes toward authority held by its members blocked their access to the open door of the new Warden. Those who took advantage of that access were the new employees who were conscious of the traditional chain of command only as a device by which their functions were frustrated. Other non-custodial employees in the past had resigned in the face of these frustrations or had accepted the attitudes and goals of custody with their acceptance of its communication channels. This group was spared the custodial orientation (with its narrow definition of purposes, roles and possibilities within the prison) by a practice of turning to one another and the license it took in turning to the Warden for definitions. The new men were members of the official staff, but they were not members of the official community in the sense of sharing the goals and values which gave an integrity to that group. . . .

As the new men by-passed conventional channels and turned to the Warden for definitions, they found that officer sensitive to the limits on his discretion imposed by custodial control of communication. His efforts to inquire through the custodial force into rumors of corruption in the prison had been frustrated for a year, forcing him to employ an outside investigator. The dismissal of several guards as a result of that inquiry, based in part on testimony taken from inmates, had lowered custodial morale and strained relations with that group. In this situation, the new men were able to form themselves into a policy caucus around the Warden and participate in the making of the definitions they sought. In turn this gave the functions represented by the new men (industry, education, and treatment) a hearing in policy decisions which they had not previously enjoyed.

When other units gained a share in policy definitions, the techniques of controlling decision by controlling the information on which it was based reacted against custodial officials. The new group was able to inject a wider range of pertinent considerations for policy than had reached the Warden in the past. As officials charged with treatment responsibilities gained access to the decision-making forum, this constituted a virtual representation of the interests and welfare of the inmates. This representation was reflected in a number of minor policy changes.

One of the first projects of the liberal group was to establish a clear conception of its own functions in the institution. To that end it produced a formal diagram of the organization. In contradiction to the actualities of custodial domination and the effective goals of the agency, the organizational chart placed the functions of treatment and industry on a level with the guard force. This, in itself, was a critical redefinition of roles if not of powers. Then, discarding its advisory capacity, the next step of the liberal group was to formalize its position as a policy agency for internal affairs. The guard force, the largest numerical group of employees, had only minority representation on the policy committee, and other officials of importance in the old power hierarchy were excluded altogether.

The next project of the liberal group was a Policy and Philosophy Manual. There was little formal statement of policy in the traditional prison between the establishing statute and the descriptive "wake 'em, work 'em, etc." of the guards. An authoritarian system is necessarily weak in operational ideology because it must resolve issues by appeal to the superior official rather than by appeal to principle. Authoritarian discipline is subverted by the publication of principles to which an appeal from persons can be made. Given a constitution or a law of the twelve tables, the weakest man in the community is armed with a weapon against the strongest. However, a Manual was published for the institution, and it asserted "rehabilitation through treatment and constructive industry" as the primary institutional purpose. It stated that "the democratic approach to management is the soundest" and contained commitments to

> The delegation to lower management levels of all possible responsibility and authority commensurate with sound management.
>
> A practice of constant consultation, dissemination of information, and discussion of problems up and down the management chain.

These concepts were directly inconsistent with authoritarian hierarchy and control. Custodial officers were members of the council that produced the document, but they made no effective resistance to its publication. Unable to communicate effectively in the new policy forum, suspicious and on the defensive, the guard force withdrew from the area of general policy and fell back on its control over the actual operations, procedures and communications in the prison yard. The liberal group had no impact on that area until it could translate its formalized principles into operating procedures.

The Procedural Revolution

From a legalistic point of view, it would seem that the revolution in the prison had been accomplished by 1950. The liberal group had gained formal status, drafted a "constitution" and seized control of the policy-making centers thus created. In terms of the daily operating procedures of the institution, however, the change had scarcely begun. While work supervisors continued to report and take orders through the guards, their programs and the emphasis of their work continued along essentially traditional lines. The policy-making group had gained status without gaining influence. It wrote new regulations and the guards continued to enforce the old. At this point—one not uncommon in the administration of penal or other institutions—a reformulation of general policy had exerted little visible impact on actual procedures.

While efforts of the policy group to legislate patterns of behavior and standards of action were defeated in the execution, that group was able to adjust institutional patterns of communication to the new policy. The principle that all those affected by a decision should have an understanding of the issues and a voice in their determination dictated the holding of discussion meetings in several sections of the organization. Led by the treatment director, these discussions proved most effective in the newly established and more complex units of the industrial program. There they provided a means by which the interests of the work supervisors were advanced past the custodial hierarchy, and the supervisors responded briskly to the chance. As an outcome of these meetings, prison rules were revised to abandon the time-honored salute in all contacts between inmate and supervisor and to give up other elements of regimentation on the work line which had hindered productivity in the past. The abandonment of these status distinctions at work opened the way to more active communication on the job, improved production, the development of workshop communities of interest, and habits of interaction quite inconsistent with the continuing demands of life in the cell blocks. The more open contacts between supervisors and inmates provided a basis for turning later to the supervisors rather than the guards for direct reports on the men. As might be expected, efforts to conduct similar discussion sessions with the custodial force brought little response.

At the start of 1951, an inmate council was established with a right to debate any issue and advance proposals for staff consideration. This Council, with an adviser from the treatment unit, formed working committees for such areas as food, hobby, and craft work, education, recreation, and public relations. It would seem especially significant in terms of the type of analysis advanced here that the Council called itself "the voice of the inmates."

Later developments began to challenge the realities of custodial control in one area after another. In times past, punishment, inmate promotions, jub assignments, good-time allowances, and every type of petty privilege had been administered by custody in terms of consideration of control. Seniority and the appearance of adjustment within the walls were used as a basis for the distribution of privilege. This reinforced the dominance of conservative and con-wise old prisoners. When the administration of privileges was, in effect, delegated to senior inmates, that served the interest of control as much by strengthening the inmate social structure as by applying sanctions to individuals. The administrative processes involved in this management of incentives were mainly informal and summary. That does not mean, however, that the operating decisions were not rational on the criterion of custodial control. A basic tactic of the liberal group was to alter the method and, hence, the dominant motive by which those operating decisions were made.

The treatment office claimed a voice in decisions on privilege and punishment on the grounds that privilege should be "meaningful" and that incentives should be concentrated behind their recently defined "goals of the institution." In defense of treatment-oriented personnel, it must be admitted that they had little conception of how all operations had been geared to the goals of security. By failing to share in institutional goals as defined by the guard force, they failed to comprehend the rationale of traditional procedures. They had little understanding of the economy of scarcity which prevailed in the yard or the extent to which a privilege or a larger sphere of movement extended to the "wrong" inmate could disturb the prison's social order. The philosophy of the treatment unit accented the importance of the individual, and this is the crucial basis on which the changes introduced may be called a "democratic" revolution. The focus of treatment men on the individual—a focus permitted by their lack of custodial responsibilities—was crucial in their conflict with the authoritarian tradition.

Participation in the expanding group of activities sponsored by treatment became the basis of a record. At the same time, the more complex processes of production required work supervisors to reward inmates on the basis of productivity as well as conduct. A report of the inmate's work record was channeled directly to the treatment office. Such records were inserted as relevant to daily operating decisions, and the decisions responded to the interests which were communicated most effectively. The traditional "time off for good behavior" became a committee decision in which six factors, only one of which was conduct, were weighted equally. The interest of teaching men a trade was taken as a ground for moving the administration of transfers to the treatment unit and away from custodial administration. By that time, the terminology and ideology of "individual development" rather than "good conduct" had been imposed on the reports of supervisors.

The treatment unit, armed with an expanding record, first asserted an informed interest and then assumed the management of functions in one area after another, extending finally to recreation and entertainment. These changes in the location of effective discretion within the agency tended to leave the custodial force with nothing but its guns as a basis of control. Rising disorder in the inmate community indicated that such a basis is weak indeed. The present section has indicated that the range of discretion possessed by a unit of administration tends to be as wide and no wider than the store of information on which decision is based.

THE IMPACT OF ADMINISTRATIVE CHANGE

As new concepts of policy were incorporated into the procedures of daily administration, these had a direct effect on the patterns of communication and interpersonal contact within the prison. The communication patterns of both official and inmate societies were altered to the point that they no longer served to support the traditional power hierarchy or gain acceptance for its authority. This section will trace the development of a rebellion among members of the once disciplined custodial force and, with reference to the prison's disciplinary records, the rise of anarchy in the inmate population. . . .

The Revolt of the "Old Guard"

While significant changes took place elsewhere in the institution, the custodial force retained the traditional patterns of communication from an earlier day. Just as the new officials had avoided indoctrination with custodial attitudes, the bulk of the guard force remained isolated from the new concepts and principles of the policy manual. Three years after its publication, few of the guards knew of its existence. Written declaration from above proved incapable of challenging the rationalizations which emerged within the group. Men whose daily work required them to be constantly ready to shoot an inmate arrived at a conception of inmates as persons who might justifiably be shot.

The system of limited communication to subordinates, which supported an authoritarian hierarchy in both official and inmate groups, was supplemented by a grapevine which supplied each level of the hierarchy with self-justifying and conservative values. Acceptance of these values as legitimate was the price of peer group acceptance in all ranks. Thus, a limited communication pattern within the guard force protected the traditional set of custodial attitudes from challenge or criticism. At the same time, their isolation frequently left watch officers less well-informed than the inmates they guarded, reversing the conditions of the past and removing the legitimate basis of the guard's authority.

The guards tended to blame the treatment unit and its programs for the decline in their status which inevitably followed. The over-all consequences of procedural change were to flatten the status pyramid of the prison community by providing equal access to influence and information, narrowing the gaps of social distance which made up a formal hierarchy of authority.

In order to understand the resistance of the custodial force, it is necessary to see the situation as the guards viewed it. New officials violated the chain of command at every turn and dismissed the traditional prerogatives of rank. The failure of treatment officers to maintain distinctions of class threatened the psychology of domination so central to control, and led guards to see the treatment officials as on a level with the inmates themselves. Policy discussions with the Inmate Council challenged control based on secrecy and fear simply by supplying the rational basis for actions which had appeared to be arbitrary before. The inmates had more direct and effective representation in policy than the guards. Custodial accounting for the movement of men was confounded by the treatment activities. Finally, the guards felt with some reason that they knew far more about the behavior of prisoners in the authoritarian institution than did treatment officials. The guards were in the most favorable position to see inmates exploiting new activities in pursuit of the old goals of dominance and power. . . .

The old guard launched a counterattack with the only weapons remaining to it. The Inmate Council, meeting with its staff adviser in the yard, was free from harassment. However, completely literal enforcement of old regulations against movement and communication brought the follow-up activities of Council committees and treatment-sponsored clubs to a halt. Inmates who were "getting out of their place" through participation in new activities were the subject of disciplinary reports. Gaining access to the treatment office was made so complex and, for selected inmates, so humiliating that many who valued their self-respect in the yard abandoned the effort. Requests sent through the custodial channels to the treatment office were often lost. The custodial force perpetuated a distinction in the yard between "right inmates" and "politicians," who were assumed to be using contact with the treatment office for their own advantage. Guards manipulated traditional inmate values by asking men returning from the treatment office how much they had "beaten their time." In the face of those pressures, inmates employed in the Treatment Unit arranged for passes to work until lock-up and stayed out of the yard. In spite of the expanding number of privileges which could be manipulated by contacts in the treatment office, the influence of its inmate employees was neutralized.

By the beginning of 1953, the revolt of the old guard reached the height of its effectiveness. Conservative inmates had withdrawn from the Inmate Council, and the younger men who replaced them were exploiting the Council to an extent which challenged the faith of even the liberal officials. The inmate clubs and associations sponsored by the Treatment Unit had collapsed, and voluntary class attendance was in decline. Violence and escape had risen to a point at which new emphasis on custodial values of repression and control was required. The Deputy Warden, once a leader for liberal changes, sided with custody in the staff conferences and threatened a split in that group.

For all practical purposes, the guard force had regained control over the operation of the prison. However, it had lost control over formal policy statements as it lost its monopoly over communication channels. The old guard, ambitious for legitimacy as well as practical success, sought alliances outside the prison with men discharged earlier and with community groups which supported their position. Represented by a minority bloc in the legislature which was seeking an issue, the old guard took its policy contest into the field of politics.

Legislative hearings on the prison opened with a series of charges which indicated, by their nature, their source in the active custodial force. A stand was taken on those matters which seemed most like mismanagement to the old guard: promotion and discipline. However, what the guards called favoritism was proved to be a sound promotion on the basis of "merit." What the guards considered abuses of discipline in the failure to back up subordinates was defended as a policy of judicial fairness. The staff was able to meet the legislative inquiry with a convincing mass of records and documentary material while the guards, in making the charges, were limited to the information they could leak. Hence, the position of the old guard, which had a great deal of merit from the standpoint of authoritarian control or custody and a strong prospect of success in the conflict with the institution, was flatly rejected in the more democratic forum of the legislature. By pressing for a definition of policy in a forum beyond the range of their effective influence and communication, the guards gained only the endorsement of the liberal position and a final repudiation of their own.

The prison had changed in its character from a military dictatorship to an institution in which the role of armed force was subordinated to the objective of treatment. While some guards persisted in their belief that all control over the inmates had been lost, a decline in escape, violence and disorder indicated, and the inmate community generally recognized, that the treatment unit had assumed control. . . .

Change and Social Disorganization

Discussion thus far has indicated that a shift in communication patterns and their control produced a drastic shift of power within a highly formalized organizational structure. The course of that change was delayed, modified, but seldom reversed by formal definitions of status and authority. The power of a unit to define a course of action for others was directly related to its store of information and capacity to transmit that information to the locale of decision. A change parallel to that in official society may be traced in the inmate community with even greater clarity in the absence of any official legitimacy for the power structure which existed there.

The first period of policy change was marked by little disturbance and relatively high morale in the yard. The investigation which crippled guard-inmate commerce brought no sanctions against the dominant inmate clique. While some activities by which inmate leadership supported its position were cut off, others appeared, and the inmate leaders were able to monopolize new privileges and claim credit for the sunshine. Control over the orientation of new men maintained the conservative inmate group in power as long as the guard force controlled the procedures of prison life. The early periods of low custodial morale and the revision of disciplinary procedures were followed by an outbreak of escape and some rise in disorder, but records show that these figures had returned to normal by 1949.

After that time, however, new activities and relationships in the treatment and production units began to create new communities of interest in the inmate body with a functional leadership of their own. As activities began to involve more and more co-operative supervision by officials, the "rat concept" of the old inmate culture and the sanctions against contact with officials were weakened. Old leaders often abandoned the opportunities for contact and information which appeared in connection with new work lines when accepting these opportunities involved accepting new relationships with officers and their fellows. The leaders drew into a more overt alliance with guard officials and sustained their position by traditional means in the prison yard. During the first part of the transition, the social consequences of the new work situations were isolated from the power structure and social processes of the prison yard, but the Council opened new avenues to recognition even there.

The old inmate leaders were like the custodial force in not being able to operate effectively in the context of group discussion and decision-making. In spite of a conservative majority of senior inmates on the first Council, a clique of new men seized the initiative in drafting the Council's constitution and bylaws, writing in provision for themselves. New officials thought the Council was a substantial privilege for the inmates, involving some small measures of control as well as a voice in prison affairs. To old inmate leaders it was a small boon in comparison to the position they had once enjoyed. The first months of the Council's operation provoked widespread inmate resistance and opposition, ending with the resignations of several old leaders. However, that move came too late to discredit the Council as a route to influence in the prison for a different class of men.

By the middle of 1951, the monolithic structure of inmate society had developed broad cracks. The marginally criminal first offenders, the lowest caste in the old prison, had found a focus of interest and organization in the Treatment Unit and the Council. As official frankness, publication of rules, and a formal orientation program made new men independent of the indoctrination by old cons, another group of tough, young, reform-school graduates declared their independence from old inmate leadership and embarked on a radical course of exploitation and troublemaking. In the following year, neither the traditional "code" nor old leadership commanded the respect which permitted them to define roles or adjust conflicts in the community. In the absence of controlling definitions, disputes were increasingly submitted to the arbitration of force, and the status of the physically powerful and aggressive men advanced.

Factions in the yard corresponded to those which split the administration in 1953. Conservative leaders allied with the old guard to neutralize the influence of inmates associated with the treatment program. However, the mounting disciplinary reports for that year did not reflect a direct conflict between those two elements. It was the young toughs, unwilling to accept definitions from any other group, who were out of control. In the face of these disturbances, created by an element of the inmate body that literally took orders from no one, the guard force and security measures were increased. The failure of these measures to restrain increasing disorder indicates the importance of informal social control, even in a society governed mainly by force and fear. . . .

This was the type of situation in which young men turned to follow "heroes" who dramatically asserted the ideals of toughness and resistance. Men made desperate by long sentences once had been absorbed into inmate society by the acceptance of values and definitions which made for adjustment. Now such men were encouraged by youthful followers to live up to newspaper reputations by sensational escapes and Promethean rebellion. It was the adverse publicity from such escapades which helped to establish the setting for the revolt of the old guard. At one critical point, a mass break-out was averted by posting machine guns on the roof and transferring inmate leaders of the younger group to another prison. Inmate society was close to a condition of anarchy in which the only recognized authority was that provided by physical force. This is not to say that attacks against officials were the rule. Official control over the instruments of force prevented this. What is significant to the analysis here is the complete failure of leadership and authority within the inmate community itself —the transfer of influence from the leader to the hero.

RECONSTRUCTION

A change in customary patterns of communication appeared to produce disorder and the collapse of authority in both official and inmate societies. This result occurred by way of the subversion of status attached to positions and conflict for the acceptance of inconsistent definitions. The emergence of a new order and stability in the prison seems anticlimactic by contrast. It involved little more than the development of patterns of communication by which all elements of the community gained the definitions on which stability is based.

Press reports of the legislative hearing which debated penal policy seem to have had a stabilizing influence on the inmates. Issues which had seemed, at first, to be little more than an administrative contest for power were defined for everyone on the level of principle. Inmates themselves entered into the debate on policy with an unprecedented interest. The position of the old guard was supported by testimony from one of the old leaders, but two of the major "heroes" of the inmate community submitted a letter to the legislative hearing in support of the new administrative position.

When the legislative debates were over, the Warden met with the inmates in a series of open discussions which are credited with a major role in restoring order. He took the lead in providing definitions and explanations of the situation so necessary to a sense of security but which no inmate group in the period of factionalism was able to supply. The role of the young toughs declined in the inmate community, and rates of escape and violence immediately dropped.

The central fact in the defeat of the old guard and those of their senior officers who remained was its recognition of the staff committee as an authoritative source of definitions for the prison. Prior to the legislative endorsement of a liberal position, the guards thought of themselves as custodians of the true or real institutional goals. It was this conviction which had armed them to circulate inconsistent definitions and also to remain aloof from the new policy centers. To the extent that the guards accepted the legitimacy of the new policy source, this acceptance worked to reduce tension in two ways. It reduced the circulation of contradictory definitions which had generated conflicts in the inmate body, but it also led the guards to a more active communication with and participation on policy councils. In the period of "tightening up the organization," policy has begun to incorporate more and more of the custodial point of view. Regular meetings between the Superintendent and the watches serve to bring considerations of security to bear on each decision.

With the defeat of the old guard, systematic efforts to isolate the influence of treatment-oriented inmates ceased, and a new social order began to emerge in the prison yard. Direct contacts between inmates and officials were taken as a matter of course. As a result, the idea of the "rat," with its implications for all inmate social process and structure, is almost forgotten at present. . . .

The transition involved a transfer of power from one unit of the agency to another. However, this change in the administration must be considered something more than simply a palace revolution. Inmate culture reflects certain qualitative differences in the present prison government. Wider access to officials constitutes a wider distribution of influence within the prison community which is reflected by a concern for inmate interests and welfare in policy. It protects against much of the exploitation and abuse which characterized inmate society in the past. While disciplinary rates have returned toward normal after the crisis, they will never be as low as was the case in the authoritarian prison. They reflect a greater initiative and a wider range of total activity in the inmate body. Even more significantly, they reflect a willingness of the inmates to accept official sanctions in the arbitration of inmate conflicts. The inmate community has abandoned many of the sanctions by which it imposed conformity on its own members.

Voluntary enrollment in treatment and education programs has shown a constant increase since the period of conflict. Such participation has become accepted as a means of gaining recognition in inmate society as well as official rewards. The programs sustain an atmosphere in which inmate attitudes are colored by ideas other than those generated within their own society and conditions in which a majority of the men are willing to accept officially sponsored ideas. An uncensored, inmate-edited newspaper, published in the treatment office, supplements the Warden's meetings with the men and prevents other inmate groups from gaining a monopoly on definition and interpretation.

Attempts by radical groups to capture the Inmate Council and to manipulate privileges administered through that agency have been defeated by inmates with little official intervention. The Council is not a strong and active organization, but it does insure that the inmates who speak with the most authority among their fellows are those in closest touch with the officials. The most striking distinction between the present inmate society and the past is the relative absence of powerful inmate leaders. Inmates elected to the Council by their fellows have less influence than the leadership which emerged in the authoritarian environment. Newly admitted inmates are no longer assigned to the lowest social status, social mobility is greater, and men with talent are recruited into activities in the yard by which status may be earned. A significant difference between past and present inmate society is indicated by the program of orientation carried on cooperatively by officials and the Council.

CONCLUSIONS

The three propositions advanced for analysis are supported by the evidence of this study. The unit which dominated the work of the old prison supported its position by control over the communication system. As those communication patterns were altered, a new policy emerged. Control over policy permitted the staff committee to formalize a drastic reassignment of roles and purposes in the institution, and this shift was followed by changes in the traditional patterns of contact for both official and inmate societies. The new principles and policy center did not become authoritative in practice until they gained the support of new communication patterns. During the interval in which communication patterns failed to correspond to the formal authority of the institution, anarchy and disorganization demanded an increased resort to force. On the basis of this evidence, it may be asserted that a pattern of communication serves as a functional equivalent for force in maintaining or subverting a stable system of authority. . . .

Allen H. Barton

and

Bo Anderson

Change in an Organizational System: Formalization of a Qualitative Study

Quantitative social research in the last twenty-five years has relied heavily on the sample survey. By this method very large populations can be accurately described through the study of only one or two thousand persons. The most efficient design for descriptive purposes is the random sample, with the individuals selected so as to be widely scattered among the whole population. Yet precisely this design makes it difficult to study processes which involve mutual effects among people and among groups. The atomistic survey is particularly misplaced in the study of organizations.

This article, published here for the first time, is one of a series sponsored by the Documentation Project for Advanced Training in Social Research, Columbia University. It may be cited as Publication A-323 of the Bureau of Applied Social Research, Columbia University.

Organizations are systems of individuals and groups which act upon one another. Changes in the behavior of one status group within an organization must affect the behavior of other groups, which in turn may have consequences feeding back to the group which changed first. The consequences of change in a system cannot be predicted by any simple two-variable notions of causation in which "A" invariably leads to "B."

The object of this paper is to see how the system aspect of organizations can be dealt with in empirical research. Progress toward methods capable of studying the operation of systems has come from several sources. One requirement is that data be gathered at several points *in time*. The technique of trend or panel studies adds this time dimension to surveys.[1] Studies of small groups using quantified observations of behavior permit analysis of changes in different natural phases or under changing experimental conditions.[2] A few studies have traced changes in organizations over time, using such variables as could be derived from organizational records.[3]

A second requirement for system analysis is that data be obtained from the *different units* which act upon one another within the system. Some surveys have gone beyond the individual respondent by getting his description of the people with whom he interacts, for example, by asking him what the politics of his family, friends, or co-workers are.[4] Surveys have begun to use clustered samples within formal groups, such as college faculties [5] or printing shops,[6] so that the group context

[1] Bernard Berelson, Paul F. Lazarsfeld, and William N. McPhee, *Voting* (Chicago: Univ. of Chicago, 1954), is an example of the panel method applied to mass political behavior. A discussion of the method and more examples are found in Paul F. Lazarsfeld and Morris Rosenberg, *The Language of Social Research* (Glencoe, Ill.: Free Press, 1955), Section 3, "The Analysis of Change through Time."

[2] Robert F. Bales, "The Equilibrium Problem in Small Groups," in A. P. Hare, E. F. Borgatta, and R. F. Bales, *Small Groups: Studies in Social Interaction* (New York: Knopf, 1955), summarizes research along these lines done at the Harvard Laboratory of Social Relations.

Henry Lennard and Arnold Bernstein, *The Anatomy of Psychotherapy: Systems of Communication and Expectation* (New York: Columbia, 1960), studies a two-person interaction system over time in a natural situation.

[3] For example, S. M. Lipset, M. A. Trow, and J. S. Coleman, *Union Democracy* (Glencoe, Ill.: Free Press, 1956), Chaps. 3 and 17; and Julia S. Brown, "Union Size as a Function of Intra-Union Conflict," *Human Relations*, 9 (1956), 75–89.

[4] Berelson, Lazarsfeld, and McPhee (see n. 1).

[5] Paul F. Lazarsfeld and Wagner Thielens, Jr., *The Academic Mind* (Glencoe, Ill.: Free Press, 1958).

[6] Lipset, Trow, and Coleman (see n. 3).

of individuals can be directly measured by aggregating the responses of all members. Sociometric data on contacts among group members, obtained when *all* members of a group are surveyed, provide more refined information on sets of related individuals.[7] A few studies have interviewed both sides of a role relationship, such as workers and their foreman,[8] superintendents and their school board,[9] students and faculty members.[10] These methods obtain data on related parts of a system rather than isolated individuals, although they seldom have been used to cover *all* the major parts of any system.

What has not been done is to combine these methods in the study of an organizational system. No one has yet studied quantitatively the attitudes and behavior of different strata within an organization, at two or more time periods, with data on contacts between people and groups. We cannot therefore present a series of examples for methodological clarification. However, there are a number of *qualitative* case studies which deal with organizational processes, using largely subjective measures of the variables involved. We will examine one such study, in order to illustrate the concept of an organization as a system and to suggest how quantitative methods *might* be used to study organizations as systems. Our findings may also shed some light on the techniques of purely qualitative research.

Richard H. McCleery's *Policy Change in Prison Management* [11] is a brief report on a study of change in the social system of a prison. It describes the prison in equilibrium under an authoritarian system in which the custodial goal of strict physical orderliness was stressed above all else; the disorders and difficulties which followed a change in top personnel and policies; and the eventual restoration of equilibrium under policies which emphasized the rehabilitation function.

By observing what happened when certain features of the authoritarian regime were removed, he obtained suggestions of the functions which these features had been performing for the main-

[7] T. M. Newcomb, *Personality and Social Change* (New York: Holt, Rinehart and Winston, 1943), provides an example of this method, combined with a panel study, applied to the survey of change in attitudes of college students.

[8] Robert L. Kahn and Daniel Katz, "Leadership Practices in Relations to Productivity and Morale," in Dorwin Cartwright and Alvin Zander, *Group Dynamics: Research and Theory* (Evanston, Ill.: Row, Peterson, 1953), pp. 612–628, summarizes several such studies.

[9] Neal Gross, W. S. Mason, and A. W. McEachern, *Explorations in Role Analysis* (New York: Wiley, 1958).

[10] Newcomb (see n. 7).

[11] Richard H. McCleery, *Policy Change in Prison Management* (East Lansing: Michigan State Univ., Governmental Research Bureau, 1957).

tenance of order, as well as suggestions of their dysfunctions for the rehabilitation goal. Observing the growth of the new equilibrium as the "liberal" regime gradually responded to the problems of the transition period, he found evidence of the availability of alternatives to the old methods which permitted a higher achievement of the nominal goals of the prison: rehabilitation and effective custody.

THE ANATOMY OF THE SYSTEM

McCleery's first step is to describe the "anatomy" of the system, the groups or strata which formed the prison's structure. The following major status groups are distinguished: the top administration (essentially the warden, later joined by a policy committee of department heads); the custodial staff (guards and guard officers); the treatment staff (workshop supervisors, psychiatrist, and later the directors of programs of education and recreation); the inmate elite of old cons with privilege and power; and the mass of the inmates.

VARIABLES IN THE SYSTEM

The monograph consists of qualitative descriptions of these status groups and their relationships at various stages in the process of change. By qualitative, we mean that McCleery simply reports that a variable has a high or low value, or that it has increased or decreased.[12] The major types of variables considered are attitudes toward prison programs; the amount of communication between status groups; the degree of control over such communication held by intermediary groups; the types of sanctions employed to encourage or inhibit various behaviors; and the response of various groups to these sanctions.

TIME PERIODS

Not all variables are reported for all time periods, but generally the author uses his qualitative observations just as one would use data from a trend or panel study, or an analysis of interaction records over time. His narrative description may be summarized in a set of trend

[12] McCleery's monograph is based on his unpublished dissertation, *Power, Communications, and the Social Order* (Chapel Hill: Univ. of North Carolina, 1956). Both of these reports are essentially qualitative.

charts, with qualitative signs substituted for figures. Five main time periods seem to be distinguished: (1) the authoritarian equilibrium under the old warden, (2) the period of initiation of reforms when the new warden succeeded him, (3) a period of extension of reforms, (4) a period of sabotage by the guards and rebellion by certain groups of prisoners, and ultimately (5) a new equilibrium rather more liberal than the original one in its emphasis on fair treatment and rehabilitation.

OBSERVATIONS OF CHANGE OVER TIME

McCleery's starting point is in the communications system. The new warden's first act was to open communications channels with the treatment staff; direct communications between administration and the prisoners was expanded gradually; the preferred communications position of the custodial staff declined to a point where this group was virtually isolated, requiring a moderate rise to achieve the new equilibrium (Table 1a).

Table 1a. AMOUNT OF COMMUNICATIONS BETWEEN STATUS GROUPS

	Authoritarian equilibrium (1)	*Initiation of reforms* (2)	*Extension of reforms* (3)	*Sabotage and rebellion* (4)	*Liberal equilibrium* (5)
Administration–Treatment	LOW	HIGH	HIGH	HIGH	HIGH
Administration–Custody	HIGH	MED	LOW	LOW	MED
Administration–Inmates	LOW	MED	HIGH	MED	HIGH
Custody–Treatment	HIGH	HIGH	LOW	LOW	MED
Custody–Inmate elite	HIGH	HIGH	HIGH	HIGH	*
Custody–Inmate mass	LOW	LOW	LOW	LOW	MED
Treatment–Inmates	LOW	MED	HIGH	MED	HIGH
Inmate elite–Mass	HIGH	HIGH	MED	LOW	*

* By the last period the old inmate elite had disappeared as a status group.

A crucial attitude area considered was the acceptance by the various groups of the goal of "treatment" or rehabilitation. The authoritarian prison gave very low priority to this goal. New personnel leading the treatment staff, and their new access to communications within the prison, permitted the treatment goal to be spread to the top administration, to the treatment staff, then to the mass of the prisoners and to some extent to the custodial staff (Table 1b).

Table 1b. ACCEPTANCE OF TREATMENT GOAL AMONG VARIOUS STATUS GROUPS

	Time Periods				
	(1)	(2)	(3)	(4)	(5)
Administration	MED	HIGH	HIGH	LOW	HIGH
Custodial staff	LOW	LOW	LOW	LOW	MED
Treatment heads	HIGH	HIGH	HIGH	LOW	HIGH
Treatment staff	MED	HIGH	HIGH	LOW	HIGH
Inmate elite	LOW	LOW	LOW	LOW	*
Inmate mass	LOW	MED	MED	LOW	HIGH

* By the last period the old inmate elite had disappeared as a status group.

Decisive variables in achieving the prison's goals were the types of sanctions and opportunities with which the prisoners were confronted by the various staff groups. The authoritarian prison was characterized by unpredictable, arbitrary allocation of rewards and punishments; a key reform was the replacement of this arbitrariness by "due process" and full explanation. At the same time the amount of educational, recreational, and other positive activities available to the inmates was greatly increased, whereas the use of "rituals of domination" by the custodial staff was reduced. The toleration of inmate-elite privileges and positive support of their power by the custodial staff were gradually reduced to the point that the "inmate elite" in the old sense disappeared as a status group (Table 1b).

Table 1c. STAFF BEHAVIOR: SANCTIONS AND OPPORTUNITIES

	Time Periods				
	(1)	(2)	(3)	(4)	(5)
Administration's arbitrariness in discipline, assignments, etc.	HIGH	MED	LOW	LOW	LOW
Rehabilitative activities offered by treatment staff	LOW	MED	HIGH	HIGH	HIGH
Custodial staff's maintenance of rituals of domination	HIGH	HIGH	MED	MED	LOW
Custodial staff's toleration of inmate-elite privileges, power, rackets, etc.	HIGH	HIGH	MED	MED	LOW

Finally we have the response of the mass of the inmates to the system—the output which the system is intended to influence. On the positive side there is the amount of inmate participation in the treatment program, which is presumably related to ultimate output of long-run change in behavior. On the negative side there is the amount of disorder within the prison—overt violence, riots, escapes, violations of rules—which threatens its custodial purpose. Both of these variables underwent wide fluctuations; the explanation of these sometimes paradoxical shifts and of the values which they achieved in the new equilibrium are the matters with which McCleery is mainly concerned (Table 1d).

Table 1d. RESPONSE OF INMATE MASS TO STAFF BEHAVIOR

	Time Periods				
	(1)	(2)	(3)	(4)	(5)
Inmates' participation in treatment program	LOW	MED	HIGH	LOW	HIGH
Inmates' amount of disorderly behavior, violence	LOW	MED+	MED—	HIGH	MED

We will not raise here the important question of the reliability of qualitative observations—whether different observers using the same methods in the same prison would report the same things. It is important to note that all of these variables could in principle be quantitatively measured by such devices as attitude scales, sociometric questions, analysis of formal communications content, self-reports or systematic description of behavior, statistical analysis of official records, ratings by informed participants, etc. How practical such measurements would be in a prison during a crisis period is another question, but they can undoubtedly be applied to more "normal" types of organization.

SYSTEMS OF RELATIONSHIPS

On the basis of these observations of change over time, McCleery suggests a great many causal relationships which form subsystems of links and feedbacks. For example, of the authoritarian system he says,

> Custodial control of communications, and the interactional patterns thus established, imposed custodial attitudes, values and behaviors throughout the industrial program, negating its formal position and purpose (p. 11).
>
> Supervisors [of the work program] came to think, act and dress like the guards. They justified labor in terms of disciplinary rather than productive or training results, maintained sharp class distinction on the job, and repressed the rare examples of initiative which appeared among their inmate employees (p. 12).

> Accepting that definition of labor . . . inmates opposed the industrial program and gave the minimum tolerable effort to it. Supervisors, in turn, borrowed custodial attitudes which explained failures in production on the basis of the malice and incompetence of the inmates. The institutionally shared belief in the limited possibilities of prison industry further reduced its role (p. 12).

The operation of this set of relationships can be diagramed as follows (Chart 1):

This set of causal relationships might have been inferred from examining the way the authoritarian system worked; it was strongly supported by McCleery's observation of what happened when the crucial factor of control over communications was changed by the new warden, and the other factors changed thereafter.

From a number of statements in McCleery's report it is possible to reconstruct a rather intricate system of social control which served to maintain a low rate of disorderly behavior within the authoritarian prison:

> The absence of published regulations or official orientation for new men, the secrecy and arbitrariness of disciplinary action, the shocking unfamiliarity of the prison world to men just arrived, and the demands imposed by regimentation—all these combined to make the new inmate dependent on the experienced prisoner (p. 17).
>
> Over time, a few senior inmates proved their "rightness" to a

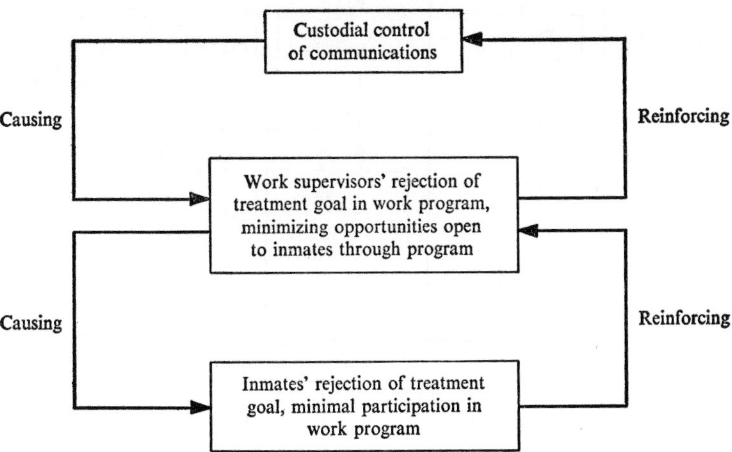

Chart 1. The process of degeneration of the work program under custodial control of communications

number of primary groups. . . . Their wider range of contacts made them able to influence transfers, manipulate the system by which goods were stolen, gambled and exchanged, and give warning of official action (p. 18).

Hence the custodial goals of peace, order and adjustment dictated an alliance between senior officers and inmate leaders in the interests of stability and to the end of minimizing the role of the hero [the charismatic rebel against the prison authority]. . . . In order to maintain these contacts with inmates which provided warnings of danger, officials were willing to tolerate a considerable amount of rule evasion, pilfering, and petty exercises of power by the inmate leaders. These privileges stabilized the inmate society (pp. 19–20).

Here is one of the key mechanisms by which the equilibrium of the authoritarian system was maintained—a set of relationships which permitted the maintenance of order at the expense of rendering impossible the other nominal goal of the prison, rehabilitation. This system too can be presented in the form of a flow diagram (Chart 2).

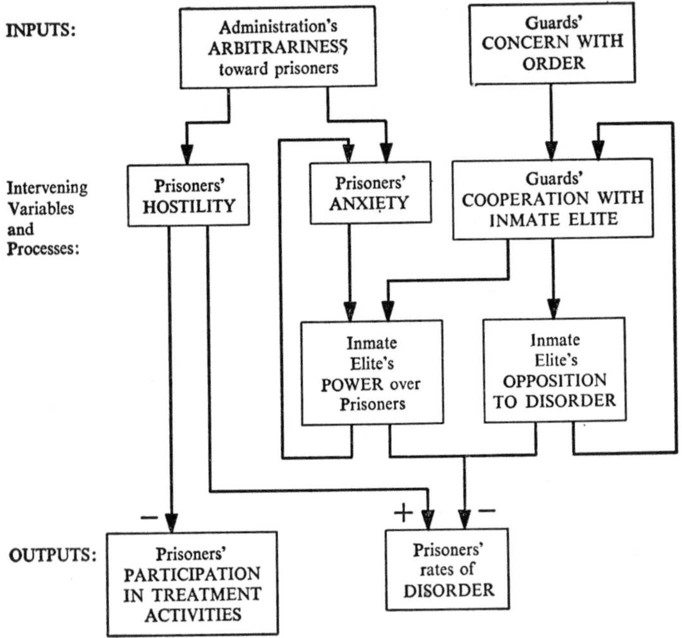

Chart 2. The system of informal control in the authoritarian state

In this system, the maintenance of a power elite among the prisoners is dependent on a steady input of arbitrary administrative behavior producing anxiety. The powers exercised by the inmate elite group give them something to offer the custodial staff in return for privileges, which in turn strengthen the inmate elite. The cooperation of the guards in the maintenance of their privileged position makes the inmate leadership "accommodative" rather than rebellious or reform-minded and willing to use some of their powers to hold down the rate of disorderly behavior among the prisoners. This set of conditions therefore favors a low rate of disorder. At the same time, since the arbitrariness of the administration creates a strong hostility toward the prison among the rank-and-file prisoners, their participation in treatment activities is minimized. Thus one goal of the prison is achieved, but the other is not. As long as external authorities tolerate this partial failure of output, the organization system remains balanced.

A SIMPLIFIED ARITHMETICAL MODEL OF THE SOCIAL CONTROL SYSTEM

The ways in which the observed events are explained by the qualitative analyst may be clarified by a simplified mathematical model of the social control system of the prison. We will not consider all the many variables and stages found in the original text, and only the simplest arithmetical forms of relationships will be employed.

We will assume that the rate of prisoner Disorder (D) is increased by Hostility (H) toward the prison administration but reduced by the Power (P) exercised over the prisoners by the inmate elite.

$$D = uH - vP \tag{1}$$

We will also assume that Hostility is created by two factors: the degree of Arbitrariness (A) of the prison authorities in administering the rules, and a constant factor, the general Frustrations (F) which are inherent in any prison, regardless of how well run.

$$H = wA + F \tag{2}$$

We assume that the degree of Power (P) of the inmate elite to prevent Disorder is dependent on the degree of Arbitrariness (A) of the prison administration (through the mechanisms of creating anxiety and dependence on the experienced and manipulatively skilled prisoners, which will not be explicitly included here).

$$P = yA \tag{3}$$

Finally, we will assume that the rate of prisoner participation in the rehabilitation program (R) decreases as the prisoners' Hostility (H) increases, subject to some constant factor of the attractiveness of the activities (U):

$$R = U - zH \tag{4}$$

We have thus pulled out of the more complex model one section which illustrates the point that a given change in input can produce intervening changes which act in opposite directions on the output (Chart 3).

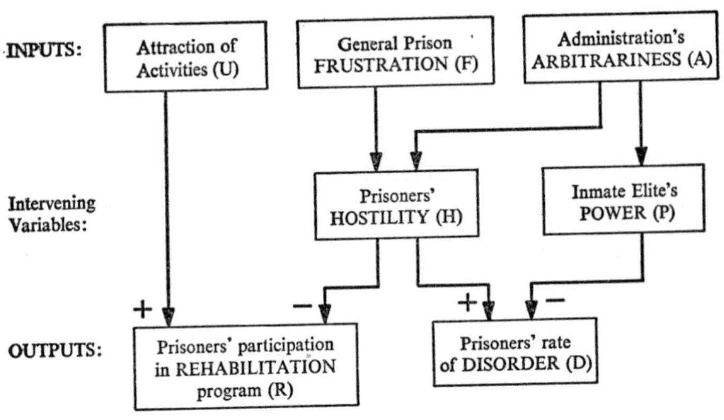

Chart 3. Simplified system of informal control in the authoritarian prison

The net result of a change in A will depend on the strength of the two opposing relationships through which it affects D.

All of these variables could be measured by various attitude scales, rating devices, behavior records, and similar measures. Let us assume for simplicity that all the relationships are linear and that our scales and measures have been so calibrated that in the equations given above all the coefficients (u, v, w, y, z) are equal to 1. The constant Frustration factor (F) is set equal to 20 in this example, and the constant attractiveness of the rehabilitation activities (U) equals 40. Then if we know the input values of administrative Arbitrariness, we can compute the intervening and the output variables. Table 2 shows several possible situations.

Table 2. A MODEL OF INPUTS AND OUTPUTS IN THE PRISON SYSTEM

	Inputs			*Intervening Variables*		*Outputs*	
	Administration's ARBITRARINESS (A)	Prison FRUSTRATION Constant (F)	Activities Attraction Constant (U)	Prisoners' HOSTILITY (H)	Inmate Elite's POWER (P)	Prisoners' Rate of DISORDER (D)	Prisoners' REHABILITATION Activity (R)
Situation 1	20	20	40	40	20	20	0
Situation 2	10	20	40	30	10	20	10
Situation 3	0	20	40	20	0	20	20

Assumptions: $H = A + F$ $P = A$ $D = H - P$ $R = U - H$

Given this particular system of relationships, the rate of disorder remains the same, regardless of the degree of arbitrariness of the prison administration. A reduction in arbitrariness reduces hostility and thus might be thought of as an improvement likely to reduce disorder. In fact, it also weakens the informal control mechanism just enough to allow the disorder rate to stay unchanged. If the administrator's only goal is to minimize disorder, he can choose any of the three situations. On the other hand, if he is also concerned with increasing participation in rehabilitative activities, he can do so by reducing arbitrariness without changing the rate of disorder.

As far as this model is concerned, the degree of arbitrary behavior of the administration could be increased indefinitely, thereby raising prisoner hostility higher and higher, without increasing disorder, since the increased control keeps pace. In reality such relations would hold only over a certain range, beyond which the mechanisms would break down. At some level of ruthlessness either the informal controls would fail to keep pace and a rebellion would break out or the prisoners would be so crushed that their hostility would again decline.

Suppose now that we assume a somewhat different system, in which there is a much stronger relationship between administrative arbitrariness and the inmate elite's power to control prison disorders. This can be represented by supposing that the coefficient y in the equation $P = yA$ is not 1 but 2. Then the situation will be quite different. The power of the inmate elite to hold down disorder will be much greater in Situation 1, but decreases more rapidly as administrative Arbitrariness declines (Table 3).

Table 3. A MODEL OF THE SYSTEM WITH ONE RELATIONSHIP ALTERED

	Inputs			*Intervening Variables*		*Outputs*	
	Administration's ARBITRARINESS (A)	Prison FRUSTRATION Constant (F)	Activities Attraction Constant (U)	Prisoners' HOSTILITY (H)	Inmate Elite's POWER (P)	Prisoners' Rate of DISORDER (D)	Prisoners' REHABILITATION Activity (R)
Situation 1	20	20	40	40	40	0	0
Situation 2	10	20	40	30	20	10	10
Situation 3	0	20	40	20	0	20	20

Assumptions: $H = A + F$ $P = 2A$ $D = H - P$ $R = U - H$

Under these circumstances we obtain the apparent paradox that a greater liberalization of prison policy, reducing the prisoners' hostility, results in increased disorder. This comes about because the informal controls on the expression of hostility in the form of disorder are weakened even faster than hostility is reduced. The prison administrator who acted in ignorance of this relationship would meet with "unanticipated consequences." If disorder is to be minimized in this system, arbitrary policies must be maintained. On the other hand, he cannot achieve prisoner participation in rehabilitation programs without reducing administrative arbitrariness and incurring the cost of increased disorder. This dilemma will exist unless by some *change in the structure of the system* he can create an alternative source of control over disorder, not dependent on the inmate elite.

THE WELFARE FUNCTION OF THE ADMINISTRATOR

If the administrator is restricted to choosing among these situations, his choice will depend on his goals, on his weighing of different outputs. If we assume that his only goal is to minimize disorder, he will prefer Situation 1 above. This corresponds to the actual goal of the authoritarian prison administration, as reported by McCleery. If his only goal is participation in rehabilitation programs, he will prefer Situation 3. If he weighs the two goals equally, he will find all three situations equally satisfactory (or unsatisfactory).

A formal way of describing the various possible administrative preferences would be in the form of a utility function:

$$\text{Goal-attainment } (G) = pR - qD \qquad (5)$$

With various possible functions p and q, the relative preferability of situations would be as shown in Table 4.

Table 4. ALTERNATIVE MEASURES OF GOAL ATTAINMENT OF THE PRISON

	Outputs		*Various Goal-Attainment Indices*			
			a. For system where P = A			
	D	R	$G_1 = R$	$G_2 = (-D)$	$G_3 = \frac{R - D}{2}$	$G_4 = \frac{R - D^2}{20}$
Situation 1	20	0	0	−20	−10	−20
Situation 2	20	10	10	−20	− 5	−10
Situation 3	20	20	20	−20	0	0
			b. For system where P = 2A			
Situation 1	0	0	0	0	0	0
Situation 2	10	10	10	−10	0	5
Situation 3	20	20	20	−20	0	0

The goal definition G_1 assumes that rehabilitation is the only goal; G_2 assumes that order is the only goal; G_3 weighs the two outputs equally. G_4 departs from the linear form; it assumes that small amounts of disorder are quite tolerable but that the undesirability of increased disorder rises very rapidly relative to the desirability of increased rehabilitation. Thus, for the system in which reduction of prisoner hostility "costs" a good deal in loss of control over prisoner behavior, this goal definition results in the best situation being a compromise.

The model so far has shown the consequences, under specified conditions, of varying administrative policies with respect to arbitrariness. If the output of the system is then related back to its input (the administration's arbitrariness), we have a closed system. By making an assumption about how the administration behaves in response to various patterns of prisoner behavior, we are able to predict which alternative situation the administration will produce. This prediction can be represented formally by saying that the administration will vary its arbitrariness to maximize its goal achievement. We assume here that the other two inputs, the general frustrations of imprisonment and the attractiveness of the rehabilitation activities, are constant; in reality, of course, they might also be variables which the administration could manipulate to achieve its goals (Chart 4).

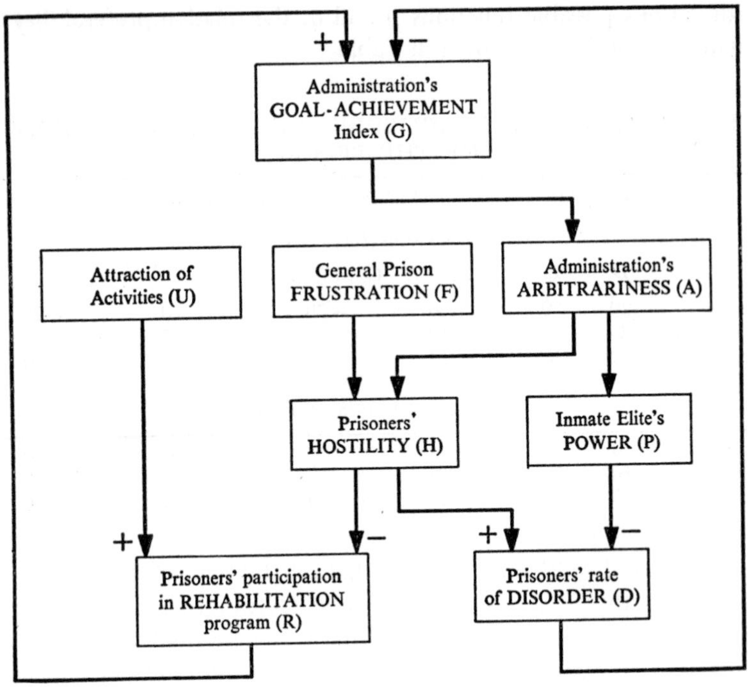

Chart 4. The prison as a system in equilibrium

PARTICIPANTS' PERCEPTIONS OF THE SYSTEM

There is an important assumption underlying the notion that the administrator's behavior responds in determinate ways to the output of the system. This is that he knows what the output is, and how it is related to his own acts. As was suggested above, he might be ignorant of at least some of the relationships in the system. Administrators may therefore have different policies not only because of commitment to different goals but because of different perceptions of the system. One might represent these "perceived systems" by the kind of chart used here. The processes by which perceived systems respond to reality cannot be discussed here.

This simple model has left out the behavior of the custodial staff and of the treatment staff. If such subgroups are to be covered, we should have to consider their *goal commitments,* their *perceptions* of the system, their *power* to influence different variables in the system, and the administrator's power to influence them. The behavior of the administration, the guards, and the treatment staff under the authoritarian regime is accounted for by McCleery partly in terms of their limited perception of what was possible in the prison system. Changes in their behavior were related in part to changes in perceptions and in part to the power of higher authorities.

A Dynamic Model

What actually happened in the prison was not only that a given policy change led to unanticipated results but that it led to one result in the short run and a different one in the long run. The short-run result of the liberal reforms was a great increase in disorder, but after a period of crisis the rates fell again to tolerable levels.

McCleery gives a complex explanation of this period of disorder; basically it arose because certain changes lagged behind others. The old mechanisms of informal control broke down; the new programs did not immediately create new primary group controls favorable to a more liberal prison. The result was a period during which prisoner aggressiveness broke out in a rash of disorders, against which the official controls of discipline and force were not effective. Only gradually did a new informal control through prisoner group consensus arise to hold disorder in check.

To illustrate what is involved in such a situation where lags in some variables cause short-run effects quite different from long-run effects, we will pick out certain variables involved in the process of transition and construct simple dynamic model, using a form of period analysis. We assume, as in our static model, that disorder is increased by hostility toward the prison administration but reduced by the power exercised by the prisoner elite; that participation in rehabilitation activities is decreased by hostility; and that the degree of control of the inmate elite over disorderly behavior is dependent on the degree of arbitrariness of the prison administration in dealing with the prisoners generally.

Now, to the previous formula for hostility we add a new factor: that it is produced not only by the present state of administrative arbitrariness and the prison-frustration constant, but also by a carry-over of past hostility:

$$H_t = wA_t + F + xH_{t-1} \tag{2a}$$

This corresponds to an assumption that it takes time for aggressiveness to be worked off even after the causes of aggressiveness are reduced.

A numerical example can be produced in which a system starts from equilibrium with a certain level of disorder, responds to the reduction of administrative arbitrariness with increased disorder, but eventually returns to the same level of disorder at which it had started—with less hostility and less power in the hands of the inmate elite. We will assume that $u = 1$, $v = 1$, $w = 1$, $z = 1$, $y = 2$, $F = 10$, $u = 40$, $x = \frac{1}{2}$.

Table 5. SHORT- AND LONG-RUN EFFECTS OF CHANGE IN ADMINISTRATIVE ARBITRARINESS

	Inputs			*Intervening Variables*		*Outputs*	
	Administration ARBITRARINESS	Prison FRUSTRATION Constant (F)	Activities Attraction Constant (U)	Prisoners' HOSTILITY (H)	Inmate Elite's POWER (P)	Prisoners' Rate of DISORDER (D)	Prisoners' REHABILITATION Activity (R)
t_0: Authoritarian regime	10	10	40	40	20	20	0
t_1: Authoritarian regime	10	10	40	40	20	20	0
t_2: Reform initiated	0	10	40	30	0	30	10
t_3: Reform continued	0	10	40	25	0	25	15
t_4: Reform continued	0	10	40	22.5	0	22.5	17.5
t_5: Reform continued	0	10	40	21.25	0	21.25	18.75
t_n: New equilibrium	0	10	40	20	0	20	20

Assumptions: $H_t = A_t + F + \frac{1}{2}H_{t-1}$ $\quad D_t = H_t - P_t$
$P_t = 2A_t$ $\quad R_t = U - H_t$

In the example (Table 5) t_0 and t_1 are the last two periods of the authoritarian administration. The reform introduced at t_2 produces an immediate increase in the amount of disorder, which gradually falls off again to reach its former level. (We could also produce a brief lag in the increase in disorder, corresponding more closely to the actual observations in the prison, by making the power exercised by the inmate elite depend in part on past power.)

If the coefficient in the power equation were higher—for example, if $P = 3A$—the authoritarian equilibrium would involve even less disorder, reform would generate a sudden rise, and disorder would level off again somewhat higher than the original rate. If the coefficient were less than 2, the initial rate of disorder would be higher, there would be a small increase, and then it would fall to a lower level than before. In all these cases the decline in hostility follows the same curve; the difference is in how sharply the power variable drops.

If the change suggested above were reversed by a more authoritarian administration taking over, there would be a short-run fall in the rate of disorder. This "success" of old-line methods would, however, be followed by a rise to the same rate as before and accompanied by a decline in participation in rehabilitation activities. If authoritarianism were continually stepped up in an effort to keep disorder below this equilibrium point, the level of hostility might get beyond the bounds within which the control mechanism can suppress its expression, and the system would break down in massive disorders.

CONCLUSION

In this paper we have attempted (a) to formalize a qualitative analysis of organizational processes, and (b) to illustrate what is meant by a *system* of relationships within an organization, in order to suggest ways in which quantitative data on organizational systems might be analyzed.

The cost of quantitatively studying a large number of "cases" is great when each case is an organization composed of many individuals and subgroups. The economy of research suggests that a few key quantitative studies should be guided and supplemented by many less expensive qualitative case analyses similar to the one discussed here. The improvement of qualitative data gathering and analysis is therefore an important methodological problem for social research. A formal analysis of what skilled practitioners actually do is one of the means by which this improvement will come about.[13] By making qualitative researchers more conscious of their operations, and more aware of the common logic which underlies both kinds of analysis, qualitative research may become more systematic and more relevant to ongoing quantitative studies. The formal devices illustrated here include the "anatomizing" of the system into subgroups characterized by a set of variables; the use of systematic tables for recording variables qualitatively observed over several time periods; the formulation of "system schemes" to portray relationships among sets of variables

[13] Allen H. Barton and Paul F. Lazarsfeld, "Some Functions of Qualitative Analysis in Social Research," *Sociologica,* Vol. 1 of "Frankfurter Beiträge zur Soziologie" (Frankfurt: Europaeische Verlagsanstalt, 1955), 321–361. Also Howard S. Becker, "Problems of Inference and Proof in Participant Observation," *American Sociological Review,* 23 (December 1958), 652–660.

which are suggested by the observed changes; and the use of simple arithmetical models to explore possible consequences of change in given variables for the system.

Quantitative data on organizational systems can come from several types of studies. By *comparative studies* or *surveys of large numbers of organizational units,* in which data are gathered on all relevant status groups within the units studied rather than on just a single stratum, it should be possible to examine organizational systems in various states of equilibrium or change. By *panel or trend studies* within single organizations which obtain data from the several interacting status groups over time, the sequences of change in the system can be brought to light. Panel or trend studies conducted during periods of organizational change are especially useful for this purpose, because they permit us to observe "natural experiments." It is possible in some cases to conduct *controlled experiments* on simulated or actual organizations, which greatly facilitate the making of causal inferences.[14]

Social researchers have not generally faced the problem of analyzing quantitative data on complex systems over time. It is clear that simple methods of two-variable and three-variable analysis are not sufficient, and that some form of "models" must be used. It is not easy to say how closely such empirical data could be related to the construction of precise mathematical models.[15] The kinds of measurement used in quantitative social research are still very crude; ranking people or organizations, or locating them in a few ranked classes, is more characteristic than applying scales with equal intervals and a meaningful zero point.[16] The question of what kind of mathematics might be relevant for models of social systems and at the same time appropriate to the nature of social science measurements is a large one. The use of "simulation models" in which computers reproduce complex social processes is one promising line of development.[17]

[14] Nancy Morse and E. Reimer, "The Experimental Change of a Major Organizational Variable," *Journal of Abnormal and Social Psychology,* 52 (1955), 120–129.

[15] Herbert A. Simon, *Models of Man* (New York: Wiley, 1957), Chaps. 6 and 10.

[16] S. S. Stevens, "Mathematics Measurement, and Psychophysics," in S. S. Stevens (ed.), Handbook of Experimental Psychology (New York: Wiley, 1951). See also Bert F. Green, "Attitude Measurement," in Gardner Lindzey (ed.), *Handbook of Social Psychology* (Cambridge, Mass.: Addison-Wesley, 1954), Chap. 9.

[17] William N. McPhee, "The Uses of a Computer Model of Voting," *Public Opinion Quarterly,* 23 (Fall 1959), 440–441.

7. Methods for the Study of Organization

»»

Many areas of organizational analysis compete for the titles: relatively neglected, quite neglected, and most neglected. The study of methods, on the other hand, seems to be a field in which much work is conducted and progress is constantly reported. The issues are basically these: to learn to apply to the study of organizations methods which served fruitfully in the exploration of other fields; to adapt techniques which were developed specifically for the study of other subjects as, for instance, small groups to the study of organizations; and to establish research methods which will answer the special needs of the field, which are generated by the "emergent properties" of this type of social unit.

The major difficulty rests in the fact that till now social sciences have applied mainly qualitative research techniques, such as the case-study method, to the study of larger social units, and mainly quantitative techniques, such as surveys, to the study of individuals. The problem is to bridge this gap by applying *quantitative techniques to the study of organizations.* To do so requires the development of methods of data collection which will make possible the gathering of quantitative materials on organizational variables, and methods of data processing which will allow us to draw conclusions concerning the state of organizational variables from information collected from or about individual respondents. Until this is accomplished, quantitative studies will continue to be predominantly studies of individuals in organizations rather than studies of organizations.

Lazarsfeld and Menzel make a major step in this direction by analyzing the logical and methodological differences between the properties of individuals and social units. Coleman follows with a review of applications of this kind of logic to various research and sample designs, as well as analytical methods in actual research. One of the major innovations, reported both by Coleman and by Weiss and Jacobson, is the application of the sociometric approach to the study of large social units. Stinchcombe, in his presentation, and also Barton and Anderson give us two samples of an application of another recent methodological trend in organizational analysis: formal analysis applying mathematical models.

Lazarsfeld and Menzel are concerned with the methodological characteristics of various statements on "collectives" and "members." These distinctions can be applied to any unit and its participants, or to any unit and its subunits. For the purpose of organizational analysis, the major interpretation would be seeing the organization as a "collective," and its participants or groups of participants as "members."

Analytical properties of collectives are induced from information collected from or on members themselves; "structural" properties are based on information concerning their relations; and "global" properties are based on information, not on properties of members, but on collectives as such. Members' properties are "absolute" (concerning the individual, alone); *Relational* (his relations to others) or *Comparative* (depending on the member's place in a distribution of the members); or *Contextual* (following from a property of the collective). These and other conceptual distinctions which are introduced, differentiate and determine the nature of the various types of propositions dealt with in organizational analysis. The discussion therefore supplies a methodological paradigm for organizational analysis which may serve as a check list for the types of variables to be covered, and for classification of propositions which are made. It gives a clear meaning to the concepts, such as emergent properties, group climate, organizational character, which are often used in a vague way. It indicates the kind of measurements which will be used to determine the values of the various organizational variables.

Coleman reviews the methodological innovations in statistical analysis required by the study of organizations and the study of relationships therein. New *sampling* methods have been developed which make it possible to sample individuals as parts of a context, and to take into account their relations to, and place in, the organizational structure. Coleman concludes by discussing new *analytical* methods which have been devised to establish the effect of the context, the patterns of interaction, and the heterogeneity of the unit on the single actors, or for characterization of the unit as such.

Frequently, students of organizations try to explain behavior of individuals by means of their membership in a certain organization or organizational unit. This procedure assumes that the member is somehow affected by the unit. The channels through which the properties of the unit affect the properties of individuals are many (although they are rarely specified). A member may *perceive* the unit realistically and thus be affected. He may be *recruited* in ways which will ensure that his properties are in line with those of the unit, or he may be *socialized* in such a manner after recruitment. Often it is implicitly assumed that he is *influenced by other members* of the unit. This belief implies that the member interacts with other members and that he is emotionally attached to them, and/or respects their opinions. Until recently, in organizational studies, this was more often assumed than demonstrated. One of the major reasons for this tendency as that standard methods for determining patterns of interaction and inter-individual attachments were developed for the study of small groups and could not be applied to large-scale organizations. Sociograms are a typical example. Recently methods have been developed to overcome this limitation.

Weiss and Jacobson report on the application of sociometry to the study of complex organizations. The major problem was to handle a large number of relationships. This was done by applying a matrix analysis following earlier works by Festinger, Forsyth, and Katz. The method made it possible to distinguish between respondents which were members of primary groups and those which were not; to place primary groups as well as individual respondents in the organizational structure; to determine liaison relations among groups; and to relate these findings to other variables.

Stinchcombe gives us a brief illustration of another recent methodological trend: the revival of formalization in sociological analysis, stressing the use of mathematical models. Like Weiss and Jacobson, he makes Festinger's matrix his starting point. But rather than analyze networks of friendship, he uses the matrix to describe and analyze the network of formal relations, especially advice and command. The major object is to put the traditional organizational chart into formalized terms, so that positions in an organization can be precisely described and related as well as used as variables in further analysis. Barton and Anderson, whose contribution is included in Part 6, on organizational change, supply another illustration of this "formal" approach.

Paul F. Lazarsfeld
and
Herbert Menzel

On the Relation between Individual and Collective Properties

INTRODUCTORY CONSIDERATIONS

1. Purpose

Social scientists often make use of variables to describe not only individual persons but also groups, communities, organizations, or other "collectives."[1] Thus one reads, for example, of "racially mixed census tracts," of "highly bureaucratized voluntary organizations," or of a "centrally located rooming-house district." At other times the variables, although describing individuals, are based on data about certain collectives, as in a comparison of "graduates of top-ranking medical schools" with "graduates of other medical schools." This paper attempts to clarify some of the operations involved in the con-

This article, published here for the first time, is one of a series sponsored by the Documentation Project for Advanced Training in Social Research, Columbia University. It may be cited as Publication A-322 of the Bureau of Applied Social Research, Columbia University.

[1] Individuals and collectives made up of individuals do not, of course, exhaust the matters which social scientists describe. Social-science propositions may, instead, have various other units for their subjects. Not infrequently the subjects are acts, behavior patterns, customs, norms, "items of culture," and the like, as in the assertion that "items of culture that are . . . not much woven into a pattern . . . are least likely to encounter resistance to their diffusion."—Ralph Linton, *The Study of Man* (New York: Appleton, 1936), pp. 341–342. "Beliefs and practices" have been sorted into four classes according to the pattern of their differential distribution among mobile and nonmobile holders of high and low positions in a stratification system."—Peter M. Blau, "Social Mobility and Interpersonal Relations," *American Sociological Review*, 21 (1956), 290–295.

struction and use of such variables in empirical research, and provides a nomenclature for the different ways in which information about individuals and about collectives may be interwoven in these properties. The properties will be classified according to the measurement operations involved in their construction.

2. Some Features of Generalizing Propositions

The intended meaning of the variables often remains ambiguous if they are not examined in the context of the propositions in which they are used. It is therefore necessary at the outset to highlight certain features which are common to all generalizing propositions, whether or not they involve collectives. (As an illustration, reference is made to the proposition "Children of rich parents go to college in greater proportion than do children of poor parents.")

a. Generalizing propositions assert something about a set of *elements* (children).
b. For the research purposes at hand, these elements are considered *comparable*. In other words, the same set of *properties* (wealth of parents; going to college) is used to describe each element.
c. Each element has a certain *value* on each property. The values (rich parents, poor parents; going to college, not going to college) may be quantitative or qualitative.
d. The propositions assert interrelationships between the properties of the elements.

3. Present Concern

The propositions with which the present discussion is concerned have the additional characteristic that their elements are dealt with either as collectives or as members of collectives. An example of the first kind is "There is a negative correlation between the rate of juvenile delinquency of American cities and the proportion of their budget given over to education." An example of the second kind is "Those recognized as leaders do not deviate very far from the norms of their group."

4. Special Meaning of "Collective" and "Member"

The terms "collective" and "member" are used here in a specific sense which needs clarification. A collective may be an element of a proposition; that is, it is one of a set of units which are regarded as *comparable* in the sense specified above: the same set of properties is used to describe all the elements. These elements are *collectives* if each is considered to be composed of constituent parts, called *members,* which are regarded as comparable in their turn. "Comparable" is used in the same sense as before: all members are described by a single set of properties. (This is usually not the same set as that used to describe the collectives.)

In other instances members are the elements of the propositions. Elements will be called "members" if they are considered to be constituent parts of larger units, called "collectives," which are regarded as comparable in the same sense as before.

Thus one set of properties is always used to describe or classify all the members, and another single set of properties is used to characterize all the collectives. It is clear that under these definitions one can speak of "collectives" only when their "members" are also being referred to, and of "members" only when their "collectives" are also involved. Furthermore, there must be a multiplicity of members if the term "collective" is to be meaningful. It is perhaps less obvious but will be seen later that there must also be a multiplicity of collectives—i.e., the members of more than one collective must be referred to—if the distinctions between properties to be described below are to be relevant.

By contrast, the notion of "element" is needed to characterize any generalizing proposition whatsoever. It is applicable even in situations where the notions of "member" and "collective" are not involved at all.

5. Distinction between "Individuals" and "Members"

In the examples that come to mind most easily, the members of collectives are individual persons. Thus, for example, cities are the collectives and people are the members in the following two propositions:

(1) "The oldest settlers of cities are most likely to hold political office," or (2) "The more industry there is in a city, the higher the proportion of Democratic voters." The first proposition has members and the second has collectives as elements. In the same sense, a precinct can be treated as a collective, with the inhabitants as members. However, the members of a collective are not necessarily individual persons. A city, for example, can be described as a collective with the voting precincts as members. It follows that what appears as a collective in one context (e.g., precincts), can appear as a member

in another. In any analysis of a piece of writing in which some of the elements are collectives, it is always necessary to specify clearly of what members the collectives are composed (for the purposes at hand).[2]

The following graph will help to keep this terminology in mind:

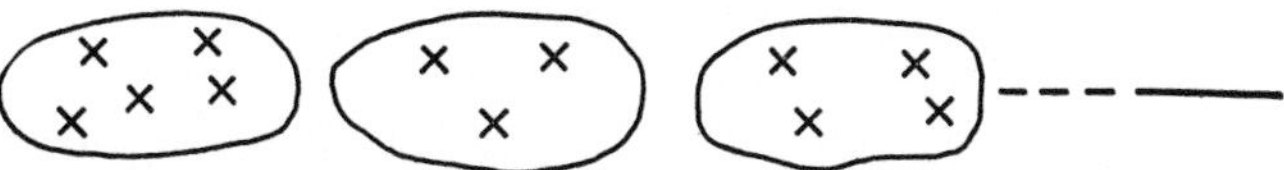

The circles symbolize the collectives, the crosses within it their members. The dots indicate that we are dealing with collectives as elements of a proposition. This is the situation with which we deal in the first part of this paper. In Sections 10 and 11 we discuss research where members are the focus of attention. They are then the elements of propositions, but their membership in one of a series of collectives is one of their characteristics.

6. Possibility of "Three-Level" Propositions

In some studies, more than two levels appear: for example, inhabitants, precincts, and cities may all be elements of the same study. This whole matter could, therefore, be elaborated by pointing out the various relationships which can exist between inhabitants, precincts, and cities. The next few pages are restricted to collectives which have only one kind of member; the members in most illustrations will be individual persons, but we will also present some examples in which the members themselves are larger units. Only much later (in Section 16) will examples of "three-level" propositions be taken up, in which units, e.g., "union shops," are simultaneously considered to be both members of their locals *and* collectives of individual workers.

7. Propositions about Collectives as Substitutes and in Their Own Right

Propositions about collectives are sometimes made as substitutes for propositions about individual persons, simply because the neces-

[2] It is, of course, also possible to make propositions about cities without reference to any members at all, just as it is possible to make propositions about individuals without reference to any collectives. Thus one may, e.g., correlate city size with number of churches, or location with building materials used, just as one can correlate individual income and education. In neither case are the distinctions made in the present paper relevant, because the individuals are not treated as "members" and the cities are not treated as "collectives" as here defined (i.e., as composed of "members"—constituent units described by their values on some one set of properties). It is thus clear that the typology of properties here presented is not always pertinent.

sary data about individual persons are not available. For example, a high Republican vote in "silk-stocking" districts is sometimes accepted to show that wealthy people are likely to vote Republican, when no records about individual votes and individual incomes are available.[3] For this reason it is often not realized that a large number of sociologically meaningful empirical propositions can be made of which only collectives are intended to be the elements. Thus, for example, an anthropologist may show that the political independence of communities is correlated with their pattern of settlement. A student of social disorganization may ask whether city zones with a high incidence of juvenile delinquency also show a high incidence of commitments for senile dementia. A small-group experimenter may hypothesize that "the probability of effective utilization of the insights that occur is greater in certain communication patterns than in others."[4] Much discursive writing also consists, in a hidden way, of such propositions.

A TYPOLOGY OF PROPERTIES DESCRIBING "COLLECTIVES" AND "MEMBERS"

8. Properties of Collectives

It is often useful to distinguish three types of properties which describe collectives: analytical properties based on data about each member; structural properties based on data about the relations among members; and global properties, not based on information about the properties of individual members.[5] The following examples may clarify these distinctions:

[3] This procedure can lead to very misleading statistics, as pointed out by W. S. Robinson in "Ecological Correlations and the Behavior of Individuals," *American Sociological Review*, 15 (1950), 351–357. Sounder methods for inferring individual correlations from ecological data are proposed by Leo A. Goodman, "Ecological Regressions and Behavior of Individuals," *American Sociological Review*, 18 (1953), 663–664, and by Otis Dudley Duncan and Beverly Davis, "An Alternate to Ecological Correlation," *ibid.*, pp. 665–666.

[4] For details on these and additional examples, see Paul F. Lazarsfeld and Morris Rosenberg (eds.), *The Language of Social Research* (Glencoe, Ill.: Free Press, 1955), pp. 302–322. Compare also Herbert Menzel, "Comment," *American Sociological Review*, 15 (1950), 674.

[5] This classification of properties of collectives corresponds closely to the classifications presented earlier by Cattell and by Kendall and Lazarsfeld and reprinted in Lazarsfeld and Rosenberg (eds.), *op. cit.*, pp. 291–301. Analytical properties are Cattell's population variables and Kendall and Lazarsfeld's Types I, II, and III. Structural properties are Cattell's structural variables and Kendall and Lazars-

a. *Analytical.* These are properties of collectives which are obtained by performing some mathematical operation upon some property of each single member.[6]

> The average rental paid in a precinct and the proportion of its inhabitants who have "Old Immigrant" (English, German, Scottish, Scandinavian) names are analytical properties of a collective (precinct) composed of individuals.[7] The proportion of the communities of a given state that have their own high school is an analytical property of a collective (state) the members of which are communities. The diffusion of a message in a city, defined as the per cent of the target population knowing the message, is an analytical property of the city.[8]
>
> The standard deviation of incomes in a nation appears as an analytical property in the following example. The effect of postwar legislation in Great Britain was to make the income distribution much narrower. Economists have predicted that under these conditions people will save more, because they will spend less money on display consumption which might help them be socially acceptable in the higher strata.
>
> Correlations are sometimes used to characterize collectives and then also constitute analytical properties. The correlation of age and prestige in a given community, for example, has been used as a measure of its norms regarding old age. Sometimes more indirect inferences are involved. MacRae shows that in urban areas voting is highly correlated with occupation, while this is not the case in rural districts. He concludes from this vote that in rural districts there is a stronger spirit of community and cohesion.[9]

---

feld's Type IV. Our global properties are Cattell's syntality variables and Kendall and Lazarsfeld's Type V. See also n. 25.

[6] It should be understood that the distinctions here proposed do not depend on who performs the operations involved. For example, "average income of a city" would be classified as an analytical property regardless of whether the investigator (a) obtains individual income data from all inhabitants directly and then computes the average, (b) obtains individual income data from the files of the tax collector and then computes the average, or (c) looks up the average income in the published census reports. Compare also n. 17.

[7] Phillips Cutright and Peter H. Rossi, "Grass Roots Politicians and the Vote," *American Sociological Review,* 23 (1958), 171–179.

[8] Melvin L. DeFleur and Otto N. Larsen, *The Flow of Information* (New York: Harper, 1958).

[9] Duncan MacRae, Jr., "Occupations and the Congressional Vote, 1940–1950," *American Sociological Review,* 20 (1955), 332–340. For another example, see the

b. *Structural.* These are properties of collectives which are obtained by performing some operation on data about the relations of each member to some or all of the others.

> Assume, for example, that a sociometrist has recorded the "best-liked classmate" of each student in a number of classes. He can then describe the classes by the degree to which all choices are concentrated upon a few "stars." Or he might, alternately, classify them according to their cliquishness, the latter being defined as the number of subgroups into which a class can be divided so that no choices cut across subgroup lines. In these examples the collective is the school class, and the members are the individual students; "concentration of choices" and "cliquishness" are structural properties of the classes.

> For an example in which the members are larger units, consider a map of the precincts of a city, which indicates the number of Negroes residing in each. Let a "Negro enclave" be defined as a precinct in which some Negroes live, but which is completely surrounded by precincts without Negroes. The proportion of the precincts of a city which are Negro enclaves would then be a structural property of the city.

c. *Global.* Often collectives are characterized by properties which are not based on information about the properties of individual members.

> American Indian tribes have been characterized by the frequency with which themes of "achievement motive" make their appearance in their folk tales.[10] Societies have been classified as to the presence of money as a medium of exchange, of a written language, etc.[11] Nations may be characterized by the ratio of the national budget allotted to edu-

---

evidence used to demonstrate differences in the norms of two housing projects in Leon Festinger, Stanley Schachter, and Kurt Back, "The Operation of Group Standards," in Lazarsfeld and Rosenberg, *op. cit.*, pp. 373–377.

[10] See David C. McClelland and G. A. Friedman, "A Cross-cultural Study of the Relationship between Child Training Practices and Achievement Motivation Appearing in Folk Tales," in Guy E. Swanson, Theodore M. Newcomb, and Eugene L. Hartley (eds.), *Readings in Social Psychology* (New York: Holt, Rinehart and Winston, 1952), pp. 243–249.

[11] See, e.g., Linton C. Freeman and Robert F. Winch, "Societal Complexity: An Empirical Test of a Typology of Societies," *American Journal of Sociology*, 62 (1957), 461–466.

cation and to armaments. Army companies may be characterized by the cleanliness of their mess equipment.

Voting precincts have been classified according to the activities and attitudes of their Republican and Democratic captains, including hours spent on party duties, number of persons known to the captain personally, and his expressed commitment to the party.[12] In experiments in message diffusion by leaflets dropped from airplanes, cities have been treated to different degrees of "stimulus intensity," defined as the per capita ratio of leaflets dropped.[13] All these are global properties.

The density of settlement is a global property of a district. Having a city manager form of government is a global property of a city. The insistence on specified initiation rites as a prerequisite to membership is a global property of a religious cult or of a college fraternity. Accessibility from the nearest big city is a global property of a village. A scale score assigned to each state according to the combination of duties assigned to the state board of education (rather than left to local authorities) is a global property of each state.[14]

"Emergent," "integral," "syntalic" and other terms have been used in meanings very similar to that of our term "global." It is not at all certain which term is most useful.[15]

Notice that all three of the above types of properties—analytical, structural, and global—describe collectives.

[12] Cutright and Rossi, *loc. cit.*

[13] DeFleur and Larsen, *op. cit.*

[14] Robert Redfield, *The Folk Culture of Yucatan* (Chicago: U. of Chicago Press, 1941); and Margaret J. Hagood, and Daniel O. Price, *Statistics for Sociologists* (rev. ed., New York: Henry Holt and Company, 1952), pp. 144–152.

[15] Although global properties of collectives are not based on information about members, the above examples are, of course, listed here on the assumption that assertions about the members are made somewhere in the same proposition or at least in the same body of work; otherwise the distinction between "global" and "absolute" properties would become pointless (cf. n. 2). It may also bear repeating here that any discussion of a "collective" requires clear specification of what its members are considered to be. The proportion of the buildings of a city which are devoted to cultural activities was given as an example of a "global property" of a city on the assumption that the city is treated as a collective of inhabitants; i.e., that statements involving the inhabitants are made in some connection with this measure of "cultural level." It is, of course, also possible to treat a city as a collective of buildings; then the proportion of buildings devoted to cultural activities would become an analytical property. Which of these two types of property it is can be judged only from the context. (See also Section 13.)

9. A Subsidiary Distinction among Analytical Properties of Collectives

An interesting distinction may be made among the analytical properties. The first two examples given above were the average income of a city, and the proportion of the communities of a given state that have their own high school. These properties of collectives have what one might call a similarity of meaning to the properties of members on which they are based. The wealth of a city seems to be the same sort of thing as the wealth of an inhabitant. The endowment of a community with a high school and the rate of high-school endowed communities in a state have a parallel meaning. This is not true for the remaining examples of analytical properties given above—the standard deviation of incomes in a nation, or correlations like that between age and prestige in a given community. Correlations and standard deviations can apply only to collectives and have no parallel on the level of members. The standard deviation of incomes in a city, for example, denotes something quite different—lack of homogeneity, perhaps—from individual income, the datum from which it is computed.

Another variable of this sort is "degree of consensus." When a Democrat and a Republican are competing for the mayoralty, the degree of political consensus in a particular club might be measured by the extent of the club's deviation from a fifty-fifty split. In this instance the analytic property is measured by a proportion, but it is not the simple proportion of adherents of either party; clubs which are 80 per cent Democratic and those which are 20 per cent Democratic are regarded as equal in consensus.

Whereas correlations, standard deviations, and similar measures always have a meaning peculiar to the group level, averages and proportions may or may not have a parallel meaning on the individual and collective levels.[16] Lack of parallel meaning is perhaps most clearly illustrated in the concept of a "hung jury," that is, a jury rendered indecisive by its inability to reach the required unanimity. Such a state of affairs is most likely when the individual jurors are most decisive and unyielding in their convictions.

[16] Compare the notion of "counterpart" in Edgar F. Borgatta, Leonard Cottrell, Jr., and Henry J. Meyer, "On the Dimensions of Group Behavior," *Sociometry*, 19 (1956), 233.

10. Properties of Members

Another set of distinctions can be made between properties describing members in contexts where collectives have also been defined.

a. *Absolute* properties are characteristics of members which are obtained without making any use either of information about the characteristics of the collective, or of information about the relationships of the member being described to other members. They thus include most of the characteristics commonly used to describe individuals.

   In the proposition, "Graduates of large law schools are more likely to earn high incomes at age 40 than graduates of small law schools," income is an absolute property of the members (the individual students).

b. *Relational* properties of members are computed [17] from information about the substantive relationships between the member described and other members.

   Sociometric popularity-isolation (number of choices received) is a relational property. Many other sociometric indices fall into this category. For example, if each member of a small group has rated each other member on a 5-point scale of acceptance-rejection, each member can be characterized by the total score he received (popularity), by the total score he expressed (active sociability), by the average deviation of the scores he accorded the others (discrimination in his acceptance of other members), etc.[18] In a study of the diffusion of the use of a new drug through a community of doctors, the physicians were classified according to whether

[17] It may be worth repeating here that the distinctions proposed are independent of who performs the operations involved. Thus, e.g., "sociometric popularity" would be classified as a relational property when measured in any of the following three ways: (a) the investigator counts the number of choices accorded to a member by his colleagues in answer to a sociometric questionnaire; (b) the investigator observes the frequency of interactions between the member and his colleagues; (c) the member is asked, "How many visits did you receive from colleagues during the last week?" These distinctions are, of course, important in themselves but not relevant to the present typology (cf. n. 6).

[18] Some sociometric indices are listed in Hans Zeisel, *Say It with Figures* (4th ed.; New York: Harper, 1957), pp. 110–114, 148–153. The list includes indices not only of relational properties but of comparative and structural properties as well.

or not they had a friend who had already used the new drug on a certain date.[19]

Some investigators have clarified the structure of relational properties by the use of matrices.[20] This new device can be fruitfully applied to some older papers.[21]

The distinction between relational properties of individuals and structural properties of collectives deserves emphasis. The former characterize members of collectives in their relations to one another. The latter characterize collectives and are aggregates over the relational properties of their members.

c. *Comparative* properties characterize a member by a comparison between his value on some (absolute or relational) property and the distribution of this property over the entire collective of which he is a member.

Sibling order is a comparative property of individuals in the proposition, "First-born children are more often maladjusted than intermediate and last born children." Note that each individual is characterized by comparison with the age of the other individuals in his family; in the resulting classification, many of the "last-born" will be older in years than many of the "first-born." Being a "deviate" from the majority opinion in one's housing project unit is a comparative property.[22]

Another example is contained in the following proposition: "Students who had the highest I.Q. in their respective high school classes have greater difficulty in adjusting in college than students who are not quite at the top in high school, even when their actual I.Q. score is equally high." Here the comparative property (being at the top in high school or not) is established in terms of the I.Q. distribution in each student's respective high school; the proposition pertains to a set of college students which includes boys from several high schools (collectives).

[19] Herbert Menzel and Elihu Katz, "Social Relations and Innovation in the Medical Profession: The Epidemiology of a New Drug," *Public Opinion Quarterly*, 19 (1956), 337–352.

[20] See Zeisel, *loc. cit.*, and Leon Festinger, Stanley Schachter, and Kurt Back, "Matrix Analysis of Group Structures," in Lazarsfeld and Rosenberg, *op. cit.*, pp. 358–367. In both instances matrices are also used to develop indices for structural properties of groups.

[21] See, e.g., Robert R. Sears, "Experimental Studies of Projection," *Journal of Social Psychology*, 7 (1936), 151–163.

[22] Festinger, Schachter, and Back, *loc. cit.*, pp. 367–382.

d. *Contextual* properties describe a member by a property of his collective.

> Consider an example cited previously: "Graduates of large law schools are more likely to earn high incomes at age 40 than graduates of small law schools." In this proposition, "being a member of a large law school" is a contextual property of individuals.
>
> Contextual properties are also used in the following propositions: "Union members in closed shops are less militant than union members in open shops." "Residents of racially mixed districts show more racial prejudice than those of racially homogeneous districts." "The less the promotion opportunity afforded by a branch (of the army), the more favorable the opinion (of soldiers) tends to be toward promotion opportunity." [23] In these propositions, being a member of a closed shop, residing in a mixed district, or being a soldier in a branch with frequent promotions are all examples of contextual properties.

Contextual properties are really characteristics of collectives applied to their members. Thus the classification of "collective properties" developed above could be repeated here as a subdivision of contextual "individual properties." [24] Note also that a contextual property, unlike a comparative property, has the same value for all members of a given collective.

11. Contextual and Comparative Properties Meaningful Only Where More Than One Collective Is Involved

It is not meaningful to speak of contextual or comparative properties when the elements under study are all members of the same collective—for instance, when only graduates of one law school are being studied—for the following reasons. Any *contextual* property would, in that case, have the same value for all the elements; hence nothing could be said about the interrelationship of this property and any other property. Any *comparative* property would, under these circumstances, classify the elements in exactly the same way as the absolute property from which it was derived, except that the calibration may be grosser. (If only children of one family are considered,

[23] S. A. Stouffer, *et al., The American Soldier* (Princeton, N.J.: Princeton, 1949), I, 256.

[24] It is sometimes helpful to talk of "collective properties" instead of the cumbersome "properties of collectives"; the same holds for "individual properties." It is important, however, not to be misled by this linguistic condensation.

the classification into "first-born," "intermediate," and "last-born" differs from that by age only in the grosser calibration. Similarly, if I.Q. scores of graduates of one law school are replaced by classification into lowest, second, third, and highest I.Q. quartile within their school, nothing will change except that the number of categories is reduced.)

12. Special Case Where the Typology Can Be Applied in Two Alternate Ways

A difficulty comes about when all the members of a set of collectives (or a representative sample of the members of each) constitute the elements of a proposition which includes a contextual property. Suppose, for instance, that the income ten years after graduation is recorded for all who graduate from fifty law schools in a certain year. A possible finding might be, "The income of law school graduates is correlated with the size of the school they graduated from." This is a proposition about students, relating their income (an absolute property) to the size of their law school (a contextual property). The same proposition could be interpreted also as one where the elements are the law schools; the average income of the students would then be an analytical property of each law school; its size would be a global property of these collectives.

13. The Present Classification Is Formal Rather Than Substantive

As stated at the outset, the scheme suggested above is intended for the classification of properties according to the operations involved in their measurement. Although a classification by the underlying concepts or forces that the properties may be intended to represent might have numerous parallels to the present classification, it would not be the same.[25] In the present methodological context, for example,

[25] Cattell's classification of population, structural, and syntality variables (cf. n. 5 above), which is closely paralleled in form by our analytical-structural-global distinction, seems to be based on a mixture of measurement criteria and considerations of causality. The latter gain the upper hand in the critique of Cattell's scheme by Borgatta, Cottrell, and Meyer: e.g., "Aggregate measures, to the extent that they cannot be accounted for as population variables (in direct parallel measures), may be considered syntality variables. . . . Further, changes in population variables attributable to social interaction should be regarded as syntality variables."—Borgatta, Cottrell, and Meyer, *loc. cit.*, p. 234. Peter M. Blau's "Formal Organization: Dimensions of Analysis," *American Journal of Sociology,* 63 (1957), 58–69, contains an analysis in terms of intended underlying concepts

"number of libraries in a community" and "occurrence of aggressiveness themes in folk tales current in a tribe" are classified as global properties because they are not based on information about the properties of individual members. Yet it would be convincing to argue that these properties are relevant to the behavioral sciences only because properties of individuals, of the relations among individuals, or of the resulting social structures are inferred from them. Similarly, the title of office held by a person in a hierarchy would here be classified as an "absolute" property, even when the researcher is actually interested in the incumbent's power over subordinates which the title implies.

At some points arbitrary decisions have to be made. On an intuitive basis we decided to consider the number of members in a collective (e.g., population size) as a global property, although one might argue that it is analytical, obtained by counting the "existence" of each member. Even more ambiguous is the classification of rates, based on the behavior of ex-members—e.g., suicide rates. No definitive practice is proposed for such borderline cases.

COMBINATIONS OF TYPES OF PROPERTIES

The types of properties which have been defined can appear in various forms of combinations.

14. Several Types in the Same Proposition

Very commonly, as many of the above examples have shown, one proposition will make use of properties of several types. An additional illustration of this can be drawn from a study of political processes within the International Typographical Union, which has been operating under an internal two-party system for many decades. The shops of this union were classified according to their degree of "political consensus"; shops in which 67 per cent or more of the mem-

---

which parallels the present discussion of measurement operations in certain respects.

In addition, the literature contains, of course, classifications of group properties which are based on quite different criteria. See, e.g., John K. Hemphill and Charles M. Westie, "The Measurement of Group Dimensions," in Lazarsfeld and Rosenberg, *op. cit.*, pp. 323–324; and Robert K. Merton, "Provisional List of Group Properties," in his *Social Theory and Social Structure* (rev. ed.; Glencoe, Ill.: Free Press, 1957), pp. 310–326. The Hemphill-Westie categories are subjected to a factor analysis and compared with certain other schemes in Borgatta, Cottrell, and Meyer, *loc. cit.*, pp. 223–240.

bers favored the same party were regarded as high in consensus, the remainder as low. Individual members were graded according to the amount of union political activity they engaged in. It was expected that men in shops where political consensus was high would be more active in politics than those in shops where consensus was low. The hypothesis, however, was borne out only in small shops (i.e., those with thirty men or less). The finding could therefore be expressed in the following proposition: "For workers in small shops, there is a correlation between consensus of the shop and degree of political activity of the men; for workers in large shops, there is no such correlation." In this proposition there appear two contextual properties (size and consensus of each man's shop) and an absolute property (political activity).[26]

The following hypothetical example again shows the use of several types of variables in one proposition—in fact, in each of several propositions. Ten preliterate tribes living in a certain country are classified according to the number of wars they have fought during the last hundred years. This characteristic, in the present terminology, is a global property of each tribe. A representative sample of one hundred men from each tribe is given a test of "aggressiveness"—an absolute property, from which a summary score for each tribe is computed, as an analytical property. At this point, the correlation between average aggressiveness and the number of wars can be computed. One may regard this computation as either a correlation between an analytical and a global property of ten collectives, or a correlation between an absolute and a contextual property of one thousand individual persons.

Now a factory is opened in the district, and some men from each of the ten tribes find employment there as laborers. Each is given the test of "aggressiveness"; each is also observed for a period of one month, and the number of fights he starts with other employees is recorded. Then the following two correlations can be computed:

a. The correlation between the score on the aggressiveness test and the number of fights. This is a proposition the elements of which are people and the properties of which are conventional psychological characteristics—absolute properties, in the present terminology.

[26] See S. M. Lipset, Martin Trow, and James Coleman, *Union Democracy: The Inside Politics of the International Typographical Union* (Glencoe, Ill.: Free Press, 1956).

b. The correlation between the number of fights and the number of wars reported for the tribe from which each individual came. This is again a proposition the elements of which are people. But one of the variables (number of wars) now is a contextual property.

The comparison between these two propositions is interesting. In proposition (a) actual fighting is related to the psychological trait of aggressiveness. In proposition (b) actual fighting is related to something that one might call the normative background of each person.

15. Properties of One Type Constructed from Properties of Another Type

The types of properties outlined can also be compounded in that a property of one type may be constructed from properties of another type. Contextual properties, for example, have been defined as properties describing a member by a property of his collective. But what property of his collective is to be used? In most of the examples given, contextual properties of members were based on global properties of their collectives, as in the phrase "men from tribes that have engaged in many wars." But contextual properties can equally well be based on any other kind of property of a collective—for example, on a structural property, as when doctors are classified according to whether or not they ever practiced in cities ridden by medical cliques. One might test whether those who formerly practiced in cliqueless cities have less tendency to form cliques in their new location.

This compounding is also illustrated by examples, cited earlier in another connection: "being a worker in a big shop" and "being a worker in a shop with high consensus." The first of these is a contextual property constructed from a global property; the second is a contextual property constructed from an analytical property.

16. Several Types from the Same Data

In some instances one body of research will construct properties of several different types from the same data, as in the following excerpts from a report on the adoption of modern farming practices by Kentucky farmers.

> 393 farm operators . . . in thirteen neighborhoods were interviewed. . . . Information was obtained on the extent to which each of the operators had tried and was following 21 farm practices recommended by the agricultural agencies. For each respondent, an adop-

> tion score was calculated. This score is the percentage of applicable practices which the operator had adopted. For example, if 18 of the practices applied to the farm operations being carried on and the operator had adopted 9, his score was 50. Neighborhoods varied widely in the mean adoption scores of residents, which range from a low of 25 in one neighborhood to a high of 57 in another. . . . The neighborhoods were combined . . . into three types of neighborhoods: "low adoption areas," "medium adoption areas," and "high adoption areas." . . .
>
> The following operational hypothesis . . . is suggested: In areas of high adoption, those from whom other farmers obtain farming information have higher adoption rates than farmers in general; but, in areas of low adoption, the adoption rates of leaders are similar to adoption rates of farmers in general . . . the hypothesis is supported by data. In the "low adoption areas" the mean score of all farmers was 32 and that of the leaders 37, while in the "high adoption areas" the mean score of all farmers was 48 and that of the leaders 66.[27]

Here the farm operator's "adoption score" is used as an absolute property of information leaders and of farmers in general. It is also used as the datum from which the classification of neighborhoods into "high adoption areas" and "low adoption areas" is computed. This classification is an analytical property of the neighborhoods; when used, as in the proposition quoted, to characterize the farmers resident in the neighborhoods, it becomes a contextual property of the farmers.

17. Simultaneous Characterization of the Same Elements as Collectives and as Members

Complexity of another sort arises when one set of elements appears both as members and as collectives in the same proposition. Up to this point examples of such "three-level propositions" have deliberately been excluded. It is now appropriate to introduce such examples. Consider, for instance, the following assertion: "Women's clubs which are internally divided into cliques have less easy-going relationships with other women's clubs than have clubs which are not so divided." Here the elements (women's clubs) are first categorized according to a structural variable (internal division into cliques), and then an assertion is made about a relational property

[27] C. Paul Marsh and A. Lee Coleman, "Group Influences and Agricultural Innovations: Some Tentative Findings and Hypotheses," *American Journal of Sociology*, 61 (1956), 588–594. Other varying examples of the use of properties describing or referring to collectives will be found in Lazarsfeld and Rosenberg, *op. cit.*, pp. 287–386.

(relationship with other clubs) of the elements in each structural category.

In the study of political processes within the International Typographical Union, which was cited earlier, each printer's vote in a union election was recorded. A liberal and a conservative candidate competed for union office. Each printer's vote was compared with his own conservative-liberal predisposition, determined by an attitude scale. The individuals could thus be classified as voting according to or contrary to their own predisposition. Up to this point, no collective is involved; there is merely a combination of two absolute properties into one. This combined absolute property of each printer was then compared with two contextual properties: the majority vote in his shop, and the majority vote in the local to which his shop belonged. The question was whether the climate of opinion in a man's shop or that in his entire local is more important in affecting his decisions. The answer could be determined only by examining cases where the shop and the local were in conflict. It was found that more people voted contrary to their own predisposition when it was in conflict with the majority of their shop (but not of their local) than when it was in conflict with the majority of their local (but not of their shop). In this instance each person is first characterized as voting according to or contrary to his predisposition. This absolute variable is then correlated with two contextual variables, both describing the same members (persons), but each having reference to a different level of collectives (shops or locals).[28]

18. Outlook

The preceding analysis can be extended in many directions; three of them shall be briefly sketched. For one we can introduce status differences among the members of the collectives. Colleges have professors and administrators, factory teams have workers and foremen, platoons have soldiers and noncoms. This may call for extending the notion of structural properties if, e.g., we distinguish various types of supervision; or analytical properties may be generalized if we classify colleges according to the degree to which the administration and the faculty share the same values. Stouffer has made ingenious use of such status differences by developing what one could call partitioned analytical properties. He wanted to know whether the food provided for army units had an effect on soldiers' morale. If he had asked the

[28] Adapted from Lipset, Trow, and Coleman, *op. cit.*

soldiers to rate the food he would not have known whether their morale did not affect their rating of the food. So he asked the non-commissioned officers to judge the food and correlated their average rating with the average morale score of the soldiers; the elements of the correlation were of course the army units studied.[29]

A second line of analysis opens up if the elements of a proposition are pairs of individuals: people who are friends tend to vote the same way; egalitarian relationships are more enduring than those which are hierarchic. It would be artificial to call such notions "propositions about collectives." Obviously dyads can be characterized in an even more complex way: pairs of doctors who commonly discuss cases with each other as equals are more likely to use the same type of drug than are pairs of doctors who stand in an advisor-advisee relationship to each other.[30] A scrutiny of recent sociometric literature is likely to provide distinctions going beyond those offered in this paper.

Finally, the utility of the present approach deserves argument. Obviously no one wants to make methodological classifications for their own sake. They are, however, useful in reminding us of the variety of research operations that are possible, and in clearing up misunderstandings. It can, for example, be shown that many arguments about atomism versus "holistic" approaches in current sociological literature can be clarified by an explication of the formal types of properties which enter into speculative or empirical propositions. In another publication, the senior author has summarized passages from several recent works of social research which relate, often in quite complex ways, the characteristics and attitudes of individuals, their propensity to choose friends inside and outside of variously overlapping collectives, the composition of these collectives in terms of members' background and perceptions, and the recent occurrence of certain events in the history of the collectives. He attempted to show that such "contextual propositions" go a long way toward satisfying the frequently heard demand that social research should "consider structures" or "take the total situation into account." [31]

[29] Stouffer, *et al., op. cit.*, I, 353–358.

[30] James Coleman, Herbert Menzel, and Elihu Katz, "Social Processes in Physicians' Adoption of a New Drug," *Journal of Chronic Diseases*, 9 (1959), 18.

[31] Paul F. Lazarsfeld, "Problems in Methodology," Robert K. Merton, Leonard Broom, and Leonard S. Cottrell, Jr. (eds.), *Sociology Today* (New York: Basic Books, 1959), pp. 69–73.

James S. Coleman

Relational Analysis: The Study of Social Organizations with Survey Methods

Survey research methods have often led to the neglect of social structure and of the relations among individuals. On the other hand, survey methods are highly efficient in bringing in a large volume of data—amenable to statistical treatment—at a relatively low cost in time and effort. Can the student of social structure enjoy the advantages of the survey without neglecting the relationships which make up that structure? In other words, can he use a method which ordinarily treats each individual as an isolated unit in order to study social structure?

The purpose of this paper is to describe some important developments in survey research which are giving us a new way of studying social organization.

It is useful to trace briefly the history of survey research, to indicate how it has grown from "polling" to the point where it can now study problems involving complex human organization. A look at this history indicates two definite stages. The first was a polling stage which was concerned with the *distribution* of responses on any one item: What proportion favored Roosevelt in 1936? What proportion was in favor of labor unions? This type of concern continues even today among pollsters, and to the lay public it is still the function of surveys to "find out what people think" or to see just how many feel thus and and so.

Among sociologists, however, this purely descriptive use of survey research was soon supplanted by an *analytical* one. First there began

Reprinted from *Human Organization,* 17 (1958–1959), 28–36, by permission of the author and publisher, The Society for Applied Anthropology.

to be a concern with how different sub-groups in the population felt or behaved. From this, the analysts moved on to further cross-tabulations. Finally, some survey analysts began, through cross-tabulations and correlations, to study complicated questions of why people behaved as they did. By relating one opinion item to another, attitude configurations and clusters of attitudes emerged; by relating background information to these attitudes, some insight was gained into the *determinants* of attitudes. It was in this analytical stage, then, beyond the simple description of a population, that survey research began to be of real use to social science.

But throughout all this one fact remained, a very disturbing one to the student of social organization. The *individual* remained the unit of analysis. No matter how complex the analysis, how numerous the correlations, the studies focused on individuals as separate and independent units. The very techniques mirrored this well: samples were random, never including (except by accident) two persons who were friends; interviews were with one individual, as an atomistic entity, and responses were coded onto separate IBM cards, one for each person. As a result, the kinds of substantive problems on which such research focused tended to be problems of "aggregate psychology," that is, *within*-individual problems, and never problems concerned with relations between people.

Now, very recently, this focus on the individual has shown signs of changing, with a shift to groups as the units of analysis, or to networks of relations among individuals. The shift is quite a difficult one to make, both conceptually and technically, and the specific methods used to date are only halting steps toward a full-fledged methodology. Nevertheless, some of these methods are outlined below, to indicate just how, taken together, they can even now provide us with an extremely fruitful research tool. This tool has sometimes been used for the study of formal organization but more often for the study of the informal organization which springs up within a formal structure. In both cases, it shows promise of opening to research, problems which have been heretofore the province of speculation.

PROBLEMS OF DESIGN AND SAMPLING

The break from the atomistic concerns of ordinary survey analysis requires taking a different perspective toward the individual interview. In usual survey research and statistical analysis, this interview is regarded as *independent* of others, as an entity in itself. All cross-tabulations and analyses relate one item in that questionnaire to another item in the same questionnaire. But, in this different approach, an individual interview is seen as a *part* of some larger structure in which the respondent finds himself: his network of friends, the shop or office where he works, the bowling team he belongs to, and so on. Thus, as a part of a larger structure, the individual is *not* treated independently. The analysis must somehow tie together and interrelate the attributes of these different parts of the structure.

So much for the basic change in perspective—away from the atomistic treatment of the individual interview, and toward the treatment of each interview as a part of some larger whole. This basic perspective has several implications for the kind of data collected and for the sample design. Perhaps the most important innovation in the kind of data collected is sociometric-type data in the interview, that is, explicit questions about the respondent's relation to other specific individuals. Each person may be asked the names of his best friends, or the names of his subordinates in the shop upon whom he depends most, or any one of a multitude of *relational* questions. For example, in a study of two housing projects by Merton, Jahoda, and West,[1] one way to map out the informal social structure in the community was to ask people who their best friends were. Having obtained such data from all the families in the project, so that each family could be located in the network of social relations in the community, it was then possible to examine the relation between this social structure, on the one hand, and various values and statuses on the other. Specifically, this information allowed these authors to show that in one housing project social ties were based very largely on similarities in background and religion; in the other, social relations were more often built around common leisure interests and participation in community organizations.

More generally, the incorporation of sociometric-type data into survey research allows the investigator to *locate* each interviewed individual within the networks of voluntary relations which surround him. In some cases, these networks of voluntary relations will be superimposed on a highly articulated formal structure. In a department of a business, for example, there are numerous hierarchical levels and there are numerous work relations which are imposed by the job itself. In such cases, sociometric-type questions can be asked relative to these formal relations, e.g.: "Which supervisor do you turn to most often?"

[1] Robert K. Merton, Patricia S. West, and Marie Jahoda, *Patterns of Social Life: Explorations in the Sociology of Housing*, forthcoming.

or, "Which of the men in your own workgroup do you see most often outside of work?" or, "When you want X type of job done in a hurry to whom do you go to get it done?" or, "When you need advice on such-and-such a problem, who do you usually turn to?"

Another kind of data is that which refers to some larger social unit. For example, in some research on high schools currently being carried out at the University of Chicago, it is necessary to find the paths to prestige within a school, so that the boys are asked: "What does it take to be important and looked up to by the other fellows here at school?" Then the responses to this question—aggregated over each school separately—can be used to characterize the *school* as well as the individual. Because of this, the question itself makes explicit reference to the school.

But apart from the kinds of data collected, there are also important *sampling* considerations. In this kind of research, it is no longer possible to pull each individual out of his social context and interview him as an independent entity. It is necessary to sample parts of that context as well or, to say it differently, to sample explicitly with reference to the social structure. There are numerous ways of doing this; only a few, which have been successfully tried, are mentioned below.

a. Snowball Sampling:

One method of interviewing a man's immediate social environment is to use the sociometric questions in the interview for sampling purposes. For example, in a study of political attitudes in a New England community, Martin Trow has used this approach: first interviewing a small sample of persons, then asking these persons who their best friends are, interviewing these friends, then asking *them* their friends, interviewing these, and so on.[2] In this way, the sampling plan follows out the chains of sociometric relations in the community. In many respects, this sampling technique is like that of a good reporter who tracks down "leads" from one person to another. The difference, of course, is that snowball sampling in survey research is amenable to the same scientific sampling procedures as ordinary samples. Where the population in ordinary samples is a population of individuals, here it is two populations: one of individuals and one of *relations* among individuals.

[2] Martin A. Trow, "Right Wing Radicalism and Political Intolerance: A Study of Support for McCarthy in a New England Town." Unpublished Ph.D. dissertation, Columbia University, 1957.

b. Saturation Sampling:

Perhaps a more obvious approach is to interview *everyone* within the relevant social structure. In a study of doctors in four communities, *all* the doctors in these communities were interviewed.[3] Sociometric-type questions were then used to lay out the professional and social relations existing among these doctors. This "saturation" method or complete census was feasible there, because the total number of doctors in these communities was small—less than three hundred. But in the study mentioned earlier which used snowball sampling, such an approach would have been practically impossible, for the community was about 15,000 in size. Thus this "saturation sampling" is only feasible under rather special circumstances. A borderline case is the study of high schools mentioned earlier. There are 9,000 students in the ten schools being studied. Only because these students are given self-administered questionnaires, rather than interviews, is it possible to use a saturation sample, and thereby characterize the complete social structure.

c. Dense Sampling:

Another approach is to sample "densely." This is a compromise between the usual thinly dispersed random sample and the saturation sample. An illustration will indicate how this may be useful. In a study of pressure upon the academic freedom of college social science teachers, carried out by Paul Lazarsfeld, at least *half* of the social science faculty in every college in the sample was interviewed.[4] Thus, by sampling densely, enough men were interviewed in each college so that the climate of the college could be characterized, as well as the attitudes of the individual respondent.

d. Multi-stage Sampling:

Any of the above approaches to sampling can be combined with an element found in many sample designs: the multi-stage sample. For example, in the academic freedom study referred to above, it would have been impossible to have a dense sample of social science teachers in *all* the colleges in the United States, so a two-stage sample was used:

[3] J. S. Coleman, E. Katz, and H. M. Menzel, "Diffusion of an Innovation among Physicians," *Sociometry*, XX (Dec. 1957).

[4] P. F. Lazarsfeld and Wagner Thielens, *The Academic Man: Social Scientists in a Time of Crisis*, The Free Press, Glencoe, Ill., 1956.

first sampling colleges, and then teachers within colleges. In doing this, of course, the crucial question is what balance to maintain between the sampling of colleges and the sampling of teachers within colleges. Enough colleges are needed to have representativity, yet few enough so that the sampling within each one can be dense. In a study of union politics, reported in *Union Democracy*,[5] we perhaps made a wrong decision: we interviewed in 90 printing shops, spreading the interviews so thinly that only one man out of three—at most—was interviewed within the shop. This meant that we had only a very few interviews in each shop, and could not use the interview material to characterize the climate or atmosphere of the shops, except in the very largest ones.

These sampling procedures are, of course, not the only possible ones. An infinite degree of variation is possible, depending upon the problem and upon the kind of social structure involved. The most important point is that the individual interview can no longer be treated as an independent entity, but must be considered as a part of some larger whole: in the sampling, in the questions asked, and in the subsequent analysis.

ANALYTICAL METHODS

The real innovations in this new kind of research are in the techniques of analysis. I will mention several of these with which I am most familiar, to give an indication of the kinds of problems this research examines and the way it examines them.

a. Contextual Analysis:

The first, and the one closest to usual survey research, might be termed contextual analysis. In essence, it consists of relating a characteristic of the respondent's social context—and the independent variable—to a characteristic of the individual himself.[6] A good example of this occurred in *The American Soldier*, where the attitudes of inexperienced men, in companies where most others were inexperienced, were compared to attitudes of similarly inexperienced men in com-

[5] S. M. Lipset, M. A. Trow, and J. S. Coleman, *Union Democracy*, The Free Press, Glencoe, Ill., 1956.

[6] Peter Blau has emphasized the importance of such analysis in formal organizations for locating the "structural effects" of a situation upon the individuals in it. See his "Formal Organization: Dimensions of Analysis," *American Journal of Sociology*, LXIII (1957), 58–69.

panies where most others were veterans. It was found that inexperienced men in green companies felt very differently about themselves, and about combat, than their counterparts in veteran companies. That is, when men were characterized by both individual characteristics and by their social surroundings, the latter were found to have an important effect on their attitudes.

In the union politics study mentioned above, one of the major elements in the analysis was an examination of the effect of the shop context on the men within the shop. We had access to voting records in union political elections for these shops, and these made it possible to characterize the shop as politically radical or politically conservative and as high or low in political consensus. Then we could examine the different behavior or attitudes of men in different kinds of shops and compute a "shop effect." An example is given in Table 1. Each man

Table 1

		Shops of high political consensus	Shops of low political consensus
Percent of men active in union politics		29%	7%
	N	(125)	(28)

is in a shop of high or low political consensus, depending on whether the men in the shop vote alike or are evenly split between the radical and conservative parties. And each man has a certain degree of political activity. In this table, the shop's political consensus and the man's political activity are related. The table indicates that in shops of high consensus, men are politically more active than in shops of low consensus. The inference might be that high consensus provides a kind of resonance of political beliefs which generates a greater interest in politics. In any case, the table exemplifies the use of an attribute of a *shop* related to an attribute of a *man* in the shop. This general kind of analysis, which bridges the gap between two levels of sociological units —the individual and his social context—seems to be a very basic one for this "structural" approach to survey research.

b. Boundaries of Homogeneity:

A second kind of analysis attempts to answer the question: How homogeneous are various groups in some belief or attitude? In a medical school, for example, are a student's attitudes toward medicine more like those of his fraternity brothers or more like those of his laboratory partners? This question, incidentally, has been posed in a study of medical students presently being carried out at Columbia University.[7] The answer is, in the particular medical school being studied, that his attitudes are far more like those of his fraternity brothers. In other words, in this medical school, the "boundaries of homogeneity" of certain attitudes about medicine coincide very largely with fraternity boundaries.

The major problems in answering questions of group homogeneity are problems of index construction. Consider the above example: each student has twenty or thirty fraternity brothers, but only three laboratory partners in anatomy lab. How can the effects of variability between groups, due to small numbers in a group, be separated out from the actual tendency toward homogeneity of attitude? It can be done, and indices have been developed to do so. The indices, incidentally, are much like the formulas by which statisticians measure the effects of clustering in a random sample. In Appendix A, an index for assessing the amount of group homogeneity is presented.

An example of group homogeneity may indicate more concretely how this approach can be useful in research. In the study of doctors in four communities mentioned earlier, we were interested in the social processes affecting the physicians' introduction of a new drug into their practices. Through interviewing all doctors and asking sociometric questions in the interview, we were able to delineate seven "cliques" of doctors who were sociometrically linked together. (How to reconstruct such cliques is another problem, which will be considered shortly.) The question, then, became this: At each point in time after the drug was marketed, were cliques homogeneous or not in their members' use or non-use of the drug? If they were homogeneous, then this was evidence that some kind of social influence or diffusion was going on in relation to the measured sociometric ties. If not, this indicated that the cliques delineated on the basis of questions in the interview had little relevance to drug adoption. Table 2 shows, for several time periods, just how much homogeneity there was in the cliques, beyond that which would arise by chance. An index value of 1.0 means each clique is completely homogeneous in its use or non-use of the drug. An index value of 0 means there is no more homogeneity than would arise through chance variation between groups.

Table 2 shows that there was no homogeneity until around seven

[7] Some of the work in this study (though not the work mentioned here) is reported in P. F. Kendall, R. K. Merton, and G. G. Reader (eds.), *The Student Physician*, Commonwealth Fund, New York, 1957.

Table 2

Months after drug was marketed	Amount of clique homogeneity	Percent of doctors who had used the drug
1 months	no homogeneity	14%
3	no "	32
5	no "	49
7	.07	66
9	.12	71
11	.18	76
13	.03	83
15	no homogeneity	86

months after the drug was introduced, that is, until over 50 percent of the doctors had used the drug. The maximum homogeneity was reached at about eleven months, when three-fourths of the doctors had begun to use the drug. Then after that, the homogeneity receded to zero again.

This result helped to reinforce a conclusion derived from other findings in the study: that the social networks measured in the study were effective as paths of diffusion at certain times but not at others. However, apart from the substantive results of the study, this example indicates how such analysis of the boundaries of homogeneity may be useful for the study of the functioning of various social organizations.

c. Pair Analysis:

Neither of the above kinds of analysis has required the use of sociometric-type data. An important kind of analysis which does use such direct data on relationships is the analysis of *pairs.* Here, the pair formed by A's choosing B becomes the unit of analysis. Speaking technically, "pair cards" may be constructed for each sociometric choice, and then these cards used for cross-tabulations. In other words, instead of cross-tabulating a man's attitude toward Russia with his attitude toward the United Nations, we can cross-tabulate the man's attitude toward Russia with the attitude toward Russia of the man he eats lunch with at the cafeteria.

One of the most important problems which has been studied in this way is the similarity or difference in attitudes or backgrounds between the two members of a pair. That is, do people have friendship relations with those who are like them politically, with people of the same age, with persons in the same occupation?

This kind of problem can be illustrated by Table 3, which contains hypothetical data. This table, which looks very much like an or-

Table 3

		Chosen boy	Chosen girl	
Chooser	boy	45	15	40
	girl	20	20	60
				100

dinary contingency table, must be treated in a slightly different fashion. It allows us to raise the question: do boys tend to choose boys more than would be expected by chance? and, do girls tend to choose girls more than would be expected by chance? The answer, of course, depends upon what we take as chance. However, chance models have been worked out, so that one can assign measures of the tendency to choose others of one's own kind. One of these is outlined in Appendix B. For the above example, this measure (varying between 0 and 1) says that the tendency to in-choice for boys is .38 and that for girls is .17. By comparing such indices for numerous attributes, one could get a good glimpse into the informal social organization of the group. For example, in the medical study mentioned earlier which is being carried out at Columbia University, the values of in-choice tendency for friends shown in Table 4 were found:

Table 4

Subgroups	Tendencies toward in-choice
Class in school	.92
Fraternity	.52
Sex	.33
Marital status	.20
Attitudes toward national health insurance	.37

By looking at the relative sizes of these index values, we get an idea of just how the informal social relations—that is, the friendship choices—at this medical school mesh with the formal structure, and with the distribution of attitudes.

In the study mentioned above of drug introduction by doctors, these pair relations were used as the major aspect of the analysis: by examining how close in time a doctor's first use of a new drug was to the first use of the doctor he mentioned as a friend, it was possible to infer the functioning of friendship networks in the introduction of this drug.

These examples of pair analysis give only a crude picture of the kinds of problems which can be studied in this fashion. The important matter is to break away from the analysis of *individuals* as units to the study of *pairs* of individuals. To be sure, this involves technical IBM problems and problems of index construction along with conceptual problems, but the difficulties are not great.

d. Partitioning into Cliques:

Another important kind of problem is the partitioning of a larger group into cliques by use of sociometric choices. This problem is a thorny one, for it involves not only the delineation of cliques, but, even prior to this, the *definition* of what is to constitute a clique. Are cliques to be mutually exclusive in membership, or can they have overlapping memberships? Are they to consist of people who all name one another, or of people who are tied together by more tenuous connections? Such questions must be answered before the group can be partitioned into cliques.

A good review of some of the methods by which cliques and subgroups can be treated is presented in Lindzey and Borgotta.[8] The two most feasible of these are the method of matrix multiplication [9] and the method of shifting rows and columns in the sociometric choice matrix until the choices are clustered around the diagonal.[10] This last technique is by far the more feasible of the two if the groups are more than about twenty in size. When the groups are on the order of a hundred, even this method becomes clumsy. An IBM technique was successfully used in the study of doctors and the study of medical students, both mentioned above, in which the groups were 200–400 in size. At the University of Chicago, a program has been developed for Univac, using a method of shifting rows and columns in a matrix, which can handle groups up to a thousand in size.[11] The necessity for

[8] G. Lindzey (ed.), *Handbook of Social Psychology*, Addison-Wesley, Cambridge, 1956, Chap. II.

[9] See L. Festinger, "The Analysis of Sociograms Using Matrix Algebra," *Human Relations*, II, No. 2 (1949), 153–158 and R. D. Luce, "Connectivity and Generalized Cliques in Sociometric Group Structure," *Psychometrika*, XV (1950), 169–190.

[10] C. O. Beum and E. G. Brundage, "A Method for Analyzing the Sociomatrix," *Sociometry*, XIII (1950), 141–145.

[11] A description of this program, written by the author and Duncan McRae, is

some such method becomes great when, for example, one wants to map out systematically the informal organization of a high school of a thousand students.

CONCLUSION

These four kinds of analysis, contextual analysis, boundaries of homogeneity, pair analysis, and partitioning into cliques, are only four of many possibilities. Several other approaches have been used, but these four give some idea of the way in which survey analysis can come to treat problems which involve social structure. In the long run, these modes of analysis will probably represent only the initial halting steps in the development of a kind of structural research which will represent a truly sociological methodology. In any case, these developments spell an important milestone in social research, for they help open up for systematic research those problems which have heretofore been the province of the theorist or of purely qualitative methods.

There is one new development which should be mentioned, although the frontier is just opened, and not at all explored. This development is the construction of electronic computers with immediate-access storage capacities a hundred times the size of an 80-column IBM card. Such computers make it possible, for the first time, to lay out a complex social structure for direct and systematic examination. Instead of examining the similarity of attitudes between socially connected pairs, after laborious construction of "pair cards," it becomes possible to trace through a whole structural network, examining the points in the network where attitudes or actions begin to diverge. Methods for doing this have not yet been developed but, for the first time, the technical facilities exist, and it is just a matter of time until analytical methods are developed. IBM cards and counter-sorters were methodologically appropriate for the individualistic orientation which survey research has had in the past; electronic computers with large storage capacities are precisely appropriate for the statistical analysis of complex social organization.

Unfortunately, it has not been possible here to present any of the tools discussed above fully enough to show precisely how it is used. In giving a broad overview of a number of developments, my aim has

---

available upon request from the author and the program itself is available for copying, for those who have access to a Univac I or II.

been to point to an important new direction in social research, one which may aid significantly in the systematic study of social organization. In the two appendices which follow, indices for the study of "boundaries of homogeneity" and for "pair analysis" are developed, adding some concrete techniques to this broad overview.

Robert S. Weiss
and
Eugene Jacobson

A Method for the Analysis of the Structure of Complex Organizations

Sociometric techniques have been used most frequently in the study of small group structure.[1] The utilization of sociometry in the study of large and complex social systems, such as the bureaucratic organization, has generally been limited to the construction of indices, e.g., frequency of communication, or amount of out-group as compared with in-group contact. These indices are then treated as characteristics of individual members of the organization, and the structural context in which they were developed is generally lost.

The use of sociometry to determine the overall structure of a complex organization probably owes its rarity to an absence both of basic structural concepts and of efficient methods for the manipulation of large masses of sociometric data. This paper proposes both a set of structural concepts and a methodology, which together state a practical approach to the sociometric analysis of complex structures.

The approach is based on certain assumptions about the nature of

Reprinted in part from Robert S. Weiss and Eugene Jacobson, *American Sociological Review*, 20 (1955), 661–668, by permission of the authors and the publisher, The American Sociological Association.

[1] See, for example, Gardner Lindzey and Edgar F. Borgatta, "Sociometric Measurement," in Gardner Lindzey (editor), *Handbook of Social Psychology*, Cambridge: Addison Wesley Press, 1954.

large organizations. To begin with, a complex unit, such as the government agency, the labor union, the church, the military unit, the school, and the industrial plant, can be seen as having a fabric of roles that constitutes the "structure" of the organization. Individual members contribute in accordance with the prescriptions of the roles they perform and co-ordinate their activities with each other in accordance with the relationships of their roles to other roles in the structure. This structure can be assumed, in most cases, to remain relatively constant despite changes in personnel through promotion, transfer, retirement, or recruitment. If a member of a relatively stable organization is replaced, the new member will ordinarily be expected to re-establish the work relationships that the previous incumbent had maintained, with changes only in the more peripheral contacts.

An organization's structure reflects the coordination patterns within it, and its analysis and description is essential to the understanding of the division of labor, the communication processes, and the adjustment and growth mechanisms of the complex unit. As a first approximation, the organization chart, when it exists, provides an introduction to this analysis and description. But even the best chart is an over-simplified description of the organization. Rather than being designed to reproduce the structure, it is usually intended primarily to establish lines of authority and to define the limits of administrative units. It is useful as a description of the actual structure only to the extent that working contacts are confined to charted authority relationships or relationships within administrative units.[2]

Intensive study of a complex organization will generally require a more complete description of structure than that provided by the standard organization chart. It is the purpose of this paper to present an objective and reproducible method for arriving at this description. The method consists of an analysis of the role relationships reported by members of the organization at a given point in time.

HOW THE METHOD WAS DEVELOPED

The Human Relations Program of the Survey Research Center has been conducting studies of the determinants of effectiveness of com-

[2] A set of research monographs, *Studies in Naval Leadership*, published 1949–1954 by the Personnel Research Board of the Ohio State University, under the direction of Carroll Shartle, presents extensive empirical analyses relating some aspects of organization chart representations of structure and sociometric choice. The work directed by Ralph Stogdill and reported by Ellis Scott is particularly relevant.

plex organizations since 1947.[3] In the winter of 1949 a study in a government agency was designed to investigate relationships among variations in patterns of communication and variations in employee attitudes. Methods for measuring the relevant attitudes in the areas of job performance, relationships with superiors and subordinates, organization goals, communication, power, and individual career mobility were available. But the corresponding task of measuring variations in patterns of communication and interaction demanded the development of descriptive and analytic methods not previously used. The structural analysis that follows is the product of an attempt to develop a systematic description of interaction patterns.

THE BASIC DATA

The structure of the complex government agency was found through what was basically a sociometric analysis. The procedures differed from those used to find choice patterns in a small group primarily in that more people were involved and the choice criterion was different. The number of persons, in this case about 200, made it necessary to replace the ordinary cut-and-try analysis with more systematic procedures.[4] The criterion used was one calculated to produce data which would be co-ordinate to the elements of structure. We assumed that the elements of structure were role relationships; reports of work contacts were used as a criterion.

To obtain the basic information about attitudes and patterns of interaction, each of the 196 members of the professional and administrative staff of the agency was interviewed privately in sessions that lasted from one to three hours. When the interview was about two-

[3] Studies completed by 1952 are summarized in Daniel Katz and Robert Kahn, "Some Recent Findings in Human Relations Research in Industry," in E. G. Swanson, T. M. Newcomb and E. L. Hartley (editors), *Readings in Social Psychology*, New York: Henry Holt and Company, 1952.

[4] Some systematic analysis methods have been proposed, notably by Duncan Luce and Albert D. Perry, "A Method of Matrix Analysis of Group Structure," *Psychometrika*, 14 (1949); and by Luce, "Connectivity and Generalized Cliques in Sociometric Group Structure," *Psychometrika*, 15 (1950). In these studies a group was defined as consisting of a set of individuals who were of a certain degree of closeness to each other. This definition proved inappropriate for the problem discussed in this paper. It seemed, on theoretical, intuitive, and practical grounds that "groups" of individuals should be defined in terms of their separateness from each other rather than in terms of their degree of inner connectedness, if the ultimate objective is the description of a complex organization consisting of a set of groups.

thirds completed, each respondent was asked to fill out a "Personal Contact Checklist" form.[5] Instructions were

> Now go back over the past two or three months and think of the people (in the organization) with whom you have worked most closely. We would like to get the names of the people with whom you work most closely. Write their names in here. You will notice that we want some who are higher than you in the organization, some lower than you, and some at the same level.

After the respondent had listed his co-workers, he was asked to indicate the frequency of his contacts with them, reason for the contact, subject matter discussed, and the relative importance of the contact, each on a four or five point scale.

About 2400 work relationships were reported by the 196 respondents. Of these, 44 per cent were reciprocated. That is, if individual A reported that he worked with B, B also reported that he worked with A. Reciprocation was strongly related to reported frequency and importance of contact. Eighty per cent of the 409 contacts reported as "several times daily" and of "utmost" or "great" importance were reciprocated. Only 19 per cent of the 565 contacts reported as "several times monthly" or "several times yearly" and of "some," "little," or "no" importance were reciprocated. Reciprocated reports of work relationships were primary data for the bulk of the analysis, although some use of unreciprocated choices was made to clarify ambiguous contact patterns.

DEVELOPMENT OF A MATRIX

To reduce this mass of reported contacts to a graphic representation of the organization structure, the matrix analysis suggested by Festinger[6] and by Forsyth and Katz[7] was used as a guide. An IBM punching and listing procedure was used for the construction of the 196 x 196 matrix.[8]

[5] This sociometric form is reproduced in Eugene Jacobson and Stanley Seashore, "Communication Practices in Complex Organizations," *Journal of Social Issues*, Vol. 7, No. 3 (1951), pp. 28–40.

[6] Leon Festinger, "The Analysis of Sociograms Using Matrix Algebra," *Human Relations*, 2 (April, 1949), pp. 153–158.

[7] Elaine Forsyth and Leo Katz, "A Matrix Approach to the Analysis of Sociometric Data," *Sociometry*, 9 (November, 1946), pp. 340–347.

[8] The listing technique developed by Orabelle Poll, working with Ian Ross, is described in O. Poll, H. Ruderman and D. Zipperstein, "Methodological Report of a Sociometric Study of Personnel in a Government Agency," Survey Research Center, 1950, hectographed.

A schematic diagram of this matrix is shown in Figure 1. Individuals who report a contact appear in the left margin. Those reported as contacts appear along the top margin. Respondents were listed

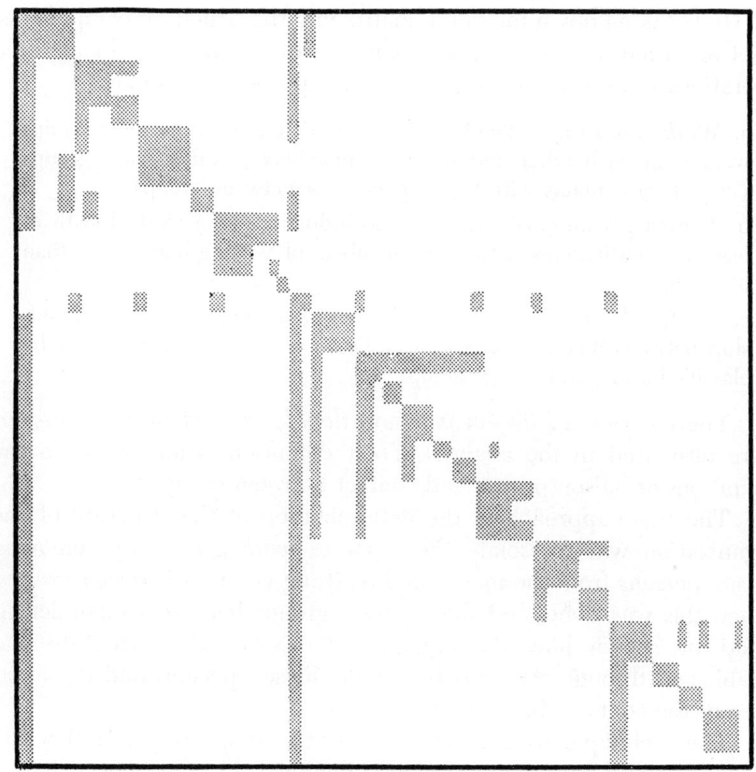

Fig. 1. Schematic impression of original matrix

sequentially in organization chart order, and, as a result, most persons were located in the matrix near most of the others with whom they worked. The dark blocks along the diagonal from the upper left to the lower right indicate clusters of reports. The long vertical lines indicate individuals who were reported as contacts by a large number of respondents.

ANALYSIS OF THE MATRIX: SEPARATING THE WORK GROUPS

In breaking down the initial matrix into the structural components, a set of structural concepts that identified the elements and suggested operations to be used in the analysis was proposed as follows:

a. *Work group* was defined as a set of individuals whose relationships were with each other and not with members of other work groups (except for contacts with liaison persons or between groups).

b. *Liaison person* was defined as an individual who worked with at least two individuals who were members of work groups other than his own.

c. *Contact between groups* was defined as a single working relationship between members of sets of individuals who would otherwise be classified as separate work groups.

The concepts of *liaison pair* and *double contact between groups* were also used in the analysis. Their definition is analogous to the definitions of liaison person and contact between groups.[9]

The basic approach to the determination of the structure of the organization was to isolate the separate *work groups* by removing *liaison persons* from the matrix and omitting *contacts between groups.* When this was done, and the separate groups had been identified, it could be shown how the organization coordination structure was established through the activities of the liaison persons and the existence of the contacts between groups.

The technique used in isolating work groups required that the matrix be symmetric across the main diagonal. In other words, it was necessary that there be an entry in the cell corresponding to B's report of contact with A whenever there was an entry in the cell corresponding to A's report of contact with B. The original unreciprocated matrix could be made into a symmetric form either by adding entries in the

[9] These concepts correspond in many respects to the concepts of articulation point, bridge, articulation pair, and double bridge in the mathematics of graph theory. The concept of separate work group corresponds to the graph theory concept of component. These correspondences are described in Robert S. Weiss, "An Application of Graph Theoretical Concepts to the Analysis of Sociometric Information," Survey Research Center, 1953, hectographed. An elementary introduction to the concepts of mathematical graph theory appears in Frank Harary and Robert Z. Norman, *Graph Theory as a Mathematical Model in Social Science,* Ann Arbor: Institute for Social Research, 1953.

proper cells when a report was not reciprocated, or by deleting unreciprocated entries. The second method was chosen because the close relationship between reciprocation and importance and frequency of contact suggested that the simplification would not be at the cost of essential information.

From this symmetric matrix, the work groups were isolated through the following procedures:

1. The large matrix was separated, more or less arbitrarily, along the diagonal from upper left to lower right corner into smaller matrices called *segments* that retained as many of the total contacts as possible. There is good reason to believe that the structure finally developed is one that will be arrived at in all details no matter what original arbitrary segment division is made, but the labor required will vary somewhat depending on segment inclusiveness.[10]

2. The individual who had the greatest number of contacts outside of his segment was tentatively considered to be a liaison person and was removed from the matrix, together with his contacts. Then the individual with the next greatest number of contacts outside his segment was removed, and so on, until no person remained in the matrix who had more than one contact outside his segment.

3. Within each segment, persons who had no contacts with others in the segment were removed from the matrix and tentatively considered to be isolates.

4. Rows and columns within the segments were reordered to bring persons who reported contacts with each other into adjacent positions. When the reordering was accomplished, the separate groups were, in most cases, identified by inspection.

5. More than 80 per cent of the structure could be, unambiguously and economically, identified by the procedures outlined above. The remaining blocks of interaction within segments, however, demanded a more detailed and rigorous analysis to determine whether they were ultimate separate units or whether they were still capable of being separated. If they were separable, that meant that they contained liaison persons. All persons who had the contact pattern that would allow them to contact all other persons in the unit with a minimum number of steps were considered to be potential liaison persons.[11] If

[10] The analysis reported here has been replicated from written instructions with essentially identical results. The directions are included as an appendix to Robert Weiss, *Processes of Organization,* to be published by the Institute for Social Research.

[11] These potential liaison persons are, in the language of graph theory, *central*

their removal from the group caused it to break into separated units, they were classified as liaison persons.

6. Upon completion of step 5 above, there were three lists of persons:

a. members of separated work groups

b. tentatively identified liaison persons

c. tentatively identified isolates

7. Only reciprocated reports had been used up to step 6. The unreciprocated data were then used to make more certain assignment of liaison persons and isolates. Tentative isolates who reported frequent contact with one of the separated groups, or who were reported as frequent contacts by one of the separated groups, were assigned as members of groups. Tentative liaison persons, whose frequent contacts were all with one of the separated groups, even though some were not reciprocated, were considered to have membership in that group.

8. The end product of this set of operations was two lists of persons:

a. About 82 per cent of the respondents could be classed as members of the twenty-two primary separate work groups that formed the basic framework of the organization. These people had the bulk of their contacts within their respective groups.

b. The twenty-two work groups were held together by a network of liaison persons who were the remaining 18 per cent of the respondents. One-third of these liaison persons had many contacts with each other and few with any single work group. They were characterized as a *liaison set*. The rest of the liaison persons were assigned to the primary work groups in which they had frequent contacts as *liaison group members*, or remained as *liaison individuals*.[12]

---

to the unit. The assumption is that the set of central individuals includes the set of liaison persons, but exceptional cases can be constructed. A method for locating liaison members of a set has been developed by Frank Harary and Ian Ross, "Identification of the Liaison Persons of an Organization Using the Structure Matrix," *Management Science*, 1 (April–July, 1955), pp. 251–258. The less rigorous technique used in the original analysis is described in *Processes of Organization, op. cit.* Contacts between groups may also be found by these techniques. The two participants in a contact between groups appear as liaison individuals under most conditions. Certain problems in this area have not, however, been solved as yet.

[12] Only one person could be classed as an isolate. This individual was an observer on leave from another organization.

For a matrix of 200 persons, after the data have been punched, tabulated, and

DESCRIPTION OF THE STRUCTURE

The first result of the analysis was a representation of the structure of the organization as it existed in fact. In Figure 2 the squares repre-

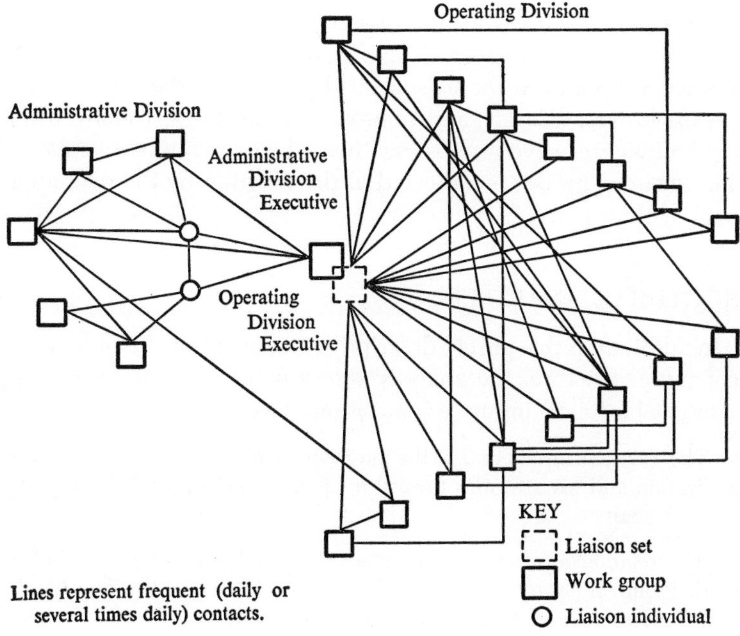

Fig. 2. Schematic representation of the structure of the organization

sent work groups (separate groups plus *liaison group members*), the two circles in the Administrative Division represent *liaison individuals* without group assignment, and the dashed square in the center of the diagram is the *liaison set* of persons, none of whom have group assignment but who work closely with each other. The lines connecting these elements indicate the existence of one or more working relationships among the elements.

reproduced in reciprocated matrix form, the analysis described here can probably be compiled by one person in something under forty hours. Some parts of the analysis can be completed by an electronic digital computer, such as MIDAC. Ian Ross, University of Michigan, has developed a program for the analysis of interaction data from groups of up to forty individuals.

The individuals who work in the Administrative Division of the organization have few contacts with persons in the Operating Division. There is only one frequent working relationship reported; this is between a minor executive in the Administrative bureau and one of the Operating Division work group members, and probably results from an unusual task that required temporary collaboration. Co-ordination between the Divisions is achieved partly by the dual membership of one person who is a member of high status both in the Administrative executive group and in the liaison set that includes the Operating Division executives. Weekly and semi-weekly meetings, usually formal, bring the two executive groups together. The overlapping membership of the executive groups is indicated in the diagram by the overlapping corners of the square.

STRUCTURAL ANALYSIS

In addition to this purely descriptive treatment of the organization as a unique structure, the analysis allows us to look for relationships that might be found in any organization. Two examples are

a. The relationship between the position of an individual in the organization and his attitudes toward his job, coworkers, and the organization's goals.

b. The relationship between the goals and methods of operation of a work group or larger segment of the organization, on the one hand, and the structure of that work group or segment.

Position and Attitudes

The position of each member can be described in a number of ways: his assignment to one work group rather than another; the relative centrality or peripherality of his position in the structure; whether his position was that of a liaison person, ordinary work group member, or relative isolate; his relationship to others in his work group; and a large number of other relevant indices. We have related several of these measures to identification with the organization, attitudes toward supervision and communication, and other relevant attitudes. Results obtained do not lend themselves readily to generalization. There are systematic relationships, particularly between internal structure of the working groups and attitudes toward supervision and communication, but few of the attitudes seem to be dependent primarily upon structure. Most of them are conditioned by the respondent's past experience and aspirations, and the nature of the roles he is required to perform. These findings appear in other reports.[13]

Goals, Methods of Operation, and Structure

The structures of the two major units, the Administrative Division and the Operating Division, differed in a number of respects, including size of work group, extent of contact among work groups, methods of co-ordinating work groups, and structure of the executive group. It was possible to relate these structural differences to the nature of the different goals of the Divisions. The major goal of the Administrative group was the administration of internal policy in a consistent fashion and with sufficient attention to detail to make errors unlikely. The structure of this Division is hierarchic, with little direct contact between executive and work group member. The work groups tend to correspond to formally prescribed units and to be relatively isolated from one another.

The structure of the Operating Division which has a very different major goal contrasts sharply with the structure of the Administrative Division. The major goal of the Operating Division is to respond flexibly and effectively to a changing environment. Since accountability is less important than effective co-ordination in this Division, work groups tend to be small and there is a great deal of contact among them irrespective of formal requirements. The executive group has direct contact with the work groups and there is much less evidence of adherence to hierarchic "channels" of interaction than appears in the Administrative Division. The structure is less like that formally prescribed, less hierarchic, and probably more fluid.

The effect on structure of particular forms of division of labor was investigated by comparing work groups where each member was responsible for a specific job with groups where each member was responsible for certain operations involved in performing the group task but not for any finished unit of work. Clear differences in co-ordinative relationships within these two kinds of groups emerged. In groups whose members were each responsible for all operations on a portion of the total task, the formally prescribed co-ordinative relationships, those between supervisor and supervised, predominated. In groups

[13] One analysis that used some of these data has been published in Dwaine Marvick, *Career Perspectives in a Bureaucratic Setting,* Ann Arbor: University of Michigan, 1954. A formal method for using the sociometric data as a basis for establishing a status ranking is reported by Orabelle Poll as *The Application of Scaling Techniques to Partially Ordered Stratification Systems,* M.A. Thesis, Department of Sociology, University of Michigan, 1951. Other material is presented in *Processes of Organization, op. cit.*

whose members each specialized in a few operations, on the other hand, informal co-ordinative relationships, between individuals not hierarchically related, were more common.

A number of other areas for investigation have been proposed. Once the basic structural data about a complex organization are available, variations in pattern can be related to indices of overall unit effectiveness. In this study, another analysis is under way relating distribution of contact patterns within sub-groups to organization morale.

SUMMARY

We have described a methodology for the determination of the structure of a complex organization, including techniques for gathering, classifying, and analyzing data. This methodology has proved useful in furnishing an accurate description of the structure of a complex organization and in allowing us to investigate the effects on individuals of their position in the structure and the relationship between the goals of parts of the organization and their structure.

Morris Zelditch, Jr., and Terence K. Hopkins

Laboratory Experiments with Organizations

This paper examines the possibility of experimenting with the properties of complex, formally organized social systems in the laboratory. It discusses, first, a few general functions of laboratory experiments; second, whether the properties of organizations prevent their being constructed in the laboratory; and, finally, the ways in which various types of laboratory experiments are relevant to organizational theory.

This paper is published here for the first time. Hopkins gratefully acknowledges the support of the Social Science Research Council Pre-Doctoral Research Training Fellowship, 1957–1958.

LABORATORY EXPERIMENTS

The experiment in the laboratory is a rather special kind of inquiry and should not be confused with its cousins, the field experiment and laboratory observation. To *experiment* is so to manipulate the conditions under which some event is made to occur that the effects produced by different sets of initial conditions can be contrasted. In this paper only studies containing such intentionally produced contrasts are called experiments. By *laboratory* is meant any setting that allows the investigator to control rigorously the conditions under which he makes his observations. The scope of this paper, then, is rather narrow. In particular, these definitions exclude the *field experiment,* which does not rigorously control conditions of observation, and *laboratory observation,* which does not contrast effects.

The reasons for choosing to conduct a laboratory experiment fall into two groups: (1) those concerning why one would choose to experiment; and (2) those concerning why one would do so in the laboratory.

1. As for the first, the reasons for experimenting depend upon the character of the hypotheses to be tested and the empirical conditions required to test them. In general, experimentation is desirable when (a) the hypotheses under examination are explanatory rather than descriptive (i.e., are of the form: if x, then y); (b) they are related logically to other hypotheses predicated of the same process or system; (c) the primary purpose of the investigation is theory construction; and (d) the conditions required to test the hypotheses are not readily obtained in existing natural situations. Each of these requires brief comment.

a. In general, descriptive hypotheses assert something directly true of the "real" world as it naturally exists. Altering any of its states therefore yields precisely the information that is *not* desired. Experiments, consequently, are primarily relevant to explanatory hypotheses.

b. Investigation of a set of systematically related hypotheses in the natural world encounters many obstacles.[1] It is usually difficult, and sometimes impossible, to assess the way in which various factors function without deliberately acting on the complex of antecedent con-

[1] For a clear analysis of the interrelation of a system of variables, in which some of these problems are evident, see Allen H. Barton and Bo Anderson, "Change in an Organizational System: Formalization of a Qualitative Study," this volume, pp. 400–418.

ditions. These difficulties lead one to experiment if separating such factors is the investigator's principal interest.

c. The relevance of a theoretical concern is crucial to cutting through a good deal of the dispute over the "artificiality" of laboratory experimentation. Events in the laboratory often bear little or no resemblance to events normally occurring in the real world, and for this reason may appear to many "unnatural" and to some trivial. But the theoretical importance of events is not determined by their frequency in nature. It is determined by their relevance to theoretical concepts. And theories often contain concepts that refer to events occurring only rarely, if at all, in the real world. Such concepts are simpler, more general, and, in a sense that is more accurate than usual, less "superficial" than more graphic concepts. Though the events to which they refer seldom occur, then, these concepts prove more capable of interpreting the real world. But to examine the types of events to which they refer often requires the construction of "artificial" systems. Such systems are never descriptive of the real world, but they are not intended to be. Their purpose is to construct and test theory, not to match reality as commonly experienced.

d. The conditions required to test hypotheses are often difficult, uneconomical, or even impossible to obtain by nonexperimental means in natural situations.[2] In surveys or other types of field studies, for example, the investigator can exercise *ex post facto* control over spurious causal factors, but he can do so only for factors which have occurred to him as relevant. Those he knows nothing about must obviously go unexamined. In a properly conducted experiment, this problem is met by randomly allocating treatments to subjects. By assigning the treatments in this way the effects of extraneous uncontrolled factors tend also to be random. The experiment, therefore, in comparison with other research methods, permits much greater control over confounding factors, and thus over spurious causal interpretations. Another example arises out of the inaccessibility of certain states in the real world. The most important instances, perhaps, are due to high correlations among factors the effects of which the investigator wishes to separate. It may be desired, for example, to purify a complex, multidimensional concept (such as "democratic" leadership); but one may be unable to obtain in natural situations the "pure" contrasts required to separate the relevant factors.

2. It remains to consider why one would experiment in the labora-

[2] Only a brief and incomplete discussion is possible here. For a more detailed argument, see M. Zelditch and William Evan, "Laboratory Simulation of Bureaucratic Organization: A Methodological Analysis," in preparation.

tory rather than in the field. The term "laboratory," it will be recalled, is used here to refer to any setting in which the investigator has a high degree of control over the conditions of observation. (It thus denotes an analytic concept and should not be read as referring to separate buildings, white coats, university settings, etc.) This degree of control is obtained in two ways: (a) through control over the empirical system being observed, and (b) through control over the measurement process. Therefore, to the extent that the investigator can insulate a system from extraneous influences ("isolate" it), and introduce precise measurement devices, he is conducting his experiment in a laboratory.

To conduct research in such a setting has a number of positive consequences. Most obviously, it facilitates the precise measurement of the results of the experiment, both because of the instrumentation possible and because random error due to the influence of extraneous processes is reduced. Less obviously, but equally important, it facilitates the simplification that is the essence of experimentation. The experimenter can construct and reconstruct organizational routines solely in accordance with research needs and without regard to the administrative need to maintain an effective organization intact. This permits him, of course, much greater freedom in the manipulation of treatments. But it also provides him with the social means he needs to carry out the experiment he originally designed—in particular, to preserve the character of the different treatments. To be able to allocate subjects to treatments and to keep them there, for example, permits him not only to control for any effects that personality differences might produce, but also to prevent people who are receiving different treatments from interacting during the experiment and thereby confounding the effects. The social and physical segregation of the research allows him to regulate the flow of inputs into the system under study and thus to keep the treatments from being affected by extraneous external factors. Finally, not only external influences, but even extraneous internal influences may be eliminated; thus all contamination of the process which is the immediate concern of the experimenter is reduced as far as possible.

LABORATORY GROUPS AND FORMAL ORGANIZATIONS

To execute an experiment, the experimenter must have a considerable degree of authority over his subjects; methodological control, that is, must be translated into social control. If his concern converges with the policy problems of a real organization, or if his experiment requires relatively little alteration of an organization's operating routines, the experimenter may be able to use actually operating, fully manned units and to exercise control through an organization's established system of authority. If his concern is largely theoretical, or if his experiment requires highly artificial conjunctions of properties or settings, actual organizations are, rather naturally, often reluctant to turn themselves over to his care. Moreover, to experiment with fully manned, operating systems may be very costly.

An alternative to experimenting with actual organizations is to use small, temporary, often specially recruited groups of subjects to "simulate" complex organizations. But this solution, which is the principal focus of interest in this paper, gives rise to problems of its own. On the surface, at least, such groups would not appear to provide a likely context in which to study the operation of complex, formally organized social systems. Not only are they small and temporary, but their routines are usually *ad hoc* and their significance to their members slight. Most actual organizations, on the other hand, are just the opposite; they are large and durable, have institutionalized routines, and are of considerable importance in the lives of their members. How is it possible, then, to make valid statements about organizations from experiments on laboratory groups? The answer to this question occupies the remainder of this section, the purpose of which is primarily to counter the commonly held opinion that, owing to the obvious differences between actual organizations and experimental groups, the experimental study of formal organization is condemned from the start to results irrelevant to organizational theory. The general argument is first illustrated, and then applied to the problems raised by differences in size, duration, institutionalization, and meaningfulness of participation.[3]

General Argument

Events in laboratory groups and events in actual organizations, like events in any two different social settings, can be related to one another only if both are relevant to the same set of propositions in a theory. Otherwise put, the two systems must have at least some properties in common. They may not have very many common properties, but to the extent that they have any, common generaliza-

[3] It should be pointed out that these properties are dealt with, not because they define what is meant by a formal organization, but because they are assumed by many to be important correlates of what is meant by this concept. The criteria defining a complex, formal organization are briefly set forth below.

tions about both systems are possible. The question under consideration reduces, therefore, to whether there are at least some propositions in organizational theory which refer only to properties of the sort that the experimenter is capable of reproducing in the laboratory. For example, it is usually not feasible to use experimental groups to test propositions about the effects or conditions of very large size or very long duration. But a proposition *can* be tested using such groups if the following conditions are met: (1) at least two values can be obtained for each relevant variable; (2) it is not essential to the hypothesis where, in the possible range of each variable, these values are located (for example, extreme values are not stipulated); (3) scale properties (e.g., size) either do not occur at all in the proposition or they occur only in place of other properties (e.g., degree of role differentiation) on the erroneous assumption that they are necessary correlates of these other properties.

By way of illustration, consider the following proposition from Gouldner: in a complex organization overt conflict between superiors and subordinates occasions an increase in the number and specificity of the organization's rules.[4] If complexity is taken to mean so many specialized roles that the services of many people are needed for the system to operate, it would be difficult to test the proposition experimentally. Or, if conflict means a very high degree of conflict, it is doubtful that one should reproduce the property, whether or not it could be reproduced. On the other hand, if complexity means only *some* degree of specialization, so that size *per se* is not made particularly relevant, and if conflict means *some* conflict but not necessarily extreme conflict, the proposition can be experimentally tested in the laboratory.

It remains to show that such typical properties of experimental groups as their temporary duration, small size, peripheral significance to members, and lack of institutionalization either are not necessarily properties of experimental groups or are not necessarily correlated with theoretically important properties of organizations.

Scale Properties: Duration and Size

Time enters propositions in organizational theory in three ways: (1) some assertions pertain to processes that take a period of time to complete themselves, such as the assertion that conflict leads to formalization; (2) some refer to properties that remain stable or constant over

[4] See Alvin W. Gouldner, *Wildcat Strike* (Antioch, Ohio: Antioch Press, 1954), Chap. 8.

a period of time; (3) some contain the length of time the organization has existed (its "age") as a property. Whether or not it is important that most organizations are long-lasting and most experimental groups short-lived depends upon how time is used in the propositions being tested. If the length of time a process takes to work itself out, or the period over which certain properties remain constant, are not specifically stated, or are inconsiderable, then it hardly matters at all. And "age" does not appear to be particularly important; it seems relevant, not for itself, but for what it implies or stands in place of, which in this case is presumably institutionalization. But this is a very different issue from that of time *per se*.

The characteristically short life of experimental groups has one important implication which should be elaborated. Limited duration may mean that experimental groups operate for considerably less time than it normally takes for important processes to work themselves out. Experimental time is usually measured in hours, but it may take months, for example, for the participants in an organization to develop personal relations that are strong enough to make particularistic influences important to the organization's day-to-day operation. It is true that to some extent the experimenter's ingenuity can overcome this limitation. He can both start the experimental system well along in the development required and use various techniques to speed it up. In studying conflict, for instance, instead of passively waiting for it to be produced by the situation he can allocate to roles persons who are known to have different norms, or to dislike one another personally; or he can so control their interaction, for example by substituting prewritten messages for theirs, that the required development of conflict is attained relatively rapidly. So long as the theory does not specify that a change is to come about gradually over a long period of time, then, something can be done. Nevertheless, at least in the present state of knowledge, definite limits exist on the experimenter's ability to speed up important processes, and these limits imply a restriction on the range of problems in organizational theory which it is possible to study experimentally.

With respect to size, the issue is much simpler. Large size, in our view, is not in itself a critical characteristic of organizations. Rather, what appears to be important here is complexity, which is often indicated by size but is quite distinct from it. To date, it is true, the tasks assigned in experiments have tended to be simple and the resultant group structures rather uncomplicated. But this correlation between the small number of participants in experimental groups and the simple forms their activity assumes has come about, not because of some necessary connection between size and complexity, but because so far very few experiments have been informed by sociological concerns. Consider how formidably complicated one might make a group's structure if such mechanisms as subgrouping, multiple roles, and overlapping memberships were systematically employed. Nine people, for instance, can be arranged into three three-man units. Systems of such limited complexity are not exact equivalents of large-scale structures, of course. But one neither needs nor wants exact equivalents. They are not needed, because in so far as the explanation of events in terms of one or another of these mechanisms is valid, the same mechanism should produce comparable effects. And they are not wanted, because one wishes to observe the effects of the mechanisms and not the effects of other factors which the theory being tested anyway ignores.

Institutionalization and Involvement

The routines in experimental groups are commonly *ad hoc* in character. Those in actual organizations just as commonly are not; they are anchored at least in the organization's structure and usually in the larger structure of occupational roles as well. They are normatively defined and the norms defining them are widely held. This difference is important and may prevent experimentation, because experimentally created organizations are not likely to develop, even approximately, the degree of institutionalization characteristic of organizations outside the laboratory. But then, they may not need to. As before, so here, what matters are the theoretical statements concerning institutionalization and the possibilities of creating at least some degree of it in an experimental setting.

To begin with, the relevant theory may state only that some patterns of interaction are institutionalized in organizations and not that some *particular* organizational patterns or specialized roles are institutionalized, in which event no special problem need arise. All experimental groups are formed on the basis of institutionalized relations of some sort, and the experimenter may utilize any of the patterns characteristically a part of the anchoring relation in order to meet the required condition. Since the basis is often the professor-student relation, he can make use of these particular statuses, or he can use any of the norms that are usually institutionalized in the college community, such as those governing discussion in groups.

The theory may very well stipulate, however, that certain specific kinds of roles are part of the structure, e.g., employer-employee relations in a bureaucracy. Then, it is true, the experimenter may be in difficulty if he uses just any set of subjects and attempts to create the required degree of institutionalization in the course of the experiment. It is quite feasible, however, to activate norms and statuses structured prior to and outside of the experimental situation. The legitimacy of bureaucratic office, for example, is rather widely accepted in the general population, and the experimenter who wishes to study bureaucratic role relations can activate the appropriate attitudes in his subjects by a variety of means. (See, for an example, the description given below of the Evan-Zelditch experiment.) A rather different solution, not so obvious as the first but perhaps more practical ordinarily, is role playing. Here subjects enact roles which are familiar to them or are made familiar to them by instruction, even though the setting is one in which those roles are not ordinarily activated.[5]

The *ad hoc* character of the routines used in experimental groups, then, is hardly necessary. To the extent that the theory under examination calls for variously institutionalized routines, the experimental situation can be constructed to meet this requirement. It is true that few experiments so far have actually met it, but this deficiency reflects not the nature of experimental groups so much as the content of the theories tested.

That participation in experimental groups is not so meaningful or involving as participation in more enduring or rewarding groups does not seem to introduce any new difficulties. By any of the techniques already suggested the experimenter can activate roles appropriate to complex organizations and in this way create in the course of the experiment fairly high levels of involvement, if that is what is wanted. For other problems the usually low degree of involvement of participants in experimental groups may be just what is wanted.

TYPES OF ORGANIZATIONALLY RELEVANT EXPERIMENTS

The aim of this section is to classify experiments as more or less relevant to organizational theory. For this purpose an *organization* is defined as a social system having, besides the properties generic to social systems, the following characteristics. It is *highly formalized:*

[5] See for a very good example of this technique, Alvin Zander and Arthur R. Cohen, "Attributed Social Power and Group Acceptance: A Classroom Experimental Demonstration," *Journal of Abnormal and Social Psychology,* 51 (1955), 490–492.

an organization has explicitly formulated policies and rules; these define what actions should and should not occur; and the rules are operative at least to some extent. An organization is *highly differentiated,* both functionally and structurally: it is divided, first, into distinct subunits differing at least with respect to coordinating functions, and second, into statuses which within the subunits also differ at least with respect to coordinating functions. It is *integrated through strictly defined subordination:* [6] (a) all subunits in the system are ranked (differentially evaluated); (b) higher-ranking subunits exercise control over a prescribed set, and in principle only that set, of lower-ranking subunits; and (c) the system is unified structurally through linking statuses. (Such statuses are simultaneously located in two adjacently ranked subunits and have high rank in the inferior unit and low rank in the superior unit.) [7] Finally, it is a *structurally complex* social system: it has at least three subunits; at least two of them differ in rank; and, consequently, it exhibits at least three status-levels.

Experimental groups may be classified according to (1) the degree of their complexity (the last criterion above); and (2) the extent to which they satisfy the remaining three criterion properties. This double classification yields the following four types:

TYPE I. *The miniature replica.* The experimenter in this case creates systems having a complete minimum set of units and ranks as well as all three other criterion properties.

TYPE II. *The part replica.* This system satisfies the first three criteria but contains less than the minimum set of units and ranks. In such a system the experimenter may simulate the missing units or ranks so that subjects think of themselves as participating in a complex organization.

TYPE III. *The "near" organization.* The experimenter creates all or some of the minimum number of units and ranks, and at least one but not all three of the other criteria.

TYPE IV. *The simply structured unit.* The experimenter creates a system consisting of only a single unit, and it exhibits none of the defining properties of an organization.

[6] This somewhat ungainly phrase, adapted from Weber, is intended to distinguish a *hierarchy* in general, from the rather special kind of hierarchical order found in formalized organizations.

[7] For a fuller development of this concept, see Chester I. Barnard, *The Functions of the Executive* (Cambridge, Mass.: Harvard, 1938), pp. 110 ff. See also Terence K. Hopkins, "Bureaucratic Authority: The Convergence of Weber and Barnard," in this volume, pp. 82 ff.

The miniature replica is used in an experiment described by Enke.

> The Rand Logistics Laboratory wished to compare two Air Force logistics plans. Two Air Defense Command systems were artificially created, and each was supplied with air bases, supply depots, storage sites, headquarters command, suppliers, etc. and subjected to a fixed flying program, that is, each had the same aircraft, the same spare parts, the same breakdowns at the same numbered flights. Each Command was also subjected to the same (fixed) external constraints, which included factory costs and delays, transportation costs and delays, storage costs and delays, etc. Finally, each was also subjected to two "wars," one at the end of the first simulated year of operation and one at the end of the second.
>
> The component organizations in the two ADCs were each actually manned by only one or a few men, and an hour of experimental time simulated a day of real time. The experiment nonetheless lasted for several months, simulating the total expected life of the aircraft. The participants were physically located on a large floor area, each organization having a desk or partitioned area. The whole could be seen from a top deck and it was from here that the experiment was supervised. The two ADC systems were of course physically isolated from each other.[8]

The Air Defense Commands created by Rand's Logistics Laboratory were "miniature" in that the scale properties were not role-for-role (and hence, not person-for-person) or minute-for-minute re-creations of real organizations.[9]

The part replica is exemplified in an experiment conducted by Evan and Zelditch.

> Forty-five college students were "hired" as coders by a (fictitious) national research organization at $1.25 an hour. They were to code face sheets and were trained for half an hour three at a time, by a coding instructor who identified himself as head of the project. Each was given a code book, a book of general organizational rules, a time sheet, code sheets, a set of face sheets, and the name and extension of the supervisor, with whom they could communicate if trouble arose but only by phone. After being instructed, subjects were taken to

[8] S. Enke, "On the Economic Management of Large Organizations: A Laboratory Study," *Journal of Business of the University of Chicago*, 31 (1958), 280–292.

[9] It might be noted that, from one point of view, the experiment is not on organizations so much as on inter-organizational relations. If this perspective is adopted, one would want to add that by assigning one or two men to each of the "organizations," the *inter*-organizational processes are "isolated" from the effects of variations in *intra*-organizational structure.

separate rooms, in which the only other person was an observer, who did not interact with the subject. The code book given the coder was technically deficient in a number of respects, and he was instructed to telephone his supervisor whenever he had any questions. In response to such questions the supervisor exhibited one of three levels of knowledge: more than the coder, the same as the coder, or less than the coder. The coder's performance and his conformity to rules and commands were the dependent variables; legitimacy was examined as the intervening variable.

The experiment was divided into two time periods. During the first all supervisors had more knowledge than the coder. At the end of it, the supervisor called his coder to announce that he had to leave and that there was another supervisor who should be consulted should trouble arise. For the second time period, subjects were randomly allocated among the three knowledge-level treatments. (The "new" supervisors were simply the old ones rotated once.) At the beginning of this second period all subjects received new questionnaires and code sheets, brought by a runner, in order that all could begin this phase alike. Where the knowledge-level contrasted with the official authority structure subjects decreased in conformity and altered the basis on which supervisors were regarded as legitimate, but there were no marked effects on performance. Total elapsed time of each replication was two hours.[10]

Only a small part of an organization, as defined above, is actually operating in this experiment. The concern of the experimenters here does not require that the whole of an organization be activated, but only that the "part" that is activated be influenced in determinate ways by the fact that it is a part of a complex organization. In effect, the experimenters *create* a larger organization than they *activate*. This is done in three ways. First, the subjects are "hired" and led throughout to believe that they have a temporary job in a "real" organization. (The purposes of the experiment are subsequently explained to the subjects.) Second, the subjects are briefly exposed at the very beginning of the experiment to the top or third level of the organization, the "project director," although subsequently he plays no actual part in the system. Third, inputs from other parts of the organization are simulated, inputs such as the rules, codebooks, and finished questionnaires, as well as the runner bringing the new questionnaires. (The manipulation of inputs into the part-replica, it might

[10] W. M. Evan and M. Zelditch, "A Laboratory Experiment on Bureaucratic Authority," ms. in preparation.

be noted, is probably capable of greater exploitation than is shown in this illustration. In principle, the problem is the same as that of simulating the external environment of an organization as a whole.)

The "near organization" is most closely approximated by studies using the Bavelas-apparatus.

> Subjects in these studies sit in cubicles fashioned by partitioning a circular table. Each partition has a slot at the base through which messages may be passed. Communication is by written message only. The experimenter may form any pattern of communication he wishes by opening or closing the slots in the partitions. One may create, for example, a condition in which one subject is central and all the others peripheral by closing off all channels except those between the central subject and each of the others.
>
> This condition may then be contrasted with another in which communication is decentralized. Typically subjects are given various problem-solving tasks in the form of puzzles: they may for instance be given five cards, one per subject, among which six symbols are so distributed that only one symbol is common to all five cards, and the subjects' task is to identify which is the common symbol. The experimenter measures such effects as the creation of social hierarchies, the speed and accuracy of the solution, and the morale of the subjects.[11]

Bavelas creates what is, in a sense, an analytic slice of an organization. The property simulated is in fact not one of the criterion properties, but it clearly derives from them, because the stipulated means of integrating an organization necessarily entails mediated communication.[12] On the other hand, he does not systematically create other properties of an organization; nor do the subjects think of themselves as members of such an organization, or as occupying organizational statuses; nor do they even perform a task that resembles typical organizational tasks.[13]

[11] See, for example, A. Bavelas, "Communication Patterns in Task-oriented Groups," in D. Cartwright and A. Zander, *Group Dynamics: Research and Theory* (Evanston, Ill.: Row, Peterson, 1953), pp. 493–506.

[12] By mediated communication is meant *human* mediation, not mechanical mediation. Communications from A to C pass through B. (Mechanical means of communication can be used in either the A to B relation, or in relations among units.) What makes systems operating through the Bavelas apparatus "near" organizations, then, is not that written messages are used but that the communications network typically assumes a certain form.

[13] It perhaps should be said explicitly that this comment is not intended as a criticism of Bavelas. His studies have different aims—in a sense more abstractly theoretical aims—than the studies previously described. Also, it should be observed that the apparatus as such would lend itself to the creation of properties other than mediated communication.

The simply structured unit is a residually defined class, the members of which are alike only in that they are not complex and have no distinctively organizational properties. Nevertheless, it has been suggested that the investigation of simply structured units may be relevant to the study of complex, formal organizations in two ways. First, subunits within an organization may behave in various respects like simply structured units. Experiments with such units on the relation of cohesion to productivity, for example, may be relevant to students of organizations in this way.[14] Second, it has also been held that simply structured units and complex, formal organizations have certain properties in common simply because both are social systems.[15] Certain propositions are therefore considered true of both, despite their many differences. For example, laboratory investigation of the relation between the functional problems of simply structured units and their structural differentiation may possibly contribute to our knowledge of structural differentiation in more complex systems.

The notion that experiments on simply structured units might be relevant to organizational problems is very attractive because it adds a very large literature, of high technical quality, to the resources of the organizational theorist. But it is, at the same time, one of those seductive notions that have serious drawbacks. It is possible, for example, to build an entire program of experiments on organizational problems around the investigation of the simply structured unit, with these two grounds as the principal justification.[16] But even though it would have *some* pertinence, such a program would be essentially tangential. Organizational theory is not a theory of all social systems, though organizations share some properties with all other social systems. Nor is it a theory of the conjunction of simply structured

[14] For an excellent example of a relevant experiment, see S. Schachter, N. Ellertson, D. McBride, and D. Gregory, "An Experimental Study of Cohesiveness and Productivity," *Human Relations*, 4 (1951), 229–238.

[15] See N. J. Demerath and J. W. Thibaut, "Small Groups and Administrative Organizations," *Administrative Science Quarterly*, 1 (1956), 139–154, who say, "Certain phenomena and patterns observed in small groups have their parallels, analogues, or homologues in administrative organizations, or vice versa. Therefore, some principles, laws, or theories of behavior may be found applicable to both organizations and small groups," p. 149. The most prominent exponents of such a view have been T. Parsons and R. F. Bales, particularly in *Working Papers in the Theory of Action* (Glencoe, Ill.: Free Press, 1953). Parsons' movement back and forth between systems at different emergent levels may be studied by comparing this work with "Suggestions for a Sociological Approach to the Theory of Organizations," in this volume, pp. 32 ff.

[16] See Demerath and Thibaut, *op. cit.*

units, although organizations contain many such units. It is a theory the special object of which is a class of formal, complex systems. Experimental inquiries are most directly relevant to it when they examine such systems. And it is perfectly possible to examine them experimentally. If it is true that size is only loosely correlated with complexity, that the age of a system is frequently irrelevant, that laboratory groups can be so constructed that their routines are both institutionalized and meaningful to their participants—then it is also true that complex, formal organizations can be created in the laboratory. It is this sort of system, rather than the simply structured unit, on which the experimenter interested in advancing organizational theory should concentrate.

Arthur L. Stinchcombe

On the Use of Matrix Algebra in the Analysis of Formal Organization

Introduction

A formal organization, especially one with a bureaucratic administration, is a network of regular, legitimate communications channels. The role of an official in a formal organization has both a functional aspect, what the official does, and a positional aspect, with whom and in what manner he communicates.

For example, an official may have both an engineering and a staff (advising) role, or he may both make production decisions and command specified others to follow them. In an ordinary organization chart, the name of the office tells the functional aspect, and its position on the chart (and the lines between it and other officers) show its place in the communications system.

In this note I will try to develop a formal method of represent-

This is a revised version of a paper published in *Berkeley Publications in Society and Institutions*, 4 (1958), 56–65.

ing the structure of the communications network which will allow the place of an office in that network to be represented by numerical indices. Then formal similarities of the position of offices in communications systems can be separated from substantive similarities of work done. The relations between positions and functions can then be investigated more easily.

The proposed method is an extension of the application of matrix algebra to sociometric problems by Festinger, Schachter, and Back.[1] Instead of allowing only numbers as entries in the cells, we will generalize the cell entries to classifications of social relations. There are at least two major types of formal communications relations, advice and command.[2]

This means that we want to deal with two types of asymmetrical relations with the same matrix. It is possible to define operations on matrices with three entries (two relations and a zero entry) which preserve most of the virtues of the matrix approach.

A Descriptive Matrix of a Hypothetical Example of Formal Organization

We may arrange officers in an imaginary formal organization along the top and sides of a square matrix as below. Then represent the social relations between the officers according to the following scheme: starting at the top of the *column* representing an office, if the officer of the column gives *advice* to the officer in the first *row*, put an *A* in the first cell. If he gives *commands* to the officer in that row, put a *C* in the first cell. If he does neither, put no entry. (Including no entry on the diagonals.) Continue down the column; then do the same for the other columns.

In the example I have assumed that the President of a company gives orders to the General Manager (who in turn gives orders to the Foreman, cf. column 2), to the Engineer, and to the Accountant. The General Manager I have assumed to give advice to the President concerning problems of production, and to give orders to the Foreman. The Engineer is assumed to give advice to the people directly concerned with physical production, the General Manager and the

[1] Leon Festinger, Stanley Schachter, and Kurt Back, "Matrix Analysis of Group Structures," reprinted in P. F. Lazarsfeld and Morris Rosenberg, *The Language of Social Research* (Glencoe, Ill.: Free Press, 1955), pp. 358–367. Originally printed in *Social Pressures in Informal Groups* (copyright 1950, Harper), pp. 132–147.

[2] There may be others; for instance, *c* has the power to veto *r*'s proposals, *c* and *r* are both members of a policy-making committee, *c* furnishes unanalyzed information to *r*, which he analyzes before giving advice, etc.

Foreman. The Accountant is assumed to advise the President on the financial position of the company, and the General Manager on the relative profitability of different departments. Such seems to be at least a possible arrangement of the relations between this particular group of officers in a small company. Of course, the matrix could be expanded, to include four foremen, or to add other offices.

	Given by				
Given to	President	General Manager	Foreman	Engineer	Acc'tant
President		A			A
Gen. Manager	C			A	A
Foreman		C		A	
Engineer	C				
Acc'tant	C				

Fig. 1. Matrix of a hypothetical formal communications net

SECOND-ORDER RELATIONS

Now we may "multiply" this matrix by itself in the following manner: Take the cells in each column and "multiply" them by the cells in all the other columns, entering the results in the former column in the "squared" matrix, in the row corresponding to the row in the latter column of the original matrix. The operation of "multiplication" is defined as the letter from the former column followed by the letter from the latter column.

Another way of describing this operation: In each cell in the "squared matrix," enter the products found in the following way: take the column in the original matrix corresponding to the column of the cell you want to fill in, and take the corresponding row in the original matrix; then "multiply" the first cell in the column by the first cell in the row, the second cell in the column by the second cell in the row, etc. This "multiplication" is done by writing down the column entry first and then the row entry right next to it. Mark all these products down in the cell of the squared matrix, separated by a + sign.[3] This gives the following result:

[3] If a_{rc} is the entry in the rth row, c^{th} column of the original matrix, and a^2_{rc} is the entry in the corresponding cell in the "squared" matrix, then

$$a^2_{rc} = a_{1c}a_{r1} + a_{2c}a_{r2} + \dots + a_{nc}a_{rn}.$$

The order of the elements of "products" is not to be ignored in combining them.

Given to \ Given by	President	General Manager	Foreman	Engineer	Accountant
President	CA+CA			AA	AA
General Manager	CA+CA	AC			AC
Foreman	CC+CA			AC	AC
Engineer		AC			AC
Accountant		AC			AC

Fig. 2. "Square" of hypothetical matrix (Figure 1)

To illustrate the method of derivation of this matrix, we may take the example of the first column in the "squared" matrix. The President gives commands to the General Manager. The General Manager in turn gives commands to the Foreman (*CC* in the third row of the first column) and gives advice to the President (*CA* in the top cell of the first column); the President gives orders to the Engineer, who in turn gives advice to the General Manager (*CA* in the second cell, first column) and to the Foreman (*CA* in the third cell); finally the President gives orders to the Accountant, who in his turn advises him (*CA* in the first cell) and also advises the General Manager (*CA* in the second cell). This completes the first column in the "squared" matrix.

Now consider the Engineer's column in the "squared" matrix. The Engineer gives advice to the General Manager, who in turn advises the President (*AA* in the top cell) and commands the Foreman (*AC* in the third cell). He also advises the Foreman, but the Foreman gives neither commands nor advice to any of the other officers; so this has no result in the squared matrix. And so on. (It should be noted again that it is essential to preserve the order of *A* and *C* in "multiplication." It is quite different to give orders to someone's advisor and to give advice to someone's boss.)

From this description of the derivation, we can see that this "squared" matrix catalogs the "social relations at second remove" between the officers. Thus the Accountant advises someone (namely the General Manager, but this doesn't show up) who advises the President; he also advises someone who commands the General Manager (*AC* in the second cell of the fifth column). The squared matrix, in other words, gives only the mediated relations between officers; it gives no hint of who the mediator is.

There are four types of these mediated relations:

1. *AA:* advising someone who advises the officer of the row;
2. *AC:* advising someone who commands the officer of the row;
3. *CA:* commanding someone who advises the officer of the row;
4. *CC:* commanding someone who commands the officer of the row;

besides the two direct relations:

A: advising the officer of the row;
C: commanding the officer of the row.

We may choose names for each of these types of relations:

A and *AA* we may group together as "advice-giving."
AC (advising someone's boss) we may call "influence."
CA (commanding someone's advisors) we may call "coordination."
C and *CC* we may classify as relations of "command."

USING BOTH MATRICES IN CHARACTERIZING ROLES

Now consider the matrix formed by "adding" the cells of the original matrix to the cells of the "squared" matrix:

Given to	Given by: President	General Manager	Foreman	Engineer	Accountant
President	2 CA	A		AA	A+AA
General Manager	C+2 CA	AC		A	A+AC
Foreman	CC+CA	C		A+AC	AC
Engineer	C	AC			AC
Accountant	C	AC			AC

Fig. 3. Summary of first- and second-order communications relations

This matrix gives a summary picture of the nature of the first and second order social relations in the structure.[4] There are a number of ways to analyze the matrix that might be of use. For example, it may be useful merely to note the fact that the foreman has no unmediated relations to the President, but he does have mediated ones. It might also be noticed that the Engineer's advice to the Foreman is complicated by the fact that he also advises his boss (both an *A* and an *AC* in column 4, row 3).

But perhaps the most immediately useful manipulations of the matrix are those of merely counting the number of times different types of relations appear in the columns or in the rows. This procedure gives numerical measures of the positional aspect of roles in the communications network. If we count down the columns, we get a measure of the number of each type of social control relations in which the designated official serves as originator. Thus (ignoring the diagonal cells for the moment):

Types of Communications			Officer		
	President	*General Mgr.*	*Foreman*	*Engineer*	*Acc'tant*
Commands (*C* and *CC*)	4	1	0	0	0
Coordinates (*CA*)	3	0	0	0	0
Influences (*AC*)	0	2	0	1	3
Advises (*A* and *AA*)	0	1	0	3	3

Fig. 4. Originating aspects of communications positions (column count)

That is, most of the social control the President wields is either by command or by "coordination" (giving orders to those who give advice) or the "control of the flow of information." The General Manager, in our example, has some command function, no "coordination" function, considerable "influence," and some advisory function. The Engineer has little "influence," and what powers he has are almost purely advisory. The Accountant has both "influence" and advisory methods of controlling others.

If we look at the rows, on the other hand, we can get a picture of the type of social controls impinging on each official:

The main control over the President is by advisory relations. The General Manager gets both commands and advice, but is also subject to "influence" (people talk to his boss), and to "coordination" (the

[4] Of course, it would be possible to conduct further multiplications, "cubing" the original matrix, but with noncommutativeness, this would lead to eight types of third-order relationships, giving a total of 14.

Types of Communications	*President*	*General Mgr.*	*Officer Foreman*	*Engineer*	*Acc'tant*
Receives Commands (*C* & *CC*)	0	1	2	1	1
Rec's Coordination (*CA*)	0	2	1	0	0
Rec's Influence (*AC*)	0	1	2	2	1
Rec's Advice (*A* & *AA*)	4	2	1	0	0

Fig. 5. Receiving aspects of communications positions (row count)

advice he gets is controlled from above). The Foreman gets less advice and "coordination" directed at him, and more commands and "influence." The staff officers have fewer controls over them than do either top or line management, but what there are are more imperative.

Conclusion

This extension of mathematical methods of analyzing networks of social relations from sociometric experience has only reached the stage of methodological theorizing. The use of this method in actual research on formal organizations would require standardization for organizations of different size, clear operational definitions of the content of communications between officials, and so forth.

But this method of analysis promises to be more fruitful than the clumsy topological representations of organizational communications nets, because it is more easily subject to mathematical manipulation and because it is flexible enough to deal with a number of different types of communication.

Name Index

Subject Index